EARLY HISTORY OF KAUSAMBI

EARLY HISTORY

OF

KAUSAMBI

FROM THE SIXTH CENTURY B. C.

TO THE ELEVENTH CENTURY A. D.

NAGENDRA NATH GHOSH, M. A.

GYAN

Published by

Gyan Publishing House
5, Ansari Road
Daryaganj, New Delhi-110002
Phone: 011-47034999, 9811692060
E-mail: books@gyanbooks.com

Distribution Network
gyanbooks.com
India, USA, Canada, UK, Australia, France

ISBN: 978-81-212-9128-6 (PB)
First Published, 1935

2nd Impression 2023

Printed at: Gyan Press, Delhi.

EARLY HISTORY OF KAUSAMBI
AUTHOR: NAGENDRA NATH GHOSH

Allahabad Archaeological Society Series No. I

EARLY HISTORY of KAUŚĀMBĪ

FROM THE SIXTH CENTURY B.C.
TO THE ELEVENTH CENTURY A.D.

By

NAGENDRA NATH GHOSH, M.A.

HEAD OF THE DEPARTMENT OF HISTORY AND CIVICS, EWING CHRISTIAN COLLEGE, ALLAHABAD; AUTHOR OF 'THE GROWTH OF THE INDIAN CONSTITUTION'; COLLABORATOR WITH MAJOR B. D. BASU IN 'INDIA UNDER THE BRITISH CROWN'; HONY. LIFE MEMBER, ALLAHABAD ARCHAEOLOGICAL SOCIETY, MEMBER, NUMISMATIC SOCIETY OF INDIA

Published under the auspices of
The Allahabad Archaeological Society

1935

Dedicated

With Profound Respect and Admiration

to

The Memory

of

General Sir ALEXANDER CUNNINGHAM, C.S.I.

1814—1893

Father of Indian Archaeology

Colonel A. Cunningham, while he was the Chief Engineer of the North-Western Provinces, laid before Lord Canning in November 1861, a memorandum praying for a complete and systematic archaeological investigation of the ancient historic ruins of Upper India. This led to his appointment as the first Archaeological Surveyor to the Government of India. As director of the Archaeological Survey (1870—1885) he brought to light the immense importance of the archaeological ruins of more than fifty ancient cities—including Kauśāmbī—in the United Provinces. (A.S.R. Vol. I).

PREFACE

A few of my articles on the early history of Kauśâmbī were published in papers and journals from time to time, and a paper on a controversial point of its history in the second century B.C. was read at the SIXTH ORIENTAL CONFERENCE, held at Baroda. All these formed the nucleus of the present monograph. In it I have endeavoured to present an account of the ancient greatness of Kauśâmbī, now reduced to a ruined fortress. The facts have been arranged to give the story a continuous form, which, however, has been broken on account of the paucity of materials available on the subject.

The materials for these pages have been drawn mainly from primary sources—Sanskrit and Pâli literature. The references in the ancient texts have been used after careful sifting in the light of epigraphic, archaeological and numismatic evidences. Secondary sources have been consulted where it was necessary, either for acceptance or rejection of the views stated therein. References to Kauśâmbī in modern literature are scanty, and statements in some places appear to be incorrect.

I have visited Kauśâmbī and its adjunct, the Pabhosâ Rock, several times. My personal observations of the situation of the place *vis-a-vis* the Yamunâ and the Pabhosâ Rock have greatly helped me to use some of the Pâli and epigraphic references regarding the subject.

Sir Alexander Cunningham has used the spelling 'Kosâmbi,' evidently following the Pâli Texts. But I have preferred the Sanskrit spelling 'Kauśâmbī' and also used the corrected version in the quotations from the authors who used the former spelling. In the matter of transliteration I have followed the system approved by the INTERNATIONAL ORIENTAL CONGRESS of 1894, with this slight difference that I have preferred the sign - to ^ for the long â instead of ā to represent आ, and other slight variations which will explain themselves.

I wish to acknowledge with sincere thanks my indebtedness to Dr. Hem Chandra Raychaudhari, M.A., Ph.D., lecturer in History, Calcutta University, for his kindly going through those portions of the MS. which I considered of controversial nature, and offering some valuable suggestions. I am further grateful for the kind assistance I received from my friend and colleague, Prof. C. H. Hazlett, M.A. for carefully revising the MS. My acknowledgment is also due to Mr. Braj Mohan Vyas, the Secretary of the Allâhâbâd Municipal Museum, for helping me to prepare a list of the Kauśâmbī relics housed in the Museum, which provided materials for my note on the archaeological importance of Kauśâmbī.

I must also thank my friend Tripiṭakâcharya Râhula Sankrityana for having seen through the final proofs, and my student Sm. Devi Shanker Bajpai for preparing the index.

I am grateful to Dr. Radha Kumud Mookerji M.A., Ph. D., P.R.S., Professor and Head of the Department of Indian History, Lucknow University, for the trouble he has taken to read the book and write an Introduction to it.

N. N. GHOSH

EWING CHRISTIAN COLLEGE
ALLAHABAD
January 30, 1935

CONTENTS

CONTENTS

CONTENTS

LIST OF MAPS

The following is list of plates of the finds in Kauśâmbī at present housed in the Allahabad Museum

TRANSLITERATION

a.....................अ
â.....................आ
i.....................इ
ī.....................ई
ṛ.....................ऋ
au....................औ
ṇ.....................ण,
c.....................च
ṭ.....................ट
t.....................त
th....................थ
ḍ.....................ड
d.....................द
dh....................ध
ś.....................श
ṣ.....................ष
s.....................स
ṁ.....................Anusvâra
ḥ.....................Visarga
h.....................ह
kṣ....................क्ष

ABBREVIATIONS

Ang. Nik. — Anguttara Nikâya.

Aśoka — *By* Dr. D. R. Bhandarkar.

Asoka (G. L.) — *By* Dr. Radha Kumud Mookerji.

A.S.R. — Reports of the Archaeological Survey of India.

Bd. — Brahmâṇḍa Purâṇa.

Bh. — Bhâgavata Purâṇa.

C. A. G. I. — Cunningham's Ancient Geography of India.

C. A. I. — Coins of Ancient India *by* General Cunningham.

C. C. I. M. — Catalogue of the Coins of the Indian Museum, Calcutta.

C. H. I. — Cambridge History of India, Vol. 1.

Dh. A. — Dhammapada Aṭṭhakathâ. (P. T. S.)

D. N. — Digha Nikâya (P. T. S.).

Dv. — Dīpavaṁsa.

Dvd. — Divyâvadâna.

E. H. I. — Early History of India, *by* Dr. V. Smith.

G. A. I. — Geography of Ancient India *by* General Cunningham.

Ep. Ind. — Epigraphia Indica.

ABBREVIATIONS

G. E. B. — Geography of Early Buddhism *by* Dr. B. C. Law.

Hv. — Harivaṁśa.

Ind. Ant. — Indian Antiquary.

Jat. — The Jâtakas.

J. B. O. R. S. — The Journal of the Behar and Orissa Research Society.

Jayaswal. — History of India from 150 A.D.—350 A. D.

J. R. A. S. — The Journal of the Royal Asiatic Society.

Mat. — Matsya Purâṇa.

Mbh. — The Mahâbhârata.

Mv. — Mahavaṁsa.

M. N. — Majjhima Nikâya.

Pradhan — The Chronology of Ancient India. *by* Dr. S. N. Pradhan.

P. V. — Peta Vatthu.

Pargiter. — The Kali Age, *by* F. E. Pargiter.

P. H. A. I. — Political History of Ancient India. *by* Dr. H. C. Raychaudhari.

Ram. — Ramâyaṇa.

S. B. — Sacred Books of the Buddhists.

Smv. — Sumangalavilâsini.

S. N. — Saṁyutta Nikâya.

Sat. Br. — Śatapatha Brâhmaṇa.

S. nip. — Sutta Nipâta.

ABBREVIATIONS

V. T. — Vinaya Texts.
Va. — Vâyu Purâṇa.
Watters — On Yuan Chwang's Travel in India *by* Mr. Watters.

ON THE ANTIQUITY AND IMPORTANCE OF KAUŚÂMBĪ

Kauśâmbī, whose site is to be undoubtedly identified with ruins existing at Kośam,[1] 38 miles from Allâhâbâd above the Yamunâ, is a very ancient city known to us from tradition and history. It is commonly known from Pâli canon as a Buddhist town, being the capital of the Vatsa King Udayana, a contemporary of the Buddha. But the existence of the city can be traced to hoary antiquity, long anterior to the time of the Buddha who flourished in the 6th century B. C. We find references to the city of Kauśâmbī in the Epics[2] and in the Purâṇas[3] which speak of time older than the Pâli canon. We find mentioned therein kings who ruled the kingdom of Kauśâmbī long before Udayana had graced the throne.

I. Traditional Accounts of its Origin

There are several traditional accounts of the origin of the city of Kauśâmbī, but none of them has any semblance of connection with the other.

[1] See later, p. 83.
[2] Mbh I, 63, Ram I, 32.
[3] Mt. Va, Bd.

They are often contradictory. They have no corroborative evidence to prove their historical value. But the name of Kauśâmbī occurring therein undoubtedly proves the great antiquity of the city. According to the Mahâbhârata we can trace the origin of the city of Kauśâmbī to a prince of the Cedi King, Uparicara Vasu. The latter, a king of the Kuru Dynasty, conquered the beautiful kingdom of Cedi. He had five powerful sons—Bṛihadratha, Pratyagraha, Kuśâmba, Mabella and Yadu. Each of them was installed over a new kingdom which became famous after his name. The reference is at best a faint one, and can be used only inferentially. A clear account of the foundation of the town of Kauśâmbī can be had in the Ramâyaṇa.[4]

Once upon a time Ṛiṣi Viśvâmitra, accompanied by Râma and Lakṣhmaṇa, halted in the evening at a pleasant spot on his way to Mithilâ after the destruction of the *râkṣas* Mârici and his followers, and told the princes the following story:

"Long ago there was a king named Kuśa, devoted to sacred rites and religion. His wife was named Vaidarbhi. He had four sons—Kuśâmba, Kuśanâbha, Asurtaraja and Vasu. One day Kuśa sent for his sons and asked them to found new kingdoms

[4] Ram I, 32, 6

and earn Kṣatriya virtue by ruling them. They founded several towns. *The powerful Kuśâmba founded Kauśâmbī*, Kuśanâbha founded Mahodaya, Asurtaraja founded Dharamâraṇya and Vasu founded, Girivraja."

The above are the Epic traditions of the origin of this famous city. During the time of the Buddha, the kingdom of Kauśâmbī was known as the country of the Vatsas, and its king Udayana as Vatsa Râja. The Epic account and that given in the Harivaṁśa[5] agree in tracing the origin of the Vatsa people to a king of Kâśi, Pratardana by name. They, however, differ in other details of the story in which the account of the origin of the Vatsas formed a part. The Harivaṁśa account is clearer on one point, because after having said प्रतर्द्दनस्य पुत्रौ द्वौ वत्स भार्गौं बभूवतुः it adds. वत्सस्य वत्सभूमिस्तु भृगुभूमिस्तु भार्गवात् ।

II. The Puranic Data as to its Antiquity

In addition to the information we obtain as to the origin of the Vatsa people of the territory of Kauśâmbī from the Harivaṁśa which can be styled as an *upapurâṇa*, there is plenty of data available in some of the oldest and most important Purâṇas which prove the great antiquity of Kauśâmbī. What

[5] Hv. I, 29.

is more important, these Purâṇic accounts, unlike those of the Epics, wonderfully agree with one another in details, barring slight discrepancies in some of the names given in the dynastic lists of kings, perhaps due to the differences in the accents of the spoken languages of the regions where the subsequent recensions of the earlier Purâṇas had been made. Following the Matsya Purâṇa[6] we find that when Hastinâpur was carried away[7] by the Ganges, the Kuru or the Bhârata King Nicakṣu[8] who was fifth in descent from Parikṣit, the grandson of Arjuna, abandoned Hastinâpur and dwelt in Kauśâmbī.[9]

From the above account we may conclude that Kauśâmbī existed as a city to tempt Nicakṣu to remove his capital there. There is no word in the Purâṇic accounts to suggest that Nicakṣu *founded* it. Of course, improvements and probably enlargement of the place were made after it had become the capital of the Kuru Kings. But that the place existed as an important town under the name of Kauśâmbī at the time of Nicakṣu's migration, is clear. The learned scholar Dr. Ray

[6] Pargiter, p. 5.

[7] *Gaṅgay âphṛte tasmin nagare.* Vs. has it more distinctly: *Yo Gangay âphṛte Hastinâpure.*

[8] Bh. Nimicakra.

[9] *Kausaṁbyaṁ sa nivatsyati*

Chaudhary evidently holds that view. He said, "Epic Traditions attribute the foundation of this famous city (Kauśâmbī) to a Cedi prince and the origin of the Vatsas is traced to a king of Kâśi."[10] He also refers in this connection to *Satapatha Brâhmaṇa* where the name of Proti Kauśambeya occurs and according to the commentator Harisvâmin, Proti Kauśambeya was a native of Kauśâmbī.[11] This is certainly another proof of its antiquity, if Harisvâmin's interpretation is correct.

In addition to the references to Kauśâmbī in ancient Sanskrit literature dealt with above, which speak for its remote antiquity, the name of the city occurs in the Pâli Piṭakâs, the Jâtakas, in the later non-canonical Buddhist literature, Lalitavistara, Meghadūta, Kathâsaritsâgara, Ratnâvali and the accounts of the Chinese Pilgrims, Fa-hien and Hiuen Tsang. The memory of Kauśâmbī was thus perpetuated from age to age in our ancient literature, a fact which speaks for its importance in the history of India during the early mediaeval periods.

[10] P. H. A. I., p. 92.
[11] Ibid-Sat Br. XII 2. 2. 13

KAUŚÂMBĪ IN THE TIME OF THE BUDDHA

It is not possible to say more of the pre-Buddhist history of Kauśâmbī than is contained in the Epic and Purâṇic traditions already referred to. Purâṇas also give a list of kings of Kauśâmbī from Nichakṣu downwards which will be considered later. In the early Buddhist time, however, we are on more solid ground as to its history. There are copious references to the city of Kauśâmbī in Pâli literature, both canonical and non-canonical.

I. Economic Condition

Centre of Trade and Traffic

That it was a great city in the time of the Buddha is evident from a conversation found in the Mahâparinibbâna Sutta of the Dīgha Nikâya between the Buddha and his close disciple Ânanda. When the Buddha expressed his desire to die in the town of Kusinârâ,[1] Ânanda said: "Let not the Exalted One die in this wattle and daub town in the midst of the jungle, in this branch township. For, Lord, there are other great cities such as

[1] Modern Kâsia near Gorakhpore, U. P.

Campâ,[2] Râjagaha,[3] Sâvatthi,[4] Saketa,[5] Kauśâmbī and Vârâṇasī." Kauśâmbī is thus included in the Dīgha Nikâya among the six great cities in the time of the Buddha. Situated on the bank of the Yamunâ, it was a rich commercial city at that time. Like Taxilâ, Śrâvastī, Vârâṇasī, Râjagriha and Vaiśâlī, Kauśâmbī was a wealthy city in which millionaire merchants, lesser merchants and middle men resided.[6] In the Sutta Nipâta[7] we are told that it (Kauśâmbī) was the most important entrepot of goods and passengers coming to Kośala and Magadha from the south and west. In the *Sumangalavilāsinī*, which is a commentary on the Dīgha Nikâya, written by the famous exegete Buddhaghosha, we find the names of some bankers of Kauśâmbī. They were Ghosika or Ghosita, Kakoda and Pāvāriya who built beautiful hermitages (Ârâmas) in their respective gardens for the

[2] The capital of the Aṅga country which comprises the modern districts of Bhâgalpur and Munghyr. The site of ancient Campâ is marked, according to Cunningham, by the two villages, Campanagar and Campapura, that exist near Bhâgalpur.

[3] Sanks. Râjagriha near Gayâ.

[4] Sanks. Śrâvastī now identified with the ruins at Saheṭ Maheṭ in the district of Gonda, U. P., near Balrâmpur.

[5] Sâketa grew into the Capital city of Kosala on the ruins of Ajodhyâ. In the time of the Buddha, Sâketa was the second city, next to Śrâvasti, and occasionally used as the seat of Government. The city of the ancient Sâketa is to be identified with modern Ajodhyâ.

[6] Buddhist India, p. 102

[7] S. Nip. 1011-1013

residence of *Bhikkhus*. We can gather from the Vinaya Texts[8] that the terminus of the main river route from east to west was Kauśâmbī. Sahajâti was its nearest river station down the Yamunâ, near the confluence. It is identified with the ruins now existing at Bhīṭâ, about eight miles from Allâhâbâd.[9] Upwards the river was used for the cargo and passenger boats plying from the east along the Ganges as far as Sahajâti and along the Yamunâ as far west as Kauśâmbī. The traffic downwards was as far as Kośala, Magadha and Campâ and right up to the mouth of the Ganges and thence either across the Bay or along the coast to Burma.[10] Roads coming from the southwest and northwest also converged on Kauśâmbī for import and export of goods from those quarters. Thus Kauśâmbī was in the time of the Buddha the greatest river port for import and export of goods for the whole of North and Mid-India and had commercial relations even with Burma.[11]

[8] V. T. 1, 81, 3, 401, 382.

[9] I have visited Bhīṭâ several times. The place is full of ruins which speak for its antiquity. Some of the archaeological finds have been brought to the Allâhâbâd Museum. The discovery of a terra cotta seal in Bhīṭâ bearing the inscription of Sahajâti undoubtedly identifies the present ruins of Bhīṭâ with the ancient city mentioned in the Vinaya Texts—See Jayaswal, p. 225.

[10] Buddhist India, p. 104.

[11] Ibid.

II. Political Condition

One of the Sixteen Janapadas

In the Anguttara Nikâya[12] we learn that the Vatsas ruled the kingdom of Kauśâmbī with its capital of the same name and that Kauśâmbī was one of the sixteen *Janapadas* (Kingdoms) in India existing in the time of the Buddha. The other fifteen Janapadas were: 1 Aṅga,[13] 2. Magadha,[14] 3. Kâśi, 4. Kośala,[15] 5. Vajji,[16] 6. Malla,[17]

[12] Ang. Nik. I 213; IV. 252, 256, 260.

[13] The state east of Magadha with its capital Campâ. According to Cunningham, the site of the ancient city of Campâ is to be identified with the two villages—Campanagara and Campapura—which still exist near Bhagalpur.

[14] Corresponds roughly to the present Patna and Gayâ districts of Behar. Its capital at the time of the Mahâbhârata was Girivraja or old Râjagṛiha. Bimbasâra built new Râjgriha at a few miles distance and it was the capital known in the time of the Buddha. The ruins of Râjagṛiha are still extant among hills near Gayâ.

[15] Roughly corresponds to modern Oudh. Its earliest capital was Ajodhyâ. In the time of the Buddha the capital was Śrâvasti (Sâvatthī), the ruins of which have been identified with Saheṭ Maheṭ in Gonda district, near Balrâmpur.

[16] A republican state north of Videha of the clan known as the Licchavis with its capital at Vaiśâlī (Vesâli) now identified with Besarh in the Muzaffarpur district of Behar.

[17] The territory of another republican people, the Mallas, divided into two parts which had their capital cities of Pâvâ and Kusinârâ. Kusinârâ is to be identified with the ruins at Kasiâ, 21 miles from Gorakhpore, U. P., and Pâvâ with Padronâ, 12 miles north of Kasiâ. It is interesting to note that it is in the Mallan town of Pâvâ that the

7. Cedi,[18] 8. Kuru,[19] 9. Pañcâla,[20] 10. Maccha,[21] 11. Sūrasena,[22] 12. Assaka,[23] 13. Avantī,[24] 14. Gandhâra,[25] 15. Kamboja.[26] The king of Kauśâmbī in Buddha's time was Udayana (Udenâ of the Pâli canon).

King Udayana

1. *His Predecessors and Parentage*

Purâṇas give a list of kings who reigned in Kauśâmbī before Udayana. Nicakṣu, who transferred his residence here from Hastinâpur, was the

Buddha was taken ill, and in the other Mallan town of Kusinârâ he died. These were the last two towns which the Buddha had seen immediately before his *Parinibbâna.*

[18] Corresponds roughly to modern Bundelkhand.

[19] Corresponds roughly to the modern Delhi province and the Meerut district, U. P. Its ancient capitals were Hastinâpura and Indraprastha.

[20] Corresponds roughly to Rohilkhand and a part of the central Doab. It was divided into two parts—Northern Pañcâla with its capital at Ahicchatra (modern Ramnagar in the Bareilly district, U. P.) and Southern Pañcâla with its capital at Kâmpilya (modern Kampil, in the Furrukhabâd district, U. P.)

[21] Corresponds roughly to the modern territory of Jaipur.

[22] The country with its capital at Mathurā, U. P.

[23] Acc. to S. nip verse 1977, it was in the Dakkhināpatha, close by the river Godâvarī.

[24] Roughly corresponds to modern Malwâ, Nimâr and the adjoining parts of the Central Provinces.

[25] Corresponds roughly to Kâshmir and Taxilâ.

[26] A state immediately north of Gandhâra, identified with Rajpura described by Hiuen Tsang to have existed in the modern N. W. F. P.

fifth king after Parīkṣita, the grandson of Arjuna Pândava. King Udayana, as can be seen from the genealogical table drawn from the Purâṇic data,[27] was the seventeenth king from Nicakṣu. Thus his descent is traced from the Kuru or Bhârata kings of Hastinâpur. The great Sanskrit dramatist Bhâsa also calls him a scion of the Bhârata dynasty in the *Svapna Vâsavadattam*. Very little is known about the kings of Kauśâmbī earlier than Udayana. According to a Jain tradition[28] Śatânīka II, the father of Udayana, attacked Campâ, the capital of Aṅga, during the reign of Dadhivâhana. According to the Purâṇas the father of Udayana was Śatânīka. In the Matsya Purâṇa we find:—

"Tigmâd Bṛahdratho bhâvyo vasudâno Bṛhadrathât Vasudânâc Chatâniko bhaviṣy Odayanas tataḥ."

The Purâṇic account of his parentage agrees with the Tibetan account. According to the *Dulva* his father's name was Śatânīka. "The King of Kauśâmbī, Catanika, had a son born to him at the same time as the future Buddha was born and as the world was illuminated at his birth, as with the sun, he was called Udayana."[29]

But the account of his birth found in Pâlī literature is different both as to the name of his

[27] See Appendix I, p. 35.
[28] J. A. S. B., 1914, p. 321.
[29] Rockhill—Life of the Buddha, p. 17.

father, which is Parantapa, and as to the incident of his birth. In Buddhaghosha's commentary on the Dhammapada we find the following story of the birth of Udayana:—

King Parantapa of Kauśâmbī one day was with his queen outside the palace; the queen was in a family way and the king had made her put on a scarlet cloak and had placed on her finger a ring of rare value. Just then a *Hatthilinga*, a monster bird, flew down from the sky and, taking the queen for a piece of flesh, carried her off. The queen, fearing for her life, kept quiet, thinking that if she made any noise the bird would let her fall. The *Hatthilinga*, arriving at the Himavanta forest, dropped her in the fork of a banyan tree in order to devour her. When he began to fly around the place where he intended to perch, the queen seized the opportunity and, clapping her hands, shouted lustily, and the bird, startled at the unexpected noise, flew away. At that time the sun went down, and from the effect of past sins committed by the queen, the wind began to blow and violent rain came on. The queen, having passed a sleepless and miserable night in the fork of the tree, gave birth to a son in the morning. To the son she gave the name of *Udayana*, because at his birth she had experienced the three seasons, the cold season, the hot season, and the rainy season. In that forest lived a Ṛiṣi of the forest from whom Udayana learned the mystic formulae for charming wild elephants, and with their help and showing the ministers the ruby ring and the scarlet cloak given to him by his mother recovered his father's throne after the latter's death.[80]

Neither Pâli literature nor the Tibetan Dulva discloses who Udayana's mother was. We however obtain a clue to Udayana's maternity from a different source—the Sanskrit source. The point has been clearly brought out by Dr. Bhandarkar.

In his Carmichael Lectures, 1918 (pp. 58 and 59), he states that in the plays of Bhâsa Udayana is called *Vaidehīputra*. This clearly indicates that Udayana's mother was a princess of Videha. The name is, however, unknown.

2. *Udayana's Queens*

Udayana had four queens. Tradition has preserved long stories of the adventures of Udayana and three of his queens. In every case the marriage was accomplished in a romantic manner.

Queen Vâsula-Dattâ. In the commentary on verses 21-23 of the Dhammapada we find the romantic story of Vâsula-dattâ, daughter of King Pajjota of Avantī. Pajjota was a man of fierce temper and unscrupulous character. Being told that Udayana, king of Kauśâmbī, surpassed him in

[80] Dh. A.—Udena Vatthu

glory, Pajjota determined to attack him. Being advised that an open campaign would not succeed against that powerful king, he took to stratagem. He had an exact likeness of an elephant made of wood and carefully painted; then he had machinery fixed inside to be worked with ropes, placed sixty men within to pull the ropes and started off across the boundary of King Udayana's territory. On being informed by a hunter that a beautiful elephant was in sight King Udayana took the bait, plunged into the forest in pursuit of the prize, became separated from his retinue, and was taken prisoner by Pajjota's men, who were in hiding on either side of the road. King Pajjota set a guard over him and on the third day offered him his life and freedom if he would give him the mystic power of charming elephants. King Udayana said that he would give the charm to any one who paid him homage. Pajjota planned a trick. He told his daughter Vâsula-dattâ that she would have to learn a charm from a dwarf, and told Udayana that a hunch-back woman would receive the charm from behind the curtain. So careful was the king to prevent an improper intimacy between the two! But when the prisoner day after day rehearsed the charm and his unseen pupil was slow to catch it, Udayana one day called impatiently, "Oh, you hunch-back!

How thick-headed and thick-lipped you must be!" The princess very indignantly retorted, "What do you mean, you wretched dwarf, to call me a hunch-back?" "The king told me so," he replied and pulled the corner of the curtain to see, and then asked who she was, and the trick was discovered. He then went inside, and there was no more talk that day of learning the charm, or of repeating lessons!

Then they laid a counter-plot. Vâsula-dattâ told her father that in order that she might succeed in learning the charm it would be necessary for her to procure an herb under a certain conjunction of the stars, and she should have the right of exit and the use of an elephant. Her wish was granted. Then one day when her father went to amuse himself in the garden, Udayana placed the princess on a swift elephant and fled. When King Pajjota found it out he sent soldiers in hot pursuit. But Udayana avoided capture by scattering gold and silver pieces along the road, so that when the pursuers stopped to gather them up, he forged ahead and reached his frontier fortress. Then the pursuers drew back and the royal couple entered the city in safety and in triumph. Then with due pomp and ceremony she was anointed as his queen, surrounded by five hundred female attendants.

Apart from the romantic interest of the marriage in the above story, it is illustrative of the fact that political rivalry existed between Kauśâmbī and Avantī and that King Udayana 'surpassed' King Pajjota in glory and power. Even if we may not believe the entire story as a fact, we can at least glean from it that this political rivalry between the two states ended, as usual in those days, in a matrimonial alliance between them.

Queen Sāmāvatī. Udayana's second queen was Sāmāvatī. The story of his marriage with her is also interesting. One day King Udayana on opening the door of his summer palace and looking out saw the young Sāmāvatī and asked whose daughter she was. Now, Sāmāvatī was the daughter of Seth Vaddavati of the Vaddavati country. At a time when that country was ravaged by famine and pestilence she came to Kauśâmbī and had been adopted by *Seth* Ghosita as his daughter. Sāmāvatī, after being handsomely dressed, was conducted to Udayana, who, the moment he saw her, fell in love with her and raised her to the rank of a great queen surrounded by five hundred attendants.[31]

Queen Mâgandiya. Pâli canon does not give us any clue as to the name of the third queen of

[31] Ibid.

Udayana. We get the name and also the romantic story of the marriage purely from non-canonical Buddhist literature, the Dhammapada Aṭṭhakatha of the famous exegete Buddhaghoṣa.

In the famous Kururathâ country there lived Brahmin Magandīya. He had a daughter whom he named Mâgandīa. She was very beautiful. Princes and sons of merchants demanded her hand in marriage, but he refused their suits with the reply that they were not worthy of her. One day the Buddha went to the village of Magandaya. The Brahmin seeing the Buddha thought that he was a fit husband for his daughter and approaching him said: "Lord, my daughter is extremely beautiful and you also are remarkable for your beauty. You may therefore have my daughter for your wife". The Buddha thereupon spoke to him on the futility of personal beauty and politely declined the offer. On this the Brahmin went away highly irritated and took her to King Udayana. The king was highly pleased at her appearance and fell in love with her and made her his queen, surrounded by five hundred female attendants."[82]

Queen Padmāvatī. The name of the fourth queen of Udayana we learn from the famous

[82] Ibid.

Sanskrit drama Svapnavâsvadattam of Bhâsa. She is Padmâvatī, the daughter of Ajâtaśatru of Magadha. Her brother Darśaka figures prominently in the story. It was probably a political marriage for the purpose of cementing friendship with Magadha, which was then a powerful kingdom.

3. *Udayana's Relations with the Neighbouring States*

Wedged between the two powerful neighbouring states of Avantī in the west and Magadha in the east, and with its capital city commanding the trade-routes by land and water in Mid-India, the city of Kauśâmbī was coveted by both Pajjota and Ajâtaśatru. The powerful king, Ajâtaśatru of Magadha, had extended his territory in the west as far as Kâśī, which touched the eastern confines of the kingdom of Kauśâmbī. King Pajjota invaded the kingdom of Kauśâmbī but was unsuccessful, and had to buy peace by giving his daughter in marriage to its king, Udayana.[83] Udayana secured the eastern frontiers of his kingdom by entering into a matrimonial alliance with the king of Magadha. These two royal marriages were essentially necessary for the maintenance of the political independence of Kauśâmbī, which

[83] See *ante* p. 15.

served as a buffer state between Avantī and Magadha. "Had not Udayana contracted these alliances," says Dr. Law, "Kauśâmbī would have fallen an easy prey to the overgrowing powers of Magadha and Avantī."[34] King Udayana conquered the country of the Bhaggas over whom his son Bodhi ruled as his viceroy.[35] Dr. Ray Chaudhary suggests that the Bhaggas were the descendants of the Epic and Purâṇic Bhârgavas.[36] If this illuminating supposition is correct, a close connection between these two peoples—the Bhaggas and the Vatsas—existed from a very early time, long before the time of the Buddha. During Udayana's time, however, they were known to be a republican people whom Udayana had conquered. Udayana was a war-like king and kept his army always in readiness. The elephants formed a considerable portion of his army.[37] He had his frontiers guarded by fortresses.[38] He beautified the city of Kauśâmbī with numerous palaces, tanks, and gardens.[39] He preserved forests and appointed forest guards to keep watch over them.[40]

[34] G. E. B., p. 23.
[35] M. N. II. 85.
[36] P. H. A. I., pp. 93, 130 f.
[37] Dh. A.
[38] Ibid.
[39] Ibid.
[40] M. N. III. 156-157.

KAUŚÂMBĪ IN THE TIME OF THE BUDDHA
(continued)

I. Udayana's Conversion to Buddhism

It was while the Buddha was passing the sixth year of his ministry, before the rains had set in at Kapilavastu, that he thought of introducing his doctrine in Kauśâmbī. Having left Kapilavastu he visited Vaiśâlī and Râjagṛiha and then came to Vârâṇasī. From that place the Buddha together with his disciples started for Kauśâmbī. King Udayana was reviewing his troops, which had been assembled for a military expedition to the city of Kanakavâtī, when he saw the Buddha approaching. Being angry at the untimely appearance of this messenger of peace who might delay or stop his military operations, he exclaimed: "All such messengers of bad luck must be put to death." With that he took a sharp arrow and shot at the Buddha. As the arrow flew through the air these words were heard:

"From malice is misery brought forth.
He who here gives up to sacrifice and quarrels
Hereafter will experience the misery of hell.
Put away misery and quarrelling".[1]

[1] Rockhill—The Life of the Buddha, p. 74.

When the king heard these words he became submissive to the Blessed One, and with clasped hands sat down near the Buddha, who began to instruct him on the futility of strife and quarrelling and on the utility of conquering egoism and not human enemies. Egoism is the greatest enemy of man. "Let discernment be your sword; faith, charity, and morality your fort; virtue your army and patience your armour. Let diligence be your spear, meditation your bow and detachment your arrow."[2] With these beautiful words the Buddha concluded his sermon to Udayana.

The above account of the conversion of King Udayana to Buddhism we get from the Tibetan sources. But the circumstances leading to Udayana's conversion to the new faith are different according to Pâli sources, only the fact of his early hostility to Buddhism being common to both. The Pâli canon and the Jâtakas tell us that it was Piṇḍola Bhāraddvāja, a highly respectable member of the Order, and not the Buddha himself, who converted Udayana to the new faith.[3] It may be that the actual conversion of the king took place after the Buddha visited Kauśâmbī. We are told

[2] Ibid.
[3] Buddhist India, p. 7.

in the Jâtakas that once when Udayana was on a picnic excursion with his women-folk, the Buddhist monk Piṇḍola appeared in the neighbourhood to preach. One day his women-folk left Udayana, when he was asleep, to go to hear the religious discourse of Piṇḍola. Being highly enraged at this, Udayana had him tortured by having a nest of brown ants tied to his body.[4] At another time, we are told in the Divyâvadâna, the pavilion of his queen Sâmâvatī, who had become an ardent follower of the Buddha, was burnt down, and the queen and her attendants perished in the flames.[5] Once again, a hermit's life was threatened by Udayana, and the hermit fled to Śrâvasti.[6] Such a king, who had been bitterly hostile to Buddhism, became a follower of the Buddhist church after coming into contact with Piṇḍola Bharaddvāja.

II. Buddha's Visit to Kausambi

Kauśâmbī—a Scene of Buddhist Activity

Even though we may discard the Tibetan account of Udayana's conversion and accept the Pâli version of the event as found in the Jâtakas, we have it on the authority of the Pâlī canon that

[4] Jâtaka 4, 375.
[5] Dvd. 533.
[6] Watters, p. 368.

the Buddha himself visited Kauśâmbī, delivered several *suttas*,[7] and built up the monastic life there. Pinḍola was a native of Kauśâmbī, being the son of Udayana's chaplain.[8] He had gone to Rajâgṛiha, entered the Order, and in due time attained the six-fold abhiññā (supernatural knowledge). It is therefore probable that the monk Pinḍola had preceded his master to preach Buddhism in his native city of Kauśâmbī and that the Buddha followed him. It is difficult to say how many times the Buddha actually visited Kauśâmbī. But from the study of the *suttas* and the circumstances which served as occasions for them, one can hazard a guess that the Buddha visited the city and sojourned in the territory of King Udayana at least twice, if not oftener. We have it on the authority of the *Majjhima Nikâya* that while the Lord was sojourning in the territory of the king of Kauśâmbī, the latter's son Prince Bodhi was instructed into Buddhism by the Buddha himself.[9] Buddhaghosha tells us the story of the Magandiya's hostility to the Buddha and of her jealous intrigue against Queen Sâmavâtī. The latter's devotion to Buddhism and admiration for the

[7] Kosambiya sutta; Sandaka sutta; Bodhi-Râjkumâra sutta; etc.

[8] G. E. B., p. 17.

[9] M. N. II. 91-97.

Buddha were taken advantage of by the former to alienate the king's affection from her.[10] These events presumably took place during the Buddha's first visit to Kauśâmbī, which occurred in the sixth year of his ministry. The perusal of the *Kosambiya Sutta*[11] suggests that the Buddha delivered it during his second visit when minor differences marred the harmony of the monastic life at Kauśâmbī, when strife and discord broke out among the almsmen there. When as a result of these differences and disputes the almsmen of Kauśâmbī 'were living in a state of uproar and contention, hurling taunts at one another, unable to win over others, nor won over by others, to accord and agreement,'[12] the Buddha while on a visit to that city delivered the famous *Kosambiya-Sutta*, the theme of which was amity and its root, and the means of making up the differences with a view to establishing goodwill among the almsmen. This second visit of the Buddha to Kauśâmbī, during which he delivered the above *sutta*, occurred, according to all authorities, about the ninth year of his ministry.

After the conversion of King Udayana Kauśâmbi became an important scene of activity

[10] Dh. A.
[11] M. N. I. 322-325.
[12] Ibid.

of the Buddha and his followers. The conversion of the king to Buddhism was followed by that of other royal personages including Prince Bodhi. After that there was a steady flow of conversions of the people of Kauśâmbī into the new faith. Gradually the *vihâras* and *ârâmas* for the residence of the *bhikkhus* sprang up in the city and its suburbs. *Ghositârâma* was the most famous of them. It was built by the wealthy merchant of Kauśâmbī, Ghosita.[18] It is from the *Ghositârâma* that the Buddha delivered the *Kosambiya Sutta*, the *Sandaka Sutta*, and the *Upakkilesa Sutta*. The theme of the Kosâmbiya Sutta has already been dealt with. The *Sandaka-Sutta* was a discourse on false guides, and the *Upakkilesa Sutta* was a homily against strife and disputes. The burden of instruction of all three discourses was almost identical, it being felt necessary by the Buddha to put repeated emphasis on these instructions to guard against false doctrines which created minor *schisms* among the brethren. This famous and beautiful pleasance, Ghositârâma, the residence of the Buddha at Kauśâmbī, was built on the south-eastern corner of the city of Kauśâmbī, just on the bank of the Yamunâ. The ruins of this Vihâra were seen by the Chinese pilgrims, Fa-Hien and Hiuen Tsang.

[18] Smv., pp, 317-319.

ON THE CHRONOLOGY OF KING UDAYANA

Dates are the sheet-anchor of history. A great deal of uncertainty and difficulty with regard to the historicity of King Udayana of Kauśâmbī will be removed if we can once ascertain the probable date of his reign. Then the king of Kauśâmbī who figures so prominently in Buddhist legends and traditions, in Pâli canonical and Sanskrit literature, will at once become a living historical personality and the events of his reign assume a political significance. The task is beset with dangers, but the importance of it justifies attempting it. The data available are meagre, and are mainly literary. The method adopted, therefore, to fix the chronology of Udayana is mathematical deduction, some later-day dates of impeccable certainty gathered from Mauryan history providing the major premises for our reasonings and conclusions. The periods of reign assigned to dynastic kings in the Purâṇas and the Ceylonese Chronicles—the *Dipavaṁsa* and the *Mahavaṁsa*—and references in Pâli canonical Texts have provided the links in the chain of arguments.

The only scholar known to me who has

until now made any attempt to give a date to King Udayana's reign is Dr. Pradhan. He calculates Udayana to have reigned from 500 B.C. to 490 B.C.[1] While unable to accept the date of Udayana's accession given by Dr. Pradhan as correct I must admit that he has hit the most satisfactory approximate time. Dr. Pradhan's purpose, however, was not to find a satisfactory solution of the problem of the chronology of Udayana's reign, but to find the date of the Great War of the Mahâbhârata. The finding of the dates of dynastic kings on the Purâṇic data was only ancillary to his main purpose, namely 'to arrive at a satisfactory solution of the problem of dating the Mahâbhârata War', to which he devoted the last four chapters of his book.

The date of Alexander's invasion of India (327-325 B.C.) and the date of his death (323 B. C.) are important landmarks for the chronology of early Indian history. It is not that we do not find dates mentioned in the Purâṇas, but the system used therein is defective. It was necessary to start from a date of impeccable basis to construct the Mauryan chronology. The Greek data provided us with that starting point. Candragupta's accession to the throne took place a few

[1] Pradhan, p. 247.

years after Alexander's retirement from India and probably after the great general's death. B. C. 321 has been accepted as the most probable date of Candragupta's accession.[2] It may have been a few years earlier or later, but certainly not earlier than 325 B.C. and not much later than 321 B.C. So, accepting 321 B.C. as the year of accession of Candragupta to the throne of Magadha, we may bring into use the data provided in the ancient literature for the purpose of finding the dates of pre-Mauryan kings of the various *janapadas* who were contemporaries of the Buddha and of whom King Udayana was one. Another important fact to be noticed in this connection is the date of the Buddha's *mahâparnibbâna*. Calculating on the basis of the length of the reigns of Śaisunâga and the Nanda kings given in the Purâṇas, Dr. Vincent Smith built up a chronology of the pre-Mauryan kings of Magadha, and places Ajâtaśatru's accession in c. 502 B.C. and the period of his reign 27 years.[3] Thus, accepting the Buddha's *mahâparnibbâna* to be in 487 B.C., as he does, Vincent Smith makes Ajâtaśatru survive the

[2] Thomas-C. H. I. vol. I. pp. 471-473. According to Dr. Vincent Smith the accession of Candragupta is 322 B.C. (E. H. I. p. 196). Mr. N. Bhattashali attempts to make it B.C. 313 (J. R. A. S., 1933) which is difficult to accept.

[3] E. H. I. Appendix C., p. 44. f.

the Buddha only two years. But according to the *Mahâvaṁsa* Ajâtaśatru reigned eight years after the death of the Buddha. Add eight years to 27, then substract the sum from B.C. 502, and you will get B.C. 483 as the year of the Buddha's death. Thus while Dr. Smith was surprisingly accurate in building up the chronology on the Purâṇic data, his neglect of the Ceylonese chronicles led him into the slight discrepancy pointed out above.[4]

We can arrive at the same approximate conclusion with regard to the date of the Buddha's death by a different process, with the help of other independent data. According to the *Dīpavaṁsa* and the *Mahâvaṁsa* the coronation of Aśoka took place 218 years after the death of the Buddha.[5] Now, according to the Ceylonese chronicles Candragupta reigned for 24 years and his son Bindusāra reigned for 28

[4] Dr. Charpenthier makes the date of the *parinibbana* 477 B.C. (vide his article in Ind. Ant., p. 173. ff.) The Buddhists hold the Mahâparinibbāna to have occurred in 443 B.C. According to the Maha-Bodhi Society's reckoning the year 1934 is the 2477th year of the Mahâparinibbâna. It is difficult to accept any of these views.

[5] Dv. VI. I. "Dve satâni ca vassâni aṭṭhârasa vassâni ca Sambuddhe parinibbute abhisitto Piyadassano" Mu. (P. T. s.) ch. v. p. 30:

"Jinanibbâṇato pacchâ pure tassâbhisekato sâṭṭhârasaṃ vassasatadvayaṃ evam vijâniyaṃ."

years.[6] Therefore, accepting B. C. 321, the year of Candragupta's accession, as a correct landmark of the Mauryan chronology, Aśoka's accession to the throne falls in 269 B.C. Now, according to the Kalinga Edict Aśoka conquered the kingdom of Kalinga in the eighth year after his coronation.[7] Again, some years passed between his accession to the throne and his coronation. According to Dr. Smith the gap is one of four years.[8] Therefore Aśoka's coronation took place in 265 B.C., if the Ceylonese chronicle is to be believed. Add

[6] All authorities—the Purâṇas, *Dipavaṁsa*, *Mahavâṁsa*, Buddhaghoṣa, and the Burmese tradition—agree as to the length of Candragupta's reign. The Purâṇas differ from the Ceylonese accounts as to Bindusāra's period of reign, which was 25 years according to the former and 28 years according to the latter.

[7] XIII R. E. *Aṭhavashâbhisitabâ devânam piyasha Piyadashine lâgine A (stava) sha-avhisita (sa de) vana priasa Priadraśi (sa) raño*

Kalinga v. j.
Kalingya vijita (.).

[8] Dr. Smith rejects the Ceylonese tradition and accepts the northern tradition as to the cause of the delay of Aśoka's coronation. According to the former Aśoka killed his 99 brothers before he could firmly establish himself on the throne. According to the latter, he fought his elder brother Susima alone. The story of the northern school, according to Dr. Smith, was invented by monks to place a dark background of Aśoka's early wickedness behind the bright picture of his mature piety. Mr. K. P. Jayaswal thinks that the delay was due to the fact that Aśoka attained his 25th year, the traditional age of royal *abhiṣeka*, three or four years after his accession. (J. B. O. R. S. 1917, p. 348).

218 years to 265, and you get 483, which is the year of the Buddha's *parinibbâna*.

If then 483 B.C. is the most credible date for the death of the Buddha, he must have been born in 563 B.C., as he was eighty years old when he chose his *parinibbâna* at Kusinârâ. There may be a great deal of controversy as to the exact date of his birth, but there is none as to the length of the life he lived, which is acknowledged to be eighty years mentioned in the Pâlī canons. And as the Pâlī texts—our only available source on the subject—inform us that he was 29 years old at the time of his great Renunciation, and 36 years old when he attained the Buddhahood, this last event must have happened about 527 B.C. We also learn from the Pâli texts that the Buddha visited Kauśâmbī at least twice—in the sixth and in the ninth year of his ministry. The first visit of the Buddha to Kauśâmbī, therefore, took place in 521 B.C. and the second in 518 B.C. During both these visits King Udayana reigned in Kauśâmbī. Now that we have been able to find the probable period of his reign, let us see if we can hit the probable date of his accession. It was during his first visit to Kauśâmbī, we have already noted, that the Buddha delivered the Bodhi-Râjakumâra-Sutta for the instruction of the prince of Kauśâmbī while he was the viceroy of the Bhagga country. Prince Bodhi was supposed to have passed his period of adolescence by that time to be considered fit to be put in charge of the government of a province.[9] So if Prince Bodhi was at least twenty-one years old when he was the viceroy of the Bhagga country, and when the Buddha paid his first visit to his father's kingdom, King Udayana was at least forty-two years old at a modest estimation in 521 B.C. King Udayana was evidently in the prime of his youth when Vâsuladattâ, the princess of Avanti, and the mother of Bodhi-Kumâra, fell in love with her father's handsome captive. So we presume that King Udayana married Vâsuladattâ in 543 B.C., when he

[9] I surmise it was a newly conquered province, which, according to my friend Tripiṭakācârya Râhula Sankrityâna, the great Pâlī scholar and tourist, is identical with the present Mirzapur District, the Suṁsumâra Giri being identical with the present Chunar hill. He first stated this in his book *Buddhacaryā*, pp. 75 and 175. I had also a talk with him on this subject, and was satisfied on the point that the Suṁsumâra Giri of the Bhagga country mentioned in the Majjhima Nikâya irresistibly suggests the Chunar hill as the nearest place of that description to Kauśâmbī. The place was evidently conquered by Udayana about whose war-like activities we find plenty of references in Pâli and Tibetan texts. The Bhaggas are mentioned in the *Mahâparinibbâna sutta* of the Dīgha Nikâya as a republican clan. This lends added point to our suggestion that a minor prince could not have been appointed to rule over a sturdy, independence-loving republican people.

was twenty years old. If the Prince, the first fruit of the wedlock, (and the only issue that we know of)[10] was born a year later, i.e. in 542 B.C., he was twenty-one years old in 521 B.C., the year of the Buddha's first visit to Kauśâmbī. We know from the Pâli sources that Udayana was *reigning* on the throne of Kauśâmbī when the incident leading to his romantic marriage with Vâsuladattâ took place; and if he was at least a year on the throne before that event, he ascended the throne in 544 B.C. Thus we may venture to determine King Udayana's chronology as follows:

Birth	563 B.C.
Accession	544 B.C.
Matrimonial Alliance with Avantī	543 B.C.
Birth of Bodhikumâra ..	542 B.C.

According to Peta-Vatthu commentary Udayana survived the Buddha,[11] but it does not mention the number of years. If the fact of survival mentioned in the Pâli commentary is to be believed, Dr. Pradhan's suggestion that Udayana died in 490 B.C. has to be rejected.

[10] Kat. Sat. Sag.
[11] Pet. Vat. Com. 140.

That event has to be placed certainly after 483 B.C. And considering 81 years of age is a sufficiently good old age for a man to live we may place the date of Udayana's death in 482 B.C. more reasonably than in 490 B.C., which conflicts with the evidence found in the Peta Vatthu commentary.

APPENDIX I

The genealogical tree of the kings of Kauśâmbī from Parikshit to Kṣemaka[1]

Parikṣit.
|
Janmejaya.
|
Satânīka.
|
Asvamedhadatta.
|
Adhisīmakrishna.
|
Nicakṣu.
|
Uṣna.
|
Citraratha.
|
Suciratha.
|
Bṛiṣnimant.
|
Suṣena.
|
Sunītha.
|
Nṛcakṣu.
|
Sukhiva.
|
Paripluta.
|
Sunaya.
|
Medhâven.
|
Nrpañjaya.
|
Tigma.
|
Bṛhadratha.
|
Vasudâman.
|
Satanika II.
|
Udayana.
|
Naravahana-Bodhi.
|
Daṇḍapani.
|
Niramitra.
|
Kṣemaka.

[1] Va, 99. 249-277. Mt. 50, 56-87; Bh. IX, 22, 33-44; Kat. Sar. Sag.

FROM THE DEATH OF UDAYANA TO THE THIRD CENTURY B. C.

I. The Last Four Kings of the House of Udayana

The Purâṇas mention only four kings of Kauśâmbī after Udayana. They are *Vahinara*, *Daṇḍapāṇi*, *Niramitra*, and *Kṣemaka*. According to the Pâli canon the son and successor of Udayana was Bodhi. Dr. Pradhan has prepared a list of the lineal descendants of Arjuna Pândava. Among those of this line who reigned in Kauśâmbī he names the son and successor of Udayana as *Vahinara-Naravâhana-Bodhi*. Dr. Pradhan has evidently drawn this list from the Purâṇic and Pâli data as well as from Kathâ-Sarit-Sâgara, as the name suggests. He, however, does not mention the Pâli data in the list of authorities given by him in the foot-note.[1] But it can be safely assumed that the Purâṇic Naravâhana can be identified with the Pâli Bodhi-Kumâra. Pâli literature, however, does not make clear whether Bodhi actually reigned as king of Kauśâmbī after Udayana.

[1] Pradhan, p. 65.

There is no positive evidence either way. The doubt of such a scholar as Dr. Rhys Davids whether Bodhi-Kumâra succeeded to his father's throne[2] is evidently based on the fact that nowhere in the Pâli Pitakâs is he ever mentioned as *King* Bodhi. He is always mentioned there as Bodhi-Kumâra or *Prince* Bodhi. But it should be noted that the Pâli Pitakâs have been collated and made up of the sayings of the Buddha in the First Great Buddhist Council in the *Sattapaṇṇi* Cave at Râjagriha a few weeks after the death of the Buddha.[3] The Buddha having died before Udayana he could not possibly have seen Prince Bodhi installed on his father's throne. He could therefore have had no opportunity to mention him in his sayings as King Bodhi. We are therefore entitled to assume on the authority of the Purâṇas that Naravâhana-Bodhi was the second king of Kauśâmbī from Udayana. The only information of a political nature that we get about Bodhi-Kumâra from the Pâli Piṭakâs is that he was the

[2] C. H. I., p. 187.

[3] A. G. I., p. 187. Also see *Sumangalavilâsinī*: "On the 21st day of the Buddha's *parinibbâna*, five hundred *theras* who were all arhats and possessed of analytical knowledge were selected. The Sattapaṇṇi Cave in Râjagriha was selected as the place of the meeting of the Council and the recital of the Buddha's sayings."

viceroy of the Bhagga country,[4] and that he ruled that country from his viceregal seat at Sumsumâra Giri.[5] The Bhaggas were a republican people[6] at the time of the Buddha. They were the descendants of the Epic Bhârgavas,[7] and as such were closely connected with the Vatsas, as cousins. The Bhagga country and the Suṁsumâra Giri have been identified, as we have seen, with the present Mirzapur District and the Chunar hill respectively.[8] Bodhi built a beautiful palace in his capital and called it 'The Lotus'.[9] He was expert in riding elephants.[10] He was evidently a capable prince and a worthy son of his father. The *Matsya* describes him as the 'brave king Vahinara.'[11]

The Buddha was staying at Suṁsumâra Giri when the new palace *The Lotus* was completed. Prince Bodhi, desiring to have it sanctified by the dust of the holy Buddha, invited him to a feast in his palace, and served the meal to him and his followers with his own hands. The Lord's meal

[4] See *ante* p. 32, note.
[5] M. N. II. 91-97.
[6] D. N. II., p. 167.
[7] See *ante* p. 19.
[8] See *ante* p. 32, note.
[9] M. N. II, 91-97.
[10] Ibid.
[11] "*Viro rajo Vahinarah*". Pargiter, p. 7.

over and done, the prince like a humble seeker after truth, sat on a low seat to one side of the Buddha, and listened to the instructions contained in the famous *Bodhi-Kumâra-Sutta*, as a result of which he took refuge in the 'Buddha, Dhamma and Saṁgna', and asked the Lord to 'accept him as his follower, who has found an abiding refuge while life lasts.'[12] This conclusively proves that Bodhi became an ardent follower of the Buddha while he was a prince, and must have been an ardent and great patron of the new faith after he became king.

Neither the Pâli literature nor the post-Buddhist Sanskrit literature mentions anything of the three Paurava or Kuru kings of Kauśâmbī after Bodhi, mentioned in the Purâṇas. The second and the third king after Udayana were, as has already been seen, Danḍapāṇi and NIRAMITRA. The fourth king was Kṣemaka with whom, according to Pargiter, 'the Kuru line of kings came to an end in the Kali Age.'[13]

II. NANDA RULE

After Kṣemaka no king of Kauśâmbī, as we have seen above, figures in the Purâṇic lists. This probably means the extinction of the independence

[12] M. N. II, 97.
[13] Pargiter, p. 66.

of Kauśâmbī, which was presumably absorbed in the Nanda Empire. The NANDAS of Magadha were the direct descendants of the Śaiśunâga kings, and were considered Sudras on account of the last of the Śaiśunâga kings, Mahânandin, marrying a Śūdra woman and thereby losing caste for his children.[14] Mahânandin's son, Mahâpadmananda, is the first of the Nanda kings of Magadha. The Nandas, nine in number, comprising only two generations, Mahâpadmananda and his eight sons, included nine kings who reigned in Magadha one after the other. The total period of the reigns of the nine Nandas, according to all the Purâṇas, covered one hundred years. They had inherited the suzerainty of North India from the Śaiśunâgas and largely extended it. The Nanda dynasty came to an end in 321 B. C., when Candragupta Maurya ascended the throne of Magadha. So the period of Nanda sovereignty started in 421 B.C. Now, three generations of kings reigned in Kauśâmbī between Udayana and Kṣemaka. Allowing 24 years for each step and assuming Udayana to have died in 482 B.C., as we have seen,[15] Kṣemeka ascended the throne in 410 B.C., and probably lost his independence during the rule of the first Nanda king

[14] C. H. I., p. 313.
[15] See *ante* p. 34.

who was admittedly a great conqueror.[16] Thus Kauśâmbī in all probability remained a part of the Nanda Empire through the greater part of the fifth century B.C. and the first two decades of the fourth century B.C.

III. Mauryan Rule

Kauśâmbī was undoubtedly subject to the **Mauryan Rule.** Although we have no evidence to connect Kauśâmbī with the rule of Magadha in the time of Candragupta Maurya, it is improbable that his empire which stretched from Magadha far upto the northwest, including the present Afghanisthan and Beluchisthan, should not have included it. Fortunately there is epigraphic evidence to show that Kauśâmbī was a 'district' in the empire of Aśoka, ruled by a *Mahâmatra*. The Allâhâbâd Stone Pillar of Aśoka contains his two inscriptions. One is known as the Queen's Edict and the other as the Kauśâmbī Edict. The latter, i.e., the Kauśâmbī Edict, contains a *śâsana* or order to the 'Mahâmâtra of the district of Kauśâmbī' to expel a Bhikshu or Bhikshuni as soon as he or she is detected in the act of creating a schism. Beyond this, the political history of Kauśâmbī during this period is a complete blank.

[16] Hâthigumphâ Inscription.

KAUŚÂMBĪ IN THE SECOND CENTURY B. C.

I. King Bahasatimita (Bahasatimitra)

The veil of darkness is satisfactorily lifted in the second century B.C. when we get the name of a king of Kauśâmbī from numismatic and epigraphic sources. Four copper (including bronze) coins found by Cunningham at Kosam, the site of the ancient Kauśâmbī, have been assigned by numismatists to the second century B.C.[1] Three of these coins are in the Indian Museum, Calcutta, and one is in the possession of the Asiatic Society of Bengal. One of these coins bears the name of Bahasatimita who ruled in Kauśâmbī.[2] This numismatic evidence derived from the Bahasatimita Coin finds a valuable corroboration from the Pabhosâ Cave Inscription.[3] The Pabhosâ Rock is about two miles west of the

[1] C. C. I. M. p. 155.

[2]

Metal.	*Obverse.*	*Reverse.*
AE	Bodhi tree in railing, with 'taurine' to l., below, in early Brâhmi character, (Ba) hasatimita (sa).	Defaced; probably a bull; in poor condition.

C. A. I., PL. V. 14.

[3] Ep. Ind. vol. II, pp. 242-243.

ruins of Kauśâmbī. The inscription records that Asadhasena, king of Ahicchatra and maternal uncle of king Bahasatimita, had a cave constructed for the residence of the Kassyapiya Arhats, in the tenth year of Odaka.[4] It has not yet been definitely ascertained who this Odaka was. The plain reading of the inscription would suggest that he was the king of Kauśâmbī and was in the tenth year of his reign when Âṣâdhasena constructed the cave. Mr. K. P. JAYASWAL renders 'उदकसम दसमे सवछरे' in the tenth year of Odraka's reign and suggests that he was the 'fifth of the Sunga kings.' Prof. Rapson accepts this suggestion and bases on it his conclusion that Bahasatimita was a 'feudatory king of the Sungas.'[5] There are difficulties in the way of accepting Mr. Jayaswal's suggestion, and they are greater in the way of accepting Prof. Rapson's conclusion. They will be discussed later under a separate heading. Prof. Rapson's conclusion would lead us to believe that Bahasatimita was a contemporary of Âṣâdhasena, the donor of the cave. But there is nothing in the inscription to bear out this belief. It only indicates a close relationship of the donor with the king Bahasatimita of Kauśâmbī,

[4] See Appendix II, p. 58, where this has been more fully discussed.

[5] C. H. I., p. 524.

which entitled the former to construct the cave in the territory of the latter, and in the close vicinity of his capital. I suggest that the name of Bahasatimita occurs in the inscription merely to indicate this relationship with the donor, and that Odaka was actually reigning in Kauśâmbī when the cave was constructed. The relationship of the donor with Odaka may not have been so close. The inscription perpetuates both names, that of the former king who was a relative of the donor, and of the then king in whose territory the cave was constructed. The donor is the king of Ahicchatra, (mod. Râmnagar in Rohilkhand) which was the capital of the ancient Northern Pañcâla. Allowing for the controversial portion of the inscription, one fact emerges certain from the two evidences[6] discussed above, and that is that Bahasatimita was the king of Kauśâmbī in the second century B.C., and that the two royal houses of Kauśâmbī and Pañcâla were closely connected by matrimony in that period. We have seen that Kurus reigned for a considerable time over Kauśâmbī; it is also a fact that the Kurus and the Pañcâlas were matrimonially connected in the Epic Age. We now find again in the second century B.C. that the two royal houses were closely connected by matrimony.

[6] The Bahasatimita Coin and Pabhosâ inscription.

Bahasatimita was also related by matrimony to the royal house of Mathurâ. This is proved by the famous Morâ inscription,[7] now in the Mathurâ Museum, in which the name of the king of Kauśâmbī and of his daughter Yaśamâta appear, the latter as the author of the dedicatory inscription. The inscription is as follows:

Jivaputaye Râjabharâye Brihâsvâtimita (dhi) tu Yaśamâtayē kâritaṁ.

It is written in Brâhmi characters of the Maurya-Śunga period and records the dedication of a well. Translated into English it means, "made by order of Yaśamâtâ, the daughter of Brihaspatimita, the king's consort (and) the mother of living sons."[8] Dr. Vogel has given good reasons to suppose that Brihaspatimita or Brihaspatimitra of the Morâ inscription is the Bahasatimita of the Kauśâmbī coin. He assigns the inscription on palæographical grounds to the third or second century B.C., and that is the approximate date, as we have seen, that has been adopted for

[7] The site of the discovery of the above inscription was Morâ, 7 miles west of Mathurâ city. Dr. Vogel, while he was officiating Director of Archaeology (1910-11) found at that place eight pieces of large-sized bricks on which the inscription was incised in Brâhmī characters of the Maurya-Śunga period. J. R. A. S., 1912, p. 120.

[8] Dr. Vogel's translation. Evidently the learned epigraphist takes the partially preserved letters (*dhi*) *tu* to mean *duhitâ* or daughter.

Bahasatimita's coin.[9] Unfortunately the name of the king of Mathurâ to whom Bahasatimita married his daughter Yasmâta is not mentioned in the inscription. The inscription is an important one and falls in the same category as the Pabhosâ inscription, as establishing the relationship of the royal house of Kauśâmbī with that of Mathurâ, in the second century B.C.

II. Was Bahasatimita a Feudatory King of Kausambi Under Odraka, the Fifth Sunga King?

The question arises: Was Kauśâmbī a feudatory state of the Śungas in the time of Bahasatimita? On the suggestion of Mr. Jayaswal that Odaka of the Pabhosâ inscription was the fifth Śunga king Odraka of Magadha, Prof. Rapson has concluded that Kauśâmbī was a feudatory state of the Śungas about that period.[10] In another place he states it more clearly thus: "We may infer from the inscriptions at Pabhosâ that, in the second century B.C., Pañcâla (Ahicchatra) and Vatsa (Kauśâmbī) were governed by the same royal family, and that both kingdoms acknowledged the suzerainty of the Śungas."[11]

[9] See *ante* p. 42.

[10] C. H. I., p. 521.

[11] Ibid., pp. 525-526.

The suggestion of Mr. Jayaswal is of doubtful value, because (1) there is no strong reason to suppose that the name Odaka in the inscription should not bear, as we have seen,[12] the plain meaning of his being the king of Kauśâmbī at the time when the inscription was recorded; (2) Odraka or Andhraka, the fifth Śunga king, is stated in the Purâṇas to have reigned for two years,[13] whereas the inscription suggests that he reigned for at least ten years. Appraising Mr. Jayaswal's suggestion as 'acute and plausible' and basing his conclusion thereon, Prof. Rapson meets the second difficulty by supposing that the Purâṇic date was a 'probable error creeping into the text of the Purâṇas.'[14] But he has not adduced any reasons for his suggestion. Even allowing that Mr. Jayaswal's suggestion that Odaka of the Pabhosâ inscription was the fifth Śunga king, and that of Prof. Rapson that the Purâṇic date was an error, the learned Professor's conclusion that Bahasatimita was a feudatory prince of Kauśâmbī under Odraka is untenable due to several other considerations:

[12] See *ante* p. 43.

[13] *Vasumitraḥ suto bhâvyo daśa varśâni pârthivaḥ tato' ndhrakaḥ same dve tu tasya putro bhaviṣyati*—Vasumitra will reign for ten years. Then his son Andhraka will reign for two years.—Pargiter, P. 34,

[14] 5. C. H. I., p. 521.

First, Prof. Rapson does not deny that the Bahasatimita of the Pabhosâ inscription and of the Kauśâmbī coin is the same person. But the Kauśâmbī coin does not contain any other name than Bahasatimita. If he was a feudatory king, the coin issued by him would have contained the name of his liege-lord in addition to his own. The issuing of coins is a privilege commonly enjoyed by independent sovereigns. And if in some instances this privilege was extended to feudatory rulers, those coins contained the names of the vassal king and the liege-lord. For instance, consider the silver coins found by Sir John Marshall at Taxila of Sapedana and of Satavastra who were the governors of the eastern provinces of the great Indo-Parthian King Gondopharnes or Gondophares.[15] These coins bear the portrait and symbol of the liege-lord Gondopharnes with the lofty title of 'GREAT KING, SUPREME KING OF KINGS' as well as the name of Sapedana or Satavastra, as the case may be, with the humbler title of 'GREAT KING, KING OF KINGS.' Prof. Rapson suggests that the allegiance of Sapedana and Satavastra to their suzerain, Gondopharnes, was 'merely nominal.'[16] His

[15] Marshall—A Guide to Taxila, p. 14.
[16] C. H. I., p. 580.

suggestion is correct, for even nominal allegiance would warrant joint names. But this cannot be said of the Bahasatimita's coin.

A similar proof can be obtained from some of the copper coins of the last Indo-Greek king Harmaios,[17] issued presumably during the latter part of his reign when he came under the control of the Kuṣâṇa king Kujula Kadphises. These coins bear the name of Kujula Kadphises in *Kharoṣṭhī* and that of Harmaios in Greek letters. Sir John Marshall says that 'Kujula Kadphises and Hermaios wrested the Kabul valley and Taxila from the Parthians.'[18] If Marshall is to be believed, Hermaios was an independent king of a portion of the northwestern portion of India and not of Kabul, when the Kuṣâṇa chief sought his help to oust the Parthians from their eastern possessions. It is, however, clear that after their conquest Hermaios was allowed by Kujula to rule the Kabul valley, and probably also Taxila, and the privilege of issuing coins, but had to acknowledge at least the nominal sovereignty of Kujula, as his coins bearing joint names indicate. Hermaios

[17] *Vide* C. C. I. M., vol. I, p. 33. I. AE. Coin with the joint names of Harmaios and Kujula Kadphises. The *obv.* contains the bust of the Greek king and his name in Greek letters. The *rev.* contains the words '*Kuyulakasasa kusanayavugasa dhramathidasa*' and the figure of Heracles standing.

[18] A Guide to Taxila, p. 16.

is the last Indo-Greek king hitherto known to us from the numismatic sources, and it is evident that his entire possessions were afterwards directly ruled by the Kuṣâṇa chief, probably after the former's death.[19]

On the other hand, there are coins of Hermaios, both silver and copper, which were evidently issued by him earlier than the joint copper coins discussed above, during the days of his independence. For instance, a silver coin of Hermaios[20] contains on the *rev.* busts of king and queen and their legends and titles and on the *obv.* in Kharoṣṭhī, '*maharajasa tratarasa Heramayasa*', below '*Kaliyapaya.*' Another silver coin bears the name and the bust of the king alone.[21] There are several other silver and copper coins of Hermaios of this kind,[22] indicative of his independence, in clear contrast with his subordination to Kujula as shown by the copper coins bearing the joint names.

[19] Dr. Ray Chaudhary says, "Kujula Kadphises, the Kushân king, succeeded Hermaios in the Kabul valley." P. H. A. I., p. 311. Acc. to Dr. V. Smith Kujula 'subjugated' him during his life-time. C. C. I. M. vol. I, p. 4.

[20] C. C. I. M., p. 31; 1. I. M. AR.

[21] Ibid., p. 32. I. M. 1. AR.

[22] Ibid., pp. 32-33. There are 26 such coins catalogued by Dr. Vincent Smith from the collections in the Indian Museum, and the Bengal Asiatic Society, Calcutta.

We may also cite, as examples, some coins bearing joint names struck by the Indo-Scythian kings, Azes I. and Azilises, indicative of the subordination of the one to the other. King Azes I. struck some coins bearing his own name in Greek on the obverse, and that of Azilises in *Kharoṣṭhī* on the reverse. Then again there are some coins of Azilises which bear his own name in Greek and that of Azes in *Kharoṣṭhī*. Dr. Bhandarkar and Dr. Smith point out that these two joint types of coins 'prove that Azilises, before his accession to independent power, was the subordinate colleague of an Azes and that an Azes similarly was subsequently the subordinate colleague of Azilises.'[23] Instances can be multiplied, but the few I have discussed should be enough for our purpose.

So in the absence of a second name on the Bahasatimita's coin, and in the absence of any other symbol to suggest its feudatory relation with the Śunga king Odraka of Magadha, I take it that Bahasatimita was an independent sovereign.

Second, The above view finds additional support when we consider the political conditions of the Śungas in the time of their King Odraka. Puṣyamitra overthrew the last of the Mauryas and founded

[23] P. H. A. I., p. 299.

the Sunga dynasty in Magadha in 184 B.C. The Mauryan empire had broken up during the days of Asoka's weak successors. Puṣyamitra brought back almost the whole of Northern India, including, of course, Kauśâmbī, to the imperial suzerainty of Magadha.[24] But the Sunga supremacy was short-lived, confined probably to the reign of Puṣhyamitra or at best to that of his two immediate successors. Prof. Rapson doubts whether 'Puṣhyamitra was able to hold it to the end and hand it on to his successors.'[25] There is no doubt that Puṣyamitra was the only Sunga king about whose exploits we hear from other sources besides the Purâṇas. Of course, his son Agnimitra, while he was viceroy of Vidiśâ,[26] and his grandson Vasumitra figured as heroes in one of Kalidasa's dramas—Malavikâgnimitra, the former as the lover of the princess of Vidarbha,[27] the latter as the guardian of his grandfather's sacrificial horse. This is all we know of them while they were princes and acted as provincial

[24] "Pushyamitra's authority embraced the territories in the Gangetic basin, corresponding with modern Behar, Tirhut, and the United Provinces of Agra and Oudh. It did not include the Punjab." E. H. I., pp. 198-99

[25] C. H. I., p. 527.

[26] Modern Besnagar near Bhilsa and 120 miles east of Ujjain (C. I).

[27] Modern Berar.

viceroys of Puṣyamitra. But as kings we hear nothing more of their exploits except their names in the dynastic lists of the Purâṇas. The total reigns of Agnimitra and of his two sons Vasuyeshtha and Vasumitra are abnormally short, amounting together to 25 years.[28] The total reigns of the next four Sunga kings are likewise short, covering in all 17 years.[29] No account of their activities is to be found anywhere. Prof. Rapson says, "No certain traces of the latter Śungas or of their feudatories have yet been found in the region of Magadha."[30] Under the title 'the later Śungas' Dr. V. A. Smith groups all the Śunga rulers from Agnimitra, the son of Puṣyamitra, downwards as unimportant kings with no record of achievements, and each enjoying an abnormally short period of reign, during whose time the empire began to break up. So it is clear that the Śunga empire which started breaking up during the life-time of its founder's son and grandsons could not possibly retain its hold on such a distant province as Kauśâmbī in the time of the fifth Śunga king Odraka. This becomes clearer from another consideration. Puṣyamitra's reign, as we have seen, started in

[28] Pargiter, p. 70.
[29] Ibid.
[30] C. H. I., p. 107.

184 B.C., and lasted for 36 years. His son Agnimitra and his two grandsons Vasujyeṣtha and Vasumitra, together reigned for 25 years. If we add up the total reigns and substract the sum from 184 B.C., which is the date of Puṣyamitra's accession, we get B.C. 123, the year when the fifth Sunga king Odraka is supposed to have ascended the throne; and this date falls within the period assigned to Bahasatimita's coin.[31] I therefore conclude that Kauśâmbī was an independent state in the time of the fifth Sunga king Odraka and that Bahasatimita struck coins in his own name as its sovereign. As an additional evidence of the view I hold, the instance of Agnimitra's coins may be cited. A large number of coins have been found in Râmnagar (District Bareilly, U. P.) in the ruins of the ancient Ahicchatra, the capital of Northern Pancâla. These coins bear the royal names of Agnimitra, Bhadraghoṣa, Bhânumitra, Bhūmimitra, Indramitra, Phalgunimitra, and Sūryamitra.[32] On account of Agnimitra's name being found on one set of coins, some numismatists mistook them to have belonged to Agnimitra Sunga of the Purâṇic lists, and the hero of the *Malavikâgnimitra* drama.[33] Cunningham has clearly shown that these coins do

[31] C. C. I. M., p. 155.
[32] Ibid., p. 185.
[33] Ibid.,

not belong to the second Sunga king but to an independent king of Ahicchatra bearing that name.[34] It is therefore not unreasonable to suppose that the Pancñâla coins, issued out of the mint of Ahicchatra, and the Kauśâmbī coins, a large number of which have been found in Kosam, the site of the ancient Kauśâmbī, fall in the same category and were issued when these two states enjoyed an independent status.

Third, Consider the Barhut Gateway inscription of Dhanabhūti, which is in clear contrast with the Pabhosâ Cave inscription of Aṣâḍhasena. The former clearly proves the sovereignty of the Sungas over Barhut, the latter does not contain any word to prove the Sunga sovereignty over Pabhosâ. The Barhut inscription records that "*within the dominion of the Sungas* the gateway has been caused to be made and the workmanship in stone produced by Vâtsiputra Dhanabhūti, son of Gotiputa Āgaraju who was the son of king Gârgiputra Viśvadeva."[35] 'Sunganam raje' in

[34] C. A. I., p. 80.

[35] Sunganam raje rano Gagiputasa
Visadevasa pautena Gotiputasa
Āgarajusa putena Vâchiputena
Dhanabhūtina kâritaṃ torânaṃ
Silâkaṃmaṃto ca upaṃna—Barhut Text that can be actually read in stone or in Cunningham's eye copy; (a) pillar of E. Gateway.

the Barhut inscription clearly proves, as I have said, Sunga supremacy over the region of the inscription, but there is no such word in the Pabhosâ inscription to prove, I repeat, that the place was '*within the dominion*' of the Sungas. The words in the Pabhosâ inscription are only 'in the tenth year of Odaka (*Odakasa dasamesabacchare*).[36] It is hard to believe that any inscription in the territory of a subordinate prince should not have contained any word to convey his relation to his sovereign prince. The Barhut inscription of Dhanabhūti, on the contrary, shows that it was the practice in those days for a subordinate prince to express the relationship.

So I hold that Prof. Rapson's conclusion of Sunga sovereignty over Kauśâmbī in the time of the Pabhosâ inscription appears to be incorrect in the light of the facts discussed above and which may be summarised again as follows:

(1) *The Bahasatimitra coin, which does not contain any other name except his own and which was issued in the time when the Sunga empire had broken up, proves that the author of the coin was an independent power.*

(2) *The Sunga Empire had broken up before*

[36] See appendix II where the Pabhosâ inscription has been fully discussed.

their king Odraka ascended the throne and was confined probably to Vidiśa and its immediate neighbourhood by the time Odraka became king.

(3) *The words in the Pabhosâ inscription are in clear contrast with those in the Barhut inscription. The latter conclusively prove the Sunga sovereignty over Barhut, the former do not prove the Sunga sovereignty over Pabhosâ.*

APPENDIX II

THE PABHOSA ROCK INSCRIPTION[1]

The Pabhosâ Rock is about two miles west of Kosam, the site of ancient Kauśâmbī. The inscription is in two parts incised in two different places on the rock. One is incised on the rough surface of the west wall of the cave, and the other on the rock outside the cave. Each in itself is incomplete, and forms part of one whole. The two inscriptions must be read together to get the full meaning. The inscription on the outer rock outside the cave is as follows:

TEXT

१ राज्ञो गोपाली पुत्र स
२ वह् सति मित्र स
३ मातुलेन गोपाली या
४ वैहिदरी पुत्रेण [आसा]
५ आसाढ सेनेन लेनं
६ कारितं [उदाकसम] दस
७ मे सवछरे कश्शपीयानं
८ [ता] नं — — — ोि — ि — — — [॥]

[1] EP. Ind. vol. 11., pp. 242-43.

Appendix II

TRANSLATION

"By Âsâḍhasena, the son of Gopâli Vaihidari (i. e. Vaihidara-Princes), and maternal uncle of king Bahasatimita, son of Gopâli, a cave was caused to be made in the tenth year of Odaka for the residence of the Kassyapiya Arhats."

According to Dr. Buhler the Kassyapiya Arhats mean either the Buddhist Arhats of the Kassyapiya school or the pupils of Bardhamana who was a Kaśyapa by *gotra*.[2] The fact that there is a beautiful Jaina temple on the flat surface of the rock which can be reached by a flight of magnificent stone stairs lends support to the correctness of the latter suggestion of the learned scholar. There is also a Jaina Dharamśâlâ in the village of Pabhosâ where on a tablet of red sandstone a votive inscription recording the building of a Jaina temple has been found.[3]

The other part of the inscription found inside the cave runs as follows:

TEXT

१ अधीक्षत्राया रायो शोणकायन पुत्रस्य वंग पालस्य

२ पुत्रस्य रायो तेवनी पुत्रस्य भागवतस्य पुत्रेण

३ वैहीदरी पुत्रेण आसादसेनेन कारितं [॥]

[2] Ibid.

[3] J. R. A. S. IV. 1927.

Translation

"Caused to be made by Âsâḍhasena, son of Vaihadari (Vaihidara-princes, and) son of king Bhagavata, son of Tevani (Traivarna-princes, and) son of king Vangapâla, son of Sonakâyana of Ahicchatra."

Dr. Fuhrer assigns the inscription to the 'second or first century B. C.' on palaeographical grounds.[4] King Bahasatimita of Kauśâmbī has been proved to have belonged to the second century B. C. on numismatic grounds,[5] and he was the immediate predecessor of Odaka, who, as seems likely, was the king of Kauśâmbi at the time of the inscription. The inscription is of special historical value as it enables us to construct the following genealogy of the two royal houses of Kauśâmbī and Ahicchatra in the second century B.C.

Kauśâmbī	*Ahicchatra*
	Sonakâyana
	Vaṁgapala
	Bhagawata
Gopala = Daughter	Âṣâḍhasena
Bahasatimita	

[4] Ep. Ind. vol. 11.
[5] See *ante* p. 42.

Taking Odaka to be the king of Kauśâmbī at the time of the inscription I place him immediately after Bahasatimita, for there is no king of Kauśâmbī mentioned anywhere who comes between Bahasatimita and Odaka. Why the name of Bahasatimita was mentioned at all if he was not alive as king of Kauśâmbī at the time of the inscription can be satisfactorily explained: the author of the inscription was a close relation of Bahasatimita, being his maternal uncle. There is no evidence which I can find from the inscription or from any other source to establish the relationship of Odaka with Bahasatimita or with Ashâdhasena. Even if he was the son of Bahasatimita, his relationship with Âṣâḍhasena is not close enough to be mentioned in preference to that of the latter. Kauśâmbī was an independent kingdom to which the village of Pabhosâ, where the rock exists, belonged. What was then the claim which prompted Âṣâḍhasena to seek for permission to use the rock for the purpose of dedication except his very near relationship with the royal house of Kauśâmbī in the time of Odaka's predecessor? This explains why the name of Bahasatimita with the words indicating his relationship with the author of the inscription appears in it along with that of the reigning king of Kauśâmbī who gave the permission for it.

KAUŚÂMBĪ IN THE FIRST CENTURY B.C.

The independence which Kauśâmbī enjoyed, as we have seen, during the time of the latter Śungas remained undisturbed during the whole of the first century B.C. The later Śungas retained a precarious hold on the imperial seat of India, Magadha, until 73 B.C., when they were replaced by the Kaṇvas. The Kaṇva rule in Magadha was too short to disturb the tranquillity of such distant provinces as Kauśâmbī and Ahicchatra. It lasted only 45 years[1] after which it was overthrown by the Andhras who came from the south about the close of the first century B.C. (28 B.C.) It is unlikely that the Andhras should have been able to extend their rule so far to the northwest within that short period. At least, there is no literary or archaeological reference to connect Kauśâmbī either with the imperial Kaṇvas or Andhras. On the other hand, there are coins found at Kosam which belong to the type of Bahasatimita's coins, and bear the names of their royal authors who evidently reigned in Kauśâmbī as independent kings.[2] These names are *Āsvaghoṣa, Jethamita, Devamitra,* and *Pavata.*

[1] E. H. I., p. 206.
[2] C. M. I. C., p. 146, and p. 155.

Dr. Smith assigns these coins to the second century B.C.,[3] and puts them in his catalogue after those of Bahasatimita. But it is not clear whether these kings reigned in Kauśâmbī before or after Bahasatimita. At least Dr. Smith has not thrown any light on this point. If these kings came after Bahasatimita, those coins may be on historical grounds assigned to the first century B.C., for the independent rule of Kauśâmbī under Bahasatimita could not begin long before the last quarter of the second century B.C. when the Sunga empire positively broke up, and Bahasatimita was followed by Odaka who reigned for more than ten years. The total reigns of these two kings should lead us to the close of the second century B.C., and therefore those four kings whose names appear on the coins may be reasonably assigned to the first century B.C., and as their coins indicate they reigned in Kauśâmbī as independent kings.[4]

[3] Ibid.

[4] This conclusion seems to find additional corroboration from a consideration of the political status of its neighbouring state of Northern Pancâla. A large number of coins discovered at Râmnagar, the site of the ancient Ahicchatra, the capital of Northern Pañcâla, which bear royal names, have been assigned by Dr. Smith to the first century B. C. (C. I. M. C.), pp. 185-188. This proves the independence of Ahicchatra beyond any doubt, and lends support to the view stated above.

KAUŚÂMBÎ DURING THE KUṢÂNA RULE

The independence of Kauśâmbī evidently remained undisturbed until it was absorbed in the Kuṣân empire. The discovery of a statue of the Buddha in March 1934, on which an inscription of Kaniṣka appears, lends epigraphic evidence to the fact that it was included in the empire of Kaniṣka and that it was conquered by him in or before the second year of his reign,[1] for the inscription is dated 'in the second year of Kaniṣka's reign.' The red-stone statue on the pedestal of which the inscription appears was the gift of a pious Buddhist lady to perpetuate the sacred memory of the Buddha's several visits to Kauśâmbī. Pâli canon bears testimony to the fact that the Buddha spent at least two rainy seasons in Kauśâmbī and gave discourses.[2] We have epigraphic evidence of Kaniṣka's conquest of Benares in or before the third year of his reign, i.e., a year later than that of Kauśâmbī. A giant red-stone Bodhisattva (*sic.*) statue discovered in the

[1] The inscription has been more fully dealt with on p. 107.

[2] See *ante* pp. 22-25.

Sârnath excavations and installed in the Sârnath Museum bears an inscription dated 'in the third year of Kaniṣka's reign.'[3] This shows that in his career of conquest towards the southeast, which extended as far as Magadha,[4] Kauśâmbī which fell in his way before Benâres was probably conquered in the second year of his reign and Benâres in the third.

[3] Ep. Ind., pp. 173-181.

[4] The fact that Kaniṣka carried away the famous Buddhist saint and scholar Aśvaghoṣa who acted as Vice-President of the Buddhist council held by the Emperor at Kundalavana Vihāra in Kashmir is considered by Dr. Smith as an evidence of his conquest of that city.—E. H. I., p. 260.

KAUŚÂMBĪ IN THE FOURTH CENTURY A.D.

I. Vakataka Supremacy

After the downfall of the Kuṣâna empire at the close of the second century A.D., India again broke up as usual into a number of independent states. Among the powers who ruled considerable kingdoms in the third century and the first quarter of the fourth century A.D. the Nâgas and the Vâkâtakas are the most important. We learn from the Purâṇas that the Nâgas ruled a considerable portion of Nothern India having established themselves in Vidiśâ, Padmâvatī, Kântipura, and Mathurâ.[1] The last of the Nâga kings, Ganapati Nâga of Mathurâ, is mentioned in the Allâhâbâd inscription of Samudragupta as one of the three kings of the Doâb who were killed in one day of the battle of Kauśâmbī about 345 A.D.[2] The Vâkâṭakas arose in the Central Deccan towards the close of the third century,[3] and later became a predominant power in Central India and ruled a considerable portion of Northern

[1] J. R. A. S. 1915, p. 72.
[2] See later, p. 68.
[3] P. H. A. I., p. 342.

India.[4] It may be Kauśâmbī was under the supremacy of the Nâgas in the third century A.D. We have however no epigraphic evidence to connect the Nâga supremacy with Kauśâmbī and therefore cannot be sure on this point. Excavations of the site of Kauśâmbī are expected to throw some sure light on the history of Kauśâmbī in the third century. It is probable that the Vâkâṭakas wrested from the Nâgas some of their possessions in Northern India in the beginning of the fourth century A.D., when the Vâkâṭakas became a great power and claimed imperial dignity in the time of Pravarasena I. In a recent publication Mr. Jayaswal has shown that Pravarasena I. (300-314 A.D.) ruled from his capital Chanaka,[5] and performed four *Aśvamedhas*. It was the usual practice among the imperial rulers of India observed from the earliest time known to us to have their sons and grandsons, brothers and nephews installed as rulers over different provinces. The system of the Vâkâṭaka imperial organization was the same. According to the Purâṇas Pravarasena's four sons were provincial rulers. Mr. Jayaswal's

[4] Ibid.

[5] Jayaswal, p. 70. Chanaka roughly corresponds to the present village of Nachana, 2 miles to the west of Gauj, which is 25 miles to the S. W. of Panna and 15 miles to the S. W. of Najodh, both ruling states of C. I.

illuminating suggestion is that Maharâja Srī Bhimasena, a Vâkâtaka Prince " who has left four printed inscriptions in a cave temple about forty miles southwest of Allahabad in his 52nd year was evidently the governor of Kauśâmbī."[6]

II. The battle of Kausambi: The Gupta Supremacy

Kauśâmbī was brought under the imperial supremacy of the Guptas in the time of Samudragupta. Mr. Jayaswal is of the opinion that the pitched battle in which Samudragupta won a decided victory and consequently supremacy over Northern India was fought at Kauśâmbī in 344 or 345 A.D. According to the Allâhâbâd Inscription, states Mr. Jayaswal, Samudragupta's wars in Âryâvarta were in two parts—one before the southern expedition and the other after it. The first act of Samudragupta which turned the scale of political fortunes in his favour was the pitched battle with three kings—Acyuta, Nâgasena and Gaṇapati Nâga, who were rulers of Ahicchatra, Mathurâ and Padmâvatī respectively.[7] "The

[6] Jayaswal, p. 98. Also A. S. R., p. 119, Plate XXX.

[7] Ibid., p. 132. There is also numismatic evidence to show that Achyuta was the king of Ahicchatra about that time. A copper circular coin bearing the name of Achyuta in bold character now in the Calcutta Musuem has been dated by Dr. Smith to belong to 330 A.D.—C. C. I. M., p. 188.

convenient place," states Mr. Jayaswal, "upon which rulers from Ahicchatra, Mathurâ and Padmavati[8] would have converged was Kauśâmbī or Allâhâbâd, more likely the former, as the royal route to Pâtaliputra lay through Kauśâmbī."[9] Pâli literature bears, as we have seen,[10] ample evidence of the fact that Kauśâmbī was not only an important river station for goods and passengers coming west by the river routes from Magadha, Campa and Kośala, but roads coming from the southwest, west and northwest converged on Kauśâmbī. The proclamation of this victory was inscribed by Samudragupta on the Aśoka Pillar then *in situ* at Kauśâmbī and subsequently transferred to Allâhâbâd, probably by Akbar.[11] In line 30 of the *prasasti* the proud victor in the battle exultantly mentions that all three kings—Acyuta, Nâgasena and Gaṇapati-Nâga—were killed in one day of the battle.[12] If Mr. Jayaswal's suggestion that the battle which gave Samudragupta the supremacy over Northern India was fought at Kauśâmbī is correct, as I have reason to believe

[8] Narwar, a famous city which still exists in the territory of the Mâhârâja of Sindhia.

[9] Jayaswal, p. 134.

[10] See *ante* p. 7.

[11] See p. 107.

[12] Allâhâbâd Pillar Inscription.

it is, Kauśâmbī receives an added importance in its history of the fourth century A.D. I hope further materials, which are expected to be forthcoming if the contemplated excavation of the site of Kauśâmbī by the Allâhâbâd Archaeological Society is undertaken, will provide additional corroborative evidence of this important fact.

KAUŚÂMBĪ IN THE FIFTH AND IN THE SEVENTH CENTURY A.D.

THE CHINESE PILGRIMS AT KAUSAMBI

For the history of Kauśâmbī in the fifth and in the seventh century A.D. we are primarily indebted to the two Chinese pilgrims, Fa-hien and Hiuen Tsang, who naturally visited this sacred city of the Buddhists during their sojourn in India. *Fa-hien* visited India during the latter part of the reign of Candragupta II, Vikramāditya, the son and successor of Samudragupta, and stayed in the country for six years (405-411). *Hiuen Tsang's* sojourn in India two centuries later also fell, it is interesting to note, during the *latter* part of Harṣavardhana's reign (629-643). Both the pilgrims timed their visits to India most opportunely, when the wars were finished, the imperial rule was firmly established and peace reigned supreme in the land, which enabled the pilgrims to move about in the country most freely without molestation of any kind. Both pilgrims speak highly of the conditions of roads and of the absence of thieves and robbers—a testimony which redounds to the glory of the

Indian administration in the fifth and in the seventh century A.D., of which we can be legitimately proud.

Fa-hien's notice of the city of Kauśâmbī in his record is brief; that of Hiuen Tsang is in fuller detail. Both of them are silent about the political condition of Kauśâmbī during their visits. But that is partly because Kauśâmbī was during their visits under the imperial rule of the Guptas and of Harṣvardhana, respectively, and there was no independent or subordinate king residing in the city whose guests they were; and partly because of the fact that the two travellers came to India primarily as pious pilgrims to pay respects to the Buddhist shrines, and to collect and carry home copies of the Pâli Piṭakâs, if they could find any. Consequently their notice of Kauśâmbī, in common with that of many other places, was confined to the religious conditions obtaining there at the time. The record of the pilgrims regarding Kauśâmbī, however, clearly points out one thing, namely, that it was once an important scene of Buddhist activity, and was still a centre of Hīnayâna Buddhism. Fa-hien says: "Thirteen yojans[1] to the northwest of the shrine (Deer Park, Benares) is a country called Kauśâmbī. There is

[1] One yojan is to be considered equal to eight British miles.

a shrine there, known as the garden of Ghochirârâma, in which Buddha once dwelt, and where there are still priests, mostly of the lesser vehicle."[2] Ghochirârâma is the Ghositârâma or Ghosikârâma of Hiuen Tsang and Buddhaghosha, a pleasance and *vihâra* built by the pious and wealthy Buddhist merchant Ghosita or Ghosika. Evidently the Ghositârâma was in good condition in the fifth century A.D. when Fa-hien visited Kauśâmbī. It was however reduced to ruins when Hiuen Tsang visited the place in the seventh century A.D. This may be accounted for by the fact that the Huṇas who poured into India in the latter part of the fifth century A.D. carried on a systematic ravage of the country and destruction of buildings, the Śaiva Temples and Buddhist Monasteries coming equally under their vandalic lust.

The records of Hiuen Tsang show that the monasteries in Kauśâmbī were in a ruined condition in his time. He saw ten such monasteries.[3] There were three hundred brethren living in Kauśâmbī, all following the Hīnayâna system.[4] A Buddhist temple existed in his time. "Within the royal enclosure of the capital," says the pilgrim, "was

[2] Giles—Travels of Fa-Hien.
[3] Watters. II., p. 366.
[4] Ibid.

a large Buddhist temple over sixty feet high in which was a carved *Sandal-wood Image* of the Buddha with a stone canopy suspended over it."[5] This image, according to Hiuen Tsang, was the one made at the request of Udayana.[6] Watters says (on the authority of the Chinese account) that the same image was taken to Khotan or probably to China. The ruins of the house of the wealthy and pious Buddhist banker Ghosita, the donor of the Ghositârâma, were seen by the pilgrim. The house was in the 'southeast corner of the city.'[7] It is interesting to note that the southeast corner of the present site of Kauśâmbī is exactly on the river Yamuna which flows along its southern side. Ghosita was a premier merchant of Kauśâmbī, and the position of his residence was, precisely as it should have been, on the river bank. The pilgrim also saw 'a Buddhist temple, a hair and nail relic tope and the remains of the Buddha's bath-house.'[8] The temple referred to here is different from the one mentioned above, namely, the one built at the request of King Udayana. Wherever the Buddha lived for a long time, he had occasions to shave his head and to cut his nails. They were taken by pious and devout Buddhists as sacred relics over which they

[5] Ibid., p. 368. [6] Ibid. [7] Ibid., p. 369. [8] Ibid.

built a Stūpa. The ruins of the main monastery at Kauśâmbī, the Ghositârâma where the Buddha resided with his followers during his visits to the city, were also seen by the pilgrim, the site of which was 'outside the city on its southeast side.' Thus it is evident that the *ârâma* was built outside the city and on the river bank, for the convenience of the pilgrims and monks. This account of the position of the Ghositârâma receives corroboration from an independent source, the Piṭakás, where we find that the *ârâmas* built in different places for the residence of the Buddha and his followers were as a rule outside the city. The Buddha, we find in the Piṭakás, always preferred to live outside the city, even though he had to visit large cities to carry on evangelistic work. He loved to live in the quiet of a suburban hermitage—away from the din and bustle of city life. The main monasteries, such as Ghositârâma at Kauśâmbī, Jetavana at Śrâvastī, Gandhakuṭī-vihâra at Vârâṇasi, Mahâvanakuṭâgâraśâlâ at Vaisâli, were all built outside the city.

"To the southeast of Ghositârâma," Hiuen Tsang proceeds, "was a two-storied building with an old brick upper-chamber; and in this Vasubandhu lodged and composed the *Wei-shih-lun* for the refuting of Hinayânists and the confounding of the non-Buddhists." Then he says, "In a mango wood east of the Ghositârâma were the old foundations of the house in which Asaṅga P'usa composed the *Hsien-Yang-Sheng-Chiao-lun*."[9]

Wei-shih-lun is, according to Julien, the Chinese name of the book known as *Vidyâmâtra siddhi-śâstra*. The book is an explanatory commentary on the relation of mind and matter, and aims at refuting false doctrines of Buddhism, as they appeared to be. Vasubandhu belonged to the realistic school of Buddhism and was a great authority on Mahâyâna as well as Hīnayâna philosophy. He is famous as a great exponent of Mahâyâna doctrines. He was born about 288 A.D. and was a native of Gandhâra. He came to Ayodhyâ, being invited by Samudra-gupta. According to Paramârtha, who wrote a life of Vasubandhu, the king Vikramâditya of Ayodhyâ was induced by the writings of Vasubandhu to take an interest in Buddhism. He sent his queen, with the crown prince Bâlâditya, to study Buddhism under the famous teacher. When Bâlâditya became king he invited Vasubandhu to Ayodhyâ and favoured him with special

[9] Watters, pp. 370-371. The work with its commentaries is being restored from Chinese to Sanskrit under the more correct name of *Vigñaptimatrarasiddhi-śastra* by my friend Tripitakâchârya Râhula. Half of it is already published in J. B. O. S. (1933-34).

patronage.[10] This Baladitya, according to Peri and Dr. Vincent Smith, is Samudragupta who bore the title of Bâlâditya in his youth.[11] Thus Vasubandhu's activity must have covered the greater part of the fourth century A.D. He lived most of his time at Ayodhyâ in the court of Samudragupta under whose patronage he composed most of his books. He probably came to Kauśâmbī where, as Hiuen Tsang says, he composed *Wei-shih-lun,* after Samudragupta had brought Kauśâmbī under his rule by his great victory at the battle of Kauśâmbī in about 345 A.D.[12]

Asaṅga who, the pilgrim says, also lived in Kauśâmbī and composed there the *Hsien-Yang-Sheng-Chiao-lun*, was the elder brother of Vasubandhu and a remarkable personality of that time. He, like his brother, resided in Samudragupta's court at Ayodhyâ and was equally patronised by the emperor. Like his brother he was a great exponent of Mahâyâna Buddhism and a founder of the idealistic school of *Yogâcâra.* His notable contribution to the intellectual movements of the age was the systematisation of the idealistic philosophy which afterwards produced such great logicians as Diṅnâga and Dharmakīrti.

[10] J. R. A. S. 1905.
[11] E. H. I., pp. 328-334.
[12] See *ante* p. 3.

According to this school internal or subjective ideas are the only real things: the external is a reflection of the internal, and has no real existence. The world as we see it is nothing but the creation of minds. This school is known as Vijñânavâda or the school of Yogâcâra. His famous book goes by the name of *Yogâcharya Bhūmi Śâstra*, which was partially translated by Dharmarakṣa[18] between A.D. 414 and 421. The one that he wrote at Kauśâmbī, if Hiuen Tsang's statement is to be believed, is an exposition of that book. The fact that both these brothers who were Buddhist scholars and writers of first importance in the fourth century A.D. came to Kauśâmbī and lived there at least for some time is an eloquent testimony to the fact that the city was still regarded as an important centre of Buddhism.

[18] Dharmarakṣa was an Indo-Scythian Buddhist scholar and writer. He was a contemporary of Asaṁga and his brother, being born towards the middle of the third century A.D. He was a native of the famous Buddhist town of Touen-hoang in northeastern China, which had grown into an important centre of Buddhist missionary activity as early as the 2nd century A.D. Dharmarakṣa received his education from an Indian teacher and travelled with him to different parts of Central Asia and northwestern India. He knew 36 different languages and possessed a first-hand knowledge of Buddhism. A monk of rare genius, he translated more than 200 Sanskrit texts into Chinese, of which 90 works still exist. He died about the first quarter of the fourth century A.D.

FROM THE DEATH OF HARṢAVARDHANA TO THE ELEVENTH CENTURY A.D.

Rule of The Pratihara Kings of Kanauj

In the time of Harṣavardhana, Lord Paramount of Northern India, Kauśâmbī was subordinate to the imperial government of Kanauj, which was chosen by Harṣa as his capital. Kanauj was an ancient city. It is mentioned in several passages in the Mahâbhârata, and by Patañjali in the second century B.C. It was visited by Fa-hien about A.D. 405, during the reign of Candragupta II, Vikramâditya. During that time Kanauj came to be a considerable town under the patronage of the Gupta kings. After Harṣa had selected it as his capital, it developed into a prosperous, beautiful, and crowded city, as testified to by Hiuen Tsang who visited it first in 636 and then in 643 A.D. The kingdom of Kanauj roughly corresponded to the ancient Pancâla with its two capitals—Ahicchatra and Kampila.[1] The rapid development of Kanauj

[1] Ancient Pancâla had two political divisions, Northern and Southern Pañcâlas. Ahicchatra was the capital of the northern division and Kampila the capital of the southern division.

under Harṣa threw both these towns into obscurity. After Harṣa's time Kanauj became the most important town in Northern India, and the fate of Kauśâmbī was linked up with it.

Harṣa's death in A.D. 647 was followed by the break-up of his vast empire, and for about a hundred years we know of no kings ruling in Kanauj. The earliest known king of Kanauj after Harṣa's death is Yaśovarman who, according to Râjataraṅgiṇi, sent an embassy in A.D. 731 and was later dethroned by Lalitâditya Muktâpīḍa of Kashmīr[2] and whose name holds an honoured place in the history of Sanskrit literature as that of the patron of Bhavabhūti, the celebrated author of *Mâlatīmâdhava*. The successors of Yaśovarman retained a precarious hold on the throne of Kanauj until A.D. 816, when the last of the dynasty of Cakrâyudha was deposed by Nâgabhaṭa, a Gurjara-Pratihâra king who came from Western Rajputana and established Pratihâra rule in Kanauj which lasted for more than two hundred years. That during all these years Kauśâmbī was part[3] of the kingdom of Kanauj is proved by two inscriptions. The first is the Jhunsi copper-plate

[2] Stein, transl. Râjatar., BK. IV, pp. 136-46.

[3] Referred to as *Maṇḍala* in Yasapala's inscription which was an administrative division above the village. See Beni Prasad—The State in Ancient India, p. 417.

inscription which is ascribed to Trilocanapâla. As the genealogical table given below of the Pratihâra kings of Kanauj will show, Trilocanapâla was the eighth king from Nâgabhaṭa, the founder of the supremacy of his dynasty in Kanauj.

Pratihâra Kings of Kanauj

Nâgabhaṭa. 816-825.
|
Râmabhadra. 825-840.
|
Mihira Bhoja. 840-890.
|
Mahendrapâla. 890-c. 893. — Mahīpâla. 910-940.
|
Devapâla. 940-955. — Vijayâpala. 955-990.
|
Rajyapâla. 990-1019
|
Trilocanapâla. 1019-c. 1027
|
Yaśapâla. 1027-c. 1036.

The Jhunsi copper-plate inscription of Trilocanapâla records that he granted the village of Jhunsi to a Brâhmin.[4] This shows that his rule extended from Kanauj to Jhunsi, which is on the eastern side of the Ganges across from the

[4] J. A. S. B, XXXI, p. 8; I. A. Vol. XVIII, pp. 33-35.

town of Allâhâbâd, and as such it included Kauśâmbī which is only 38 miles southwest of Allâhâbâd. The second inscription, that of Yaśapâla, the son and successor of Trilocanapâla, more definitely proves that Kauśâmbī was under the rule of the Pratihâra kings of Kanauj. This inscription, which has been noticed in detail in another connection,[5] refers to the grant of the village of Payalâsa (mod. Prâs) in the '*Kauśâmbī-maṇḍala*' to one Mathurâ Vikṭâ of Pabhosâ. This conclusively proves that Kauśâmbī was in the eleventh century an administrative subdivision of the kings of Kanauj.

[5] See *post* pp. 98-100

ON THE IDENTIFICATION OF KAUŚÂMBĪ

The information regarding the early history of Kauśâmbī given in the foregoing pages will lose much of its importance unless we can satisfactorily identify the place. I propose to discuss this problem of identification now.

As early as February 1861 Babu Shiva Prasad of the Education Department, who took a deep and intelligent interest in all archaeological matters, informed Mr. Cunningham while he was Archaeological Surveyor to the Government of India that the village of Kosam, 30 miles from Allâhâbâd, was still known as Kauśâmbī-Nagar, that it was even then a great resort of the Jains and that only a century ago it was a large and flourishing city.[1]

As far as is known to the writer a report of the ancient ruins of Kauśâmbī was first published by Sir Alexander Cunningham, as Director of the Archaeological Survey of India, in 1871.[2] He definitely identified the present village of Kosam, a little more than 30 miles across the fields, and

[1] C. A. G. I., p. 41.
[2] A. S. R. Vol. 1. 1871.

38 miles by road, from Allâhâbâd, with the ancient city of Kauśâmbī as found in the Pâli literature and described by the Chinese pilgrim in the seventh century. Sir Alexander based his conclusion on two considerations. The first is the famous legend of Ba-kula[8] which he adopted in a truncated form from Hardy's Manual of Buddhism. The legend may be summarised thus:

The infant Bakula was born at Kauśâmbī, and while his mother was bathing in the Yamunâ, he accidentally fell into the river, and being swallowed by a fish, was carried to Benâres. There the fish fell into the net of a fisherman who sold it to the wife of a nobleman. On opening the fish she found a young child still alive inside, and at once adopted it as her own. The true mother, hearing of this wonderful escape of the infant, proceeded to Benâres and demanded the return of the child which was, of course, refused. The matter was then referred to the king, who decided that both the claimants were mothers of the child—the one by *maternity*, the other by *purchase*. The child was accordingly called Ba-kula, that is, of two *kulas* or races.

Cunningham says that "The legend of Bakula is sufficient to prove that the city of Kauśâmbī

[8] Ibid., pp. 303-304.

was situated on the Yamunâ."[4] The second reason for his conclusion is that the distance of Kosam from Allahabad corresponds with that between Prayâg and Kauśâmbī as recorded by Hiuen Tsang. There is indeed an obvious danger, seen by Cunningham himself, in fixing the identity of the place on the distance given by Hiuen Tsang, which is different in two places, and in one place too far to make Kauśâmbī anywhere near Allâhâbâd. But the clear and convincing argument with which he meets this obvious discrepancy is interesting. Let me quote Cunningham's own words:

"Unfortunately the distance (between Prayâg and Kauśâmbī) is differently stated in the *life* and in the *travels* of the Chinese pilgrim. In the former, the distance is given as fifty *li*[5] and in the latter five hundred *li*, whilst in the return journey to China, the pilgrim states that between Prayâg and Kauśâmbī he travelled for seven days through a vast forest and over bare plains. Now as the village of Kosam is only 31 miles from the fort at Allâhâbâd, the last statement would seem to preclude all possibility of its identification with the ancient Kauśâmbī. But strange to say, it

[4] Ibid., pp. 451-452. The story is more fully stated by Spencer Hardy in *Manual of Buddhism*, 2nd Ed., p. 520.

[5] A Chinese *li* is equal to a little more than a British mile.

affords the most satisfactory proof of their identity, for the subsequent route of the pilgrim to Saṅkaīsa is said to have occupied one month, and as the whole distance from Prayâg to Saṅkaīsa is only 200 miles, the average length of the pilgrim's daily march was not more than 5½ miles. This slow progress is most satisfactorily accounted for by the fact that the march from Prayâg to Saṅkaīsa was a religious procession headed by the great king Harṣavardhana of Kanauj with a train of no less than eighteen tributary kings, besides many thousands of Buddhist monks and followers. According to this reckoning the distance between Prayâg and Kauśâmbī would be 38 miles, which corresponds very closely with the actual road distance as I found it. By one route on going to Kosam I made the distance 37 miles, and return route 35 miles. The only probable explanation of Hiuen Tsang's varying distance of 50 *li* and 500 *li* that occurs to me is, that he converted the *yojanas* into Chinese *li* at the rate of 40 *li* per *yojana* or 10 *li* per *kos*, he must have written 150 *li*, the equivalent of 15 *kos*, which is the actual distance across the fields for foot passengers from Kosam to the fort of Allâhâbâd, according to the reckoning of the people of Kosam itself. But whether the explanation is correct or not, it is quite certain that the present Kosam stands on the actual site of the ancient Kauśâmbī."[6]

Thus, Cunningham was sure in his mind of the identity of the place, although the evidence on which he based his conclusion was partly traditional (the Legend of Bakula) and partly argumentative. Doubts as to Cunningham's identification of Kauśâmbī have since been expressed by Dr. Vincent Smith and Mr. Watters. Evidently, the traditional evidence and argumentative reasons with which Cunningham explained the discrepancies of the distance given in the *life* and *travel* of Hiuen Tsang have failed to carry conviction to the minds of those scholars. Believing the distance from Prayâg to Kauśâmbī to be 500 *li* as given in the *travel* and ignoring Cunningham's very illuminating suggestion of the probable transcriptional error of 50 *li* for 150 *li* and the circumstances which explain the march requiring seven days to cover the distance of 38 miles, Vincent Smith located Kauśâmbī near Satna[7] and Watters somewhere near Śrâvastī.[8]

Evidences of more positive and impeccable nature than those Cunningham could get have since been available to us, and we can reject the sites suggested by Dr. Smith and Mr. Watters, and

[6] Ibid., p. 305.
[7] J. R. A. S. 1898.
[8] Watters, pp. 367-68.

accept Mr. Cunningham's identification as true. This only shows how that wonderful master-mind of pioneer researches in ancient Indian History, Sir Alexander Cunningham, could build a true theory on a comparatively slender basis. The ancient city of Śrâvastī was identified by Cunningham with ruins of Saheṭ-Maheṭ in the district of Gonda (U. P.) and that identification has since been confirmed by the find of two inscriptions during the joint exploration of the ancient mounds at Saheṭ-Maheṭ by three eminent archaeologists, Dr. Vogel, Sir John Marshall and R. B. Daya Ram Sahni during the years 1907-1909. "These two important inscriptions," says R. B. Sahni, "finally and conclusively established the identity of those remains with Srâvasti."[9] This being so, it is useless to try to identify them any longer with Kauśâmbī. The claim of Satna being the site of the ancient Kauśâmbī may also be dismissed in the light of positive evidences which undoubtedly fix the village of Kosam as the site of the ancient city of Kauśâmbī. Let us now examine the evidences which will give a quietus to, and satisfactorily solve, this important controversy.

1. Fa-hien, as I have stated elsewhere,[10]

[9] J. R. A. S. 1927.
[10] See *ante* p. 71.

visited Kauśâmbī during his Indian itinerary (A.D. 405-11). He makes the distance of Kauśâmbī 'thirteen *yojanas* from the Deer Park.' Now, thirteen *yojanas*, according to Fa-hien's reckoning, are equivalent to 104 miles[11] of British road distance, and that closely corresponds to the actual distance between Benâres and the present village of Kosam.

2. In the Pâli Texts we find the name of 'Sahajâti' as being the terminus of the Ganges route for the boats plying from the east *en route* to Kauśâmbī which was reached by plying some distance along the Yamunâ.[12] Now Sahajâti has been definitely identified with the ruins of Bhītâ about 9 miles S. S. W. from Allâhâbâd by the discovery of a terra-cotta seal containing the name of 'Sahajâti.'[13] The suggestion that one naturally makes from references in Pâli Text that Sahajâti must have been somewhere near Prayâg at the junction of the Ganges and the Yamunâ, is thus corroborated by the find of that important seal in Bhitâ. I have visited Bhiṭâ twice. The course of the

[11] G. A. I., p. 656.

[12] *Ante* p. 6.

[13] "The name of the place (Bhitâ) was Sahajâti, which is found in a terra cotta seal matrix in the house called by Sir John Marshall the 'House of Guild.' It is seal No. I which is the oldest record found in Bhitâ. It is in Mâgadhī and reads śahajâtiye niga maśa. Every letter of the seal is at least a century older (if not earlier still) than Aśokaś' letters.– Jayaswal, p. 225.

Ganges must have changed considerably from the time of the Buddha to put the present ruins of Bhiṭâ far inland from the Ganges. The ruins of Bhitâ may be reached from the Yamunâ side by walking a couple of miles from the bank. This shows that the course of the Yamunâ has not changed so much near Allâhâbâd as that of the Ganges. Thus the Pâli references to Sahajâti now identified with Bhitâ undoubtedly prove that Kauśâmbī is on the Yamunâ, above Bhiṭâ. Therefore neither Saheṭ-Maheṭ nor Satna, but Kosam, reconciles the direction and situation as given in Pâli ṭext of ancient Kauśâmbī in relation to Sahajâti. I have visited the ruins at Kosam several times. The Yamunâ still flows by the ruins, washing its high banks in the southeast corner. It was in this corner of the city that the wealthy merchant of Kauśâmbī, Ghosita, built his residence. Hiuen Tsang testifies to having seen the ruins of the house, as also of the *Ghositārāma* built by the pious merchant close to his residence. It is thus borne out by the present situation of the ruins *vis-a-vis* the Yamunâ that Kauśâmbī should be the first important stopping station for cargo and passenger boat from Sahajâti at the junction of the Ganges and the Yamunâ referred to in the Pâli Texts.

3. During my first visit to Kauśâmbī in

December 1930, the most conspicuous relic, which drew my special interest, was a stone pillar. I wrote a description of the pillar and called it an Aśoka Pillar in an article in the Leader of January 1931. A member of the Research Department in Ancient Indian History of The Allâhâbâd University took exception to my calling it an Aśoka Pillar and gave reasons for his views in an article in the same paper. I wrote a second article in reply stating why I held it to be an Aśoka Pillar, in the Leader in March 1931. In this Aśoka Pillar standing *in situ* at Kosam there is an important inscription engraved in the upper part of the shaft. This inscription, first published in R. B. Dayaram Sahni's Annual Report of the Archaeological Survey of India, 1917, has been edited in detail in the Epigraphia Indica, Vol. XI., p. 92. The inscription is dated '*Chaitrabadi Panchami*' in *Samvat* 1621, which, according to Fleet, corresponds to February 1565 A.D. As such the inscription falls in the reign of Akbar. The inscription is as follows:

TEXT

1. Srī Gaṇēsḥa Bânâna ya nâgarīka sonī.
2. mukha-darpan darpan Soninha kau.
3. dev Bhairav.
4. Saṁbat 1621 Samaai nâm Chaitra-badī.
5. Paṁchami likhitē Lakhimanu Sonarâ.

6. Baisnav Ananda-sut Briti.
7. Kauśâmbī-puri Lakhimi-dâs tathâ.
8. Khēma-krapan Laghu bhâi.
9. Tēnha kē purukh pachhilē.
10. Nalīgu Soni
11. Mahēsa-dâs Soni.
12. Horīl Soni.
13. Chamanda Soni.
14. Ratanu-Soni.
15. Chamandilē Soni kē put.
16. Anandu Râm-dâs.
17. Lakshmi-dâs.
18. Basṁta-Râm.

4. Dhanē Baisnav.
Karam Baisnav.
Manā Baisnav.
Anandu Baisnav.

TRANSLATION

"Sri Gaṇēśa ! The town goldsmiths make this. May the god Bhairava show a mirror-like face to the goldsmiths!

"Saṁvat 1621, at the time by name, the fifth day of the dark fortnight of the month chaitra, write—Lakṣmaṇ the master goldsmith, Vaiṣṇava Briti, son of Ananda, Lakshmidas of the town of Kauśâmbī (and) of the same town the brothers

Khema-Krapan (and) Laghu.[14]

"Their men (write) afterwards—Nalīgu the goldsmith, Mahēśa-dâsa the goldsmith, Horīl the goldsmith, Camanḍa the goldsmith, Ratanu the goldsmith, the son of the goldsmith Camanḍilē, Anandu Râma-dâsa, Lakṣmīdâsa, Basṁta-râma, (and) four (others),[15] Dhane Vaiṣṇava, Karam Vaiṣṇava, Mana Vaiṣṇava, and Anada Vaiṣṇava."

The most important part of the inscription which identifies Kosam with Kauśâmbī is the records and prayers of the five leading goldsmiths with thirteen of their employees to Gaṇeśa and Śiva-Bhiarava 'for favour of goldsmiths of *Kauśâmbī* town.' This undoubtedly proves that Kosam which contains the stone pillar referred to above and which inscription was engraved in the reign of Akbar was known to its residents

[14] I do not agree here with the translation. 'Laghu bhai' means younger brother. The correct translation should, to my mind, have been 'Laksmidas of the town of Kauśâmbī and his younger brother Khema-Krapan,' so instead of the five leading goldsmiths, three of the town of Kauśâmbī and two from outside, as Mr. Pargiter thinks (vide Ep. Ind. Vol. XI, p. 91), I consider only four.

[15] Pargiter—Ep. Ind. Vol. XI, pp. 89-92. The translation of the last four lines is ambiguous. I hope the translator does not mean by 'four others' the last mentioned four *persons*, as the drift of the sentence seems to convey. To me the last four lines engraved in a separate position seem to convey the idea that aforesaid names up to the 18th line given in the same position are all Vaiṣnava in *dhane*, *karme*, *mane* and *anande*.

to be Kauśâmbī even in the sixteenth century A.D. Dr. Smith's contention that the inscription simply proves that the persons mentioned in it resided in Kauśâmbī, but that it is not necessarily identical with the remains extant at Kosam, may be dismissed easily, for if Dr. Smith was right, the pillar in which the inscription appears should have been found somewhere else, probably at Satna, which he identifies with Kauśâmbī, instead of at Kosam.

4. There is a Jain Dharmaśala in the village of Pabhosâ which, as has been stated before, is at a distance of two and a half miles northwest of the remains at Kosam. I visited Pabhosâ twice in the same trips to the ruins at Kosam. Once I went first to Pabhosâ and then went to Kosam by motor road, the other time I walked to Pabhosâ from Kosam through the fields. It is about four miles by motor road and only two and a half miles straight across the fields. On a tablet of red sandstone is found a dedicatory inscription in corrupt Sanskrit. A portion of the inscription runs thus:

चन्द्र सात्पुत्रसाक श्रीहीरालालेन कौशाम्वी नगर वाह्य
प्रभासा-चलोपरि श्रीपद्मप्रभजिन दीक्षा ज्ञान कल्याण
कक्षभे श्रीजिनविम्व प्रतिष्ठा करित (कारिता)
अंरेजवहादुर राज्ये शम् ।

"On the top of the hill of Pabhosâ outside the city of Kauśâmbī one Hiralal built a temple in honour of Jina for the spread of religion, knowledge (and) welfare (in the British Empire)".

In another portion of the inscription is found the date "संवत् १८८१" and the residence of the donor "प्रयाग"

Samvat 1881 corresponds to the Christian years 1824-1825. Thus half a century before Sir Alexander's identification, Kauśâmbī is proved to have been situated close to the Pabhosâ Hill and was known to the residents of Allâhâbâd as such.

5. The well-known Kara Inscription was found on a piece of stone in the gateway of the ancient city of Kara.[16] It was first published by Mr. H. D. Colebrook in the year 1809 in Vol. IX, pp. 440-41, of the Asiatic Researches. Mr. Trubner reproduced Colebrook's article in his Life and Essays of Colebrook, Vol. III, pp. 245-246,

[16] The ancient town of Kara is at a distance of five miles northwest from Sirâthu and 41 miles from Allâhâbâd. Kara was once a place of great importance and till the foundation of Allâhâbâd was the seat of Government of a large province. Its association with Allauddin while he was viceroy of Kara is familiar to students of Khilji history. While the political importance of the place seems to have dated from the beginning of the Muslim rule in India, it appears to have been a sacred place of the Hindus even before that time, as can be gathered from Ibn Batuta's mention of it in 1340 as a place of pilgrimage and the existence of a temple Kâleśvara to the north of the town.

in 1873. Mr. Prinsep published an improved version of the inscription in The Journal of the Asiatic Society of Bengal, Vol. V, p. 731, in 1836. In 1871 Gen. Cunningham did indeed mention it in his Archaeological Survey of India Report, Vol. I, pp. 302-303, but did not use this inscription adequately for the purpose of identification of the site of Kauśâmbī. He only said: "The kingdom of Kauśâmbī or *Kosambamaṇḍala*,[17] is mentioned in an inscription taken from the gateway of the fort of Kara, which is dated in Sambat 1092, or A.D. 1035, at which period it would appear to have been independent of Kanoj."[18] He left the

[17] Cunningham's interpretation of Kosambamaṇḍala of the inscription as a kingdom is difficult to accept.

[18] It is doubtful whether Cunningham's suggestion that it was independent of Kanauj at the time of the inscription is correct. It is on the other hand more probable that both Kauśâmbī and Kara where the stone has been found were subject to the rule of King Yaśapâla of Kanauj who was the author of the inscription, the two places being at a distance of only 45 miles from one another. The fort of Kara, the ruins of which still exist overlooking the Ganges and on the gateway of which the stone containing the inscription has been found, is supposed to have been built by Jaichand the last Hindu Raja of Kanauj, who reigned in the latter part of the twelfth century A.D. The political importance of Kara in supersession of Kauśâmbī seems to have begun from the construction of the fort there and continued in the time of the Muslim rulers of Delhi who after the fall of Jaichand found it more convenient to use the fortified town of Kara as the headquarters of a new Doab province named after its capital town in preference to Kauśâmbī. I feel certain

examination of this important inscription at that point, and relied for the purpose of identification on evidences of a comparatively slender character already discussed.

It was left for the present Director of Archaeology, Rai Bahadur Dayaram Sahni, to edit it more fully and correctly in collaboration with Rai Bahadur Rama Prasad Chanda through whose courtesy he secured a fresh estampage of the inscription. He published it in The Journal of the Royal Asiatic Society, London, Vol. IV, October, 1927; and used it as an evidence for the identity of Kauśâmbī. The inscription is dated Samvat 1093 and refers to the grant of the *Payal* (*a*) *sa* in the *Kau sa* (*sa*) *mba maṇḍala* to one Mathura Vikaṭa of Pabhosâ together with its customary duties, royalties, taxes, gold and tithes in perpetuity to his descendants (Putra-Pautrâṇâm) by Mahârâjâdhirâja Yaśapâla.

Yaśapâla, as we have seen before,[19] was the ninth king from Nâgabhaṭa, the founder of the

that the engraved stone was removed by Jaichand from Payalasa which is only at a distance of five miles (J. R. A. S. 1917) from Kara to use it on the gateway of his newly constructed fort. 'I do not see any reason to believe that Kara should have been independent of Kanauj', R.B. Sahni says in his article (J. R. A. S. 1917), 'when its king could give away a village within five miles of the town.'

[19] See *ante* p. 80.

Pratihâra rule in Kanauj. It appears characteristic of the kings of this dynasty to grant lands to deserving people by way of gift. A copper-plate inscription found at Khaidra near Ahmadâbad records that the Gurjara king Sri Datta Kusâli made several grants of land to certain Brâhmans in the district of Akrūreśvara, near Jambrusra, on the south bank of the Narbadâ opposite Broach.[20] The inscription is dated A.D. 463 and was in the time when the Gurjara Pratihâras were ruling in Western Râjputâna and pushed their conquests up to the south bank of the Narbadâ in the Deccan peninsula. The Jhunsi copper-plate inscription, as we have seen before,[21] records a similar grant of the village of Jhunsi across the Ganges from Allâhâbâd. The donor of this gift is Trilocanapâla, the eighth Pratihâra king of Kanauj. The inscription which is now in the library of the Bengal Asiatic Society, is dated A.D. 1027. So Yaśapâla who made a similar grant of the village of Payâlasa to a resident of Pabhosâ has only followed the traditions of his family. Yaśapâla is presumably the immediate successor of Trilocanapâla, for the Jhunsi inscription is dated A.D. 1027 and the Kara inscription

[20] J. R. A. S. New series 1, 270-280; A. G. I., p. 369.
[21] See *ante* p. 80.

A.D. 1036, and we know of no other king of Kanauj who came between Trilocanapâla and Yaśapâla.

Now the inscription refers to three places—Kauśamba-maṇḍala, Pabhosâ and Payâlasa. Pabhosâ is only two and a half miles from Kosam, and Payâlasa has been identified by R. B. Dayaram Sahni with the present village of Pras within five miles of Kara and 30 miles N. N. W. of Kosam.[22] Trilochanapâla, mentioned in the inscription as Mahârâjâdhirâja, is a scion of the royal family of Kanauj which had ruled over Kauśâmbī since Kanauj became the imperial seat in Northern India. Taking all these facts into consideration the conclusion becomes irresistible that the present ruins of Kosam are to be identified with the ancient Kauśâmbī.

[22] J. R. A. S. Oct. 1927.

APPENDIX III

The Kara inscription as edited, translated and published by R. B. Dayaram Sahni (J. R. A. S. IV. 1927) is as follows:

TEXT

line

1. om samvat 1093
2. Āṣāḍha śudi I
3. ady=eharṁ (ha) śrimat-Kaṭe
4. mahârâjâdhirâja
5. śri-Yasa (śa) ḥ pâla [:*] Kau
6. sâ (śa) mba-maṇḍale Payal [a]
7. sa-grâme mahantam=â (a)
8. nusamâdisa (śa) ti yathâ
9. Pabhosekīya-Mâthu
10. ra-vik [a] ṭasya sâ (śâ) sana—
11. tvaṁ prasâdhi (ī) kṛtya matv [a*]
12. bhâga-bhoga-Kara-hira
13. n (ṇ) ya-pratyâdyâ-dhikaṁ
14. matv=opanetavyam=iti
15. dasa (śa) bandhena saha.....
16. alabhrata (?)
17. putra-pautrâṇâṁ

Appendix III

TRANSLATION

"Om. In the year Samvat 1093, on the first day of the bright fortnight of Aṣâḍha, today (while encamping) here at the illustrious Kata, the Mahârâjâdhirâja, the illustrious Yaśapâla commands the mahant (headman or other official) in the village of Payalâsa in the mandala of Kauśâmbī that, knowing that (the aforesaid village) has been presented (by me) as a gift to Mathura Vikaṭa (Vikaṭa) of Pabhosâ, the customary duties, royalties, taxes, gold, other income (pratyâdayâ) etc., together with the tenth part of the produce should be paid (to him).....of the sons and grandsons."

R. B. Dayaram Sahni reject Messrs. Colebrooke and Prinseps' rendering of the locality Payahâsa for Payalasa, and identifies the same with the present village of Pras just 30 miles N. N. W. of Kosam and gives convincing reasons for it.

ON THE ARCHAEOLOGICAL IMPORTANCE OF KAUŚĀMBĪ

The nearest village to the ruins of the old city is Musarfa, which is at a distance of about a mile from the place. As you reach the open fields from the village, the high bastions and the earthen ramparts of an immense fortress come into sight. As you pass on through the narrow paths between the cultivated fields you notice many stone images on either side, as well as bricks stacked at different places. These stone figures and bricks have yielded to the plough. This proves that the entire area covered by the fields and the villages round the present fortress was perhaps the suburb of the old city.

The ruin of the immense fortress has a circuit of a little over four miles, protected on all sides by earthen ramparts about thirty feet high above the fields and a number of bastions rising to above fifty or sixty feet high. Signs of shallow water-hollows at the foot of the ramparts point to the fact that there were once ditches protecting the fort.

There are two villages, Kosam Inâm and

Kosam Khirâj, lying on the west and east side, respectively, of the fortress. Inside the rampart and on the bank of the Yamunâ there are two villages called *Gaḍhava* and *Gaḍhava choṭa*, their names being no doubt derived from inside the gaṛ. These and the other adjoining villages which were once covered by the old city of Kauśâmbī contained when Cunningham wrote his report in 1862 more than 400 houses and 2000 inhabitants. At present the number of houses and of the inhabitants has considerably increased.

Brick Walls

One very special feature of the old fortress is that you will find hardly a space in the ruins within the ramparts which is not strewn with bricks. They are of various sizes ranging from 19 inches to 12½ by 2½ inches and to even smaller bricks than the present standard size. There are *pucca* pathways less than two feet wide through which we walked amongst the ruins. These pathways are probably the tops of walls of ancient buildings which lie under the earth. The large-sized bricks seen by Cunningham are considered by him to have been the ruins of old walls. Lines of old walls are found here and there and these are occasionally dug out by the villagers for making their own houses, so much so that almost every house in the neighbouring villages is constructed of these bricks taken from the ruined fort. The entire prospect of the ruined area tempts an archaeologist to try his spade forthwith. I feel sanguine that, besides the many valuable finds already collected by Mr. Brij Mohan Vyas, underneath the ruins lies a store-house of ancient relics, to be yielded to the spade, which will enlarge the stock of our knowledge of ancient and mediaeval Indian History connected with the place.

A Stone Pillar

The chief object of archaeological interest existing *in situ* in the ruins is a stone pillar. The top of it is broken and its capital is missing. It is probable that if excavations are carried further near the pillar, the capital may be found. The upper portion of the pillar is also broken. As it stands now it measures nearly 22 feet. It is built in the style of Aśoka Pillars—crystal-smooth one-columned structure. Unfortunately no inscription of Aśoka is to be found on it. Now the question is: how old is the pillar? In the absence of these two important clues—the capital and the inscription—it is difficult to be positive as to its age and its builder. But the structure of the pillar and the fact that Kauśâmbī was an important Buddhist place in the time of Aśoka point to the probable conclusion that it was built by Aśoka or by some one not very long after him, in close imitation of his other stone monoliths. It is a large stone monolith similar to those at Allâhâbâd, Delhi and in the Champâran District, excepting only that it bears no inscription of Aśoka. The capital is missing and a good portion of the upper shaft is broken. When Sir Alexander saw this pillar for a closer examination in about 1870 he found it to be only 14 feet high as it stood then above the ground. A mound of brick ruins covered a good portion of the lower shaft which he cleared to the depth of 7 feet 4 inches without reaching the end of the polished portion of the shaft. Cunningham also found two broken pieces of the upper shaft lying close by which measured respectively 4 feet 6 inches and 2 feet 3 inches. By calculating on the basis of the standing column which was then in a reclining position of 5°, and of the broken pieces, and the measurement of the thinnest part of the column, the learned Archaeologist concluded that the column was originally 36 feet high. When I visited the ruins in December 1930 along with Prof. A. C. Banerji and one of his post-graduate research scholars in mathematics, we found the column in the present erect position set right by the present Director of Archaeology, R. B. Dayaram Sahni who also evidently excavated a few feet of ground round the base. The column as it stands now is about 23 feet high and the base near the ground level measured 120 inches. Further excavation round the pillar to the depth of another 6 feet or so will, I feel certain, lead us to the end of the base and will bear out General Cunningham's conclusion of its height being 36 feet, which is also the height of another of Aśoka's monolithic pillars, namely, the Lauriya Arerâj Pillar in the Champâran District which bears a copy of the Seven Pillar Edicts. So the lack of an inscription is no convincing ground on which to reject it as an Aśokan column when there is evidence of the existence of many 'uninscribed monolithic sandstone pillars' built by Aśoka.[1]

The importance of the pillar lies in the fact that it contains a number of inscriptions 'ranging from the age of the Guptas to the present day.'[2] The early inscriptions have not yet been deciphered except the word *prabhara* at the top of a broken shaft which Mr. Cunningham ascribes to the 4th or 5th century A.D.[3] The one in the time of Akbar has been already discussed by me.[4]

[1] E. H. I., p. 165.
[2] A. S. R. Vol. I., p. 310.
[3] Ibid.
[4] See *ante* p. 9cf.

The Allahabad Pillar

The Aśoka Pillar now in Allâhâbâd Fort is rightly regarded as originally erected at Kauśâmbī. Dr. Bhandarkar says that the *śâsana* or orders of Aśoka against schism which we find engraved on pillars are at three different places, namely, Sârnath, Sânchi and Allahabad.[5] "The pillars at the former two places are believed to be in *situ*, but that at present existing at Allâhâbâd is rightly regarded as having been in Kauśâmbī."[6] This is also the view of Dr. Hultzch. He says: "Kauśâmbī Edict is addressed to the Mahâmâtras of Kauśâmbī. Cunningham concluded from it that the Allâhâbâd pillar must have been originally erected by Aśoka at Kauśâmbī."[7] He agrees in this with Cunningham but disagrees with him as to the latter's suggestion that Feroz Shâh removed it to Allâhâbâd, and holds with more reason that Akbar did it to add to the beauty of his newly built city. That this pillar was originally set up by Aśoka is clear from another consideration. Aśoka's edict on the Pillar now in Allâhâbâd is aimed at schism which was breaking the unity of the Buddhist Church. The *śâsana* runs as follows: "Whosoever breaks up the

[5] D. R. Bhandarkar—Aśoka, p. 94.
[6] Ibid.
[7] Hultzsch, *corpus*, p. XX, Vol. I.

Church, be it monk or nun, shall be clad in white raiment, and compelled to live in what is not a residence (of the clergy)."[8] The *śâsana* or the order is addressed, as is clear from the inscription, directly to the Mahâmâtras of Kauśâmbī.[9] According to Dr. Radha Kumud there were two classes of Mahâmâtras. One class of Mahâmâtras were associated with Viceroys as Ministers, to whom kings' orders were communicated by the Viceroy, or in some cases by the king himself jointly with the Viceroy. The other class of Mahâmâtras were 'Provincial Governors who were entitled to receive the king's message directly.'[10] The learned scholar is of the opinion that since the Kauśâmbī Edict is addressed by the king directly to the Mahâmâtras of Kauśâmbī, it 'must have been, therefore, the headquarters of another province.'[11] It is therefore natural to suppose that the Pillar had been erected in the seat of a provincial government, which was Kauśâmbī.

A Red Stone Image of the Buddha: Kaniska's Inscription

A very important relic recently discovered by Mr. Vyas (February 1934), is a red stone

[8] Aśoka, p. 94.
[9] ....Ye (â) Napayati Kosambiya maham (â) ta.
[10] Asoka (G. L.), p. 52.
[11] Ibid.

Buddha image. It has been placed on the left side of the entrance of the verandah of the Museum Hall, Allâhâbâd. The statue is about four feet in height. Its head and right hand are clean gone—they appear to have been cut by some sharp weapon. Barring that, the figure is complete. It bears an inscription of the time of Kaniṣka, dated in the second year of his reign. Mr. Goswami, a post-graduate Fellow of the Calcutta University, took the first estampage of the inscription which he has rendered thus:

"In the 2nd year of the reign of Kanishka Bhikkhuni Buddhimitrâ put up this Bodhisattva at this place sanctified by the Buddha's several visits."

With the assistance of Mr. Vyas I secured an estampage of the inscription. The words are written in clear Kuṣaṇa script. The first seven letters indicate 'in the reign of Kaniṣka.' The inscription is incised on the front of the pedestal which measures 16″ × 3″. As far as it is known to me, it is the earliest of Kaniṣka's inscriptions hitherto discovered. The statue, barring the size, is wonderfully similar in colour and shape to the red stone Bodhisattva (*sic*) discovered at Sârnâth and now kept in the Sârnâth Museum which also contains an inscription of Kaniṣka, dated in the third year of his reign. The inscription on the statue found at Kauśâmbī undoubtedly proves that it was an important Buddhist centre in the time of Kaniṣka.

Inscriptions of the Magha Dynasty of Kausambi

Besides the inscription referred to above, three inscriptions, in excellent preservation, of the Magha Dynasty of Kauśâmbī have been discovered. They are incised on pieces of stone and have been brought to the Allâhâbâd Museum. Mr. Vyas tells me that estampages of these inscriptions have been taken by Prof. Gauri Shanker Chatterji of the Allâhâbâd University, who had the credit of discovering the inscription on the biggest stone slab. It is understood that Professor Chatterjee has been busy editing the inscription. When it is done and published it will throw important light on a period of the history of Kauśâmbī and also settle the controversy as to the name of the author of the inscription, namely, whether it is Megha as stated by R. B. Dayarama Sahni or Bhadra Magha as stated by Mr. K. P. Jayaswal.

Stone Sculptures

The following are the important sculptures which have been recovered from the ruins of Kauśâmbī and are housed in the Allâhâbâd

Museum: about a dozen or so Jina Heads and about half a dozen pieces of Jaina *Tirthankaras* in sitting posture in various *mudrâs*. The most beautiful of these sculptures is the one of Candra-prabhu Tīrthaṅkara bearing the sign of a crescent below the feet. Unfortunately its head is gone. Besides there is the figure of *Caturmukha Rudra* and of an *Ekamukha Rudra*. There are two railing pillars of the Kuṣaṇa period and four pieces of stone about one foot long and six inches wide containing on all of them images of Jain Tīrthaṅkaras. A big piece of stone about three feet long and two feet wide and four inches thick contains the images of exquisite carving of 24 Jain Tīrthaṅkaras. Unfortunately the head of every single image has been chopped off.

TERRA COTTAS

The ruins of Kauśâmbī have yielded a large number of terra-cotta figures. Mr. Vyas has been able to recover about 200 such figures which have been brought to light by the spade. This point deserves special notice of the Archaeological Department of the Government of India because when the site yields such important ancient relics merely with the help of the spade, it is sure to yield richer results by an excavation going to the depth of three to four feet. A big broken fragment of Toraṇa Lintel which when complete bore representation of the poor noble animals of the Buddhist texts was also found. The piece which is now in the Allâhâbâd Museum is about four feet long and one foot wide. The figures represented on this broken sheet are:

A bull and broken portion of an elephant, and R. B. Daya Ram Sahni thinks that in the portion which is missing there was a horse and a lion. About this piece the Director General of Archaeology, R. B. Sahni, writes: "These animals are portrayed on the abacus of the Aśoka Pillar at Sârnâth and on a miniature terra-cotta in the Lahore Central Museum but have, as far as I am aware, not been noticed elsewhere in India." Mr. Vyas has discovered two seals; one of them is a rare stamp seal with the name of a private individual in Brâhmī characters of the time of Aśoka; the second seal is a terra-cotta seal. So far as it could be made out it does not contain any inscription but the branch of a tree on which are sketched certain male or female figures. All these have been taken temporarily by the Director General of Archaeology, Rai Bahadur Daya Ram Sahni.

Coins

Among the coins collected by Mr. Vyas for

the Allâhâbâd Museum there are about two hundred from the ancient site of Kauśâmbī. These coins have been mostly found in the village of Garḍhavâ inside the ramparts of the old fort. These have all been ploughed up and have been collected by Mr. Vyas from the villagers who have picked them up from the fields. The writer has also collected a number of them and they are in his possession. The Kauśâmbī coins in the Allâhâbâd Museum have not as yet been properly classified, but some of them are very old and may be found in Sir Alexander Cunningham's book on the Ancient Coins of India. The majority of them contain on one side the figure of an elephant and on the other a crescent on Mount Meru. Mr. Durga Prasad of Benâres who has made a special study of ancient punch-marked coins thinks that they are the coins of Candragupta. Mr. Vyas has found one very important coin which contains an inscription, but the only word that is legible is 'Ma' in Brâhmī character. It is possible it may be a symbol of Candragupta Maurya. Coins which are largely obtained at Kauśâmbī are those which are described in Sir Alexander Cunningham's book as 'containing on one side a lanky bull and on the other a number of marks such as a wheel, a tree within railing, and swastika. These coins figure as numbers seven and nine on Plate V of his book. Coins of Kauśâmbī belonging to the second and first centuries B.C. have already been discussed.'[12] Besides these, a large number of cast coins have been recovered from this site. Prominent among these are those which correspond with Nos. 29, 24 and 26 in Plate I of Sir Alexander Cunningham's book. Besides these a large number of coins of the Sharqi Kings of Jaunpore as well as of the Moguls have been discovered in Kauśâmbī.

[12] See *ante* p. 31f. and p. 42ff.

INDEX

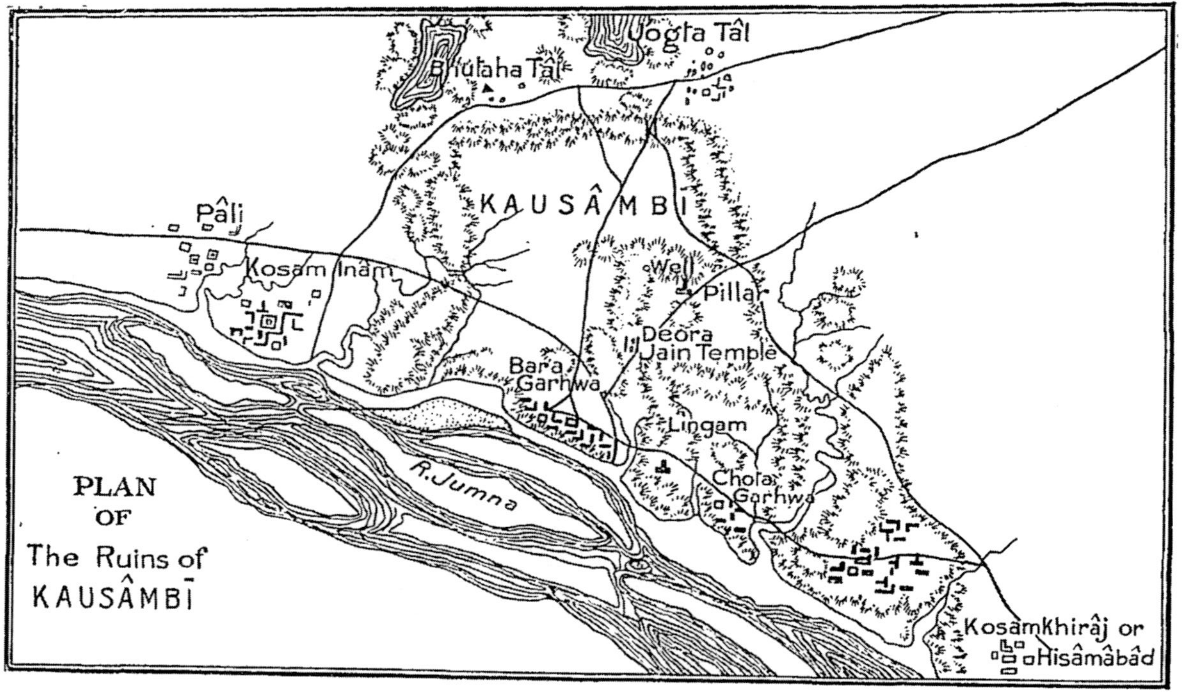

Map of the site of ruins

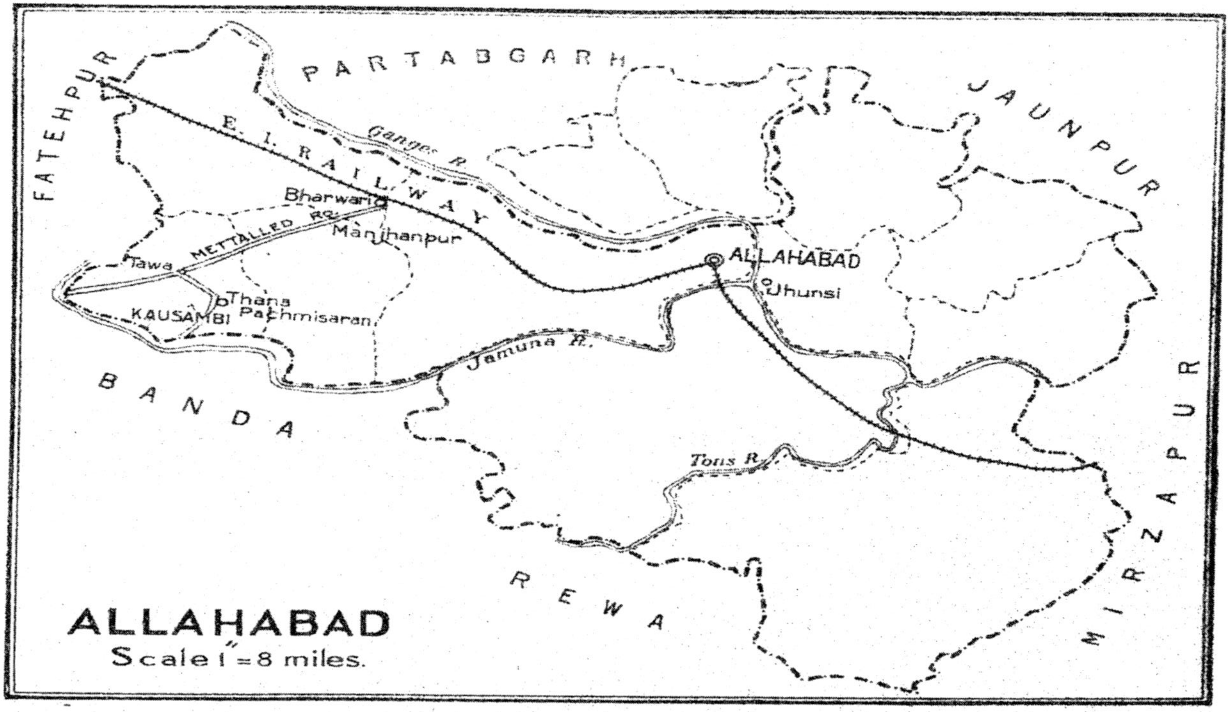

Map of the District of Allâhâbâd showing the routes to the ruins

The present ruins of Kauśâmbī

The Aśoka Pillar in *Situ*

A Red-stone Image of the Buddha found in Kauśâmbī, dated in the 2nd year of Kaniṣka's reign

[*In Allâhâbâd Municipal Museum*]

A Terra-cotta Toy Cart dated about 3rd Century A. D. found at Kauśâmbī

[*In Allâhâbâd Municipal Museum*]

Plate 5

Pre-Mauryan Terra-cotta Toys
[*In Allâhâbâd Municipal Museum*]

A Terra-cotta image of the Manasâ Devi (Snake Goddess)
[*In Âllâbâbâd Municipal Museum*]

Terra-cotta heads

[*In Allâhâbâd Municipal Museum*]

Terra-cotta heads
[*In Ailábáñád Municipal Museum*]

Plate 9

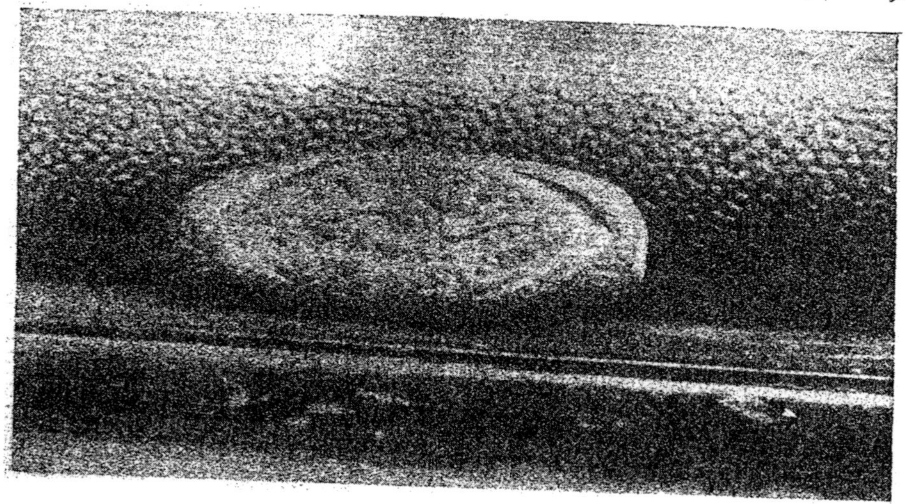

A Terra-cotta seal
[*In Allâhâbâd Municipal Museum*

दस बरस का भँवर

दस बरस का भँवर

रवीन्द्र वर्मा

राजकमल प्रकाशन

ISBN : 978-81-267-1302-8

मूल्य : ₹695

पहला संस्करण : 2007
पहली आवृत्ति : 2023
This book is printed on **Print on Demand** Technology : 2025

प्रकाशक : राजकमल प्रकाशन प्रा.लि.
1-बी, नेताजी सुभाष मार्ग, दरियागंज
नई दिल्ली-110 002

शाखाएँ : अशोक राजपथ, साइंस कॉलेज के सामने, पटना-800 006
पहली मंजिल, दरबारी बिल्डिंग, महात्मा गांधी मार्ग, प्रयागराज-211 001
1, अनमोल सोराबजी संतुक लेन, धोबी तलाव, मरीन लाइंस, मुम्बई-400 002
वेबसाइट : www.rajkamalprakashan.com
ई-मेल : info@rajkamalprakashan.com

DUS BARAS KA BHANWAR
by Ravindra Verma

एक

1.1

जब पुष्पक एक्सप्रेस झाँसी के प्लेटफ़ॉर्म पर सरकते-सरकते थमी तो सूने प्लेटफ़ॉर्म पर बिजली की रोशनियाँ चमकीं। रोशनियाँ प्लेटफ़ॉर्म की छत से उल्टी लटकी थीं। छत के परे आधी रात का अँधेरा था—जो आसमान में छिटपुट तारों के इर्द-गिर्द जमा हो रहा था।

प्लेटफ़ॉर्म पर उतरकर रतन और दो अटैचियों के साथ अकेले खड़े हुए बाँके बिहारी को याद आया कि पिछली बार भी आधी रात इसी तरह पुष्पक से उतरकर वे यहीं खड़े थे। फ़र्क यही था कि तब पुष्पक विपरीत दिशा से आई थी।

'चाय', रतन ने चायवाले को रोककर बाँके बिहारी की ओर देखते हुए कहा, 'पापा, मैं चाय पिऊँगा।'

एक ओर चायवाला रुक गया था। दूसरी ओर दोनों अटैचियों के पास एक कुली भी आकर खड़ा हो गया।

'तीन चाय', बाँके बिहारी ने संदिग्ध मुस्कान के साथ कहा। असल में उन्हें अचानक यह याद आ गया था कि पिछली बार भी रतन ने इसी तरह चाय की माँग की थी, जब वे लखनऊ से लौटे थे। और तब भी कुली के साथ दोनों ने चाय पी थी। बाँके बिहारी की वह उम्र कब की शुरू हो गई थी जब चीज़ें अपने को दुहराती हुई लगती हैं जैसे निरन्तर फैलती हुई सृष्टि की भी सीमाएँ हों।

कुली अधेड़ और चौकन्ना था। उसकी मूँछ और बढ़ी दाढ़ी के कुछ बाल सफ़ेद थे। उसने प्लास्टिक के कप से चाय सुड़ककर पहले बाँके बिहारी को देखा : एक श्वेत-धवल दाढ़ी और सन-से बालों से घिरा चेहरा था, जो सीधी काठी पर रखा था। फिर रतन को : नया गबरू जवान था जो गाड़ी से उतर आया था, मगर अभी जागा नहीं था। दूसरी बार चाय सुड़ककर कुली ने दोनों को एक बार फिर देखा और सोचा कि गबरू जवान को बूढ़े की फ़िक्र करनी चाहिए। मगर गंगा उल्टी बह रही थी।

बाँके बिहारी वीरान प्लेटफ़ॉर्म को हसरत से देख रहे थे जैसे कोई लौटकर अपने घर को देखता है। प्लेटफ़ॉर्म पर भरपूर उजाला था। पर उजाला सूना था।

सारे स्टॉल बन्द थे। सिर्फ़ चाय का स्टॉल खुला था। उसके सामने दो आदमी खड़े थे। पुष्पक से उतरे छिटपुट लोग चले गए थे। चाय पीने और कोई नहीं रुका था। सामने प्लेटफ़ार्मों को जोड़ता लोहे का पुल था जिस पर कुछ लोग धब्बों-से नज़र आते थे। रोशनी पुल के ऊपर और प्लेटफ़ॉर्म के बाहर कुछ क़दम चलती थी और थककर बैठ जाती थी। चारों ओर अँधेरे का समुद्र ठाठें मार रहा था।

जब वे चले, सबसे आगे कुली था। कुली के पीछे बाँके बिहारी और बाँके बिहारी के पीछे रतन। रतन को बाँके बिहारी मुड़-मुड़कर देख लेते थे जैसे आगे अटैचियाँ थामे कुली को देखते थे। अँधेरे में उनकी सफ़ेद मुंडी आगे-पीछे घूमती। कुली के पैर चपल थे। बड़ी अटैची उसने सिर पर रख ली थी। छोटी उसके हाथ में थी। उसकी चाल तेज़ थी। बाँके बिहारी तेज़ चलते हुए मुड़-मुड़कर पीछे देखते जाते। उन्हें लगा, पुल की सीढ़ियों पर लगी रोशनी ने उनके कानों में फुसफुसाया : सँभलकर, ज़रा सँभलकर। हँसकर उन्होंने पीछे रतन को देखा। रतन आँखें नीची किए चुपचाप चला आ रहा था जैसे उसे रोशनी या अँधेरे या शहर से कोई मतलब न हो।

ऑटो-रिक्शा में बैठकर रतन ने आँखें मूँद लीं। बाँके बिहारी आँखें फाड़-फाड़कर शहर देखने लगे, जो सो रहा था। ठंडी हवा का पहला झोंका ऑटो पर झपटा जैसे ही वह भर्र-भर्र करके आगे बढ़ा। बाँके बिहारी ने शॉल पूरी लपेटने से पहले रतन से पूछा—'ठंड तो नहीं लग रही ?' 'नहीं', रतन ने आँखें बन्द किए हुए कहा। वह सिर्फ़ स्वेटर पहने था। मार्च शुरू हो गया था। सर्दी ऑटो पर ठंडी हवाओं में लिपटी झपट-झपट पड़ती थी। बाँके बिहारी अँधेरे में रेलवे का ऑफिस, कोठियाँ पहचानते और सड़क के दोनों ओर खड़े पेड़ों को देखते रहे, जो कुछ दूर जाकर गहरे होते जाते, पेड़ों के पीछे पेड़ और उनके पीछे पेड़...जो अँधेरे में डूब जाते। सड़क पर बिजली के खम्भे जल रहे थे। फिर कुछ बन्द, अँधेरे मकानों में अपनी चीख़ें छोड़ता हुआ ऑटो इलाइट सिनेमा के चौराहे पर पहुँचकर बाईं ओर घूम गया। बाँके बिहारी की आँखें बन्द हो गई थीं। जब एक झटके से आँखें खुलीं तो सामने दूर पहाड़ी पर किला खड़ा था जैसे अँधेरे का किला हो, समूचे शहर को अपनी बाँहों में छिपाए हुए। ऊपर आसमान में छिटपुट तारे थे—तारों के अवशेष की तरह।

एक बार सहसा आसमान चमका और पहाड़ी पर किला उजागर हो गया जैसे अँधेरे में नंगा खड़ा हो।

'अम्माँ, अम्माँ', रतन की आवाज़ किवाड़ पर बजती साँकल के साथ मोहल्ले में गूँजी।

ऑटोवाला दोनों अटैचियाँ चबूतरे पर रखकर चला गया था। अँधेरे में ऑटो की भर्र-भर्र की घुलती हुई अनुगूँजें थीं।

दरवाज़ा खुला।

'छोटे', अम्माँ की आवाज़ थी जैसे किवाड़ खोलकर बाहर आई हो।

बाँके बिहारी और रतन अटैचियाँ उठाए पौर में घुसे। रतन ने आँगन में खड़े-खड़े दालान में अटैची रखी, फिर पेड़ के पीछे रखे घड़े से एक गिलास पानी लेकर पिया। उसने गायत्री से कहा कि मुझे बहुत नींद लगी है, मैं ऊपर जा रहा हूँ। वह सीढ़ियों पर धड़-धड़ चढ़ने लगा।

अम्माँ ने आँगन में खड़े-खड़े फ़ौरन बत्ती जलाई और पूछा—'भूख तो नहीं लगी ?' 'नहीं', रतन ने आख़िरी सीढ़ी पर कहा और छत पर चला गया। छत पर उसके अटारी में जाते क़दमों की आहट होती रही।

'पचास बरस से कह रही हूँ', गायत्री ने बाँके बिहारी की ओर देखकर कहा, 'कि सीढ़ियों पर ओट बनवा लो, तुमने नहीं माना। अभी नंगी सीढ़ियों पर छोटे के पैर काँपे थे।'

'वह आधा नींद में है', बाँके बिहारी बोले।

'उसकी तबियत कैसी है ?'

'आधी ठीक है।'

'आधी !' गायत्री ने पति को हैरत से देखा।

'हाँ।'

'बम्बई के डॉक्टर भी ठीक न कर सके ?'

'बम्बई नहीं, मुम्बई !'

'यह मेरे सवाल का जवाब नहीं है।'

आँगन में खड़े पेड़ की पत्तियों में उलझी हवाएँ छूटने को कसमसाईं। शाखों के झूमकर एक-दूसरे से टकराने की आवाज़ें आईं। फिर हवाओं की हवाओं से टकराने की आवाज़ें...हू-हू...सूँ-सूँ...जैसे आँगन में एक पेड़ न हो, जंगल हो।

'आधा तो ठीक है', बाँके बिहारी ने कहा।

'क्या ?'

'जवाब और रतन, दोनों।' आवाज़ ठंडी थी जैसे पेड़ की हवा बोली हो।

जैसे अपने से बोली हों, गायत्री बोलीं, 'मँझले तो कहता था कि बम्बई में जो डॉक्टर हैं, वे और कहीं नहीं।'

'अब मँझले मुम्बई में रहता है, गायत्री। बम्बई नहीं रही। कल सुबह बताऊँगा।'

शायद ऑटो की मोहल्ले की सड़क पर खिंची चीख़ से दो कुत्ते जाग गए थे और रह-रहकर भौंक रहे थे। जब वे चुप हो गए, तभी बाँके बिहारी को नींद आई। नींद में उतरना सीढ़ियों पर उतरने की तरह था, जिनका एक सिरा ख़ाली था और आँगन में खुलता था। बाँके बिहारी की आँखें आधी खुली थीं। उनके पैर अचानक पाँचवीं सीढ़ी पर काँपे। आँखें अपने आप पूरी खुल गईं : नीचे आँगन नहीं था, समुद्र था। सीढ़ी के ऊपर आसमान था, नीचे समुद्र था। वे आँखें बन्द किए नीचे उतरते गए। सीढ़ी ख़त्म ही नहीं होती थी जैसे समुद्र पाताल में उतरता जाता हो। जब नीचे उतरते हुए उन्हें अपने पैर तैरते पैरों की तरह लगे तो उनकी आँखें खुल गईं : न कहीं सीढ़ी थी, न आँगन था। केवल समुद्र था। वे समुद्र के प्लेटफ़ॉर्म पर खड़े थे, जिसके सामने पुष्पक एक्सप्रेस खड़ी थी। रेलगाड़ी के सारे दरवाज़े और खिड़कियाँ बन्द थीं। रतन कहीं नहीं था। बाँके बिहारी की आँखें रतन को ढूँढ़ रही थीं। आँखें समुद्र की लहरों पर पक्षियों की तरह घूमतीं...दूर-दूर...बहुत दूर...चारों ओर...चारों ओर गोल धरती पर समुद्र नीचे लुढ़क रहा था जैसे जुहू-तट पर सागर दूर क्षितिज पर दूसरी ओर झरने-सा गिरता लगता था...अभी चारों ओर जुहू-क्षितिज था और चारों ओर रात थी। रात में आँखें सागर-क्षितिज पर अटकी चीख़ रही थीं...रतन, रतन...। एकाएक सामने खड़ी पुष्पक एक्सप्रेस का एक दरवाज़ा खुला। दरवाज़े में बड़े, मँझले और भैया खड़े हाथ हिला रहे थे और मुस्करा रहे थे। ये तीनों एक-साथ कहाँ जा रहे हैं ? भैया अमरीका से कब आया ? छोटे इनके साथ क्यों नहीं है ?

'छोटे कहाँ है ?' बाँके बिहारी चीख़ते हैं।

गाड़ी के दरवाज़े में खड़े तीनों के होंठ हिलते हैं। मगर कोई आवाज़ नहीं आती।

'क्या ?' बाँके बिहारी फिर चीख़ते हैं।

तीनों हाथ हिलाते हैं। गाड़ी चल देती है।

जब गाड़ी की जगह ख़ाली होती है तो उसी ख़ाली जगह के पीछे छोटे खड़ा नज़र आता है। बाँके बिहारी समुद्र पर दौड़कर छोटे को गले लगा लेते हैं। वे हाँफ रहे हैं। उनकी आँखों में आँसू नहीं हैं। आँखें सागर की फेनिल लहरों को निहार रही हैं।

वे देखते हैं कि सीधी गाड़ी अचानक बाएँ मुड़ती है, फिर यू-टर्न लेकर दाएँ मुड़ जाती है जैसे रेलगाड़ी न हो, कोई ऑटो-रिक्शा हो जिसे पटरी की ज़रूरत नहीं होती।

धरती की पनीली गेंद पर बाँके बिहारी रतन को छाती से चपेटे अकेले खड़े थे।

सुबह चाय पीते हुए बाँके बिहारी ने पत्नी से कहा :

'सुनो।'

'हाँ।'

'पचास साल से तुम ठीक कह रही थीं।'

'क्या ?' वे हँसीं।

'आँगन की सीढ़ी नंगी है। उसे ढँक देना चाहिए।'

'हाँ,' उन्होंने आह भरी, 'बड़े, मँझले और भैया इन्हीं सीढ़ियों पर नंगे खेलते हुए बड़े हो गए।'

बाँके बिहारी क्षण-भर गायत्री को देखते रहे। फिर बोले—'छोटे बड़े होकर सीढ़ियों पर फँस गए हैं। हमें सीढ़ियों को ढँकना होगा।'

'एक ईंट की दीवार कमर तक काफ़ी होगी,' गायत्री ने कहा।

'मिस्त्री से पूछ लेंगे।'

फिर बाँके बिहारी ने गायत्री से पूछा :

'छोटे उठ गए ?'

'नहीं।'

'ठीक है। सोने दो।'

गायत्री भीतर चली गईं। बाँके बिहारी चाय का कप नीचे रखकर पौर में गावतकिए पर सिर टिकाए पसर गए। दरवाज़ा खुला था। ताज़ी धूप सड़क पर नर्म कालीन-सी बिछी थी। आँगन में धूप नहीं थी, जब वे अन्दर कोठे से पौर में आए। अब शायद नीम की पत्तियों से छनकर तने पर फिसलती हुई धूप नंगे फ़र्श पर आ गई होगी। घर के बाहर चबूतरे पर भी धूप घर की दीवार की ओर सरकती हुई लगती थी। घर धूप से घिर गया था।

बाँके बिहारी ने आँखें मूँद लीं। उन्हें लगा, वे अभी पैदा हुए हैं। वे अपने घर की सुबह देख रहे थे जैसे पहली बार देख रहे हों। यह सुबह अपने घर में गायत्री और उनके बीच तनी थी। अलबत्ता छोटे अटारी में सो रहे थे। छोटे शायद अब कभी पूरी तरह ठीक नहीं होंगे। डॉक्टर यही कहते हैं। वे कहते हैं कि छोटे को देखभाल, दवा-दारू चाहिए। मर्ज़ दस साल पुराना था। पहले पता ही नहीं चला। फिर कुछ वक़्त शक में गुज़रा। जिस दिन छोटे नूर मंज़िल से घर आए, उसी शाम बाँके बिहारी ने बहू को दूसरे कमरे में बोलते सुना था, 'यह नीम-पागल घर में रहेगा, तो मुन्ना पर क्या असर पड़ेगा ?' वे दो दिन बाद ही छोटे को लेकर झाँसी आ गए थे। दो बरस बाद मँझले ने छोटे को मुम्बई बुलाया। मँझले की बेटी पँचगनी में पढ़ती थी और उसका तीन कमरे का बड़ा फ़्लैट था। उसने नई फ़ैक्टरी

डाली थी। दस माह बाद छोटे ने फ़ोन पर रोते हुए कहा—'पापा, यहाँ मैं घर का नौकर हो गया हूँ, जिसे वेतन नहीं मिलता।' तब बाँके बिहारी मुम्बई गए थे और कल रात छोटे को लेकर लौटे थे।

यह सच है कि बाँके बिहारी दस बरस इसी झिलमिल भरोसे में रहे कि छोटे को उसके तीनों बड़े भाई सँभाल लेंगे। भैया अमरीका में था। उसने लिखा था कि पापा, मैं छोटे को यहाँ बुला तो नहीं सकता, मगर इलाज के लिए डॉलर भेज सकता हूँ। डॉलर से क्या नहीं हो सकता, पापा ? भैया, बाँकेलाल बुदबुदाए, डॉलर से नीम-पागल और घर के नौकर ही बनेंगे ! उन्होंने आँखें खोलीं। एक गौरैया पौर में घुस आई थी और चूँ-चूँ, चूँ-चूँ बोल रही थी। वह एक कोने से दूसरे कोने में उड़ी, फिर तीसरे से चौथे कोने में—और फिर दरवाज़े से फुर्र हो गई।

डॉलर नहीं लूँगा, बाँके बिहारी ने सोचा। नीम-पागल या घर के नौकर के लिए डॉलर दान ही हुआ न ! दान नहीं लूँगा। छोटे मेरा बेटा है। मैं उसे पालूँगा। उन्हें पता ही नहीं चला था। पहले वे उठकर बैठे, फिर खड़े हो गए थे गोया किसी महायात्रा का संकल्प हो।

बाँके बिहारी पौर के चबूतरे पर खड़े थे, जब दरवाज़े की धूप में कोई आकर चुपचाप खड़ा हो गया। ऐसा लगा जैसे कोई छाया हो।

'दद्दा, आप कब आए ?' छाया बोली।

'अरे मोहन, कैसे हो ?' बाँके बिहारी ने सिर घुमाया, 'मैं रात आया। एक्सप्रेस भी देना।'

मोहन ने पीछे मुड़कर साइकिल के कैरियर से दो अख़बार निकाले और उनके हाथ में थमा दिए। वे खड़े-खड़े एक्सप्रेस देखने लगे। मुख्य ख़बर गुजरात में दंगों की ही थी। कल ट्रेन में दिन-भर कुछ छिटपुट ख़बरें कानों में पड़ती रही थीं। यह पक्की ख़बर थी। परसों घटे 'गोधरा' का बदला कल गुजरात ने लिया था। गोधरा कहाँ था ? गोधरा यदि गुजरात में था तो क्या गुजरात ने गुजरात से बदला लिया ? हत्या, लूट और आगजनी का तांडव हुआ था। पता नहीं क्या-क्या हुआ था ? यह तो पहली ख़बर थी। ट्रेन में एक गुजराती अहमदाबाद का 'संदेश' लिये था—जिसमें गोधरा में हुए बलात्कारों की ख़बर थी। कल प्रतिशोध अभियान शुरू हुआ। शहर जले थे। अहमदाबाद का चरम पूर्व सांसद एहसान जाफ़री का कल अपराह्न दहन था। भीड़ से घिरे अपने घर के सामने दौड़ते लहूलुहान जाफ़री को ज़िन्दा जला दिया गया था। एहसान जाफ़री ! बाँके बिहारी की जीभ पर यह नाम घूमा, जो नूरजहाँ में बदल गया। नूरजहाँ—जो मेरे पोते की माँ है ! बाँके बिहारी अख़बार हाथ में लिए बैठ गए। धूप दरवाज़े की चौखट पर आ गई थी। उन्होंने

धूप को घूरते हुए सोचा : आग का कोई भरोसा नहीं। बाबरी मस्जिद ढहने के तुरन्त बाद दस साल पहले नूरजहाँ के पिता लखनऊ में खो गए थे। नूरजहाँ रोई थी। क्या नूरजहाँ फिर रोएगी ? दरवाज़े पर एकाएक धूप चमकी जैसे सूर्य ने कोण बदला हो। बाँके बिहारी को अचानक भैया याद आया जो सिलिकन वैली में जेब में डॉलर खनखनाता घूमता था। उसने पिछली बार बताया था कि वह और उसके दोस्त अमरीका में विश्व हिन्दू परिषद को चन्दा देते हैं। आख़िरकार, उसने कहा था, गोरों के देश में कोई हमारी संस्कृति के लिए काम कर रहा है। आप नहीं जानते, पापा, उसने कहा था—परदेस में अपना देस कैसे-कैसे याद आता है ! तब शाहरुख ख़ान की फ़िल्म देखना या मन्दिर जाना बहुत काम आता है। वही काम गुजरात के गाँवों में त्रिशूल-यज्ञ और भगवा-पट्टी बनकर फैला था। उन्हीं हाथों ने तलवारें थामी थीं। वही हाथ गुजरात जला रहे थे। गुजरात गुजरात से बदला ले रहा था। क्या मेरा एक बेटा दूसरे बेटे से बदला लेगा ? बाँके बिहारी की आँखों के सामने नूरजहाँ का चेहरा आ गया। उन्होंने उसे फिर एक मुसलमान की तरह देखा जैसे ब्याह के वक़्त देखा था। फिर भूल गए थे। भूला हुआ शिद्दत से दिसम्बर 1992 में याद आया था। फिर लगातार याद आता रहा। जब-जब बाबरी मस्जिद-रामजन्म भूमि का मसला गरमाता, बाँके बिहारी को नूरजहाँ का मुसलमान होना याद आता जैसे कोई दर्द बार-बार उठता हो।

अटारी में छोटे की आँख जब खुली तो हल्का-सा अँधेरा था, जो कोनों में गाढ़ा हो रहा था—नीचे फ़र्श पर कोनों में और ज़्यादा। छप्पर पर उजाले के कुछ छेद थे। सुबह का समाँ था। मगर आँगन के पेड़ से चिड़ियों के चहचहाने की आवाज़ें नहीं आ रही थीं। चिड़ियों की बातें मुम्बई के फ़्लैट में बहुत याद आती थीं—क्योंकि वे वहाँ नहीं थीं। वहाँ ऐसा दरवाज़ा भी नहीं था, जो छत पर खुलता हो। छत पर सुबह का उजाला था।

धूप नहीं थी।

छोटे निकर पहने सीढ़ियों के ऊपर खड़ा था। उसने सिर ऊपर घुमाया। नीम की पत्तियाँ हौले-हौले हिल रही थीं। चिड़ियाँ नहीं थीं। कहाँ गईं सारी चिड़ियाँ ? क्या अपना पेड़ भूल गईं ? या कोई और पेड़ याद आ गया ? सारी चिड़ियाँ आसमान में एक-साथ मर तो नहीं सकतीं ? चिड़ियों में सामूहिक हत्या या आगजनी का रिवाज़ भी नहीं था।

'अम्माँ', छोटे ने चौके में बैठते हुए कहा।

'हाँ', गायत्री दूसरी ओर चूल्हे के बग़ल में बैठे हुए बोलीं।

'चिड़ियाँ कहाँ गईं ?'

'कौन-सी चिड़ियाँ ?' गायत्री ने आँखें घुमाईं।

'अपने नीम की चिड़ियाँ ?'

'घूमने गई हैं', गायत्री हँसीं।

'कहाँ ?'

'दूसरे पेड़ों या घरों या आसमान में।'

'क्यों ?'

'यही उनका दिन-भर का काम है।'

'वे भी काम करती हैं ?'

'हाँ', गायत्री ने छोटे की ओर देखा।

चूल्हे से धुआँ उठा। गायत्री की आँखों में भर गया। उन्होंने आँखें मूँदकर खोलीं। आँखों में आँसू डबडबा आए। डबडबाई आँखों में छोटे की आकृति काँपने लगी।

धुआँ चौके के दोनों मेहराबों से अपने गुंजलक बनाते हुए आँगन में बिखर गया। छोटे चौके में दूसरी ओर मेड़ पर उकड़ूँ बैठा था। वह आँगन में लहराते धुएँ को देख रहा था। एकाएक उसे लगा कि पेड़ से आँगन में अँधेरा चू रहा है। वह देखता रहा : पेड़ से अँधेरा सूखी पत्तियों की तरह गिर रहा था।

सूर्य कहाँ गया ?

'अम्माँ', छोटे ने अचानक कहा, 'आज क्या दिन नहीं होगा ? सुबह के बाद रात होगी ?'

'यह सुबह नहीं है', गायत्री हँसीं, 'शाम है।'

'पर', छोटे ने सिर चारों ओर घुमाया, 'पर दिन कहाँ गया ?'

'दिन-भर तुम सोते रहे।'

छोटे ने हड़बड़ाकर चारों ओर देखा।

वह चौके में बैठा कुछ देर चाय पीता रहा और आँगन में गिरता अँधेरा देखता रहा। कोई पक्षी पेड़ पर बोला। क्या आज पक्षी पेड़ पर चुपचाप लौटे थे ?

1.2

दीवार खड़ी हो रही थी।

गायत्री ने पचास वर्ष पहले कहा था जब बड़े पैदा हुए। फिर बड़े और मँझले और भैया बड़े होते रहे और वे भूल गईं। अब जब छोटे मुम्बई से लौटे तो उन्हें

फिर याद आया जो उन्होंने पचास वर्ष पहले कहा था। यह छोटे का आख़िरी लौटना था।

नीम की पत्तियों में अपनी चहचहाहट छोड़कर चिड़ियाँ उड़ गईं थीं। सूर्य आसमान में कुछ ऊपर उठ आया था। छत को लाँघकर धूप आँगन में पसर गई थी। सीढ़ियों पर नीम के नीचे पेड़ की छाया थी, जहाँ दीवार खड़ी हो रही थी। बाँके बिहारी सुबह की छाया में खड़े थे। मिस्त्री ईंट पर ईंट रख रहा था। मज़दूर उसे ईंट देता जाता था। पास तसले में सीमेंट और बालू का मसाला था, जो दो ईंटों के बीच में भरा जाता था। बाँके बिहारी उसी ओर मुँह किए खड़े थे।

गायत्री दालान से पूजा की थाली हाथ में लिये आईं और आँगन में खड़ी हो गईं। उन्होंने अभी नहाया था। उनके खिचड़ी बाल खुले थे, जो सिर पर ढँकी धोती से झाँक रहे थे। चेहरे पर कुछ झुर्रियाँ निखर आई थीं। पूजा की थाली में चमेली के सफ़ेद फूल थे, जो मालिन दे गई थी।

'सुनो', गायत्री ने बाँके बिहारी से कहा।

'हाँ।'

'मैं जा रही हूँ।'

'कहाँ ?' उन्होंने दीवार से नज़रें उठाए बिना पूछा।

'मन्दिर', कहते हुए उन्होंने मुँह मोड़ लिया और आँगन से पौर और पौर से बाहर हो गईं।

जब बाँके बिहारी की नज़र घूमी, उन्होंने आँगन से पौर में जाती गायत्री की पीठ देखी। उन्होंने फिर दीवार की ओर मुँह मोड़ लिया जो आकार लेने लगी थी।

मन्दिर दूर नहीं था। घर से बाहर निकलते ही बाईं ओर बाज़ार के चौराहे पर पीपल की पत्तियाँ धूप में हिलती नज़र आती थीं। पीपल के पेड़ के नीचे मन्दिर था। पीपल प्राचीन था। उसके तने में एक हाथी समा जाता। पेड़ में जितनी डालियाँ थीं उससे सौ गुनी शाखाएँ थीं। एक नज़र में पूरा पेड़ भरो तो लगता जैसे कोई विराट् ऋषि समाधि में बैठा है।

मन्दिर उसी के नीचे था।

हरी पत्तियाँ धूप में जगमग हो जातीं, फिर धूप जाने पर काली—जैसे अँधेरे में मन्दिर पर चीथड़े फड़फड़ा रहे हों।

मन्दिर में अँधेरा था। शायद सड़क का उजाला छोड़कर अन्दर घुसने से आँखें अंधी हो जाती थीं। फिर आहिस्ता-आहिस्ता अँधेरा कुछ हल्का होता और मन्दिर की दीवारों पर कुछ मूर्तियाँ नज़र आतीं। मूर्तियों में शंकर, पार्वती और गणेश थे और कुछ सर्प और जंगल और नदियाँ दीवारों पर फैली थीं। फिर अन्दर एक और

छोटा-सा दरवाज़ा था, जो सँकरे गर्भ-गृह में खुलता था—जहाँ बीच में शिवलिंग पर एक घड़ा टँगा था, जिससे एक-एक बूँद लिंग पर गिर रही थी।

जैसे लिंग पर पानी की एक-एक बूँद गिर रही थी, उसी तरह एक दीवार से एक-एक बूँद रोशनी आ रही थी। वरना मन्दिर में अँधेरा सम्पूर्ण था।

गायत्री ने अपने लोटे का जल शिवलिंग पर चढ़ाया...आहिस्ता-आहिस्ता... कुछ बुदबुदाते हुए, जो मन्दिर में गूँजा...कुछ विशृंखलित स्वर थे, जिनका कोई अर्थ नहीं खुलता था। कोई और मन्दिर में नहीं था, न और कोई आवाज़ थी—सिवाय शिवलिंग पर पानी की बूँद की टप-टप के, जो एक नियमित अन्तराल पर सुनाई देती। फिर उन्होंने पूजा की थाली से हल्दी-अक्षत उँगलियों से उठाकर लिंग के माथे पर लगाए। फूल चढ़ाए। सफ़ेद फूलों से अँधेरा कुछ कम हुआ।

उन्होंने थाली से अकेला केला उठाकर शिवलिंग के चरणों में रख दिया।

गायत्री के होंठों से निकलती बुदबुदाहट लगातार चालू थी जैसे कोई नल खुला हो। बुदबुदाहट में फ़र्श पर गिरते पानी के नन्हे विस्फोट जैसा कुछ था। केवल दो शब्द ही दीवारों को सुनाई देते थे : 'संकटमोचन' और 'छोटे'। यही भाषा का अन्त था। अन्त के परे आँसू थे।

आँसू शिवलिंग के जल में मिलकर नीचे नाली में बह रहे थे।

दोपहर में आँगन की सीढ़ियों पर कमर तक दीवार खड़ी हो गई। अब आँगन से सीढ़ियाँ नहीं दीखती थीं। एक छोटी दीवार थी, जिस पर कलई होना बाक़ी था। मिस्त्री और मज़दूर रोटी खाने चले गए थे। बाँके बिहारी रोटी खाकर पौर में लेटे सड़क की ओर देख रहे थे। सड़क पर आदमी, औरतें, बच्चे, कुत्ते, गाय—सब चलते हुए नज़र आते थे। छायाएँ उनके आस-पास थीं जैसे कुछ दूर मकानों की छायाएँ। उनकी आँखें मुँद गईं।

'सो गए क्या ?' गायत्री की आवाज़ थी।

'नहीं', उन्होंने आँखें खोलीं, 'मैं सपना देख रहा था।'

'क्या ?'

'मैं सपना देख रहा था कि छोटे बिलकुल ठीक हो गए हैं।'

एक कुत्ता अचानक सड़क पर भौंका। फिर दूसरा भी भौंका। जैसे उनमें कोई झगड़ा हो गया हो। पौर से कुत्ते दीखते नहीं थे। उनकी आवाज़ें दूर होती गईं।

'मैंने भी कल रात एक सपना देखा', गायत्री ने कहा। उनकी आँखों में चमक थी।

'क्या ?'

'मैंने देखा कि छोटे का ब्याह हो रहा है और उसकी बहू चाँद का टुकड़ा है।'

बाँके बिहारी गायत्री की आँखों को घेरे उनका चेहरा देख रहे थे : आँखों के नीचे कुछ झुर्रियाँ उभर आई थीं। उन्हें पता ही नहीं चला कब उनके मुँह से ये शब्द फूटे :

'चाँद का टुकड़ा रेत है !'

गायत्री कुछ अचरज से अपने पति के सफ़ेद बालों से घिरे चेहरे को देख रही थीं। वे जानती थीं कि अब छोटे को इलाज के लिए न लखनऊ जाना है, न मुम्बई। वह आख़िरी बार लौटा था। अब वह अपने घर में ही रहेगा। इसीलिए सीढ़ियों पर पर्दा पड़ रहा था। गायत्री यह भी जानती थीं कि बड़े और मँझले को रुपए भेजने में दिक़्क़त होगी, भैया को कोई दिक़्क़त नहीं होगी। वह फ़ोन पर कहता भी है, 'अम्माँ, ज़रूरत हो तो बताना। मुझे कोई दिक़्क़त नहीं होगी।' कल दोपहर बात छिड़ने पर जब गायत्री ने यही बात दुहराई तो बाँके बिहारी झुँझलाकर बोले :

'मैं डॉलर नहीं लूँगा।'

'ख़र्च तो रुपयों में ही होगा', गायत्री ने कहा।

'तो क्या हुआ ?'

'क्यों ?'

'परिवार में निवेश तो डॉलर का ही होगा। मैं ऐसे विदेशी निवेश के ख़िलाफ़ हूँ जो मेरे परिवार को ही तहस-नहस कर दे।'

'कैसे ?' गायत्री हँसीं।

गायत्री और हँसीं जब बाँके बिहारी ने अपनी तर्क-सरणि बयान की जिसमें भैया का विश्व हिन्दू परिषद को अमरीका में दिया गया डॉलर गुजरात के गाँवों में त्रिशूल और तलवार बनकर लखनऊ में अपने घर में बैठी नूरजहाँ को डरा रहा था। यह साज़िश है, वे चीख़े। अमरीका मेरे घर के पीछे पड़ा है !

बाँके बिहारी उठे और दालान में चले गए जहाँ तख़्त पर एक ओर फ़ोन रखा था। उन्होंने 'हिन्दुस्तान' का स्थानीय नम्बर मिलाया। घंटी जा रही थी। किसी ने उठाया नहीं। उनके चेहरे पर एक चमक आ गई। उन्होंने एस.टी.डी. खोलने का नम्बर घुमाया और लम्बी बीप सुनकर लखनऊ का नम्बर मिला दिया।

'हलो,' वहाँ से आवाज़ आई।

'मैं झाँसी से बाँके बिहारी बोल रहा हूँ।'

'कैसे हैं सक्सेना साब ?' सम्पादक की भारी आवाज़ थी।

'अच्छा हूँ। यहाँ आपके ऑफ़िस में कोई फ़ोन नहीं उठा रहा।'

'ऑफिस बन्द है,' सम्पादक हँसे।

'क्यों ? क्या कोई मिला नहीं ?'

'हाँ, कोई ढूँढ़िए।'

'मौजूद है।'

'कौन ?'

'जो बोल रहा है।'

'लेकिन', सम्पादक ने कहा, 'आपने तो कहा था, आप काम नहीं करेंगे।'

'अब लौट आया हूँ।'

मौन। फ़ोन का तार ठंडा। कुछ घूँ-घूँ की ध्वनि।

'हलो,' बाँके बिहारी ने कहा।

'सक्सेना साब', सम्पादक का स्वर संदिग्ध था, 'आपका स्वास्थ्य ठीक है ?'

'ठीक है,' बाँके बिहारी हँसे।

'ठीक है,' सम्पादक की आवाज़ आई, 'आप कल से चार्ज ले लीजिए।'

'धन्यवाद।'

बाँके बिहारी ने फ़ोन रखकर ठंडी साँस ली। उन्होंने सोचा कि अब उन्हें अख़बार से पाँच हज़ार प्रति माह की आय हो जाएगी और डॉलर के आयात की ज़रूरत नहीं होगी। आँगन से आती ठंडी हवा के साथ कुछ तसल्ली महसूस हुई। जी हल्का हुआ। कुछ हवा में उड़ने जैसी स्थिति थी—जैसे कभी-कभी सपने में होता है। पहले लगा कि पैर की जगह पंख आ गए हैं या शायद पैर ही पंख हो गए हैं। फिर वे हवा में उड़ने लगे। चिड़िया की तरह। शरीर का भार कम हो गया। उम्र ग़ायब हो गई।

जब धूप ढली तो ऐसा लगा जैसे शाम का रंग आँगन की नई दीवार में घुल रहा है। पेड़ पर चिड़ियों के लौटने की आवाज़ आने लगी। मिस्त्री और मज़दूर चले गए। बाँके बिहारी ने चाय उन्हीं के साथ पी ली थी। बाँहों में कुछ ठंड महसूस हुई। उन्होंने बिना बाँह का स्वेटर उतारकर पूरी बाँह का स्वेटर पहन लिया। पैरों में नाईके के सफ़ेद जूते पहने जो मुम्बई में मँझले ने उन्हें ख़रीदकर दिए थे। उसने कहा था, पापा, आप इन्हें पहनकर घूमिए, चलना दौड़ने जैसा लगेगा। फिर उन्होंने दालान की दीवार पर टँगे आईने में अपना चेहरा देखते हुए बाल निकाले और दाढ़ी पर भी कंघा फेर लिया। मुस्कराते हुए उन्होंने गायत्री से कहा :

'मैं जाता हूँ।'

'कहाँ ?'

'अहमद के यहाँ।'

'क्यों ?' आँगन के बीच खड़ी गायत्री ने पूछा।

'कल से अख़बार का ऑफ़िस खुलेगा।'

'ऐसी क्या जल्दी है ?' गायत्री ने नीम की ओर देखते हुए कहा, 'कुछ दिन आराम कर लेते।'

बाँके बिहारी भी नीम की ओर देख रहे थे। वे हँसे।

भाजीबारी नरिया के आगे दाईं ओर मुड़कर जब बाँके बिहारी अहमद के मोहल्ले में घुसे तो आसमान से अँधेरा उतरने लगा था। अँधेरा आसमान की ऊपरी सीढ़ी पर था, मोहल्ले में अभी उजाला था। कोई धूसर रंग चारों ओर हवा में घुल गया था, जो मकानों से निकलता हुआ लगता था। मकानों में अँधेरा था। गली में बिजली के खम्भे अभी चुपचाप अपना-सा मुँह लिए खड़े थे—रोशनी नहीं थी। मकानों की दीवारें मटमैली-सी थीं जैसे उनका कोई रंग न हो। कहीं-कहीं नंगी ईंटें मसाले की अधूरी ओट लिये एक-पर-एक खड़ी थीं। चबूतरे ख़ाली थे। गली में धूल उड़ रही थी। बाँके बिहारी ने अपने सफ़ेद जूतों की ओर नीचे देखा। उन्हें लगा जैसे सिर्फ़ धूल जूतों के आगे चल रही है। गली में धूल चल रही थी। और कुछ नहीं था। न गली में, न चबूतरों पर, न आसमान में। कोई पक्षी नहीं था। न कोई पेड़ नज़र आता था। गली के दोनों ओर मकान थे। मकानों के दरवाज़े बन्द थे। दोनों ओर किवाड़-ही-किवाड़ नज़र आते थे। बन्द किवाड़ों को देखते हुए बाँके बिहारी के ज़ेहन में बचपन का एक दृश्य कौंधा। वे अपने मोहल्ले में घुसते हैं और सारे मकानों के दरवाज़े इसी तरह बन्द हैं। दिन था या रात ? अँधेरा था या उजाला ? क्या धूप थी ? क्या सड़क पर कोई आदमी या कुत्ता था ? कुछ याद नहीं था। सिर्फ़ बन्द मकान याद थे। तब शहर में प्लेग फैला था। शहर के लोग भागकर शहर से बाहर या दूर चले गए थे। दिन-रात शहर भाँय-भाँय करता था गोया शहर में जंगल रहता हो। बाँके बिहारी गली के दोनों ओर देख रहे थे। एकाएक उन्होंने देखा कि किवाड़ों पर न साँकल चढ़ी है, न ताला लगा है। मकान भीतर से बन्द थे। यही फ़र्क था। प्लेग में लोग घरों पर ताले जड़कर भागे थे।

बाँके बिहारी बाईं ओर मुड़े। अचानक गली चौड़ी हो गई, जो आगे जाकर बाईं ओर एक मैदान में खुलती थी। मैदान में दो सुअर लड़ रहे थे और एक कुत्ता भागकर इसी ओर आ रहा था। दाईं ओर चबूतरे से चार मुर्गियाँ दौड़ती हुई गली में आईं। फिर एक लड़का चबूतरे से गली में उतरा। लड़का चबूतरे पर कहाँ से आया था ? बाँके बिहारी ने इधर-उधर नज़र दौड़ाई। कोई दरवाज़ा नहीं खुला था। एक ओर एक टाट का परदा ज़रूर काँप रहा था। कोई आवाज़ नहीं थी। आवाज़

सिर्फ़ लड़ते सुअरों की थी। गली में खड़ा कुत्ता चुप था। लड़का दौड़ता हुआ मैदान की ओर भाग गया था। सुअरों के परे जिस ओर लड़का भागा था, वहाँ दूसरे लड़के भी थे। मैदान में कुछ दौड़ते लड़कों का हुजूम था। उनकी गिनती मुश्किल थी। उनके कपड़ों का रंग मटमैला था जो शाम की धूसर हवा में घुल रहा था।

लड़के फुटबाल खेल रहे थे। मैदान में दौड़ते लड़कों के घूमते पैरों से बाँके बिहारी ने यह जाना। उन्हें दोनों ओर कहीं गोल नज़र नहीं आया। वे यह सोचकर मुस्कराए कि क्या हर तरफ़ गोल था ! उन्होंने लड़कों की टाँगों के बीच बड़ी गेंद को आँखों से पकड़ने की बहुत कोशिश की। वे नंगी टाँगों का पीछा करते रहे। ऐसा लगा जैसे नंगी टाँगें छूँछी हवा में दौड़ रही हैं...दूर-दूर...हर तरफ़...। गेंद कहीं नहीं थी। गेंद के रंग पर ज़रूर शक होता था। आहिस्ता-आहिस्ता गेंद का अदृश्य रंग लड़कों की टाँगों पर चढ़ा, फिर उसने उनके जिस्म को लीलना शुरू कर दिया। कुछ पल मैदान में मटमैले चिथड़े फड़कते रहे, फिर वे हवा में डूब गए।

गली में सड़े पानी की गन्ध थी, जो एक ओर गड्ढे में इकट्ठा था।

जब एक बूढ़ा आदमी गली में सामने से आया तो बाँके बिहारी उसे देखकर चौंके। उन्हें लगा कि वह किसी आईने से आ रहा है। उसकी दाढ़ी सफ़ेद थी, सिर के बाल सफ़ेद थे, क़द-काठी उन्हीं की तरह थी। वह उन्हीं की तरह चल भी रहा था। मगर उसने एक काली शेरवानी पहनी थी। आईना ऐसी गड़बड़ी नहीं कर सकता, उन्होंने सोचा। फिर भी जब उस बूढ़े ने ऐन सामने रुककर कहा, 'बाँके बिहारी', तो बाँके बिहारी की समझ में न आया कि वह उनका नाम बोल रहा है या अपना !

'अरे, मुश्ताक, तुम !' अचानक बाँके बिहारी ने अपने पुराने सहपाठी को पहचाना।

वे एक-दूसरे से लिपट गए।

फिर वे विपरीत दिशाओं में चल दिए। कुछ क़दम आगे एक मुर्गी बाँके बिहारी के पैरों से टकरा गई। उसके पर फड़फड़ाए। सूनी गली के एक बन्द दरवाज़े से एक भारी आवाज़ आई—'कौन ?' नाम सुनने पर उसने फिर पूछा, 'यहाँ किस लिए आए हैं ?' आवाज़ कड़क थी। बताना मुश्किल था कि आवाज़ डरी हुई है या डरा रही है। आवाज़ के पीछे अँधेरा था।

अहमद का घर कुछ दूर था। गली में एकाएक बत्तियाँ जल गई थीं। बत्तियाँ दूर-दूर थीं। बीच में अँधेरा था जिसमें मकान डूबते हुए लगते थे। ऐसे ही एक मकान की सीढ़ियाँ चढ़कर बाँके बिहारी ने बन्द किवाड़ पर लटकती साँकल बजाई। तीन बार साँकल बजने पर अन्दर से आवाज़ आई—'कौन ?' बाँके बिहारी

का नाम सुनते ही फ़ौरन किवाड़ खुल गए। 'आदाब', अहमद ने कहा, 'तशरीफ़ लाइए।' जब बाँके बिहारी सामने मूढ़े पर बैठ गए, तो अहमद ने पूछा, 'ग़रीबख़ाने पर कैसे ?'

कमरे में शायद ज़ीरो पॉवर का बल्ब था। अहमद सामने स्टूल पर बैठा था। उसने चौखाने की तहमद पहनी थी। तहमद पर बनियान जैसा कुछ था। वह छाया की तरह लगता था। बाँके बिहारी ने एक नज़र चारों ओर दीवारों पर घुमाई थी, जिनका पलस्तर उखड़ गया था। अन्दर की ओर दरवाज़े पर टाट का पर्दा पड़ा था, जहाँ अँधेरा था। बाँके बिहारी को शक हुआ कि कहीं उनकी नज़र और कमज़ोर तो नहीं हो गई। उन्होंने अपना चश्मा नाक पर और ऊपर खिसकाया।

'अहमद,' बाँके बिहारी बोले।

'जी।'

'तुम्हारे मोहल्ले में मकान बन्द क्यों हैं ?'

'क्या सारे मकान बन्द हैं ?'

'हाँ।'

'आपको धोखा हुआ होगा,' अहमद हँसा जैसे झेंप रहा हो।

बाँके बिहारी को लगा जैसे सामने कोई साया हँसा हो। फिर उन्हें लगा कि वे चारों ओर साँवले सायों से घिरे हैं। वे कुछ चीख़ते-से बोले–'नहीं, नहीं, मुझे धोखा नहीं हुआ।'

अहमद कुछ नहीं बोला। वह उठा और टाट का पर्दा उठाकर अन्दर चला गया। बाँके बिहारी सायों से घिरे अकेले बैठे थे। सहसा उन्हें लगा कि वे ख़ुद एक साया हैं। तभी वे बुदबुदाए, 'नहीं, नहीं, मुझे कोई धोखा नहीं हुआ।'

अहमद हाथ में पानी का गिलास लेकर पर्दा ठेलते हुए लौटा। बाँके बिहारी ने पानी का गिलास लेकर सामने रखे ख़ाली स्टूल पर रख दिया। फिर अपना सवाल दुहराया :

'मकान बन्द क्यों हैं ?'

चुप्पी। जैसे चारों ओर उसी की छाया हो।

'आपने पानी नहीं पिया, सक्सेना साब', अहमद ने ठंडी आवाज़ में कहा।

'मुझे प्यास नहीं है।'

फिर चुप्पी। फिर चारों ओर उसी के साए। दीवारों के सायों के बीच हिलते हुए।

अहमद सामने बैठा था। उसका साया थोड़ा हिला। फिर आवाज़ आई :

'क्या...क्या गिलास की वजह से ?'

गिलास टीन का था।

फिर एकाएक बाँके बिहारी ने गिलास उठाया और एक ही साँस में सारा पानी पी लिया। ख़ाली गिलास स्टूल पर रखते हुए उनके मुँह से फिर स्वर फूटे :

'मकान बन्द क्यों हैं ?'

'आज दोपहर में वड़ोदरा से ख़बर आई थी', अहमद की आवाज़ तेज़ हो गई।

'क्या ?'

'मेरे चचा का पूरा कुनबा जला दिया गया।' आवाज़ बर्फ़ की तरह ठंडी थी।

'क्-क्...कैसे ?' बाँके बिहारी हकलाए।

'वे एक बेकरी में काम करते थे। वे अपनी बेकरी में जले। कुनबा अपने मोहल्ले में।'

चुप्पी सम्पूर्ण थी। साए अँधेरे में घुल गए थे।

'वे वड़ोदरा में कब से थे ?' बाँके बिहारी कुछ आगे झुक आए थे।

'डेढ़ सदी से।'

'डेढ़ सदी से ?' वे चौंके।

'हाँ', अहमद ने कहा, 'हमारा एक पुरखा रानी लक्ष्मीबाई की सेना में था। रानी की हार के बाद उनके कुछ पुराने सिपाही अंग्रेज़ों के डर से पश्चिम की ओर भागे थे। तीन-चार वड़ोदरा पहुँचकर वहीं बस गए। उनमें हमारे पड़दादा के भाई अकेले मुसलमान थे। वे तब झाँसी न छोड़ते, तो शायद आज उनका कुनबा बच जाता।' अहमद ने पहली बार आह भरी।

'अहमद।'

'जी।'

'ऑफ़िस की चाबी मुझे दे दो।'

'क्यों ?'

'कल ऑफ़िस खोलना है।'

'मैं आकर खोल दूँगा।'

'ठीक है', बाँके बिहारी ने अहमद की जानिब देखा।

जब बाँके बिहारी बाहर आए तो बिजली के खम्भों के उजाले में बस्ती कुछ नंगी हो गई थी। वे यह सोचते हुए लौटे कि झाँसी की रानी का मुसलमान सिपाही जो डेढ़ सदी पहले अंग्रेज़ों से बच गया था, उसे डेढ़ सदी बाद हिन्दुओं ने मार दिया !

1.3

'चाचा, नमस्ते !'

बाँके बिहारी ने अख़बार से नज़रें ऊपर उठाईं। नज़रें उठाते ही अख़बार की कड़वाहट घुल गई। मुस्कराते हुए बोले :

'नमस्ते, बेटा, कैसी हो ?'

'अच्छी हूँ', सपना मुस्कराई।

वह मुस्कराते हुए पौर के भीतरी दरवाज़े से आँगन में चली गई। वह पौर में एक दरवाज़े से दूसरे दरवाज़े तक मुस्कान की तरह खिंची थी, जिसकी आवाज़ अब आँगन से आ रही थी। उसे देखकर बाँके बिहारी सोचते कि काश, ऐसी ही एक बेटी घर में होती तो हमेशा मन की कड़वाहट घुलती रहती। यही सोचते हुए उन्होंने मुँह फिर अख़बार में दे दिया। चेहरे पर मुस्कान थी। वे सोच रहे थे कि सपना अब गायत्री से पूछेगी, 'चाची, रतन हैं ?' फिर उसके क़दमों की आवाज़ सीढ़ियों पर सुनाई देगी।

छत पर सुबह की नर्म धूप और साए फैले थे। नीम की शाखों और पत्तियों के डोलते हुए साए थे, जो धूप की चमक से घिरे थे। खुलते मार्च का ठंडी बयार में लिपटा उजाला था, जो अटारी के दरवाज़े पर ठिठक गया था। दरवाज़ा खुला था। अटारी के बीच चारपाई पर रतन लेटा था। उसकी आँखें बन्द थीं। चारपाई के पास खड़े हुए एकाएक सपना को लगा कि कोई शिशु चारपाई पर लेटा है। उसे शिशु को चूमने का मन हुआ। शायद यह करवट की वजह से था। यदि वह सीधा चित लेटा होता तो उसकी बढ़ी दाढ़ी के बाल-ही-बाल चेहरे पर नज़र आते। तब शिशु की शिनाख़्त मुश्किल होती। सिर्फ़ आँखें बन्द कर लेने से आदमी बच्चा नहीं हो जाता।

रतन चित हो गया। उसकी आँखें बन्द थीं। उसे पता नहीं था कि खिड़की में बैठी चिड़िया के साथ सपना भी उसकी ओर देख रही है। सपना उसे 'गुरु' कहती थी। पन्द्रह बरस पहले यह सम्बोधन शुरू हुआ था, जब रतन ने सपना को गणित पढ़ाना शुरू किया। तब वह दस साल की थी और पाँचवीं में थी। गणित में छमाही में फ़ेल हो गई थी। रतन से तीन माह पढ़कर उसके सौ में सौ नम्बर आए थे और उसने रतन को 'गुरु' कहना शुरू कर दिया था। रतन तब दसवीं में था। उसका बोर्ड-परीक्षा में ज़िले में पहला नम्बर आया था। सपना उसे नायक मानते हुए बड़ी हुई थी। उसने रतन का लम्बा होना और उसके चेहरे पर काले-काले बाल आना देखा था। तब वह लखनऊ पढ़ने चला गया था। पहली

बार छुट्टी में घर आया तो एक दोपहर इसी अटारी में उसने उसके चेहरे को दोनों हाथों से थामकर ऐन होंठों पर चूमा था। सपना की आँखों में आँसू आ गए थे। रतन हँसा था।

रतन ने अचानक आँखें खोलीं जैसे कोई सपना टूटा हो। एक पल उसने सपना को देखा। फिर हड़बड़ाकर उठते हुए उसने कहा—

'अरे, सपना, तुम कब आईं ?'

'अभी,' वह उसी की ओर देख रही थी।

'कैसी हो ?'

'अच्छी हूँ...और तुम, गुरु !' उसका स्वर भारी था।

'मैं...,' वह हँसा, 'मैं ठीक हूँ। मुम्बई घूमकर आ रहा हूँ।'

खिड़की में बैठी चिड़िया उड़ गई।

'चाची कह रही थीं,' सपना बोली, 'तुम रात-भर टी.वी. देखते हो।'

सपना का स्वर सपाट था जैसे रतन का चेहरा, जो चुप था। सपना को मालूम था कि दो-तीन बार पाँच-पाँच हज़ार की नौकरियाँ रतन ने छोड़ी थीं। कहीं टिका नहीं था। उसे यह भी पता चला था कि दो बरस पहले वह लखनऊ के नूर मंज़िल में दो सप्ताह को भर्ती हुआ था। फिर अभी मुम्बई इलाज के लिए ही गया था।

'घर लौटकर कैसा लग रहा है ?' सपना ने पूछा।

'अच्छा,' उसने सामने रखी कुर्सी की ओर हाथ से इशारा करते हुए कहा, 'तुम बैठो न !'

वह बैठ गई। सामने एक युवक था, जिसकी आँखों में कहीं कुछ खो गया था : काली पुतलियों की चमक में, या उन्हें घेरे सफ़ेद पर्दों में, या आँखों के किसी कोने में ! कहाँ ? सपना खोज रही थी।

रतन को जैसे ही सपना की खोज का पता चला, उसने अपनी आँखें छत की ओर फेरकर कहा, 'आज क्या छुट्टी है ?'

'नहीं, मेरे पीरियड देर से हैं। मुझे पता नहीं था कि तुम लौट आए हो।'

'हाँ', वह हँसा, 'लौट आया हूँ।' फिर कुछ रुककर, 'आख़िरी बार।'

'आख़िरी बार ?'

'हाँ, अब फिर कभी नहीं लौटूँगा।'

'क्यों ?'

'क्योंकि अब कहीं नहीं जाऊँगा,' वह ठहाका मारकर हँसा।

सपना पिछले पन्द्रह बरस से रतन की हँसी सुनती रही थी। उसने इस हँसी का बदलना देखा था। पहले वह एक लड़के की हँसी थी, हल्की-हल्की, दूब की

तरह। फिर अचानक वह कुछ फैलकर चटकी और भारी होने लगी थी। फटा बाँस ! वह उन दिनों रतन को 'फटा बाँस' कहकर चिढ़ाती थी। वह हँस पड़ता था। फिर धीरे-धीरे बाँस एक सुतवाँ बेंत में बदल गया। शुरू-शुरू में वह मूँछें रखता था। तब वह बी.ए. कर रही थी और रतन की पहली नौकरी थी। वह छुट्टी में घर आया था। उसने इसी अटारी में उससे कहा था :

'मुझसे शादी करोगी ?'

'सोचूँगी !'

वह खिलखिलाती हुई छत पर भागी थी। फिर सीढ़ियों पर। आँगन और पौर को लाँघकर उसने सड़क पार की थी और अपने घर में ऊपर जाकर पलंग पर औंधी लेट गई थी। उसकी उँगलियाँ बार-बार होंठों को छू रही थीं, जहाँ रतन ने अभी चूमा था। उसे पहली बार लगा था कि यह दुनिया उसी के लिए बनी है। सूरज उसी के लिए रोशनी बरसाता था। पेड़ों में पत्तियाँ और ताल में जल उसी के लिए थे। जब रात होगी तो चाँद उसी को देखने आकाश का दरवाज़ा खोलकर बाहर निकलेगा।

रतन अब भी हँस रहा था। लेकिन अब उसकी हँसी में वह भरोसा नहीं था। ठहाका रायते की तरह बिखर जाता था। ठहाके का बिखरना पिछले चार-पाँच बरस से नज़र आने लगा था जैसे कोई आईना दीवार पर अपनी जगह लगा हुआ चटक जाए। उस आईने में अपनी सूरत पर दरारें खिंच जाती थीं। शायद इसी आईने की वजह से पिछले माह सपना का ब्याह तय होते-होते रह गया। बीच में मारुति आ गई। सपना के घर की बैठक में मोठ के तहसीलदार वर्मा अपने इंजीनियर बेटे अनिल के साथ बैठे थे। सामने सपना, सपना की माँ और उसके पिता थे। सपना ने लड़के को नज़र-भर देख लिया था। दोनों की छिटपुट बात भी हो गई थी। कुंडली पहले मिल गई थी। तैंतीस गुण मिले थे। पंडितजी ने 'उत्तम' कह दिया था। लेन-देन की कोई बात नहीं थी। वर्मा साहब ने कहा था कि मुझे कुछ नहीं चाहिए, आप जो चाहें अपने दामाद और बेटी को दें। फिर अन्त में उन्होंने सपना के पिता से कहा—'चन्द्रा साहब !'

'जी।'

'अनिल शरमा रहा है। उसने मुझे बताया था कि उसे मारुति चाहिए।'

चन्द्रा सन्नाटे में आ गए। वे यह कहने को शब्द ढूँढ़ने लगे कि मैं एक अवकाश-प्राप्त शिक्षक हूँ, मेरे पास मारुति के लिए पैसे कहाँ ?

मुँह सपना ने खोला :

'अनिल, क्या यह सच है ?'

सपना की माँ उसका हाथ दबा रही थी। 'तुम चुप रहो, माँ !' उसने कहा।

अनिल ने 'हाँ' में मुंडी हिलाई।

'मुँह से बोलो, अनिल !' सपना की आवाज़ कुछ तेज़ हुई।

'हाँ', अनिल की आवाज़ धीमी थी।

सपना एक झटके से खड़ी हो गई। वह चीख़ी :

'तब तुम मारुति से ही ब्याह करना।'

बैठक में सन्नाटा छा गया।

सन्नाटे को चीरती हुई फिर सपना की आवाज़ गूँजी, 'आप लोग फ़ौरन मेरे घर से बाहर निकल जाएँ।'

जब सपना की नज़रें छत से लौटीं तो उसने देखा कि रतन उसे घूर रहा है। ताज्जुब की बात यह थी कि उसकी पलकें झपक नहीं रही थीं। जैसे पलकें ही ग़ायब हो गई हों। बस, आँखों में काला घेरा था, जो सफ़ेद परदे पर चमक रहा था।

'मैं जाती हूँ', उसने कहा, 'मुझे देर हो रही है।'

वह अपने घर की अटारी में चढ़कर आईने के सामने खड़ी हो गई। वह साँवली थी। उसकी आँखें आईने में पारे की तरह चमक रही थीं और सिर आईने के सिर को छूता था। वह लम्बी थी। बेल की तरह। यह रतन ने पहली बार कहा था जब उसने उसे दूसरी बार चूमा। वह अभी रतन की आँखों से सहमकर लौट आई थी। क्या वे सचमुच इतनी ख़ाली थीं जितनी लग रही थीं ? या सपना की आँखों पर नूर मंज़िल का चश्मा चढ़ा था ? यदि यह चश्मा न होता तो क्या वह अनिल और उसके तहसीलदार पिता से बात करना भी गवारा करती ? क्या उसके मन में भी मारुति-मोह था, जिसका उसने कोई सपना इंजीनियर की पत्नी होने की कल्पना में देखा था ? क्या गुरु के सपने पर मारुति का सपना छा गया था ?

क्या नूर मंज़िल एक बहाना बन गई ? क्या उसी बहाने का पर्दा सपना की आँखों पर पड़ा था ? क्या इसी पर्दे ने रतन की आँखों के रंग सोख लिए थे ? आईने के सामने खड़े हुए सपना एक बार काँप गई। नूर मंज़िल के बाद रतन झाँसी आ गया था। उसे सरस्वती पाठशाला में अस्थायी रूप से शिक्षक की जगह भी मिल गई थी। सत्र के अंतिम दिन एक लड़के ने उसे स्कूल के बाहर सड़क पर चाँटा मार दिया था—रतन ने परीक्षा में उसे फ़ेल कर दिया था। प्रिंसिपल ने उसकी शिकायत नहीं सुनी क्योंकि दुर्घटना स्कूल के बाहर सड़क पर हुई थी। असली कारण यह था कि वह लड़का स्कूल की प्रबंधन समिति के एक सदस्य का बेटा था। रतन को सलाह दी गई कि वह थाने में जाकर एफ.आई.आर. दर्ज

कराए। सैकड़ों आँखों के सामने पिटना और फिर उसे ही थाने जाने की सलाह मिलना—उससे बर्दाश्त नहीं हुआ था। वह थाने की बजाय बार चला गया था और रात में घर लौटने की बजाय रेलवे स्टेशन के प्लेटफ़ॉर्म की एक बेंच पर सो गया था। अगले दिन सपना को उसने यही बताया था।

यदि वह सचमुच बीमार था तो उसने दस माह स्कूल में पढ़ाया कैसे था ? मोहल्ले के दोनों लड़के जो उसके विद्यार्थी थे, बताते थे कि रतन सर बहुत अच्छा पढ़ाते हैं। रतन सर बहुत अच्छा न पढ़ाते होते तो सपना के गुरु कैसे बनते ? आईने में अपनी आँखें देखते हुए सपना को शक हुआ कि उसे कहीं रतन की आँखों में इसीलिए तो कुछ नहीं दिखा क्योंकि उसकी अपनी आँखों में कुछ नहीं था ?

यदि वह मुझे नहीं चाहती, तो पुराने दिनों की तरह सुबह-सुबह अटारी में क्यों आ जाती और एकटक मुझे खाट पर सोता देखती रहती ? उसने मुझे जगाया भी नहीं। मैं ही अचानक जागा जैसे वह नींद में मेरा पीछा कर रही हो। जब वह छोटी थी तो हँसते हुए मेरा पीछा करती थी और 'गुरु, गुरु' कहती थी। क्या वह फिर छोटी हो गई थी और नींद में मेरे पीछे भाग रही थी ? रतन खाट पर बैठा हुआ बाहर छत पर खुली धूप को देखने लगा। धूप नर्म थी। गुदगुदे भरोसे की तरह। दो चिड़ियाँ धूप में फुदक रही थीं। फुदकती हुई वे दीवार के साए में चली जातीं जहाँ धूप नहीं थी। फिर फुदकती हुई वे धूप में लौट आतीं, जो नर्म थी।

जब चिड़ियाँ उड़ीं तो रतन खाट से उठ गया। वह छत पर आया, फिर सीढ़ियों पर। सीढ़ियों पर उसने एक हाथ नई दीवार पर ऐसे रखा जैसे इसी दीवार के सहारे वह सदा सीढ़ियों से उतरा हो। वह कुछ गुनगुना रहा था। कोई गाना था, जिसके बोल उसे ख़ुद मालूम नहीं थे। रसोई में बैठी गायत्री ने सुर पहचाना और मुस्कराई। कल वह घबरा गई थी जब सीढ़ियों पर खड़े हुए छोटे चीख़ा था। वह आँगन में दौड़कर गई और उसने पूछा, 'क्या हुआ ?'

'अम्माँ !' छोटे घबराया हुआ था।

'क्या हुआ ?'

'क्या यह अपना ही घर है ?'

'हाँ, क्यों ?'

'यह दीवार कहाँ से आई ?'

'नई बनी है।'

'क्यों ?'

'तुम बहुत दिनों बाद घर लौटे हो। हमें लगा कि कहीं नंगी सीढ़ियाँ चढ़ना भूल न गए हो !'

छोटे उदास हो गया। उसने कहा—'क्या कोई अपना घर भूलता है, अम्माँ ?'

आज छोटे ख़ुश था। वह गा रहा था। गायत्री ने झटपट चाय के लिए चूल्हे पर पानी रख दिया।

जब वह घर से निकला, सूरज आसमान में कुछ ऊपर चढ़ आया था। सीधी सड़क मानिक चौक के बाज़ार से मिलती थी जैसे कोई नदी समुद्र में गिर रही हो। यह बाज़ार का समुद्र था। अभी ज्वार का समय था। ग्राहकों के अलावा शहर के कामकाजी लोग भी दुतरफ़ा भीड़ में शामिल थे। कन्धों से कन्धे रगड़ते थे। यह भीड़ शहर में रतन के साथ बढ़ी थी। रतन के इस अहसास के पीछे उसका ख़ुद बढ़ना और बार-बार शहर छोड़ना भी शामिल था। हर दीर्घ अनुपस्थिति के बाद बाज़ार की भीड़ कुछ और बढ़ी लगती थी, दुकानें कुछ और भरी-भरी और रंगीन नज़र आती थीं। वह भीड़ के रेले के साथ तिकोने पर पहुँचकर दाईं ओर मुड़ गया और कुछ क़दम चलकर एक तिपहिए में बैठ गया जिसका मुँह खंडेराव गेट की ओर था। उसने एक क्षण आँखें बन्द कर लीं। भीतर कोई थकान सिर उठा रही थी—हालाँकि अभी सुबह ख़त्म नहीं हुई थी और हवा इतनी ठंडी थी कि धूप गर्म नहीं लगती थी।

जब तिपहिया चला तो रतन ने आँखें खोलीं। सामने की सीट पर एक लड़का बैठा था और मुस्करा रहा था। 'नमस्कार, सर', उसने कहा और उसके होंठ फैल गए। शायद वह कुछ हँसा भी। या शायद रतन को ही कुछ भ्रम हुआ हो। लेकिन भ्रम तुरन्त टूट गया। उसके होंठ अभी भी पूरे चेहरे पर फैले थे। उसकी हँसी की आवाज़ तिपहिया की खड़खड़ाहट में खो गई थी। रतन को कोई शक नहीं था। उसने उस लड़के को पहचान लिया। वह उसी लड़के का दोस्त था जिसने सरस्वती पाठशाला के सामने सड़क पर उसे चाँटा मारा था। चाँटा मारने वाला विद्यार्थी यथावत् स्कूल में था, लेकिन चाँटा खानेवाला शिक्षक स्कूल छोड़कर, मुम्बई में बड़े भाई की वेतन-रहित नौकरी छोड़कर अभी खड़-खड़ तिपहिए में बैठा रोज़गार दफ़्तर की ओर जा रहा था।

सामने बैठा लड़का इसीलिए हँस रहा था।

खंडेराव गेट पार करके उस लड़के ने फिर अपने दाँत दिखाए। वह हँसा भी ज़रूर था। मगर उसकी खिलखिलाहट तिपहिए के शोर में फिर खो गई। रतन ने आँखें बन्द कर लीं। उसने कानों पर दोनों हाथ रख लिए। फिर भी तिपहिए की

आवाज़ आती रही। वह सन्न बैठा रहा। जब उसने आँखें खोलीं तो सामने फिर लड़के की हँसी थी और बाईं ओर लक्ष्मीबाई पार्क का गेट था।

'रोको', रतन चीखा।

तिपहिया लड़खड़ाकर रुका। रतन ने उतरकर पैसे चुकाए। फिर वह तुरन्त बिना तिपहिए की ओर देखे पार्क की ओर बढ़ा। यद्यपि तिपहिया आगे बढ़ा, लेकिन रतन को लगा कि कोई खिलखिलाहट उसका पीछा कर रही है। गेट बन्द था। वह बग़ल के छोटे दरवाज़े को ठेलकर अन्दर घुसा और तेज़-तेज़ धुर सीधा चलता रहा जब तक तिपहिए की खड़-खड़ न रुकी। तभी हँसी ख़त्म हुई। रतन के पैर धीमे हुए। वह आहिस्ता-आहिस्ता चलते हुए एक बेंच पर आकर पसर गया।

उसने एक गहरी साँस ली। सामने खुला आसमान था, जिसमें धूप फैली थी। क़िला एक कोने में खड़ा नज़र आता था। शहर उसी के पीछे था। पार्क में चारों ओर पेड़ और फूलों की क्यारियाँ थीं। बेंच के पीछे फ़व्वारे के चारों ओर पानी भरा था, यद्यपि फ़व्वारा अभी चल नहीं रहा था। पानी से आती हुई हवा ठंडी थी। बेंच पर पेड़ की छाया थी। सूर्य क़िले के ऊपर था। बेंच के सामने एक टाँग हवा में उठाए घोड़े पर बैठी रानी लक्ष्मीबाई की मूर्ति थी जैसे क़िले के बुर्ज से कूदकर रानी यहीं हवा में ठहर गई हो। उनका पुत्र घोड़े पर पीछे बैठा था। रतन कुछ देर हवा में ठहरी, हाथ में तलवार लिए रानी को देखता रहा। उसकी पृष्ठभूमि में उजला, नीला आसमान था।

लड़के की खिलखिलाहट फिर दिमाग़ में कौंधी। उसने आँखें मूँद लीं। जब हँसी चली गई, तब उसकी याद आ गई। मगर कुछ ही क्षणों में सपना सामने खड़ी हँस रही थी। रतन ने आँखें खोलीं और कुछ देर वह सामने देखता बैठा रहा जहाँ बीहड़ सुनसान था। पार्क में कोई नहीं था। कम-से-कम कोई नज़र नहीं आ रहा था। सिर्फ़ हवा और धूप थी।

जिस छोटे दरवाज़े से वह पार्क में घुसा था, उसी से उसी तरह लौह-अवरोध ठेलते हुए वह बाहर निकला। वह सड़क पर चलने लगा। सड़क पर दुपहिए, तिपहिए और कारें दौड़ रही थीं। एक क्षण उसे लगा जैसे केवल पहिए सड़क पर दोनों ओर दौड़ रहे हों। वह उन्हीं पहियों को देखने लगा। दाईं ओर पहियों के पीछे सरस्वती पाठशाला की इमारत थी जैसे दूसरी इमारतें थीं। उसकी सरसरी नज़र फिसलकर फिर पहियों से लिपटने लगी जैसे कोई खेल शुरू हो गया हो। वह सड़क पर पहिए गिनता हुआ रोज़गार दफ़्तर में घुसा। उसे लगा, वह किसी और दफ़्तर में आ गया है। उसने चपरासी से पूछा :

‘क्या यही रोज़गार दफ़्तर है ?’

‘हाँ।’

चपरासी ने रतन को ऊपर से नीचे तक देखा : वह नीली जींस और सफ़ेद कमीज़ पहने था, जो अमरीका में बसे भैया ने उसे दी थीं। कपड़े चमक रहे थे। जूतों पर भी ज़्यादा धूल नहीं थी।

‘क्या काम है ?’ चपरासी ने पूछा।

‘एक अर्ज़ी के बारे में पता करना है।’

चपरासी ने एक कोने में बैठे आदमी की ओर इशारा किया, जो एक कम्प्यूटर के सामने बैठा था। असल में हॉल में जितने कर्मचारी थे, सभी के सामने कम्प्यूटर थे। पिछले साल जब रतन आया था तो कम्प्यूटर नहीं थे और हॉल में भीड़-भाड़ नज़र आती थी। अब कम्प्यूटर थे, भीड़ नहीं थी।

‘मेरा नाम रतन सक्सेना है’, रतन ने कम्प्यूटर के साथ बैठे एक आदमी से कहा, ‘मैंने पिछले साल रजिस्ट्रेशन कराया था। कुछ बना ?’

कम्प्यूटर-धारी व्यक्ति ने कम्प्यूटर के कुछ बटन दबाए, फिर परदे पर पढ़ा— ‘बी.कॉम.; बी.सी.ए.।’ फिर वह हँसा।

‘कोई नौकरी है ?’ रतन ने पूछा।

‘नहीं, बड़ी मुश्किल है’, उसने आँखें ऊपर उठाकर कहा।

‘क्या ?’

‘शहर में कम्प्यूटर के जानकार कम्प्यूटरों से ज़्यादा हैं। आप उन्हीं में से एक हैं।’

‘मैं बिना कम्प्यूटर की नौकरी कर लूँगा’, रतन ने कहा।

कर्मचारी हँसा। उसने हॉल में अपना हाथ घुमाते हुए कहा, ‘आप यह हॉल देख रहे हैं ?’

‘हाँ।’

‘यहाँ से आधे आदमी इसलिए चले गए क्योंकि उन्हें कम्प्यूटर नहीं आता था।’

हॉल में सन्नाटा छाया रहा। कम्प्यूटर बेआवाज़ थे।

जब दूसरी बार कर्मचारी ने रतन की ओर देखा तो रतन ने पूछा :

‘वे कहाँ गए ?’

‘कौन ?’

‘जो इस हॉल में बैठते थे।’

‘क्यों ?’ कर्मचारी हतप्रभ था।

'मैं वहीं जाऊँगा।'

'क्यों ?'

'नौकरी वहीं होगी।'

कर्मचारी ने नज़रें फेर लीं। उसने कोई बटन दबाया। कम्प्यूटर के परदे पर अक्षर उभरने लगे।

रतन बाहर आ गया।

1.4

दालान में अचानक गायत्री की नज़र घड़ी पर पड़ी : सवा आठ बज गया था ! उन्हें आश्चर्य हुआ। फिर चिन्ता हुई। बाँके बिहारी अभी तक पौर से अन्दर नहीं आए थे। ठीक आठ बजे आने के साथ वे अक्सर यह भी कहते : 'भूख लग आई।' फिर हँसते हुए जोड़ते, 'शायद बुढ़ापे की वजह से है। भूख तेज़ हो गई है। बचपन की तरह।' पौर में पहुँचकर गायत्री ने देखा कि वे एकटक सामने दीवार पर टँगी घड़ी की ओर देख रहे हैं।

'क्या देख रहे हैं ?' गायत्री ने पूछा।

'समय।'

दीवार-घड़ी के ऊपर लगी बिजली की रॉड कुछ काँप रही थी। कुछ गड़बड़ था। प्रकाश का कम्पन पौर में तैर-तैर जाता। अँधेरे की झीनी चादर की तरह।

'भूख नहीं लगी ?'

'हाँ...' वे गायत्री की ओर देखते हुए बोले, 'नहीं, नहीं। तुम खा लो।'

फिर काँपते उजाले में उन्होंने नज़रें घुमा दीं जैसे गायत्री की आँखों में न देखना चाहते हों। वे आँगन में खुलते दरवाज़े की ओर देख रहे थे। फिर उजले सन्नाटे में उन्होंने अपनी नज़रें पौर के दरवाज़े में गड़ा दीं जैसे आँखों को चौखट में जड़ देना चाहते हों।

गायत्री पौर के दरवाज़े से थोड़ा हटकर खड़ी थीं। वे जानती थीं कि उनके और बाँके बिहारी के बीच लुका-छिपी का खेल चल रहा है। रोज़ की तरह आज भी शाम को लौटकर उन्होंने पहला प्रश्न छोटे के बारे में ही किया था। जब गायत्री ने बताया कि छोटे सुबह रोज़गार दफ़्तर गए थे और अभी तक नहीं लौटे तो वे कुछ नहीं बोले। उसके बाद भी कुछ नहीं बोले। पौर में चले गए।

यह पहली बार नहीं हुआ था। मगर गायत्री को दोपहर से ही लग रहा था

कि जैसे छोटे पहली बार शहर में खो गए हों। छोटे शहर में खोने के लिए छोटे नहीं थे। वे इतने बड़े थे कि खोने के लिए दुनिया में कहीं भी जा सकते थे। शहर से रेल की पटरियाँ हर तरफ़ जाती थीं। रेल की पटरियाँ धूप में दूर-दूर तक चमकती थीं...पटरियों पर कभी कोई गाय कट जाती...कभी बकरी...अख़बार में जो तस्वीर छपती, उसमें रेल की पटरियों पर गाय होती और ऊपर आकाश में चिड़ियाँ। रेल की पटरियों पर कटा जिस्म देर तक आँखों में झूलता रहता... कभी वह बीच से कटा होता, कभी सिर से।

गायत्री को भी भूख नहीं लग रही थी। दोपहर में ही उनका मन हुआ था कि बाँके बिहारी को अख़बार के दफ़्तर में फ़ोन कर दें। फिर वे अपनी बेचैनी दबा गई थीं। वे जानती थीं कि फ़ोन करने से कुछ नहीं होगा। बाँके बिहारी भी बेचैन हो जाएँगे। फिर तब आधा दिन बाक़ी था जैसे अभी पूरी रात बाक़ी थी। आने वाले किसी भी क्षण में छोटे पौर के दरवाज़े में तस्वीर की तरह जड़ सकते थे—जहाँ बाँके बिहारी की आँखें थीं।

'क्या कहीं फ़ोन किया ?' गायत्री ने पूछा।

'किसलिए ?'

'छोटे के लिए', आवाज़ कुछ तेज़ थी।

'छोटे फ़ोन पर होते', बाँके बिहारी मुस्कराते हुए बोले, 'तो वे ख़ुद फ़ोन न करते !' फिर जैसे उन्होंने पलटकर तीखे स्वर में कहा, 'सड़कों और चट्टानों के फ़ोन नम्बर नहीं होते, न बाग़ों और बेंचों के !'

गायत्री की दाईं आँख फिर फड़की। क्या यह आज पहली बार दोपहर में फड़की थी ? वे बोलीं, 'थाने का फ़ोन नम्बर तो है !'

बाँके बिहारी ने एकटक गायत्री की आँखों में देखते हुए कहा—'गायत्री, हुआ क्या है ? एक तीस साल का नौजवान सवेरे घर से गया और शाम तक नहीं लौटा। अभी रात शुरू हो रही है।'

रात का सन्नाटा था। सड़क पर बिजली के खम्भे की फीकी-सी रोशनी थी। जब कोई वाहन गुज़रता तो सन्नाटा बिखर जाता। लेकिन वाहन गुज़रने के बाद फिर चट्टान तन जाती। एकाएक मन्दिर का घंटा बोला। शंख फुँका। आरती हो रही थी।

गायत्री ने आँखें मूँद लीं।

फिर सन्नाटे में आँखें खोलकर उन्होंने समतल स्वर में कहा, 'तो फिर तुम्हें भूख क्यों नहीं लगी ?'

'क्योंकि तुम्हें नहीं लगी', बाँके बिहारी मुस्कराए।

वे दोनों एक-दूसरे की ओर देख रहे थे। तभी कोई छाया दरवाज़े में आकर खड़ी हो गई।

इससे पहले कि बाँके बिहारी आँखें घुमाते, उनके कानों में आवाज़ आई, 'जय रावण !'

इस उद्‌घोष से बाँके बिहारी के चेहरे पर मुस्कान आई और गायत्री के पैर आँगन की ओर मुड़ गए। मुस्कान चेहरे पर पूरी तरह फैल गई। श्याम सुन्दर हँसते हुए पौर में घुसे और चबूतरे की जाजम पर सामने बैठ गए।

'क्या हाल हैं ?' बाँके बिहारी ने पूछा।

'अच्छे नहीं हैं। गुजरात जल रहा है।' श्याम सुन्दर के चेहरे पर अचानक पर्दा गिरा। हँसी खो गई।

फिर एकाएक ट्यूब के झपकने से उनकी आँखें बन्द हो गईं। आँखें खोलते हुए श्याम सुन्दर बोले : 'भैया, ट्यूब बुझा दो। ऐसे उजाले से तो अँधेरा अच्छा !'

बाँके बिहारी ने उठकर ट्यूब बुझा दी। फिर दूसरी दीवार पर बल्ब जला दिया।

बाँके बिहारी और श्याम सुन्दर फिर आमने-सामने बैठ गए। वे लगभग एक ही उम्र के थे। मगर साथ पढ़े नहीं। कॉलेज के दिनों में ही श्याम सुन्दर शहर में नई पीढ़ी के जुझारू कम्यूनिस्ट की तरह विख्यात थे। उन्हें लोग 'कॉमरेड' पुकारते थे। शहर में मज़दूरों की हड़ताल हो या मेहतरों की, स्कूलों को बन्द कराने की ज़िम्मेदारी श्याम सुन्दर की ही थी। उन्होंने 'जय रावण' कहना कब शुरू किया, यह किसी को नहीं मालूम। लेकिन अधेड़ उम्र में जब बाँके बिहारी उनसे घनिष्ठ हुए, तब ऐलानिया उनका यही उद्‌बोधन था : 'जय रावण !' जो लोग सुनते, मुस्कराने लगते जैसे अजायबघर में आँखें फाड़े कभी-कभी हम मुस्कराते हैं। अजायबघर आँखें फाड़े घुसने और मुस्कराते हुए बाहर निकलने की जगह है। अजायबघर घर नहीं है। अजायबघर में कोई नहीं रहता। बाँके बिहारी ने श्याम सुन्दर से यही कहा। उन्होंने कहा कि यदि तुम्हें लोगों के भीतर कोई घर बनाना है तो उनकी ज़ुबान के रास्ते से ही जाना होगा। मैं अपना रास्ता ख़ुद बनाऊँगा—श्याम सुन्दर की ज़िद थी।

रावण महापंडित था। रामायण रावण का राज हड़पने की कथा है। यह राम का साम्राज्यवादी अभियान था। ब्राह्मण तुलसीदास ने उसे महिमामंडित किया है ताकि वर्णाश्रम धर्म बना रहे। श्याम सुन्दर की यही टेक थी। उनकी बैठक की एक दीवार पर दशानन की मढ़ी हुई एक तस्वीर लगी थी। शहर में यह अकेली रावण की तस्वीर थी। जय रावण !

‘क्या तुम जानते हो ?’ बाँके बिहारी पूछते।

‘क्या ?’

‘इस शहर में राम उतने ही यथार्थ हैं जितनी रानी लक्ष्मीबाई !’

श्याम सुन्दर हँसते, ‘लक्ष्मीबाई का रानीमहल है, क़िला है ! राम का क्या सबूत है ?’

‘लोगों को सबूत नहीं चाहिए’, बाँके बिहारी कहते, ‘तसल्ली चाहिए। रानी मर गई। राम कभी नहीं मरते। वे रोज़ सुबह शहर के घरों में रेहल से उठकर तरह-तरह के करतब करते हैं। लोग उन्हीं करतबों में जीते हैं।’

‘मैं लोगों को इसी फ़रेब से निकालना चाहता हूँ’, श्याम सुन्दर चीख़ते।

‘यह फ़रेब नहीं है’, बाँके बिहारी मुस्कराते।

‘फिर क्या है ?’

‘यह लहूलुहान ज़िन्दगी का मरहम है।’

श्याम सुन्दर टुकुर-टुकुर देखते।

‘यह हृदयहीन समाज का हृदय है’, बाँके बिहारी मुस्कराते रहते, ‘तुम दिल में खून उल्टा नहीं बहा सकते। रावण को राम नहीं बना सकते।’

वे दोनों अभी गुजरात की बातें कर रहे थे। श्याम सुन्दर ने बीड़ी जला ली थी। बाँके बिहारी अन्दर से चाय के कप ले आए थे। दूसरी बार दो बीड़ियाँ जलाकर श्याम सुन्दर ने जब एक बीड़ी बाँके बिहारी की ओर बढ़ाई तो उन्होंने ले ली। वे कभी-कभार पी लेते थे। इसका कारण हमेशा कोई गहरी चिन्ता नहीं होती थी। कभी-कभी गहरी चिन्ता भी कारण होती थी। जैसे अभी। इस चिन्ता के घेरे में गुजरात था या छोटे या दोनों—वे ख़ुद नहीं जानते थे। छोटे के रोज़गार दफ़्तर जाने और लौटकर न आने और गुजरात के बीच क्या रिश्ता हो सकता था ?

‘क्या सोच रहे हो ?’ श्याम सुन्दर ने बाँके बिहारी की चुप्पी देखकर कहा।

‘क्या देश में फैलती बेरोज़गारी और गुजरात के बीच कोई रिश्ता है ?’

‘सीधा रिश्ता है।’

‘कैसे ?’

‘बेरोज़गार राम-भक्तों की फ़ौज में भर्ती होते हैं। लोग उस फ़ौज को अयोध्या जाते देखते हैं और कीर्तन करने लगते हैं। फ़ौज गोधरा लौटती है और गुजरात हो जाता है !’

फिर श्याम सुन्दर ने एक दशक पीछे लौटकर शहर की उस भावभीनी अगवानी को याद किया जो उसने राम-ईंट लिये अयोध्या प्रयाण करते कारसेवकों के लिए अंजाम दी थी। शहर-भर में जगह-जगह उनके लिए पूड़ी-सब्ज़ी और

रायता और बूँदी के लड्डू परोसे गए थे। कारसेवकों के माथे पर भगवा-पट्टी थी या गले में रामनामी दुपट्टा था और होंठों पर 'जै श्रीराम !' वे शहर को 'जैश्रीराम' बुलवाते अयोध्या के लिए रवाना हुए थे। वे दक्षिण दिशा से बसों और रेलगाड़ियों में शहर में आते और शहर की मेहमान-नवाज़ी पर खुश होते हुए उत्तर की ओर चले जाते। कब रेहल का राम 'जैश्रीराम' में बदल गया, किसी को पता नहीं चला। तभी बाँके बिहारी ने म्यूज़ियम के सभागार में कहा था, 'देखिए, शहर का राम बदल रहा है। यह इतिहास से बदला लेना चाहता है। इसे बचाइए !' राम को बचाने की बात पर जब लोग हँसे तो बाँके बिहारी ने कहा कि राम को उन हाथों से बचाइए जो उन्हें अस्त्र की तरह इस्तेमाल करना चाहते हैं। जब राम ख़ुद बचेंगे, तभी वे आपको बचाएँगे ! श्याम सुन्दर की ज़िद थी कि लोगों को राम से छुड़ाना होगा। तब बाँके बिहारी ने शहर के दैनिक में एक लेख लिखा था, जिसका शीर्षक था : नए राम, पुराने राम। उनका कहना था कि नए राम 1949 में पैदा हुए जब बाबरी मस्जिद में मूर्तियाँ रखी गईं। ये प्रतिशोधी राम हैं। ये तुलसीदास के राम से अलग हैं, जो करुणा के सागर हैं। करुणा के सागर का गुजरात में लूट, बलात्कार और आगजनी से क्या सम्बन्ध हो सकता था ? बन्दरों की सेना ने भी राक्षसों की लंका में ऐसा नहीं किया था। 'जैश्रीराम' के नारे बोलते हुए अहमदाबाद के बाज़ारों से टी.वी., फ्रिज या जूते-कपड़े चुराना कोई धार्मिक अनुष्ठान नहीं था। यह निखालिस लूट थी, डाका था। उससे भी बुरा था। क्योंकि इससे राम का नाम जुड़ा था। क्या कोई कल्पना कर सकता है कि राम की सेना लंका में स्त्रियों का बलात्कार करती ? फिर गर्भ चीरकर वे शिशु को निकालते और त्रिशूल की नोक पर टाँग देते ? चाहे लंका तामसी राक्षसों की लंका ही क्यों न हो ! राम की वानर-सेना राक्षसी व्यवहार नहीं कर सकती थी। लूट और बलात्कार और आगजनी करते साक्षात् राक्षस राम की सेना नहीं हो सकते !

सामने बैठे श्याम सुन्दर ने कहा—'बाँके बिहारी, क्यों राम के झंझट में फँसे हो ?'

'रास्ता इसी झाड़-झंखाड़ से होकर जाता है', बाँके बिहारी बोले।

श्याम सुन्दर शुरू से दाढ़ी-मूँछ नहीं रखते थे। उनका चेहरा सफ़ाचट था। सिर के बाल अभी भी कुछ काले थे। उम्र की बराबरी के बावजूद वे सफ़ेद दाढ़ी-मूँछ-मंडित बाँके बिहारी से कुछ छोटे लगते थे। शायद इसका एक कारण उनकी छरहरी काठी और उस पर पैंट-कमीज़ का लिबास था, जिस पर एक खुला स्वेटर भी वे अभी धारण किए थे। उन्होंने तीसरी बीड़ी सुलगा ली थी। बाँके बिहारी की यह एक के बाद दूसरी बीड़ी थी।

दालान में फ़ोन की घंटी बजी। बाँके बिहारी कुछ दौड़ते-से अन्दर गए।

जब वे लौटे तो श्याम सुन्दर ने पूछा—'किसका फ़ोन था ?'

'लखनऊ से नमन का', बाँके बिहारी ने बैठते हुए कहा। जब उन्होंने तश्तरी में रखी अपनी बीड़ी उठाई तो वह बुझ चुकी थी। श्याम सुन्दर ने दीयासलाई उठाकर तीली रगड़ी और बीड़ी जला दी। तीली की रोशनी में दाढ़ी कुछ और चमकी।

'नमन ठीक हैं ?'

'हाँ।'

'लखनऊ ठीक है ?'

'हाँ।'

'अपना शहर भी ठीक है', श्याम सुन्दर ने एक गहरी साँस लेकर कहा, 'हम लोग कुछ अमन कमेटियाँ बनाने की सोच रहे हैं।'

'एक अमन कमेटी मुकरियाना-दरीगरान के लिए ज़रूर बनाओ, जहाँ अहमद रहता है।' बाँके बिहारी बोले।

'वह तो मुसलमानों का मोहल्ला है ! कोई गड़बड़ ?'

'नहीं', बाँके बिहारी ने कहा, 'सन्नाटा !'

जब श्याम सुन्दर चले गए, तो बाँके बिहारी साँकल लगाकर अन्दर पहुँचे। दालान में गायत्री बैठी थी। आँगन में अँधेरा था। अँधेरे में अँधेरे का पेड़ अदृश्य हवा में झूम रहा था।

'किसका फ़ोन था ?' गायत्री ने पूछा।

'बड़े का।'

'क्या कह रहा था ?'

'छोटे के बारे में पूछ रहा था।'

'क्या ?'

'यही, कैसा है ?'

'तुमने बताया कि वह घर नहीं लौटा।'

'हाँ', बाँके बिहारी दालान के उजाले में खड़े आँगन का अँधेरा देखने लगे।

'उसने क्या कहा ?'

'उसने पूछा कि छोटे के पास कितने रुपए थे। तुमने तो उसे और रुपए नहीं दिए, गायत्री ?'

'मुझसे दो सौ रुपए ले गया', गायत्री ने आँखें फाड़ीं।

'तीन सौ उसके पास थे। कुल पाँच सौ हुए। ज़्यादा हो गए।'

'मुझसे तो उसने नौकरी के फ़ॉर्म के लिए बोला था', गायत्री के स्वर में हताशा थी।

'रोज़गार दफ़्तर में रुपए नहीं लगते', बाँके बिहारी फीकी हँसी हँसे।

सन्नाटा छा गया। आँगन के अँधेरे में सन्नाटा बजने लगा।

असल में लखनऊ में नूर मंज़िल में भर्ती होने की नौबत रुपए की वजह से ही आई थी, जब छोटे एक रात घर से ग़ायब रहा था और अगली सुबह थाने से बरामद हुआ था—जहाँ उसे पुलिस रात में एक कॉल-गर्ल के घर से पकड़कर लाई थी। छोटे मुँह लटकाए घर लौटा था और खाना खाकर सो गया था। जागकर उसने बड़े को बताया कि वह बार में बीयर पीने को घुसा था। लेकिन बीयर के बाद उसने व्हिस्की पी ली। फिर वह अपने शरीर का होकर रह गया। वह पीछे चला, शरीर आगे। मर्द का जिस्म औरत के जिस्म के पीछे भागता था, वह क्या करे। इसीलिए नूर मंज़िल में डॉक्टर ने बताया था कि रतन के पास पैसा कम-से-कम होना चाहिए। यदि पैसा नहीं होगा तो दारू नहीं होगी। फिर रतन का जिस्म स्वायत्त कैसे होगा ?

पता नहीं, रतन का स्वायत्त शरीर शहर में इस वक़्त कहाँ होगा ? क्या थाने में फ़ोन करूँ ? इस ख़्याल से बाँके बिहारी चौंके। वे चौंके अपने आत्म-सम्मान के ख़्याल पर थे, जो बाद में आया था और जिसे वे पहले भूल गए थे। शहर में वेश्यावृत्ति अवैध घोषित हो गई थी। लोग कहते कि अब वेश्याओं के घर राजधानियों की तरह बस्ती में फैल गए हैं। क्या बाँके बिहारी हर मोहल्ले में चिल्लाते हुए घूमें ? हर दरवाजे की साँकल बजाएँ : छोटे हैं ? क्या छोटे हैं ?

'पता नहीं, छोटे कहाँ होंगे ?' गायत्री ने आँखें मूँद लीं।

स्वायत्त जिस्म रात में अपने घर माँ-बाप से मिलने नहीं लौटता। जिस्म का घर दूसरा जिस्म होता है। कौन जाने, रतन शहर में कहाँ भटक रहा हो ! बाँके बिहारी यह सोचकर उदास हो गए। जब रतन की पहली नौकरी शुरू हुई, तो दो-तीन रिश्ते आए थे। गायत्री ने बताया था कि रतन को तस्वीरें पसन्द नहीं आईं। उसे शक पहले ही था। पक्का कुछ बाद में हुआ। लेकिन तब तक देर हो गई थी। रतन ने दूसरी नौकरी भी छोड़ दी थी। वह बेकार था। दिन में सपना देखते हुए वह 'सपना-सपना' चीख़ा था। गायत्री तब अटारी में ही थी। उसने सुना था। सपना ने उसी साल बी.ए. पूरा किया था और वह बी.एड. करने आगरा चली गई थी। रतन घर में बैठा था और सपना के सपने देख रहा था। गायत्री ने बाँके बिहारी को बताया था। एक तो प्रस्ताव लड़की वाले के घर से ही आना चाहिए

था। दूसरे रतन बेकार था। सपना के पिता से क्या बात होती ? जब गायत्री ने कहा कि मैं सपना की माँ से बात छेड़ती हूँ, तो बाँके बिहारी चीखे़ थे :

'क्या कहोगी ? मेरे बेकार बेटे को अपनी बेटी का हाथ दे दो !'

फिर उनकी आवाज़ धीमी हो गई थी, 'गायत्री, हमारा कोई लाखों का व्यापार नहीं, जिसे मैं रतन को सौंप दूँ। मेरी तरह उसे भी अपने पैरों पर खड़ा होना होगा।'

'क्या हम सहारा नहीं दे सकते ?' गायत्री का स्वर कातर था।

'वही कर रहे हैं। लेकिन जिस गाड़ी में एक पहिए की जगह हमने अपना कन्धा लगाया है, उसमें एक और सवारी कैसे बिठा दें ?'

'रतन के भाई भी हैं', गायत्री ने तर्क किया था।

'ब्याह के बाद रतन का अलग परिवार होगा, गायत्री। हम कितने दिन चलेंगे ?'

हम कितने दिन चलेंगे ? बाँके बिहारी दालान में तख़्त पर बैठे बुदबुदाए।

1.5

अँधेरा हो चुका था।

पिछली बार भी यही हुआ था। उसने सपना को ढूँढ़ते हुए स्टैला के घर की घंटी बजाई। दरवाज़ा कमला ने खोला। वे दोनों सिविल लाइंस के एक फ़्लैट में एक साथ रहती थीं। यहाँ रतन को पहली बार दो साल पहले एक रात उसका पुराना सहपाठी गोविन्द लाया था। वह कमला से मिलने आता था। उसने कहा था, वहाँ स्टैला भी है, तुम चलो। उसने पहले ही बता दिया था कि उसकी कमला से दोस्ती की फ़ीस है। उसने यह भी कहा था कि ऐसी दोस्तियों का चलन झाँसी में नया है जब रतन को इस पर ताज्जुब हुआ। रतन का आश्चर्य दुगुना हुआ जब उसने स्टैला को पहली बार देखा। उसने अपना सिर झटका और आँखें ज़ोर से बन्द करके खोलीं जब उसे लगा कि सपना ही सामने स्कर्ट पहने खड़ी है—जो वह कभी नहीं पहनती थी। स्कर्ट के नीचे लम्बी, साँवली टाँगें धरती की ओर जा रही थीं। उसने सपना की टाँगें नहीं देखी थीं। स्टैला को छूकर ऐसा नहीं लगा था कि वह सपना को छू रहा है। उसे लगा था कि वह सपना की छाया छू रहा है।

'आओ', कमला ने कहा।

वह अन्दर घुसा। कमला उसे पहचान गई थी। इसीलिए उसने उस तेज़ गन्ध का भी ज़िक्र नहीं किया जो रतन के मुँह से आ रही थी। उसने मुस्कराते हुए

कहा—'क्या बार ख़ाली हो गया ?'

'क्यों ?' सामने कुर्सी पर बैठा रतन बोला।

वह हँसी। उसने कुछ नहीं कहा। स्टैला काली स्कर्ट पहने अन्दर के कमरे से बाहर उजाले में आई। रतन उसे देखता रहा : उसे लगा स्टैला के जिस्म पर जहाँ स्कर्ट है, वहाँ अँधेरा जमा है—बाक़ी रौशन चेहरा उजली टाँगों पर सधा है। वह मुस्कराती हुई कुछ तिरछी खड़ी हो गई। आगे और पीछे जहाँ अँधेरा था, कुछ अर्धवृत्ताकार रेखाएँ थीं। चेहरे पर ताज की तरह बालों में अँधेरा ही बैठा था।

'अँधेरा, अँधेरा', रतन बोलते हुए खड़ा हो गया, 'मैं यहाँ अँधेरा देखने नहीं आया हूँ।'

'कहाँ है अँधेरा ?' कमला पास खड़ी स्टैला की ओर देखते हुए मुस्कराई और बोली, 'दो रोशनियाँ जल रही हैं।'

स्टैला कुछ नहीं बोली। न वह तीसरी ख़ाली कुर्सी पर बैठी। वह आगे बढ़ी। उसने रतन का हाथ पकड़ा और उसे अन्दर कमरे की ओर ले चली जैसे किसी बच्चे को ले जा रही हो। कमरे को बन्द करके उसने अपनी ड्रेस खोल दी। फिर वह हँसी :

'लो, अँधेरा दूर हो गया।'

ड्रेस स्टूल पर एक ओर पड़ी थी। रोशनी में देह तलवार की तरह चमकी।

रतन रोता हुआ उससे लिपट गया। उसके मुँह से एक ही शब्द निकल रहा था, 'सपना...सपना...।'

आवाज़ धीमी होते-होते रोशनी में डूब गई।

रतन की जींस और कमीज़ स्टूल पर काली स्कर्ट के ऊपर पड़ी थीं। जींस सबसे ऊपर थी। पलंग की ओर खुली जींस की जेब में सौ-सौ के नोट झाँक रहे थे। स्टैला की एक नंगी टाँग उसी ओर थी। काँपती टाँग के अँगूठे और उँगली ने जेब से सौ के दोनों नोट निकाले और स्टूल के पीछे रखी मेज़ के नीचे फेंक दिए।

रोज़गार दफ़्तर के तिकोने पर ऑटो रुका। एक सवारी उतरी। उसने पचास का नोट दिया। ऑटोवाले के पास रेज़गारी नहीं थी। उसने रतन से पैसे माँगे। रतन ने जींस की जेबें टटोलीं—पहले आगे, फिर पीछे। जेबें ख़ाली थीं। जहाँ ऑटो खड़ा था, ऊपर बिजली का खम्भा था। रतन हड़बड़ाहट में नीचे उतरकर सड़क पर खड़े हुए फिर अपनी जेबें देखने लगा। उसके चेहरे पर हवाइयाँ उड़ रही थीं। कमीज़

और जींस मुचड़ी हुई लगतीं थीं। ऑटोवाला अपनी सीट पर बैठा था। उसके हाथ हैंडल पर थे। उसने तिरछी नज़र से रतन को देखा। फिर गाड़ी के शोर में उसने माँ की गाली दी और गाड़ी आगे बढ़ा दी। रतन रात की अकेली सड़क पर खम्भे के नीचे खड़ा था। उजाले में उसका चेहरा हवा में टँगा लगता था। यह वही जगह थी जहाँ सुबह अचानक वह दाईं ओर मुड़ गया था जबकि घर लौटने के लिए उसे बाईं ओर जाना था। सामने सड़क के दूसरी ओर लोहे के गेट के अन्दर दूर रेतीले रास्ते के आख़िरी पहाड़ी-शिखर पर जीवन साह की मज़ार थी जहाँ से तबले की थापों में लिपटे कव्वाली के आर्त स्वर तैरते हुए आ रहे थे :

ठहरा हुआ दरिया हूँ, बड़ी देर से चुप हूँ
कब उठेगी चश्मे-करम, मौला मेरी जानिब
कब तक मेरे मौला...

रतन कुछ पल ख़ाली काइनात में प्रार्थना की उन आवाज़ों को सुनता रहा। फिर वह बाईं ओर मुड़ा जहाँ शहर था। जैसे-जैसे वह बिजली के खम्भे से दूर हुआ, उसे लगा आकाश से रोशनी किसी झरने की तरह गिर रही है। उसने ऊपर नज़रें उठाईं। आसमान एकदम नीला था। चाँद—पूरा चाँद—एक ओर पेड़ों के ऊपर चमक रहा था। वह काफ़ी बड़ा था जैसे धरती के कुछ और पास आ गया हो जहाँ जीवन साह की मज़ार थी और पेड़ थे और रेत की पहाड़ी से प्रार्थना की तेज़, काँपती हुई आवाज़ें उठ रही थीं...ठहरा हुआ दरिया हूँ...कब तक मेरे मौला...। रतन की आँखें सहसा भीग गईं। वह आगे बढ़ता रहा। अगले क्षण उसने आँखें खोल ली थीं। आँसुओं से धुली आँखें खोलने पर उसे लगा जैसे चाँदनी एक परत और उजली हो गई है।

वह कब तिराहे पर दाईं ओर चाँदनी में मुड़ गया, उसे पता ही नहीं चला। सड़क के दोनों ओर घने पेड़ थे जो ऊँचे थे। जब उसने आँखें ऊपर उठाईं, वे दूर पत्तियों में उलझ गईं। पत्तियाँ हिल रही थीं। ठंडी हवा का एक झोंका उसके शरीर से लिपटते हुए निकल गया। रानी का अजायबघर दाईं ओर था। इमारत चाँदनी में चमक रही थी। जीवन साह की मज़ार उसी के पीछे थी जहाँ से सदाओं की आवाज़ें आ रही थीं। शायद आज बृहस्पतिवार था। हर बृहस्पति को यहाँ मेला लगता था। जीवन साह रानी लक्ष्मीबाई से पहले के पीर थे। लेकिन पीर का हिन्दू नाम क्यों ? रतन ने बाँके बिहारी से एक बार पूछा था। उन्होंने बताया था कि पीर न हिन्दू होता है, न मुसलमान। हिन्दू-मुसलमान दोनों पीर की मज़ार पर चादर चढ़ाते थे। प्रार्थना की सबको ज़रूरत थी।

वह सड़क छोड़कर दाईं ओर पगडंडी पर मुड़ गया। सामने रेत का सागर था। चाँदनी रेत पर चादर की तरह चमक रही थी। रेतीला रास्ता नीचे बाईं ओर छोटी-सी घाटी में जाता था जहाँ एक तालाब था। दाईं ओर घाटी से फिर ऊपर चढ़ाई शुरू होती थी जो ऊपर पहाड़ियों पर गुम हो जाती थी। पहाड़ियों की पीठें चाँदनी में कछुए की पीठ-सी चमक रही थीं जैसे रेत और पानी में कोई फ़र्क न हो। यह शहर के बीचोबीच एक अजीब रेतीला पहाड़ी इलाका था जिसके एक ओर क़िला खड़ा था और चारों ओर डामर की काली सड़कें थीं। डेढ़ सदी पूर्व इसी तरफ़ से ह्यू रोज़ की अंग्रेज़ी सेनाओं ने क़िले पर हमला बोला था। फिर इसी तरफ अंग्रेज़ों की सिविल लाइंस बनी। अब सब गड्डमड्ड हो गया था। सिर्फ़ क़िला अपनी जगह खड़ा था। चाँदनी में कुछ मायूस-सा।

सामने दूर से दो लोग आ रहे थे। उनके बीच कोई तीसरा था जो छोटा था। वे इतनी दूर थे कि रेत पर चाँदनी में सायों की तरह लगते थे। रतन को लगा कि वे जीवन साह की पहाड़ी के पीछे से उतरकर इस ओर आ रहे हैं। लेकिन वे साए आदमियों की चाल से कुछ ज़्यादा तेज़ लगे। एकाएक उसे याद आया कि शहर में यह किंवदन्ती थी कि बृहस्पतिवार की रात जीवन साह की मज़ार पर मेले में प्रेतात्माएँ भी आती हैं। क्या सामने ये प्रेतात्माएँ चली आ रहीं थीं ? क्या ये इस ओर रेत के रौशन टीलों पर नाचने आई थीं ? उनके कपड़े भी काले ही नज़र आ रहे थे जैसे प्रेतों के होते हैं। एक ओर काई-मंडित क़िला था, दूसरी ओर रेत के ढूहों पर नाचती प्रेतात्माएँ थीं। जब वे कुछ और पास आईं तो काले रंग की जगह नीला रंग नज़र आया। प्रेतात्माओं का क्या भरोसा ? जब चाहें, रंग बदल लें, रूप बदल लें। वे कुछ और पास आए तो रतन को लगा कि दो आदमियों के बीच एक औरत चली आ रही है—अलबत्ता तीनों ने शायद जींस पहनी थीं जैसा मुम्बई की सड़कों या समुद्र के किनारों पर नज़र आता था।

जब वे ऐन सामने आ गए, तो रतन के सामने रुक गए।

रतन को डरने के लिए सारे कारण थे। यह रेत पर चाँदनी का बियाबान था। यहाँ कोई पुलिस-थाना नहीं था जहाँ दौड़कर रपट हो सके। कोई राहगीर भी नहीं था जो मुँह मोड़कर मदद करे। तीनों राहगीर अचानक सामने थम गए थे जैसे लोहे के खम्भे हों।

'तुम्हारा नाम क्या है ?' एक बोला।

रतन ठहाका मारकर हँसा।

'हँसे क्यों ?' दूसरा गरजा।

'अरे', रतन ने हँसते हुए कहा, 'तुम लोग तो आदमी हो !'

'बीच में औरत है', पहला बोला।

चाँदनी में औरत मुस्कराई। शायद रतन को पूरा भरोसा नहीं था। उसे औरत प्रेतनी ज़्यादा लगी।

'तुम्हारा नाम क्या है ?' पहले की आवाज़ सख़्त थी।

'आदमी !' रतन मुस्कराया।

यह सुनकर तीनों एक क़दम आगे बढ़े। रतन एक क़दम पीछे हटा। उसके पैर लड़खड़ा गए। पहला लड़खड़ाते पैर देखकर ज़ोर से हँसा। फिर वह कुछ झुककर अपनी नाक रतन के मुँह के पास ले गया और फ़ौरन एक क़दम पीछे हटा। पीछे हटते हुए उसने कहा–'अरे, यह तो हमसे भी ज़्यादा पिए है !' यह सुनकर दूसरा भी हँसा। औरत भी।

'अपना नाम बताओ !' पहला फिर कड़का।

'रतन !'

एक पल सन्नाटा। चाँदनी में लिपटा हुआ। चारों ओर रेत। सामने प्रेत।

'बोलो...' पहले ने हड़काया।

रतन चुप रहा।

'बोलो जैश्रीराम !'

'जैश्रीराम !' रतन को लगा जैसे उसके भीतर कोई प्रेत बोला।

उसने प्रेत को पकड़ने के लिए आँखें बन्द कर लीं। प्रेत अन्दर था। उसे दौड़कर ढूँढ़ना था। ढूँढ़कर पकड़ना था। पकड़कर बाँधना था। बाँधकर, बाहर निकालना था। जब उसने आँखें खोलीं, बाहर कोई नहीं था। चाँदनी, रेत, हवा, आसमान–सब सूने थे। जैसे यह सृष्टि की पहली रात हो। उसने अपने क़दमों के आगे चाँदनी में चमकती रेत देखी। रेत पर कोई निशान नहीं थे। क्या सचमुच अभी दो आदमी और एक औरत उसके सामने खड़े थे ? क्या सचमुच उनके बीच कोई बात हुई थी ? उसने फिर सामने रास्ते पर फैली रेत को देखा। कहीं उल्टी तरफ़ उल्टे पैरों के चिह्न तो नहीं थे ? भूत-प्रेतों के पैर उल्टे होते हैं, यही सुना था। देखा कभी नहीं। रेत ख़ाली थी। या प्रेतों के पैरों के निशान नहीं होते। वे उल्टे पैरों से दुनिया में घूमते हुए कहीं निशान नहीं छोड़ते।

क्या जो कुछ हुआ रेत का सपना था ?

जैसे कोई सपना हो और वह उसमें खिंचा जा रहा हो, रतन आगे बढ़ा।

रास्ता सँकरा था। दोनों ओर रेत छोटी पहाड़ियों की ओर ऊपर ढलान पर दौड़ती चली जाती थी। बाईं ओर रानी का क़िला था जो कभी रानी का घर था। दाईं ओर अजायबघर था जहाँ रानी के ज़माने के निशान या उन निशानों की

तस्वीरें थीं। चाँदनी में आकाश के नीचे क़िले के बुर्ज पर ग़ौर से देखो तो रानी के सैनिकों और तोपों के साए हिलते हुए लगते थे। ये वही साए थे जिनकी शबीहें अजायबघर में रखी थीं।

वह बाईं ओर रास्ते पर मुड़ा, जो नीचे तालाब की ओर जाता था। वह अपने-आप मुड़ा था जैसे अदृश्य पानी का पीछा कर रहा हो। पानी की तरह। तालाब के पास खेल का मैदान था, जो धीरे-धीरे पूरा नज़र आया। चाँदनी में तालाब का पानी चमका। फिर मैदान में क्रिकेट खेलते हुए लड़के नज़र आए। वे निकर-कमीज़ पहने थे। नंगे पैर थे। विकेट की जगह पत्थर का टुकड़ा रखा था। गेंद रबर की थी। बल्ला काठ का टुकड़ा था, जिसमें ऊपर पकड़ने को हैंडल था। अलबत्ता बल्ला घुमाने, गेंद फेंकने या दौड़कर गेंद पकड़ने की प्रविधि टी.वी. के परदे की तरह थी। सिर्फ़ अम्पायर का सफ़ेद चोगा टी.वी. के लिबास की याद दिलाता था। जैसे-जैसे रतन नीचे उतरा, खेल तेज़ होता गया। सहसा एक छक्का पड़ा और गेंद चाँदनी में घूमती हुई पानी की ओर बढ़ी। उधर गेंद पानी की ओर बढ़ी, इधर मैदान में खिलाड़ी अपने सायों में बदलने लगे। गेंद के पानी में गिरते ही मैदान के सब साए चाँदनी में डूब गए। जब रतन का पैर मैदान पर पड़ा तो न मैदान में कोई खिलाड़ी था और न पानी में कोई गेंद।

जल-थल सूने हो गए थे। चाँदनी हवा में घूमती हुई हाहाकार कर रही थी। नीले आकाश में दिप-दिप करते सितारे चुपचाप मुस्करा रहे थे।

रतन मैदान में आगे बढ़ा। वह पानी की ओर आगे बढ़ता गया। किनारा ज़्यादा दूर नहीं था। किनारे पर एक पत्थर पड़ा था। पत्थर चिकना था। शायद धोबी का पत्थर था। पत्थर पर कपड़ों के चिह्न नहीं थे। पत्थर में कपड़ों की चिकनी स्मृति थी। वह पत्थर पर बैठ गया। उसका चेहरा पानी की ओर था। आँखें पानी को देख रही थीं। पानी की सतह पर चाँदनी की चादर काँप रही थी। चादर के एक छोर में चाँद बँधा था। चाँद पानी में दूसरी ओर डूबा हुआ काँप रहा था।

हवा का एक झोंका पीछे रेत की पहाड़ी से आया और पानी पर बिछलता हुआ क़िले की ओर चला गया।

उसकी आँखें अपलक जल को निहार रही थीं। पलकें देर से झपकी नहीं थीं। इन्हीं अनझपकी पलकों से स्टैला डर गई थी और इन्हीं चाकू-सी खुली आँखों से रेत पर दोनों आदमी डरे थे। दिन में रोज़गार दफ़्तर से निकलकर वह इन्हीं आँखों को लिये हुए दैनिक जागरण के दफ़्तर में गया था और उसने सम्पादक से कहा था : 'मैं एक विज्ञापन देना चाहता हूँ।'

‘कैसा विज्ञापन ?’ सम्पादक ने आँखें ऐनक से ऊपर उठाकर पूछा।

‘रोज़गार का।’

‘क्या आपका कोई कारख़ाना है ?’

‘नहीं।’

‘तो क्या कोई व्यवसाय है ?’

‘नहीं।’

‘फिर कैसा रोज़गार ?’

‘मुझे रोज़गार चाहिए।’

सम्पादक ने आँखें वापस ऐनक में लौटाईं और हँसते हुए कहा—

‘अपनी पलकें झुकाइए और वापस घर जाइए।’

‘क्यों ?’

‘क्योंकि हम ऐसे विज्ञापन नहीं छापते। शहर में रोज़गार नहीं है—यह कोई ख़बर नहीं। लावारिस विज्ञापन से क्या होगा ? अख़बार भरेगा, बस।’

‘अभी अपराध की ख़बरों से भरता है’, रतन ने बिना पलक झपकाए कहा।

‘ऐसी ख़बरों से लोगों की आँखें तो फैलती हैं’, सम्पादक फिर हँसा।

वह रेत और पानी के बीच पत्थर पर बैठा हुआ तालाब की गुफ़ा में छिपे चाँद को देख रहा था। उसे इस तरह बैठा हुआ देखकर आकाश का चाँद मुस्कराने लगा। नीले आकाश के नीचे हवा ठंडी थी। पानी की सतह पर और भी ज़्यादा। पानी में चाँद को घूरते हुए रतन को लगा कि वह कोई प्रतीक्षा कर रहा है। अब उसके मन में डर नहीं था। पानी में डूबा चाँद कोई शेर नहीं था जो उछलकर उसे खा जाएगा। मगर अनवरत कोई धुकधुकी थी। दिल अपने पिंजरे में धड़क रहा था। हवाएँ और रेत और आसमान—सब धड़क रहे थे। सितारे काँप-काँप जाते।

चाँद से कोई चेहरा निकलकर पानी से बाहर आ गया। वह पानी की सतह पर रतन की ओर चलने लगा। उसके पैर नहीं थे। वह दौड़ नहीं रहा था। चेहरा पानी पर चल रहा था। वह मुस्कराने लगा। उस चेहरे की सिर्फ़ लम्बाई और चौड़ाई थी। वह किसी तस्वीर की तरह था। पानी पर खड़ी तस्वीर मुस्कराने लगी। आहिस्ता-आहिस्ता तस्वीर पर दाढ़ी उग आई, ठूँठ-सी...और खिचड़ी बाल उलझ गए। फिर चेहरे के नीचे एक शरीर उग आया...शरीर पानी पर पट लेटा था...और उसके नीचे एक और शरीर था, जो रतन का शरीर था। पत्थर पर बैठा और पानी में लेटा—दोनों जिस्म रतन के थे।

तालाब के पानी पर नूर मंज़िल की वह रात उभरने लगी जब कमरे में रतन अपने पलंग पर लेटा था और दूसरा रोगी उसके शरीर पर आकर लेट गया था।

दूसरे रोगी के मुँह की तम्बाकू की गन्ध उसकी नाक में भर गई थी। वह कुछ देर उस गन्ध से बाहर निकलने को छटपटाया। फिर वह चीख़ा। मगर कोई आवाज़ नहीं थी। उसकी चीख़ गले में फँसी थी जैसा कभी-कभी सपने में होता है। तब अचानक अस्पताल के दो कर्मचारी दौड़ते हुए आए थे और उन्होंने उसके शरीर को मुक्त किया। दूसरा रोगी अगली सुबह मुस्कराया था जैसे पानी में चाँद मुस्कराया था। उसका ऊपर का एक दाँत टूटा था।

वह रात पानी पर उसी की ओर सरक रही थी। वह एक झटके से उठकर खड़ा हो गया। रात रुकी नहीं। रेत और पानी और क़िला लिये धरती अपनी धुरी पर घूमते हुए अदृश्य सूर्य के इर्द-गिर्द घूम रही थी। रेत पर चाँदनी उसी चाल की थाप थी जिस पर रतन घूमकर बेतहाशा दौड़ा था। उसके आगे रेत थी, पीछे रेत थी, दाएँ रेत थी, बाएँ रेत थी, नीचे रेत थी, ऊपर नीला आसमान था जैसे कोई पर्दा तना हो। वह हाँफने लगा। मगर दौड़ता रहा। उसने पीछे मुड़कर नहीं देखा। उसे लगा यदि वह पीछे मुड़कर देखेगा तो टूटे दाँत का आदमी बैताल की तरह उसकी पीठ पर सवार हो जाएगा।

रतन दौड़ते हुए एक पहाड़ी के सामने पहुँचा। उसे किसी ओर मुड़ने की फ़ुर्सत नहीं थी। वह सीधा पहाड़ी पर चढ़ने लगा। पहाड़ी ज़्यादा ऊँची नहीं थी। उतनी ही ऊँची थी जितनी जीवन साह की मज़ार थी। हाँफते हुए रतन ने मज़ार की जानिब देखा। वहाँ कोई नहीं था। सिर्फ़ कव्वाली के स्वर थे :

ठहरा हुआ दरिया हूँ, बड़ी देर से चुप हूँ...

रतन चट्टान पर खड़ा था। चट्टान काली थी। वह रेत की पहाड़ी के सिर पर रखी थी। उसने नीचे तालाब की ओर मुड़कर नहीं देखा था। न जाने कितनी देर वह जीवन साह की मज़ार की ओर आँखें किए हुए चट्टान पर खड़ा रहा। मज़ार से प्रार्थना के स्वर उठते और रेत पर हवा की तरह फैल जाते। ऐसा लगता जैसे रेत चारों ओर हवा में हाथ उठाए खड़ी है। जैसे एक युग से वह इसी तरह खड़ा हो, रतन आहिस्ता-आहिस्ता चट्टान पर बैठ गया। वह थक गया था जैसे उसने सारी धरती का चक्कर लगाया हो। वह लेट गया। उसकी पीठ के नीचे चट्टान थी। आँखों में आकाश भरा था। उसने पलक नहीं झपकाई। चन्द्रमा तैरता हुआ उसकी आँखों के सामने आ गया। उसे लगा जैसे वह आसमान की नीली झील में तैर रहा है। फिर चाँद नीचे उतरने लगा जैसे सीढ़ी पर पैर रखता हुआ आ रहा हो। चट्टान पर उतरकर वह सामने बैठ गया। रतन भी बैठ गया था। जब चाँद मुस्कराया तो रतन ने देखा कि उसका ऊपर का एक दाँत टूटा था।

वह एकाएक खड़ा हो गया। वह अपने जिस्म का सारा ज़ोर खींचकर चीख़ा। चीख़ पहाड़ी से उतरकर हवा की तरह चहुँ ओर रेत पर दौड़ी और तालाब के पानी पर तैरती हुई क़िले की बुर्ज की ओर भागी। दूसरी ओर, मज़ार की प्रार्थना से रतन की चीख़ टकरा गई। उसने टूटे दाँत और उलझे बालों के बीच चाँद में मँझले का चेहरा देखा था, जब मुम्बई के फ़्लैट में एक शाम उसने कहा :

'रुपए ! रुपयों की तुम्हें क्या ज़रूरत ? खाना-कपड़ा तुम्हें मिलता है। अपना काम करो।'

बँधुआ मज़दूर...बँधुआ मज़दूर...चारों ओर रेत पर कोई आवाज़ गूँजी...कब तक मेरे मौला...

दो

2.1

गणेश की मूर्ति मेज़ पर रखी थी। मेज़ दीवार से टिकी थी, जिस पर ऊपर आमिर ख़ान की तस्वीर अपने फ्रे़म में मुस्करा रही थी। फ्रे़म काला था। आमिर ख़ान सफ़ेद कमीज़ पहने था। रतन एक हाथ में दूध की कटोरी गणेश जी की सूँड़ के नीचे और आँखें आमिर पर टिकाए था जैसे आमिर यदि थोड़ा और मुस्कराया तो गणेशजी दूध पी लेंगे। आज सुबह ग्यारह बजे दिल्ली से ख़बर आई थी कि गणेश जी दूध पी रहे हैं। इस ख़बर की ताईद बम्बई, कलकत्ता और बंगलौर से भी हुई थी। जैसे-जैसे दिन चढ़ा, पहले ख़बर अखिल भारतीय हुई, फिर भूमंडलीकृत हो गई। यह भूमंडलीकरण का ज़माना था। हर चीज़ समूची धरती पर फैलने को तड़प रही थी। यदि गणेश को दूध पीना था, तो वे सिर्फ़ दिल्ली में क्यों पीते ? वे लंदन और वाशिंगटन में भी दूध पी रहे थे।

जब आमिर की मुस्कान थोड़ी और चौड़ी हुई, तो रतन ने तुरन्त नीचे गणेश जी की ओर देखा जिनकी सूँड़ के नीचे उसके हाथ में दूध से भरी कटोरी थी। सूँड़ में दूध लगा था जैसे दूध पीते हुए होंठों पर लग जाता है। रतन ने कटोरी मेज़ पर रखी और दोनों हाथ फैलाकर कमरे के फ़र्श पर नाचने लगा। वह आमिर की तरह मुस्कराते हुए नृत्य की भंगिमाएँ बदल रहा था। उसे यह भी मालूम था कि वह जिस ज़मीन पर नाच रहा था, वह कथक की ज़मीन थी—जिस पर घुँघरू मौसम रच देते थे।

गणेशजी ने दूध पीकर कमरे में आमिर का मौसम रच दिया था। रतन ने नाचते हुए आँखें बन्द कर ली थीं और उसका बायाँ हाथ एक क्षैतिज मुद्रा में था जैसे उसके घेरे में किसी लड़की की कमर हो। वह लड़की माधुरी दीक्षित या जूही चावला या मनीषा कोइराला—कोई भी हो सकती थी। रतन सक्सेना को कोई एतराज़ नहीं था। नाच नायक से चलता था। उसके हाथ में किसी भी नायिका की कमर हो सकती थी। इससे कोई फ़र्क नहीं पड़ता था। रतन फ़र्श पर लम्बे-लम्बे लय-भरे चक्करदार क़दम ले रहा था। उसकी आँखें बन्द थीं।

दरवाज़े में खड़ा मुन्ना तालियाँ बजाते हुए हँसा। रतन को तालियों का स्वर

ऐसा लगा जैसे हॉल की गहराइयों से मंच पर आ रहा हो जहाँ वह नाच रहा था। करतल ध्वनि जब कुछ देर लगातार होती रही तो रतन ने आँखें खोलीं। दरवाज़े में मुन्ना खड़ा हँस रहा था। उसके चारों ओर चौखट में दिन का उजाला था।

'तुम्हें मालूम है', रतन ने कहा, 'गणेशजी ने सचमुच दूध पिया।'

'कैसे' ?

मुन्ना कमरे में आ गया। दोनों मेज़ की ओर बढ़े। रतन ने दूध की कटोरी उठाते हुए कहा : 'फ्रिज से मैंने कटोरी-भर दूध निकाला था। देखो, कटोरी कितनी ख़ाली हो गई !'

मुन्ना ने कटोरी की ओर ताका।

रतन ने कटोरी फिर सूँड़ के नीचे लगा दी। दोनों दूध और सूँड़ को देखने लगे, बल्कि वहाँ जहाँ दोनों मिलते थे। सूँड़ उसी तरह दूध में डूबी थी जैसे कोई होंठ डूबते हैं। शायद सूँड़ कुछ हिली...या दूध...या दोनों !

'देखा', रतन ने चीख़ते हुए कटोरी हटा ली, 'दूध कुछ और कम हो गया।'

मुन्ना के ऊपरी होंठ पर अभी काली रेखा नहीं आई थी। वह नवीं में पढ़ता था। अभी स्कूल से लौटा था। स्कूल में भी गणेशजी के दूध पीने का शोर था। मगर विज्ञान की कक्षा में शिक्षक ने गणेश का खेल दिखाया था। उन्होंने एक मूर्ति और दूध मँगाकर कैपिलरी एक्शन की व्याख्या की थी। जब मुन्ना ने वही दोहराया तो रतन ने आपत्ति की कि कैपिलरी एक्शन से कटोरी आधी नहीं हो सकती।

'क्या पहले वह पूरी भरी थी ?' मुन्ना ने आँखें फाड़ीं।

'और क्या !' रतन ने भी आँखें फाड़ीं।

वह मुस्कराते आमिर ख़ान की जानिब देख रहा था। उसकी पहली बार नौकरी छूटी थी। या उसने ख़ुद छोड़ी थी ? यह गणेश के दूध पीने की तरह विवादास्पद था। चूँकि यह पहली बार था, इसलिए अविश्वास की ज़्यादा गुंजाइश नहीं थी। बड़े ने ज़रूर कल शाम उसे ग़ौर से देखा था और वे दूसरे कमरे में जाकर देर तक नूर से बातें करते रहे थे। नूरजहाँ और नमन पंजाब नेशनल बैंक में ही काम करते थे और हर शाम एक ही स्कूटर पर हज़रतगंज से इन्दिरानगर लौटते थे। पन्द्रह बरस पहले जब उन्होंने विवाह किया था तो नूरजहाँ की स्कूटी बेच दी थी। एक तो उन्हें नया घर शुरू करने के लिए रुपयों की ज़रूरत थी, दूसरे उन्हें अब एक ही घर में लौटना था। तब नमन 'ए' ब्लॉक में एक बरसाती में रहता था। मँझले तब साथ थे। बरसाती से एम.आई.जी. में साथ आए थे। बहुत ख़ुश थे कि उन्हें पढ़ने को अलग कमरा मिल गया। इसी कमरे से मँझले आई.ए.एस.

एलाइड में आए और भैया आई.आई.टी. में—जिसमें छोटे ने अभी गणेशजी को दूध पिलाया था।

छोटे ने बी.कॉम. झाँसी से किया था। बड़े ने तो छोटे को भी लखनऊ ही बुलाया था। लेकिन छोटे आए नहीं। छोटे ने कहा कि अम्माँ नहीं चाहती कि वे झाँसी छोड़ें। अम्माँ ने बताया कि असल में छोटे ही नहीं चाहते। छोटे झाँसी नहीं छोड़ना चाहते थे। लेकिन बी.कॉम. के बाद उसे लखनऊ इसी कमरे में आना पड़ा। यहीं रहते हुए छोटे ने बी.सी.ए. किया। यहीं उसने पहली नौकरी शुरू की। और यहीं नौकरी छोड़ दी। या छूट गई ? कल शाम यही सोचते हुए जब बड़े छोटे को देख रहे थे, तो वे उसे नहीं देख रहे थे—उसके पीछे दीवार पर टँगी आमिर ख़ान की तस्वीर देख रहे थे, जो पहले वहाँ नहीं थी। क्या यह संयोग ही था कि आमिर ख़ान की तस्वीर आई थी और नौकरी चली गई थी ?

रतन को ख़ुद पता नहीं था। यह ज़रूर था कि आमिर ख़ान को फ़िल्म-दर-फ़िल्म देखते हुए आहिस्ता-आहिस्ता रतन के मन में जिस शक ने सिर उठाया था, वह पक्का हो गया था। उसमें और आमिर ख़ान में ज़रूर साम्य था—जिसे सबसे पहले उसी ने आईने में देखा था। उसके पास आमिर की एक तस्वीर थी। वह तस्वीर को मेज़ पर रख देता। बग़ल में तस्वीर के आकार का ही एक छोटा-सा आईना रख देता। फिर वह दोनों का मिलान करते हुए मुस्कराने लगता। आमिर की तरह। उसे तब मालूम नहीं था कि हर आदमी दूसरे आदमी की तरह मुस्कराता है।

'फ़िल्मफ़ेयर' और 'स्टारडस्ट' के पन्नों में वह आमिर के बारे में ख़बरें खोज-खोजकर पढ़ता। उसकी कौन-सी फिल्म कैसी चली और निर्देशक और आलोचक उसके बारे में क्या राय रखते हैं। जूही चावला या माधुरी दीक्षित ने उसके बारे में क्या कहा ! जब माधुरी दीक्षित ने एक फ़िल्म में आमिर को होंठों पर भरपूर चूमा और आमिर ने माधुरी दीक्षित को, तो उसे अपने होंठों पर बहुत बेचैनी महसूस हुई और हाल के अँधेरे में अकेले बाल्कनी की सीट पर बैठे हुए उसे लगा कि उसकी जींस बहुत तंग है। वह फ़िल्म उसने न जाने कितनी बार देखी। यह अच्छा था कि फ़िल्म लाल बाग के गोल चक्कर में नॉवेल्टी में लगी थी जहाँ बड़े-भाभी का दिन में आने का कोई ख़तरा नहीं था। कभी-कभी तो ऐसा होता कि वह घर से ऑफ़िस जाने के लिए निकलता और लाल बाग चला जाता।

उस फ़िल्म के बाद जब वह झाँसी गया था तो उसने सपना को आमिर की तरह चूमा था और उससे कहा था कि वह उसे माधुरी दीक्षित की तरह चूमे। सपना हँसी थी। उसने कहा था, 'तुम चाहे आमिर की तरह चूमो, मैं तुम्हें अपनी तरह ही चूमूँगी।' तभी ऊपर अटारी में अम्माँ आ गई थीं। नहीं तो शायद झगड़ा

हो जाता। सपना ज़िद्दी थी। अपनी ही करनेवाली। अपनी ही मानने वाली। प्यार में भी। वह माधुरी दीक्षित की तरह गोरी नहीं थी। वह माधुरी दीक्षित की तरह लम्बी ज़रूर थी।

रतन की ऊँचाई आमिर के बराबर बैठती थी। सीना थोड़ा कम था। रंग थोड़ा गहरा था। कुल मिलाकर काफ़ी समानता थी। मुस्कान तो बिलकुल एक-सी थी। ताज्जुब इस बात का था कि कोई और इस समानता को देख नहीं पाता था। लेकिन एक दिन ऐसा आया। ऑफ़िस में मैरी ने कहा, 'आज तुम आमिर ख़ान जैसे दिख रहे हो !' वह मैरी की ओर देर तक देखता रहा। वह कुछ मोटी थी। उसका आठ साल का बेटा था।

'क्या रोज़ नहीं दिखता, मैरी ?' उसने नज़रें हटाए बिना कहा।

'रोज़ दिखते हो', वह हँसी।

वह उसके बालों को घूर रही थी, जो आमिर ख़ान की नकल पर सँवारे गए थे। वह समझा कि वह उसका मुस्कराता चेहरा देख रही है जो आमिर ख़ान की तरह मुस्करा रहा था। यह दूसरी शुरुआत थी। रतन की कलाकार के रूप में सामाजिक पहचान शुरू हो गई थी। ऐसा नहीं है कि रतन के मन में कभी सवाल नहीं उठे थे। जैसे यही सवाल था कि उसने कभी अभिनय नहीं किया था। स्कूल-कॉलेज में या उसके बाद—कभी नहीं। लेकिन यह कितनी उम्दा बात थी कि जीवन में कभी कोई नियम सार्वभौम नहीं था, जो सब पर लागू हो। अब इसको कोई क्या कहेगा कि देश का महानतम अभिनेता शुरू में फल-विक्रेता था ! मैं कम्प्यूटर प्रोग्रामर हूँ। मैं अभिनेता क्यों नहीं हो सकता ? सिनेमा का नायक बनने में एक और सुभीता था। इसमें मंचीय अनुभव की ज़रूरत नहीं थी। सिनेमा रंगमंच नहीं था जिसमें सैकड़ों लोगों के सामने अभिनय ज़रूरी हो। यह प्राइवेट रंगमंच था। फ़िल्म की शूटिंग एक कमरे के कोने में, पहाड़ की चोटी पर या सागर के सीने पर—कहीं भी हो सकती थी। दर्शक-दीर्घा की ज़रूरत नहीं थी।

रतन आमिर ख़ान के नृत्य की ही नकल नहीं करता था। वह आमिर ख़ान की तरह बोलता था, आमिर ख़ान की तरह हँसता था और उसी की तरह रोता था। सामने दीवार पर टँगा आईना मुसलसल गवाही देता रहता। गवाही के लिए वह आमिर की ओर भी आँखें घुमाता। आमिर सदाबहार मुस्कराता रहता। कल शाम यही मुस्कान देखते हुए नमन अपने कमरे की ओर मुड़ा था। नूर उसके पीछे थी। दोनों देर तक बातें करते रहे थे, जिनका उन्वान था : रतन बनाम आमिर। इस विमर्श में रतन की नौकरी का जाना शामिल था। नूर ने बताया कि पिछले कुछ महीनों में उसने रतन को कभी-कभी बेवक़्त घर लौटते देखा था। दो बार

दिन में जब उसे अपने ऑफ़िस में होना चाहिए था, नूर ने उसे हज़रतगंज के गलियारे में टहलते हुए पाया था। पूछने पर रतन ने कहा था कि वह ऑफ़िस के काम से ही यहाँ आया है। नूर जब सख़्त नज़र उसके चेहरे पर डालती तो उसका चेहरा भी सख़्त हो जाता। पिछली बार तो रतन की आँख भी झपकना भूल गई थी। उसने उल्टे नूर से पूछा था :

'भाभी, आप यहाँ क्या कर रही हैं ?'

'मैं', नूर बोली, 'मैं दवा लेने आई थी।'

वह तुरन्त आगे बढ़ गई थी।

नूर ने यह भी बताया कि पिछले दिनों कई बार शराब की ख़ाली शीशियाँ उसे रतन के कमरे में मिली थीं। उसने यह भी दुहराया कि जब उसने यही बात नमन से कही थी तो नमन यह कहते हुए हँसे थे, 'कमाऊ जवान है !' अब नमन की समझ में कुछ नहीं आ रहा था। वे दोनों रतन के कमरे में खड़े थे। बाहर शाम का उजास था। कमरे के कोनों में अँधेरा इकट्ठा होने लगा था। मेज़ पर गणेश की दूध पीती मूर्ति थी और दूध की कटोरी थी। मेज़ के ऊपर आमिर ख़ान का चित्र मुस्करा रहा था। मुन्ना आमिर ख़ान और रतन के बीच खड़ा था। नूरजहाँ का माथा ठनका। उसे पहले कभी इस तरह की उलझन महसूस नहीं हुई थी। नमन अपने ही घर में गणेशजी के दूध पी जाने के चमत्कार के बारे में सोच रहा था। वह शहर का घोषित मार्क्सवादी था। बैंक यूनियन की लखनऊ शाखा का मंत्री था। उसे शहर के भूमंडलीकरण विरोधी, फ़ासीवाद विरोधी, साम्प्रदायिकता विरोधी—सारे धरनों, जुलूसों और जलसों में देखा जा सकता था। वह जवानी की शुरुआत से ही 'इंक़लाब-ज़िन्दाबाद' कर रहा था और गणेशजी उसी के घर में घुसकर दूध पी गए थे !

'यह क्या पागलपन है ?' बड़े चीख़े।

'यह पागलपन नहीं है', छोटे ने संयत स्वर में कहा।

'फिर यह क्या है ?'

'यह गणेशजी की भूख है।'

'उन्हें...' बड़े ने हताश स्वर में कहा, 'क्या उन्हें यही घर मिला था ?'

'यह उनका चुनाव है।'

छोटे की आवाज़ बेलाग थी जैसे वह बहती नदी को देख रहा हो। बड़े गणेश को घूर रहे थे। नूर कमरे में चारों ओर घिरते धुँधलके को देख रही थी।

गणेश को देखते हुए नमन को न जाने कैसे अपने बचपन के गणेश याद आ गए। बचपन के गणेश बचपन की तरह थे। वे पार्वती के पुत्र थे जैसे नमन अम्माँ

का पुत्र था। जब अम्माँ दालान के पूजा के आले में रखी शंकर-पार्वती की तस्वीर को फूल चढ़ातीं तो नीचे चौकी पर रखी गणेश की मूर्ति पास बैठे नमन के साथ खेलने लगती। शिशु नमन को शिशु गणेश बहुत भाते। उसका ताज़ा-ताज़ा संसार था जो दूध जैसा निष्कलुष और निष्पाप था। शिशु देवता का एक और फ़ायदा था। वे खुद देवता थे। शंकर जैसे देवता उनके पिता थे। वे कुछ भी वरदान दे सकते थे। अलबत्ता तब नमन के पास माँगने को कुछ नहीं था।

फिर गणेश की जगह कृष्ण सखा हो गए थे। यह मनोरम संसार था। इसमें गोपियाँ थीं। राधा का प्रेम था। वृंदावन के कुंजों में घूमना था। जमना के तट पर दौड़ना था। तब वह नवीं में पढ़ता था जैसे अभी मुन्ना पढ़ता है। अम्माँ-पापा के साथ तीनों भाई मथुरा-वृंदावन गए थे। नमन को अपना वृंदावन के कुंजों में और जमना के कछारों में घूमना याद है। उसे लगता था कि कृष्ण सखाओं और गोपियों के साथ किसी पेड़ के पीछे से निकल आएँगे और वह हँसते हुए अपने छोटे भाइयों के साथ उनके पास चला जाएगा। इसका कारण भागवत का पाठ था, जो वह कभी-कभी अम्माँ को सुनाया करता था। उसे तब यह मालूम नहीं था।

रामायण का पाठ बाद में शुरू हुआ और देर तक चला। किशोर-काल के देवता कर्तव्यपरायण राम थे जो पिता के वचन की मर्यादा की ख़ातिर राज छोड़कर जंगल में चले गए थे। नमन की स्थिति उल्टी थी। पिता ने कहा था कि मैं तुम्हें स्नातक से आगे नहीं पढ़ा सकता। वे छोटे भाइयों से भी यही कहेंगे, वह जानता था। वह छोटे भाइयों को जीवन के जंगल में उँगली पकड़कर ले जाना चाहता था। इसीलिए उसने बैंक की परीक्षा दी और तुरन्त नौकरी पकड़ ली। तब उसने इलाहाबाद या लखनऊ में स्थानान्तरण का प्रयास किया था क्योंकि झाँसी में लड़कों के आगे जाने के रास्ते नहीं थे। झाँसी से न मँझले आई.ए.एस. में आते और न भैया आई.आई.टी. में।

झाँसी में ही नमन ने यूनियन की सदस्यता ले ली थी, जिसका सम्बन्ध सी.पी.आई. से था। पार्टी से ज़्यादा उसे जीवन समझा रहा था कि दुनिया राम से नहीं, गोल-गोल पैसों से चलती है। राम आहिस्ता-आहिस्ता पिछड़ते गए, पैसे पहियों की तरह आगे बढ़ते रहे। पैसों की दुनिया नंगी और निर्मम थी। अलबत्ता अम्माँ की दुनिया उसी तरह चल रही थी जैसी पहले चलती थी—उसमें राम और शिव स्वायत्त थे। बचपन के सूँड़ में मुस्कराते गणेश समझ में आते थे। लेकिन ये दूध पीते गणेश ? पता नहीं ये क्या करेंगे ? जब से राम बदले, किसी पर भरोसा नहीं रहा। क्या कोई पाँच बरस पहले सोच सकता था कि एक दिन हाथ में लड्डू लिये रामलला एक मस्जिद गिरने का सबब बनेंगे ?

कुछ नहीं हुआ, टी.वी. पर रात की ख़बर थी—सिर्फ़ जगह-जगह गणेश जी ने दूध पिया। मन्दिरों में दूध के कटोरे लिये भक्तों की कतारें थीं। भक्त हर उम्र के थे। सबको कोई-न-कोई हाजत थी। स्त्रियाँ कुछ ज़्यादा थीं। क्या आपको विश्वास है कि गणेशजी दूध पी रहे हैं ? संवाददाता सवाल पूछकर माइक भक्त के मुँह में लगा देता। भक्त कहता, गणेशजी की लीला है, वे कुछ भी कर सकते हैं ! गणेशजी को अपने हाथ से दूध पिलाना कोई मनोकामना पूरी होते देखने की तरह था।

'लो', नूर ने हाथ में थाली पकड़ाते हुए कहा।

रोज़ रात का खाना दोनों टी.वी. के सामने बैठकर खाते थे। मुन्ना को उतने समय ही टी.वी. देखने की इजाज़त थी। रतन शाम को ही बाहर चला गया था। अक्सर ऐसा होता। वह लौटकर ख़ुद किचन से अपना खाना ले लेता और खाकर सो जाता। मुन्ना ने खाना खाते हुए जब अपने स्कूल में गणेश के दूध पीने और कैपिलरी एक्शन की बात बताई, तो नमन और नूरजहाँ मुस्कराए जैसे उन्हें कोई मुक्ति मिली हो।

जब वे खाना खा रहे थे, पानी बरसने लगा। पहले बूँदें पड़ी होंगी। उसके पहले बादल घिरे होंगे। बादल घुमड़े होंगे। शायद काले अँधेरे बादलों का पेट चीरकर अचानक बिजली चमकी हो। फिर शायद कहीं बिजली गिरी हो। किसी पेड़ या इमारत पर। उन्हें कुछ पता नहीं चला था। वे खाना खा रहे थे और टी. वी. के परदे पर नाचती-गाती आकृतियाँ देख रहे थे। मुन्ना मन्त्र-मुग्ध था।

'रोटी खाओ न ! ठंडी हो रही है।' नूर ने मुन्ना से कहा।

मुन्ना मुँह चलाने लगा। नमन मुस्करा रहा था। उसे यह नाच उछल-कूद ज़्यादा लगता। यह क्या गोरखधंधा था ? छोटे का नौकरी छोड़ना, गणेश को दूध पिलाना और आमिर ख़ान की तस्वीर दीवार पर लगाना—आख़िर यह क्या सिलसिला था ? अभी छोटे पच्चीस का भी नहीं था। क्या वह किसी भँवर में फँस गया था ?

'क्या करोगे ?' बड़े ने छोटे से पूछा जब वह बाहर से लौटकर हॉल में घुसा, जहाँ अब टी.वी. के परदे पर गणेश और दूध पर विमर्श चल रहा था। नूर और मुन्ना अन्दर चले गए थे।

'खाना खाऊँगा।'

'फिर ?'

'सो जाऊँगा।'

'जागकर क्या करोगे ?' स्वर उखड़ गया।

'शायद नौकरी ढूँढूँगा।'

'शायद ?' बड़े हँसे।

'नौकरियाँ असल में पैदा नहीं हो रहीं, दादा', छोटे सामने सोफ़े पर बैठ गया। 'परिवार-नियोजन नहीं हो सका। नौकरी-नियोजन हो रहा है। भूमंडलीकरण चालू है।'

छोटे जब कभी इस तरह बोलता तो बड़े की जीभ दाँतों तले आ जाती। उसे लगता जैसे छोटे के मुँह से कोई और बोल रहा है। यह कोई और कौन था ? यह कोई और ही क्या दीवार पर आमिर ख़ान की तस्वीर लटका रहा था ? क्या यही गणेश की सूँड़ को दूध पिला रहा था ?

बड़े ने आँखें उठाकर फिर ग़ौर से छोटे का चेहरा देखा जैसे वह कुछ ढूँढ़ रहा हो—और ढूँढ़ने से सब-कुछ मिल जाता हो !

2.2

'बैंक का काउंटर इश्क फ़रमाने की जगह नहीं है'—जब नूर ने यह कहा तो नमन का चेहरा कुछ लाल हुआ। एक चुटकी लाली नूर के चेहरे पर पहले से थी जब नमन ने मेज़ पर पड़े काग़ज़ उठाने के बहाने मेज़ पर पड़ा नूर का हाथ छुआ और उसकी उँगली पर पड़ी अँगूठी को देखकर कहा, 'अँगूठी उतार दो, उँगली और ख़ूबसूरत लगेगी।' वह तब हँसी थी। नमन भी हँसा था। उन्हें पता नहीं था कि जीवन-भर वे इस हँसी की जुगलबन्दी को याद रखेंगे। यह एक अजीब इत्तफ़ाक था कि अक्टूबर की उस ढलती दोपहर काउंटर पर कोई और नहीं था। हाल में कुछ अमूर्त-सा शोर ज़रूर था। उसी जन-रव की पृष्ठभूमि में नमन ने कहा, 'ठीक है, तुम्हारी स्कूटी की हवा निकाल आता हूँ। शाम को मेरे साथ चलना। हम गोमती के किनारे उतर जाएँगे।'

उस शाम उनका पहला चुम्बन सम्पन्न हुआ था।

नूर ने बताया कि वह पिछले तीन माह से उसका कस्बाईपन देखकर ख़ुश हो रही थी, जब वह झाँसी से स्थानान्तरित होकर आया। उसका कहना था कि उसके चेहरे में कुछ ऐसा दो-टूक खरापन था जो अपवाद था। यह खरापन नमन की आवाज़ में भी था। जब वह माइक के पीछे होता तो कोई और नमन आगे आ जाता। उसकी आवाज़ ठोस, बेलौस थी। उसके मुँह से निकले शब्दों के पीछे भरोसे की आभा होती थी। उसकी आवाज़ को एक ऊँचा—पूरा गेहुँआ चेहरा घेरे था, जिस पर नेतानुमा काली दाढ़ी थी। पहली बार नूरजहाँ ने उसे आँखें फाड़े सुना था। दूसरी बार उसने एक लम्हे के लिए आँखें बन्द कर ली थीं। आँखें बन्द कर

लेने पर शक की कोई गुंजाइश नहीं बचती थी। उसकी आवाज़ का एक झरना था जो कल-कल करता हुआ मंच पर बह रहा था और उस झरने के किनारे बैठी नूरजहाँ उसे देख रही थी। नमन के पहले दोनों भाषण उसके तबादले के बाद पहले दोनों महीनों में हुए थे। तीसरे माह के दूसरे सप्ताह में एक शाम वे दोनों गोमती के किनारे उतर गए थे।

नमन को नूरजहाँ का चम्पई रंग पारदर्शी लगता था जैसे वह उसकी नसों में दौड़ता ख़ून देख रहा हो। शायद तभी उसे अँगूठी बाधा लगी थी। आहिस्ता-आहिस्ता बाधाएँ दूर होने लगीं। जाड़ों की एक ढलती दोपहर वे चिड़ियाघर में घास पर बैठे थे। वे चिड़ियाघर का एक चक्कर लगा चुके थे। थककर एक पेड़ के नीचे घास पर बैठ गए थे। कुछ दूरी पर चारों ओर कुछ लोग थे जो चिड़ियों, बन्दरों, हाथियों और हिरनों को देख रहे थे। गुफ़ा में बैठे दो शेरों के चारों ओर पानी की खाई थी। पानी की झील पर पानी की चिड़ियाँ तैर रही थीं। न हाथी कुछ बोल रहे थे, न शेर। पानी और धूप की सन्धि पानी पर चमक रही थी। आकाश भी पेड़ों के सिरों पर चमकता हुआ लगता। बादल नहीं थे। आकाश नीला था, उजाले में घुला हुआ। बच्चों की खिलौना-रेल दूर से आ रही थी। आती हुई रेल की आवाज़ नहीं थी। लगता था वह पटरियों के बिना हवा में तैर रही है।

'सुनो,' नूरजहाँ की आवाज़ थी।

'हाँ।'

'तुमने अभी तक प्रोपोज़ नहीं किया ?'

वह हँसा। वह घास पर अधलेटा था। उसकी आँखों के सामने अजायबघर की इमारत थी।

'यह ठीक जगह नहीं है,' नमन ने कहा।

'क्यों ?'

'चिड़ियाघर में बैठकर अजायबघर के सामने मैं प्रोपोज़ नहीं करूँगा। कल शाम गोमती के किनारे !'

वे दोनों हँसे। बाद में वे दोनों याद करेंगे कि उस क्षण उन दोनों के मन में उनका हिन्दू-मुसलमान होना बिलकुल नहीं था, जब घास पर उन्होंने एक-दूसरे का हाथ थामा। वे सिर्फ़ नमन और नूर थे : एक आदमी और एक औरत, अपने खुले हाथों से एक होने को आतुर ! बल्कि उनकी अतिरिक्त भिन्नता उनकी चाहत को और धार देती थी। वरना एक बुन्देली गड़रिए और अवध की बेग़म का क्या मेल ? नूर बाद में हँसती हुई यही मज़ाक करेगी। गड़रिया नामकरण इसलिए था कि नमन को घर में गर्मी में बनियान पहनना भी गवारा नहीं था।

शादी अदालत में हुई। शादी के बाद नूर इन्दिरानगर की बरसाती में आ गई जहाँ मँझले भी रहते थे। मँझले तब दूसरे कमरे में सोफ़ा-कम-बेड पर सोने लगे और वहीं उन्होंने अपनी किताबें भी लगा लीं। नमन ने पहले नूरजहाँ से शादी टालने को कहा था जब तक मँझले कहीं चुन न लिए जाएँ। तब नूरजहाँ ने हँसते हुए कहा था कि तुम भूल रहे हो कि मैं भी कमाती हूँ और मेरे अब्बा को मेरे पैसे की ज़रूरत नहीं है। यह एक इत्तफ़ाक था कि जब वे 'सी' ब्लॉक के एम.आई.जी. में गए, उसी वर्ष मँझले आई.ए.एस. में आए और मुन्ना इस दुनिया में।

जब मुन्ना आया तो अम्माँ ने भी नूरजहाँ को पूरी तरह स्वीकार कर लिया। उन्होंने उसका नाम पहले ही सुन्दरी रख दिया था और मोहल्ले में कहा था कि वह लखनऊ के माथुरों के घर की है जो फक् गोरे होते हैं और नवाबों की तरह उर्दू बोलते हैं। नूरजहाँ नई पीढ़ी की थी, कॉन्वेंट में पढ़ी थी। उसकी ज़ुबान से कुछ पता नहीं चलता था कि वह उर्दू बोल रही है या हिन्दी। जब कुछ औरतों की फुसफुसाहट गायत्री के कानों में पड़ी कि असल में सुन्दरी मुसलमान है और नमन ने कचहरी में शादी की है तो वे भड़क गईं—'हाँ, है। मुझे किसी के घर बेटी नहीं ब्याहनी। जिसे आना हो आए, न आना हो न आए।' सब आईं। मुन्ना का कनछेदन ओरछा में हुआ। बेतवा के किनारे। नूरजहाँ को यह बात अच्छी लगती थी कि मन्दिरों में मज़ारों की तरह औरत-आदमी सब जाते थे और कव्वाली की तरह भजन होते थे। धर्म में प्रार्थना और मेले का घालमेल था। मेला कभी-कभी प्रार्थना को दबा देता। तब सूखे अनुष्ठान रह जाते। लोग अनुष्ठान को ही प्रार्थना मान लेते। मूर्ति के भीतर ईश्वर खो जाता। तब मेले दंगे हो जाते।

बाँके बिहारी मुन्ना को देखकर ऐसे खुश हुए जैसे उन्हें नई ज़िन्दगी मिल गई हो। उन्होंने आँगन में खड़े होकर आकाश की ओर देखा। जब कोई उनका धर्म पूछता, तो वे आकाश की ओर ही देखते थे। अब उनके हाथों में मुन्ना भी था। मुन्ने को उनके हाथों से गायत्री ने लिया और उसे दालान में ठाकुरजी के चरणों में डाल दिया। सुन्दरी को भी ठाकुरजी के चरण छूने का इशारा किया। सुन्दरी ने मत्था टेक दिया। जब नूर नमन के साथ रहने आई तो उसके सामान में एक कुरान भी थी। अब यह किताब जिस अलमारी में रखी थी, उसी में रामायण थी और नमन की मार्क्स और एंगेल्स की किताबें थीं। एक रेहल भी थी, जिस पर रामायण या कुरान रखी जा सकती थी। इसे कौन कब लाया, यह किसी को याद नहीं था। इसका अलमारी में रहना याद था। इसे अम्माँ इस्तेमाल करतीं जब वे लखनऊ आतीं या नूर कभी-कभार।

रेहल देखकर नमन मन-ही-मन हँसता था। उसने बचपन से अपने घर में रेहल देखी थी। अब जब कभी वह नूर को रेहल पर बैठा हुआ देखता तो वह समझ जाता कि नूर परेशान है और जब उठेगी तो कुछ ठीक होगी। उसने एक बार नूर से कहा था कि तनाव तो पैक्सम की एक गोली खाने से भी कम हो जाएगा और उसमें वक़्त भी कम लगेगा। नूर हँसी थी। उसने कहा था—'कोई गोली तसल्ली नहीं दे सकती।' फिर उसने पलटकर कहा था—'यह कुछ वैसी ही तसल्ली है जो तुम मार्क्सवाद के यूटोपिया में पाते हो।'

उस वक़्त नमन के हाथ में एक पीतल की पट्टिका थी, जिसमें ऊपर उसका नाम लिखा था, नीचे नूर का। नाम हिन्दी में थे। यह पट्टिका उसने मुरादाबाद से मँगवाई थी। कल ही उसे मिली थी। वह इसे टाँगने हाथ में हथौड़ी और कीलें लिये बाहर जा रहा था। नूरजहाँ ने पूछा, 'यह क्या है ?' 'देखो', नमन ने मुस्कराते हुए पट्टिका उसके हाथ में थमा दी। उसने नमन के और अपने नामों को एक-साथ पीतल पर चमकते हुए देखा और देखती रही। फिर उसने नमन से कहा कि देर हो गई है, अब तुम नहा लो। उसने नमन के हाथ से हथौड़ी और कीलें लेते हुए कहा, 'नेम-प्लेट मैं बाद में टाँग दूँगी।' जब नमन कमरे से बाहर चला गया तो उसने नेम-प्लेट रामायण-कुरान के पीछे रख दी। उसे पता था कि न नमन कभी रामायण-कुरान उठाएगा, न उसे नेम-प्लेट मिलेगी। उसे पता नहीं था कि नेम-प्लेट छिपाते हुए उसने एक गहरी साँस ली थी।

असल में नमन के हाथ से नेम-प्लेट लेकर देखते हुए पीतल पर जगमग नमन और अपने संयुक्त नाम मोहक लगे थे। कुछ पल वह चमक में खो गई। तभी उसे पड़ोसी जगजीत सिंह की सूरत अचानक याद आ गई जो सिख था, लेकिन पिछले माह उसने दाढ़ी-केश मुँड़वा दिए थे। पिछले माह कानपुर में विकराल दंगे हुए थे जिसमें सिखों को गले में जलते टायर डालकर या उन्हें पेट्रोल में नहलाकर जला दिया गया था। वे सड़क पर आग पहने हुए भागे थे...वे चीख़ते थे और उनको घेरे आग भड़क जाती थी...इन्हीं सिखों में बैंक की कानपुर ब्रांच का अमरीक सिंह था, जिसकी लाश की भी शिनाख़्त नहीं हो सकी ! अमरीक पहले लखनऊ में था और नूरजहाँ की बग़ल में काउंटर पर बैठता था। ये 1984 के दंगे थे। इन्दिरा गांधी की हत्या के बाद।

अमरीक सिंह दो बार जगतसिंह के सफ़ाचट चेहरे में नज़र आया था और उसने नूरजहाँ से मुस्कराते हुए कहा—'नूर सुन, तू भी अपने नाम की दाढ़ी-मूँछ कटा ले। नूरजहाँ की जगह नूरकुमारी ठीक रहेगा।' नूर ने नमन को अपना यह सपना बताया जो उसने दिन में देखा था। नमन हँसा। 'पागल हो गई हो', यह

कहते हुए उसने उसे चूम लिया। 'क्यों ?' नूर ने फिर कहा, 'अम्माँ ने तो मेरा नाम सुन्दरी रखा ही है।'

'अम्माँ की बात और है,' नमन ने कहा।

'नहीं, अम्माँ की बात ग़ैर नहीं है', नूर बोली, 'सुन्दरी और नूर कुमारी में ज़्यादा दूरी नहीं है।'

'ससुराल में दूसरा नाम रखना हमारे यहाँ रिवाज़ है।' नमन ने जैसे सफ़ाई दी।

चुप्पी।

'अमरीक बच जाता, नमन', नूर ने सिर नीचा किए कहा', 'अगर वह जगजीत हो जाता।'

नमन एकाएक बिलकुल ख़ाली हो गया।

उसने ऐसा शहर कभी नहीं देखा था। न नूर ने, जो यहाँ पैदा हुई थी। नूर ने बचपन से शहर में शिया-सुन्नी के झगड़ों के बारे में सुना था—जब ताजिए निकलते थे। मगर हिन्दू-मुस्लिम दंगे ! यह एक नई बात थी। पुराने लखनऊ में पड़ोसी मोहल्लों में लोगों ने घरों की छतों पर पत्थर इकट्ठे कर लिए थे। रात में पहरे होते। लोग घर खोलते हुए डरते जब तक सूरज न निकल आए। दिसम्बर '92 के दिन थे। बाबरी मस्जिद ध्वंस के बाद। उस शाम इन्दिरानगर में भी लोगों ने अपने घरों के सामने दीए जलाए थे। भैया उस दिन यहीं था। वह और मुन्ना अपने हाथों में एक-एक मोमबत्ती लेकर गेट की ओर आ रहे थे जब नमन बाहर से गेट खोलते हुए चीख़े—'यह क्या कर रहे हो ?' दोनों ने सहमते हुए बताया कि पड़ोसी जगजीत सिंह ने उनसे यही कहा था।

नूर अन्दर टी.वी. के परदे के सामने बैठी थी। परदे पर बाबरी मस्जिद की ख़बरें थीं—जो अब नहीं थी।

कुछ लोग सामने सड़क पर 'जै श्रीराम' के नारे लगाते हुए निकल गए। ऐसा लगा जैसे सड़क पर बहुत धूल उड़ी हो।

यह इतवार की शाम थी।

अँधेरा हो गया था। धूल दिखाई नहीं देती थी। ठंड थी। नूर ने कार्डीगन पहना था। उसे और ठंड लगी। वह अन्दर से शाल ले आई और फिर टी.वी. के परदे के सामने बैठ गई। ऐसा लगा जैसे परदे के सामने कोई गठरी रखी हो। कसी हुई। कसी हुई गठरी। उसे ख़ुद भी ऐसा लगा। उसके एक ओर नमन बैठे थे, दूसरी ओर मदन। फिर भी उसे अचानक लगा कि वह अकेली है। उस क्षण परदे पर बाबरी मस्जिद के बिम्ब थे। वह पिछले जाड़ों में नमन और मुन्ना के साथ

अयोध्या गई थी। अयोध्या में उसने हनुमानगढ़ी का क़िले जैसा मन्दिर देखा था, जहाँ महन्त क्रुद्ध पहलवानों जैसे लगते थे और गीले फ़र्श पर कीचड़ फैला था। गढ़ी की सीढ़ियाँ भी गीली थीं। कनक भवन का प्रांगण चौड़ा था। प्रसन्न लोग टहलते हुए लगते थे। गुम्बदों पर स्वर्ण दमकता था। जब वहाँ भक्त कम होते, तो बन्दर कूदने लगते। बाबरी मस्जिद उजाड़ और सूनी-सी लगती थी, यद्यपि यात्री चारों ओर घूम रहे थे। उसकी दीवारों पर काई जमी थी और एक ओर एक पेड़ दीवार से उग रहा था। दीवारें चितकबरी थीं। उनकी उदासी गुम्बदों तक धुर ऊपर खिंच गई थी। गुम्बद पूरे बाहर निकलकर नज़र आए थे, जो अभी परदे पर टूटते दिखाई दे रहे थे। मस्जिद के गुम्बद सूने थे। मन्दिर के गुम्बदों की तरह।

दस वर्षीय मुन्ना टी.वी. के परदे की ओर एकटक देख रहा था। मदन दूसरे कमरे में चला गया था। नमन और नूर चुप थे। उनकी नज़रें परदे पर थीं। परदा बोल रहा था।

'मेरी कुछ समझ में नहीं आ रहा', मुन्ना ने कहा।

नूर ने नमन की ओर देखा। कमरे में एक पेडेस्टल लैम्प जल रहा था, जो मुन्ना के पास रखा था। रोशनी उसके शेड से छनकर कमरे में फैल रही थी, जो लगातार फीकी होती जाती थी। नूर और नमन जहाँ बैठे थे, वहाँ न अँधेरा था, न उजाला था।

जब कोई कुछ नहीं बोला, तो मुन्ना ने फिर कहा :

'पापा।'

'हाँ।'

'मन्दिर और मस्जिद एक-साथ क्यों नहीं रह सकते ?'

'रह सकते हैं', नमन ने कहा, 'मथुरा और वाराणसी में वे एक-साथ पीठ से पीठ टिकाए रहते हैं।'

'अयोध्या में क्यों नहीं ?'

'अयोध्या में मस्जिद के मलबे में कुर्सियों की खेती होगी।' नमन के मुँह से निकला।

'मेरी कुछ समझ में नहीं आ रहा', मुन्ना ने फिर कहा।

कुछ देर कोई कुछ नहीं बोला। नूर चुपचाप सुन रही थी। परदे पर बिम्ब थे और आवाज़ें थीं।

'मम्मी', मुन्ना ने कहा।

'हाँ', नूर बोली।

'मैं क्या हूँ ?' मुन्ना की आवाज़ धुँधलके में गूँजी।

'हमारे बेटे !' नमन ने कहा।

नूर तुरन्त उठी। 'मैं खाना लगाती हूँ', यह कहते हुए अन्दर चली गई।

खाना खाते हुए मदन ने नमन की ओर निगाहें उठाकर पूछा :

'दादा।'

'हाँ।'

'हिन्दुस्तान हिन्दुओं का नहीं है क्या ?'

वे अब डाइनिंग टेबल पर बैठे थे। टी.वी. बन्द था। परदे पर न कोई रोशनी थी, न आवाज़।

'मदन', नमन ने उसकी आँखों में देखा, 'घर सारे बेटों का एक-साथ होता है या नहीं होता !'

कुछ देर चुप्पी छाई रही। फिर चुप्पी तोड़ते हुए मदन बुदबुदाया—'उनका भी जो घर छोड़कर चले गए !'

नमन मुस्कराया। 'जो घर छोड़कर चले गए', उसने कहा, 'उन्होंने अपना घर अलग बना लिया। जो घर में हैं, घर उन्हीं का है !'

नूर चुप थी। एकाएक वह उठी। दूसरे कोने में जाकर उसने फ़ोन पर नम्बर घुमाया। देर तक रिसीवर कान से लगाए रही। बोली कुछ नहीं।

'किसे फ़ोन कर रही हो ?'

'अब्बा को। घंटी जा रही है। कोई उठा नहीं रहा।'

'क्या पता, सो गए हों !'

'इतनी जल्दी ?'

'हो सकता है।'

नूर ने रिसीवर रख दिया था। वह सोफ़े पर बैठ गई थी। उसने दोनों हाथों से अपना चेहरा ढँक लिया। फ़ोन की घंटी बजी। वह उठकर भागी।

'हलो।'

'कैसे हो तुम लोग ?' झाँसी से फ़ोन था।

'ठीक हैं, पापा।'

'तुम्हारे अब्बा ?'

'पता नहीं।'

'क्यों ? फ़ोन नहीं किया ?'

'फ़ोन किया था', नूर की आवाज़ लरज गई, 'कोई उठा नहीं रहा।'

'फ़िक्र न करो। सो गए होंगे।' फिर आवाज़ आई, 'बेटा, नमन को फ़ोन दो।'

नमन से उन्होंने कहा कि सुबह वह ज़रूर नूर के अब्बा के बारे में पता करे।

शहर में अभी किसी ख़तरे की ख़बर नहीं थी। जब नमन ने कहा कि मैं अभी जाकर पता लगाता हूँ, तो नूर ने बाहर देखते हुए कहा कि अभी रात बहुत हो गई है, सुबह देख लेना। नूर ने पहली बार सोचा कि अकेले अब्बा को अब पुराने शहर में किसी मुस्लिम बस्ती में ही चला जाना चाहिए।

खाने की मेज़ पर लैम्प के धुँधलके में मदन ने नमन से कहा :

'दादा।'

'हाँ।'

'कल सुबह मैं कानपुर चला जाऊँगा।'

'क्यों, ऐसी क्या जल्दी है ?'

'मुझे अमरीका से कुछ पेपर्स का इन्तज़ार है। फिर जाने की तैयारी भी करनी है।'

नूर मदन की ओर देख रही थी। जहाँ वह बैठी थी, वहाँ से लैम्प का धुँधलका सीधा मदन के चेहरे पर पड़ता था : सफ़ाचट चेहरा था, जो थोड़ी-सी रोशनी में भी चमकने लगता था। कोई शक नहीं था। भरोसे का गिलास पूरा भरा था।

'भैया', नमन ने पूछा, 'क्या तुम्हारा अमरीका जाने का फ़ैसला पक्का है ?'

'हाँ, दादा', उसने आँखें ऊपर उठाईं, 'बात सिर्फ़ अमरीका की नहीं है। असली बात काम और कमाई की है। कोई मुकाबला नहीं है।'

'यहाँ और वहाँ ?'

'हाँ।'

'देख लो', नमन मुस्कराया, 'क्या काम और कमाई काफ़ी हैं ?'

धुँधलके में कोई जुम्बिश हुई।

'अब दुनिया एक है, दादा', मदन ने ऊपर छत की ओर देखा, 'यह भूमंडलीकरण का ज़माना है।'

छत पर अँधेरा था।

फिर मदन ने पास बैठे मुन्ना की ओर देखते हुए कहा—'मुन्ना, तू बड़ा हो जा। फिर अमरीका आना।'

'अमरीका में क्या है ?' मुन्ना की आवाज़ थी।

'अमरीका में वाल्ट डिस्नी पार्क है।'

'लेकिन तब तक तो मैं बड़ा हो जाऊँगा।'

'बड़े होने पर पूरा अमरीका वाल्ट डिस्नी पार्क हो जाता है', नमन मुस्कराया था।

मदन हँसने लगा। मुन्ना भी हँसा, हालाँकि उसे हँसने का कारण मालूम नहीं

था। नूर को लगा कि उसके पास हँसने के लिए कोई कारण नहीं है। उसके होंठ अपने आप एक मुस्कान में टेढ़े हो गए थे जैसे वे स्वायत्त हों।

बत्ती बुझा देने पर कमरे में अँधेरा और बढ़ गया। पहले सिर्फ़ कोनों और छत पर उसकी परतें थीं। अब कमरे-भर में तरल-सा अँधेरा भर गया। रजाई डबल-बेड पर फैली थी। एक ओर नमन का सिर तकिए पर रखा था, दूसरी ओर नूर ने करवट ले ली थी। नमन की आँखें बन्द थीं। नूर ने जान-बूझकर उल्टी तरफ़ करवट नहीं ली थी। उसका जिस्म स्वचालित-सा हरकतें कर रहा था। जैसे कुछ देर पहले उसके होंठ अपने-आप टेढ़े हो गए थे, उसी तरह पलंग पर बाहर की ओर उसने करवट ले ली। नमन उसके पीछे था, चित लेटा हुआ—उसकी आँखें बन्द थीं। कोई और रात होती तो वह उसकी ओर मुड़कर उसे चूमता। या वह ख़ुद लुढ़ककर उससे लिपट जाती और अपने पैरों के ठंडे तलवे उसके पैरों पर रगड़कर उन्हें गर्म करती। लेकिन अभी न उसके पैर ठंडे थे, न गर्म—वे एक-पर-एक दो लकड़ियों की तरह रखे थे। उसे अपनी देह काठ की तरह लगी। उसके भीतर बैठी गठरी और कसने लगी।

यह पहली रात थी जब वे एक ही पलंग पर अकेले लेटे थे और उन्होंने एक-दूसरे को छुआ नहीं था।

2.3

पता नहीं गणेशजी की कृपा हुई या आमिर ख़ान की, रतन को दूसरी नौकरी जल्दी मिली और जल्दी ही छूट गई। एक साल भी पूरा नहीं हुआ। उसकी हीरो होंडा को शाहनजफ़ रोड पर राम एंड राम के ऑफ़िस के सामने खड़े होने की आदत ही पड़ी थी कि अचानक एक अपराह्न मामला ख़त्म हो गया। मामला उस अपराह्न ख़त्म नहीं हुआ, उस अपराह्न ख़ात्मे की शुरुआत हुई। मिस्टर भल्ला ने उसे अपने केबिन में बुलाकर कहा—'रतन, गोमतीनगर जाकर श्रीधरानी लि. का काम आज निपटा दो।'

उसने बाहर आकर अपना हेल्मेट उठाया और ब्रीफ़केस लेकर नीचे आया जहाँ उसकी हीरो होंडा खड़ी थी। वह गाड़ी स्टार्ट करके सड़क पर कुछ आगे बढ़ा ही था कि पीछे से उसी के नाम की पुकार उसके कानों में पड़ी। उसने गाड़ी रोकी। पीछे से अपनी मारुति पर हँसता हुआ मोहन आया। गाड़ी रोककर उसने पूछा—'कहाँ ?' 'गोमतीनगर', सुनकर वह बोला, 'कुछ देर बाद चले जाना। देखो, कितना बढ़िया मौसम है !' फरवरी के आख़िरी दिन थे। ठंडी हवा पर नर्म धूप फैली थी।

वे दोनों बोटैनिकल गार्डन के बाहर अपनी गाड़ियाँ खड़ी करके अन्दर चले गए। अन्दर जाकर वे बाईं ओर गली में मुड़े, जिसके दोनों ओर फूलों की क्यारियाँ थीं। पहली ही नज़र में वे चौंके। रतन फूलों के दहकते रंग देखकर चीख़ा, फिर चुप हो गया। उसे लगा जैसे बाग़ में आग लगी हो।

कतारों में खड़े फूलों पर धूप बिछल रही थी। हर रंग और ढंग के फूल थे। हर क़दम पर फूलों का कोण बदल जाता। और धूप का भी। सूर्य की किरणें फूलों पर नाचती नज़र आतीं। ऐसा लगता जैसे किरणें ही फूलों की खेती कर रही हों और यहाँ-वहाँ खड़े माली उन्हीं का हुक्म बजा रहे हों। फूलों के खेतों के बीच में पेड़ों के छोटे-छोटे झुंड थे। वे सड़क के एक ओर पेड़ों के झुंड में उतर गए। एक मोटे पेड़ की एक लहराती डाल क्षैतिज थी जैसे बन्दरों के बैठने के लिए बनी हो। मोहन उसी पर बैठ गया। फिर उसने अपनी जेब से चाँदी-जैसा फ़्लास्क निकालकर रतन की ओर बढ़ाया। रतन ने उसे ऐसे देखा जैसे वह कोई फूल देख रहा हो। मोहन के पास इतना धीरज नहीं था। उसने फ़्लास्क से एक घूँट भरा, फिर फ़्लास्क रतन के आगे कर दिया। रतन ने दो घूँट एक-साथ भरे और हुमककर चारों ओर देखा। फिर वह उछलकर पेड़ की डाल पर मोहन के साथ बैठ गया। एकाएक रतन को लगा कि धूप बाग़ में पेड़ों और फूलों और मालियों और लोगों को एक धागे में बाँधकर गाँठ लगा देगी। उसकी आँखों में लाल, पीले, सफ़ेद, कत्थई, नीले, हरे, गुलाबी और काले रंग तैरने लगे...फूलों की शक्ल में...तेज़-तेज़ घूमते हुए...जैसे वे एक सफ़ेद धागे में गुँथ जाएँगे।

'काला...,' मोहन ने कहा, 'क्या तुमने यहाँ काला गुलाब देखा है ?'

'नहीं... क्या गुलाब काला भी होता है ?' रतन ने आँखें फैलाकर मोहन की ओर देखा।

'हाँ...काला गुलाब भी होता है', मोहन हँसा, 'और दिलफ़रेब होता है।'

इस बीच दोनों के बीच फ़्लास्क हाथ बदलता रहा था।

'यह कौन-सी व्हिस्की है ?' रतन ने पूछा।

'स्कॉच।'

'इंडियन है ?'

'यह विश्व-ग्राम का ज़माना है। धरती के टुकड़ों में फ़र्क नहीं रहा।'

धूप अचानक ठंडी हवा के साथ जाती-सी लगी जैसे बाग़ की गठरी बँध गई हो। साये लम्बे होने लगे। जिस पेड़ पर वे बैठे थे, उसका साया फैलकर दूसरे पेड़ों में फँसने लगा। उसकी डाल पर बैठी आकृतियाँ धरती पर और लम्बी खिंचने लगीं जैसे भूत हों। फ़्लास्क अपने साए में बोतल हो गया।

'यार, मुझे तो गोमतीनगर जाना था', रतन अचानक बोला।

'यही गड़बड़ है', मोहन ने जंगल में देखते हुए कहा।

'क्या ?'

'दूसरे की नौकरी।'

'मतलब ?'

'मतलब...अपना काम करो तो मेरी तरह राजा रहोगे। जब चाहो उछलकर पेड़ पर बैठ जाओ और दारू पियो।'

'यह बात तो है', रतन ने फ़्लास्क मुँह से लगाते हुए कहा।

मोहन का काग़ज़ की सप्लाई का अपना पुश्तैनी काम था। उसके पिता ज़रूर बूढ़े हो रहे थे। कभी-कभी बीमार हो जाते। जब वे ठीक रहते, मोहन छुट्टा साँड़ की तरह शहर में घूमता था जैसे आज घूम रहा था। जैसे आज पुराना सहपाठी रतन मिल गया था, कोई-न-कोई दोस्त मिल जाता। मक़सद अच्छा वक़्त गुज़ारना था जिसमें हँसी हो, ख़ुशी हो और दारू भी हो। पैसे की कमी नहीं थी। धन्धा अच्छा था। वह बाप का इकलौता बेटा था।

मोहन चोंच-दाढ़ी और मूँछें रखता था जो आजकल अन्तर्राष्ट्रीय फ़ैशन था। उसके कपड़ों से रईसी टपकती थी। वह हमेशा मारुति में चलता था। फक् गोरा मोहन काली चोंच-दाढ़ी लटकाए सफ़ेद मारुति में रोबदार लगता था। शायद मारुति की वजह से या उसकी रईसी की वजह से रतन को मोहन से हमेशा ईर्ष्या होती। जब आज उसने अपनी आयातित जींस से शराब का फ़्लास्क निकाला तो यह ईर्ष्या और बढ़ गई थी। जीना इसी का नाम था। इसकी जड़ में अपना काम था। आख़िरकार धीरूभाई अम्बानी ने अपने काम से ही अपना नाम कमाया। उसकी शुरुआत मुझसे बदतर थी ! यह ख़्याल आते ही रतन डाल पर कुछ ज़्यादा झूमा और नीचे ज़मीन पर लुढ़क गया। मोहन कूदा। उसने रतन को सहारा देकर उठाया। जैकेट में ज़्यादा धूल नहीं लगी थी। ज़मीन पर धूल से ज़्यादा झाड़-झंखाड़ थे।

फ़्लास्क ख़ाली हो गया था। साए और लम्बे हो गए थे। जब दोनों ज़मीन पर खड़े हुए तो उनके साए भी पेड़ों की तरह लम्बे हो गए। इस ओर पेड़-ही-पेड़ थे—जहाँ तक नज़र जाती। सिर्फ़ एक ओर सड़क थी। वे उसी ओर बढ़े। सड़क पर मद्धिम धूप थी। सड़क के दोनों ओर खड़े पेड़ चारों ओर हाथ हिला रहे थे जैसे सड़क पर और आकाश में विचरती धूप को अलविदा कह रहे हों। यह विदा का वक़्त था। तभी अचानक मिस्टर भल्ला सामने से आते नज़र आए। उनके साथ एक सुन्दरी थी, जो उनकी पत्नी हो सकती थी और पत्नी नहीं भी हो सकती थी। वे सड़क पर चलते हुए खिलखिला रहे थे।

यद्यपि सड़क पर रतन ने उनसे बचने की कोशिश की, लेकिन वे हँसते हुए उसके सामने खड़े हो गए और बोले :

'यहाँ कैसे ?'

'जैसे आप', रतन के मुँह से निकला।

मिस्टर भल्ला ने उसे एक पल घूरा। फिर वे हँसते हुए आगे बढ़ गए। सुन्दरी मुस्कराती हुई उनसे क़दम मिला रही थी। उन्हें पता नहीं था, वे कुछ तेज़ चल रहे थे।

एकाएक धूप चली गई थी। रतन ने अचकचाकर ऊपर आसमान में देखा : पश्चिम की ओर बादल के एक बड़े टुकड़े ने सूरज को ढँक लिया था जैसे महाभारत में धूल सूर्य को ढँकती है और जयद्रथ का वध हो जाता है। न यह दिन था, न रात थी। अभी शाम भी नहीं हुई थी।

अगली सुबह रतन के ऑफ़िस में घुसते ही चपरासी ने बताया कि साहब आपको याद कर रहे हैं। केबिन में घुसते ही मिस्टर भल्ला ने रतन की ओर प्रश्न दाग़ा :

'क्या कल तुम गोमतीनगर गए थे ?'

'हाँ।'

'कितने बजे ?'

'साढ़े तीन बजे।'

'काम हुआ ?'

'नहीं।'

'क्यों ?'

'शर्मा जी वहाँ नहीं थे।'

'शर्मा जी वहीं थे', मिस्टर भल्ला टेढ़ा मुस्कराते हुए बोले, 'मैंने साढ़े तीन बजे उन्हें फ़ोन किया था।'

सन्नाटा।

'रतन, कल बाग़ में तुम्हारे मुँह से शराब की बू आ रही थी। गोमतीनगर जाने के बजाय तुम बाग़ में शराब पी रहे थे।'

फिर सन्नाटा।

'शराब पीकर एक महिला के सामने तुमने मुझसे बद्‌तमीज़ी भी की !'

'सर', रतन एक झटके से विनम्र हो गया, 'मैं समझा वे आपकी पत्नी हैं। घर की बात है।'

'जाओ', भल्ला चीख़ा, 'अब कभी ऑफिस मत आना।'

भल्ला ग़ुस्से में खड़ा हो गया था। वह बैठ गया। रतन केबिन से बाहर चला गया। फिर ऑफिस से बाहर। धूप अभी कच्ची थी। शाहनजफ़ रोड से वह सीधा अशोक रोड पर आकर दाएँ हज़रतगंज की ओर मुड़ा। सड़क पर ऑफ़िस की भीड़ ख़त्म हो गई थी। फिर भी काफ़ी भीड़ थी। रिक्शे, दुपहिए, तिपहिए, गाड़ियाँ, पैदल—सबके बीच से उसकी हीरो होंडा अपना रास्ता बनाती हुई बीयर की दुकान के सामने खड़ी हो गई। दुकान खुल रही थी। वह पहला ग्राहक था। दुकानदार उसी की उम्र का युवक था। उसने दो बोतलें रतन को थमाते हुए पूछा—'क्या सेलिब्रेट कर रहे हैं ?'

'आज़ादी', रतन ने मुस्कराते हुए कहा।

घर पर ताला पड़ा था। दादा-भाभी ऑफ़िस चले गए थे, मुन्ना स्कूल। वह दोनों बोतलें हाथों में घुमाता अपने कमरे में घुसा। बोतलें मेज़ पर रखकर वह किचन से ओपनर उठा लाया और एक बोतल खोलकर उसने उफनते झाग को अपने होंठों से लगा लिया। फिर बोतल वाला हाथ सामने तानकर, उसने दायाँ हाथ दाईं ओर फेंका और चीख़ा : 'आज़ादी !' तत्पश्चात् बोतलवाला हाथ फिर मुँह की ओर आया और बीयर के तीन घूँट शरीर में डूब गए। जैसे-जैसे बीयर जिस्म में डूबती, एक नाम बार-बार ज़ेहन में उछलता : धीरूभाई अम्बानी। उसकी शुरुआत मुझसे बदतर थी। मैं ज़्यादा पढ़ा-लिखा हूँ। ज़हीन हूँ। अभी भल्ला को ऑफ़िस में चित करके आ रहा हूँ। भल्ला भी क्या याद करेगा कि किसी से पाला पड़ा था ! इस धरती पर मेरा अद्वितीय जीवन छोटी-मोटी नौकरियों पर ख़र्च करने के लिए नहीं है। मुझे बड़े काम करने हैं। दूर खड़ी चोटियाँ मुझे अपनी ओर खींच रही हैं—गगनचुम्बी चोटियाँ, जिनके माथे पर हिम के टीके हैं। मैं अभी नीचे घाटी में खड़ा उन चोटियों के मस्तक को निहार रहा हूँ जैसे अर्जुन तीर छोड़ने के पहले अपने लक्ष्य को एक आँख से देखता है। देखो, चोटी का केवल श्वेत, उज्ज्वल, चमकता हुआ टीका। शाश्वत विजय का चिह्न !

घाटी में ठंडी हवा चल रही है। पैरों से कुछ दूर ठंडे पानी का एक चश्मा है, जिसमें कल-कल कल-कल पारदर्शी पानी बह रहा है। पानी के नीचे पत्थर के गोल-गोल टुकड़े हैं, पानी में हिलते हुए। चश्मे के दूसरी ओर चीड़ के पेड़ों का जंगल है। जंगल में पक्षियों की आवाज़ें हैं जो पानी की आवाज़ में बार-बार अपना सिर बाहर निकाल लेती हैं।

चोटियाँ सूनी हैं। वहाँ कोई नहीं है। कोई पक्षी भी नहीं। सूरज दूर खड़ा अपनी चमकीली बाँहों से उन्हें सहलाता है।

जब वह सोकर उठा, वह ख़ुश था। उसे वह सपना याद था, जो उसने

अभी-अभी देखा। आमिर ख़ान ने उसके गले में बाँहें डालकर कहा था : 'तुम्हारा हौसला बिलकुल सही है। प्रतिभाशाली लोग नौ से पाँच की नौकरी में नहीं फँसते। अगर मैं नौकरी करता, तो आमिर ख़ान कैसे बनता ?' वह मुस्कराता हुआ बिस्तर से उठा। एक क्षण तो उसे पता नहीं चला कि यह सुबह नहीं है, शाम है। फिर अचानक घंटी बजी और उसे शाम का ख़्याल आया। दरवाज़े पर दादा-भाभी और मुन्ना थे। उसने पूछा नहीं कि मुन्ना को देर हो गई या दादा-भाभी जल्दी आ गए या तीनों एक-साथ कहीं पिकनिक पर गए थे। उसके भीतर कोई रोशनी जल रही थी।

'रतन', बड़े ने पूछा, 'तुम जल्दी कैसे आ गए ?'

'छुट...छुट्टी हो गई।'

'अच्छा', बड़े हँसे, 'तभी ख़ुश लग रहे हो।'

रात को रतन ने भैया का अमरीका का पता माँगा और एक लम्बी चिट्ठी लिखी। चिट्ठी का उन्वान था : स्वतंत्र उद्योग बनाम नौकरी। बयान धीरूभाई अम्बानी की कहानी से आरम्भ होता था। ज़ोर अम्बानी की शून्य से शुरुआत पर था। फिर उसके निरन्तर फैलते व्यावसायिक वृत्तों का बखान था। उसके बरक्स इस भूमंडलीकरण के दौर में अमरीका से लेकर हिन्दुस्तान तक नौकरियों के संसार का सिकुड़ना था। अन्त में, यह सवाल पूछा गया था कि भारत में भैया कितना पूँजी निवेश करना चाहेंगे ? उसी के आधार पर रतन ने जल्दी ही प्रोजेक्ट रिपोर्ट भेजने का वादा किया था। रतन ने भैया को उनके पिछले वादे की याद भी दिलाई थी जिसमें उन्होंने रतन से कहा था कि कुछ ज़रूरत हो तो बताना, कोई संकोच न करना।

मदन की चिट्ठी से पहले उसका फ़ोन आया। नमन ने उठाया। आवाज़ इतनी साफ़ थी कि उसे शक हुआ कि कोई पड़ोस से बोल रहा है।

'क्या कानपुर से बोल रहे हो ?'

'नहीं, सान होज़े से।' वह हँसा। फिर मदन ने पूछा—'दादा, क्या रतन की नौकरी छूट गई ?'

'नहीं, ऑफ़िस तो रोज़ जाता है।...लेकिन तुमने पूछा क्यों ?'

'मुझे शक है।'

'क्यों ?'

'उसने मुझे काफ़ी बेवकूफ़ाना ख़त लिखा है।'

'क्या लिखा है ?'

वह हँसा, 'उसने मेरी भारत में पूँजी निवेश की क्षमता पूछी है।'

नमन को भी हँसी आ गई। उसने कहा, 'मैं पता लगाऊँगा।'

अगले सप्ताह मदन का ख़त भी आ गया। रतन के नाम ही था। ख़त में पूँजी निवेश की पेचीदगियों का बयान था। प्रमुख तत्व लाभ था। लाभ तभी सम्भव था जब उद्योग विश्वसनीय, अनुभवी हाथों में हो। अनुभव के दो रास्ते थे। एक, पिता के व्यवसाय में प्रशिक्षु का अनुभव। दो, किसी व्यवसाय में नौकरी का अनुभव—जो अम्बानी ने नौकरी करके प्राप्त किया था। रतन, मदन ने लिखा, कुछ बरस अभी तुम लगके नौकरी करो !

रतन को ऐसी उम्मीद नहीं थी।

बड़े भाइयों के पैसे से पढ़ा-लिखा और अमरीकी हुआ मदन अपने छोटे भाई की उद्यमशीलता के रास्ते में रोड़े अटका रहा था। कुछ लाख रुपए उसके लिए हाथ का क्या, पैर का मैल थे। लेकिन अब किसी देसी सेठिए की तरह वह दमड़ी दाँतों से पकड़ रहा था। उसने तो साफ़-साफ़ लिख ही दिया था कि बिना मुनाफ़े की गारंटी के वह कुछ भी करने को तैयार नहीं है। तब फिर उसमें और किसी और अमरीकी पूँजीपति में फ़र्क ही क्या था ? यह गोपनीय शर्त सीधे पूँजी निवेश (एफ़.डी.आई.) की भी थी। आई.एम.एफ़. और विश्व बैंक की तरह ही यह छोटे भाई की मदद करने के लिए नहीं था। इसका ठोस लक्ष्य छोटे भाई के ख़ून-पसीने से मुनाफ़ा कमाना था। यह सोचकर रतन की आँखों में आँसू आ गए। उसने भैया का पत्र अपनी छाती पर उल्टा रख लिया और आँखें मूँद लीं। रात का पहला पहर ख़त्म हो रहा था। वह अपने बिस्तर पर सिर की ओर टेबल लैम्प जलाए लेटा था। कमरे में दूसरी ओर मुन्ना सो रहा था।

दीवार पर आमिर ख़ान अँधेरे में था।

रोज़ की तरह वह आज सुबह भी ऑफ़िस के टाइम पर निकला था। नमन और नूर कुछ देर बाद जाते थे। मुन्ना कुछ पहले स्कूल चला जाता था। लेकिन वह पहले की तरह फ़ैज़ाबाद रोड पर दाईं ओर नहीं मुड़ा था, बल्कि बाईं ओर जाकर पॉलीटेकनीक के तिराहे पर दाईं ओर मुड़ गया था जहाँ गोमतीनगर की नई इमारतें शुरू होती थीं। हीरो होंडा कुछ देर बाद एक साइबर कैफ़े के सामने रुकी थी और रतन उतरकर अन्दर चला गया था। उसने अमरीका में मदन को अपने ई-मेल के पते पर पत्र का जवाब देने को कहा था और कहा था कि वह उसका बेसब्री से इन्तज़ार करेगा। उसे क्या पता था कि उसी वक़्त डाकिया मदन का ख़त अपने थैले में डाले साइकिल पर पोस्ट ऑफ़िस से उसके घर की ओर जा रहा था। फिर उसने कुछ देर इंटरनेट पर अपनी व्यावसायिक और नौकरी की सम्भावनाओं से खिलवाड़ किया था। सचमुच इंटरनेट पर उसे खेल का मज़ा आता

था। वह भूल जाता था कि वह जिस आदमी के भविष्य की खोज कर रहा है, वह आदमी असल में वह ख़ुद है।

तब उसने बाहर निकलकर कॉफ़ी पी थी और नए खुले बिलियर्ड पार्लर में घुस गया था। यह उसका नया शौक था। इसकी सबसे बड़ी विशेषता यह थी कि टेबल के इर्द-गिर्द समय एक खेल हो जाता था। छत से लटकती रोशनियों के नीचे विशाल टेबल पर दौड़ती रंगीन गेंदों में समय लिपट जाता और चारों ओर चक्कर काटते हुए ऊपर हवा में घुलने लगता। बिलियर्ड टेबल पर जो रोशनी सुबह थी, वही शाम को बनी रहती जैसे कोई शाश्वत समय हो। पता ही नहीं चलता था कब सुबह से शाम हो गई। काम खोजते हुए उसकी घड़ी बन्द हो गई थी।

इस बीच नमन ने रतन के ऑफ़िस में कई बार फ़ोन किया। कोई संतोषजनक जवाब न मिलने की वजह से पिछली बार उसने सीधे मिस्टर भल्ला से बात की। भल्ला ने बताया कि रतन पिछले माह ही यह कम्पनी छोड़ गया। फिर रोज़ सुबह वह कहाँ जाता था ? जब एक शाम अपनी जिज्ञासा उसने रतन के सामने रखी तो रतन ने जवाब दिया, 'नौकरी ढूँढ़ने।'

'नौकरी ढूँढ़ने ?' नमन हैरत में आ गया। रतन न सिर्फ़ रोज़ सुबह घर से निकलता था, बल्कि शाम को अक्सर उसी तरह लौटता था जैसे ऑफ़िस से आ रहा हो।

'हाँ।'

नमन हँसा, 'छोटे, तुम नौकरी ढूँढ़ने इस तरह जाते हो जैसे सब लोग नौकरी करने जाते हैं।'

'आपको घर बैठे नौकरी मिल गई, दादा', रतन संजीदा हो गया, 'क्या आपने कभी नौकरी ढूँढ़ी है ?'

'नहीं।'

'फिर आप क्या जाने !' रतन ने आँखें नीचे फ़र्श की ओर झुका दीं, 'इस ज़माने में नौकरी हीरे की कनी हो गई है जो धूल में मिल गई हो।'

तर्क बुरा नहीं था। लेकिन नमन के शक का दायरा बढ़ता जाता था। जब उसने रतन से उसके मदन को लिखे ख़त के बारे में पूछा तो उसने कहा कि नौकरी की जब ऐसी कड़की हो तो स्वरोज़गार ही मुक्ति का द्वार है। यह मैं नहीं कहता, रतन ने कहा, प्रधानमंत्री कहते हैं। यह सच था। यह प्रधानमंत्री ही नहीं, देश के बुद्धिजीवी और अर्थशास्त्री भी कह रहे थे। नमन जानता था कि बैंकों में वी.आर.एस. का शोर था। जब लगी-लगाई नौकरियाँ छूट रही हों, तो नई

नौकरियों का अल्लाह ही मालिक था। उधर श्रम-क़ानूनों पर लगातार प्रहार हो रहे थे।

ऐसे बीहड़ समय में रतन का दो-दो बार नौकरी छोड़ना नमन की समझ में नहीं आता था। रतन बेवकूफ़ नहीं था। उसने मदन को लिखे ख़त की कितनी मौजूँ व्याख्या की थी जैसे वह सिक्के का दूसरा पहलू हो। उसकी शराबखोरी और वक़्तखोरी के परदों के पार यह साफ़-साफ़ नज़र आता था कि नौकरी करने में उसका मन नहीं लगता था। वरना पच्चीस बरस की उम्र होते-होते दो बार नौकरी छोड़ देने या नौकरी से निकाल दिए जाने का कोई मतलब नहीं था। फिर मन कहाँ लगता था ? यह ख़तरनाक सवाल था।

अगली शाम जब रतन घर लौटा तो अँधेरा घिर आया था। नमन उसी का इन्तज़ार कर रहा था। उसने अपने सामने शराब का एक भरा गिलास रखा था और एक ख़ाली। उसने रतन को बैठक में बुलाया और सामने बैठने को कहा। फिर उसने ख़ाली गिलास भर दिया। रतन के गिलास उठाने पर नमन ने कहा, 'चीयर्स' और एक चुस्की ली। रतन ने एक बड़ा घूँट भरा।

दो पैगों तक वे परिवार और शहर की बातें करते रहे। तीसरे पैग के आधा गुज़र जाने के बाद नमन ने पूछा, 'रतन, तुम करना क्या चाहते हो ?'

'मैं...' रतन ने कहा, 'मैं माउंट एवरेस्ट पर चढ़ना चाहता हूँ।'

'लेकिन', नमन कुछ घबराया, 'तुम तो झाँसी में क़िले की चढ़ाई पर ही हाँफ जाते हो।'

रतन मुस्कराया, 'असल में मैं जहाँ रहूँ, वहाँ चोटी पर रहना चाहता हूँ।'

नमन भाई की ओर टकटकी लगाए देख रहा था।

'आप देख लेना', रतन ने आह-सी भरी, 'एक दिन मैं अम्बानी बनूँगा या आमिर ख़ान !'

तभी बत्ती चली गई।

नमन अँधेरे में रतन की ओर देख रहा था।

2.4

भारत बन्द था।

दुकानें बन्द थीं। दफ़्तर बन्द थे। कुछ दरवाज़े ज़रूर खुले थे। जैसे हवा के आने-जाने के लिए खुले छोड़ दिए गए हों। दवाख़ाने भी खुले थे। सड़कें खुली थीं। लोग कम थे। ऐसा लगता था जैसे लोग शहर छोड़कर चले गए हों। शायद

इसीलिए शहर में बसें नज़र नहीं आ रही थीं। सड़कों पर गाड़ियाँ भी नहीं थीं। पुलिस के वाहन ज़रूर थे। कुछ दुपहिए थे। कुछ रिक्शे थे। कुछ पैदल थे। धूप का साम्राज्य था। हवा नहीं थी। हवा बन्द थी। लगता था जैसे मौसम भी बन्द हो। न जाड़ा था। न बरसात हो रही थी। उमस थी।

शहर के जिस्मों में उमस कुछ अजीब थी। शरीर अपने से बाहर निकलकर कहीं और भाग जाना चाहते थे।

बाज़ार खंडहर लगते थे। सारे शटर बन्द थे। यह रात की कैफ़ियत थी। क्या यह दिन में रात हो गई थी ? सूरज सड़कों पर ऐसे चमक रहा था जैसे उसे कुछ पता ही न हो। हज़रतगंज के गलियारों में कुछ लोग लालबुझक्कड़ से यहाँ-वहाँ चले जा रहे थे। जब वे धूप में आते तो आँखें मिचमिचाने लगते। सूर्य की किरणें सीधी आँखों पर वार करतीं। वे आँखें फेर लेते।

पहले अख़बार में कभी-कभार प्रेम की एकल या संयुक्त आत्महत्या की ख़बर आती थी। ख़बर में आत्महत्या की प्रविधि का भी ज़िक्र होता था : मसलन होटल के कमरे में ज़हर खाकर या पंखे से लटककर या रेल की पटरी पर लेटकर या नदी में कूदकर। इधर किसानों की आत्महत्या की ख़बरें आई थीं जिनका एक ही कारण था : ऋण; और एक ही प्रविधि थी : कीटनाशक पी जाना—जैसे आदमी कीड़ा हो गया हो। कुछ कारख़ानों के मज़दूर भी कारख़ाने से निकाले जाने पर ज़िन्दगी से ही निकल गए। शहरों में जिस तरह पहले युवक-युवतियाँ प्रेम में पड़कर मरते थे, अब बेकारी से मरने लगे। जिस तरह अख़बार में पहले प्रेमी की आत्महत्या की ख़बर आती थी, अब उसी तरह बेकार की आत्महत्या की ख़बर आने लगी।

उसी अपराह्न विधानसभा मार्ग पर विधानसभा के सामने कोपभवन में जो भाषण हुए, उनमें यही ज़िक्र था। कोपभवन कोई भवन नहीं था। यह इमारतों और हरियाली से घिरा छोटा-सा मैदान था जिसमें एक ओर मंच था और सामने लोग बैठे थे। बैठे हुए लोगों को घेरे लोग खड़े थे। मंच आग उगल रहा था। लोग बीच-बीच में तालियों और नारों से उसे हवा दे रहे थे। मैदान खचाखच भरा था। नमन के भाषण के दौरान ख़ूब तालियाँ बजीं। उसने आँकड़ों की मदद से बताया कि भूमंडलीकरण का पहला दशक अवसान की ओर अग्रसर है और उसके राष्ट्रीय और अन्तर्राष्ट्रीय प्रवक्ताओं के सुनहरे वादे धूल में लोट रहे हैं। उसने कहा कि किसानों और मज़दूरों की आत्महत्या का दौर शुरू हो गया है। वह दिन दूर नहीं जब बैंक के कर्मचारी भी इसी राह पर चलेंगे। मध्यवर्गीय कर्मचारी किसी धोखे में न रहें ! यह पिज़्ज़ा और डिज़ाइनर कपड़ों का संसार घरों में टी.वी. का परदा

उठाकर घुस रहा है। बच्चे हज़ारों के कपड़े और जूते माँगते हैं। कल बैंकों का निजीकरण होगा और छँटनी होगी। जो बच्चे आज पिज़्ज़ा खा रहे हैं, उनके लिए रोटी जुटाना मुश्किल हो जाएगा। दोस्तो, नमन ने कहा—दो सदी पहले अंग्रेज़ों ने एक हाथ में सलीब और दूसरे हाथ में बन्दूक लेकर हमारे देश में प्रवेश किया था। इस दशक में गोरों ने फिर एक हाथ में पेप्सी और दूसरे हाथ में टी.वी. का केबिल लेकर हमारी धरती पर क़दम रखे हैं। धरती पर क़दम रखने वाले वे ख़ुद नहीं हैं। उनके अक्स हैं। ये अक्स अन्तरिक्ष में घूमते सैटलाइट के ज़रिए हमारे घरों में आते हैं। हमें पता नहीं चलता। हम अमरीकी बिम्बों के गुलाम हैं !

ज़ोरदार तालियों के बाद नमन ने फिर कहा कि सड़क के दूसरी तरफ़ जो विधानसभा का भव्य भवन अभी धूप में झिलमिला रहा है, यही कुछ सालों बाद अपनी ही छाया हो जाएगा जैसे आजकल अमावस की रात में लगता है। क़ानून अमरीका में बनेंगे, यहाँ परदे पर छपेंगे और विधानसभा में कुछ छायाएँ केवल हाथ उठाएँगी।

श्रोताओं की क़तार में सामने नूरजहाँ बैठी थी और डॉक्टर पांडे थे, जिनके साथ नमन को घर लौटना था। डॉ. पांडे बैंक के पैनल में थे और नमन के दोस्त थे। नमन ने डॉक्टर पांडे को रतन के बारे में बताया था और उसका मानसिक इतिहास-भूगोल भी बयान किया था। यह तय हुआ था कि वे आज एक-साथ इन्दिरानगर जाएँगे जहाँ डॉ. पांडे रतन से मिलेंगे। रतन का हाल सुनकर डॉ. पांडे ने कहा था कि हम जिस समय में जी रहे हैं, उसमें शिज़ोफ़्रेनिया का अन्देशा और भी ज़्यादा है। यह ऐसा समय था जिसमें देश के एक-तिहाई लोग भूखे थे और एक-चौथाई पिज़्ज़ा खा रहे थे—बाक़ी लोग पिज़्ज़ा की प्रदर्शन-खिड़की में आँखें गड़ाए खड़े थे ! सौ में से एक आदमी इस बीमारी का शिकार था। कल्पना करो, डॉक्टर ने कहा, हमारे देश में एक करोड़ शिज़ोफ़्रेनिक्स का एक शहर बस सकता है ! जब डॉ. पांडे यह बता रहे थे तो नमन को उनकी वह छवि याद आ रही थी जब एक सभा में बोलते हुए अचानक उनकी जेब में पड़े मोबाइल फ़ोन की घंटी बजी थी और उन्होंने भाषण के बीच फ़ोन कान से लगाकर कहा था—'अभी मैं मीटिंग में हूँ।' इतना बोलकर उन्होंने फिर अपना भाषण जारी कर दिया था। लोग मुस्कराने लगे थे। डॉ. पांडे वामपंथी थे। उस सभा में मन्दिर-मस्जिद मसले पर बोल रहे थे। डॉ. पांडे ने मोबाइल बन्द न करने का कारण मरीज़ की चिन्ता बताया था। इस चिन्ता और व्यावसायिक चिन्ता में ज़्यादा फ़र्क नहीं था। अलबत्ता मरीज़ की चिन्ता का पैरहन दिलकश था।

नमन और नूरजहाँ डॉ. पांडे की मारुति में बैठे थे। नमन ने अपना स्कूटर

बैंक में ही छोड़ दिया था। बन्द सफल था। दुकानें और दरवाज़े बन्द थे। सूरज भी अपने दिन की दुकान बढ़ाकर जा रहा था। अशोक रोड पर कुछ हलचल बढ़ गई थी। कुछ गाड़ियाँ और निकल आई थीं। डॉ. पांडे नमन को उसके भाषण के लिए बधाई दे रहे थे। नूरजहाँ पीछे बैठी मुस्करा रही थी। उसने भूतनाथ पर उतरकर मिठाई ली। फिर वे घर की ओर बढ़े।

रतन घर पर ही था। उससे नमन ने सुबह ही कह दिया था कि मेरे एक दोस्त तुमसे मिलना चाहते हैं, शाम को घर पर रहना। क्यों ? रतन के सवाल के जवाब में नमन ने कहा था, 'तुम्हारे कैरियर के लिए।' डॉ. पांडे और रतन आमने-सामने बैठे थे। उन्होंने एक-दूसरे से घुल-मिलकर बातें कीं। पहल डॉक्टर की ही थी। रतन को पता नहीं चला कि वे डॉक्टर हैं। उनकी बातों का विषय फ़िल्मों से लेकर उद्योग तक था, जो दिन-ब-दिन निजी हाथों में खिसक रहा था। यह ज़रूर था कि छोटे उद्योग ख़त्म हो रहे थे जैसे वे छोटी मछलियाँ हों जिन्हें बड़ी मछलियाँ निगल रही हों। शहर की हवा बदल रही थी ! बाज़ार सुरसा के मुँह की तरह बढ़ता जाता था। हज़रतगंज हर साल बदलता था और रौनक बढ़ जाती थी। रोशनियाँ अँधेरे को और चीरने लगतीं जैसे रात को चीर-फाड़ कर उसे दिन में बदल देंगी और फिर कभी रात नहीं होगी। कैसा होगा यह शहर जिसमें कभी रात न हो ?

'नए शहर को नए आदमी की ज़रूरत है', रतन ने कहा।

'कैसा नया आदमी ?' डॉ. पांडे ने रतन पर नज़र गड़ा दी। उन्होंने देखा था कि वह पलकें थोड़ी देर से झपकाता था और कभी-कभी पलकें झपकाना भूल जाता था जैसे अभी भूल गया था। डॉक्टर जानता था, यह शिज़ोफ़्रेनिया का लक्षण है।

'नया आदमी भूमंडलीकृत होगा,' रतन बोला, 'जिसकी नज़र आसमान पर होगी।'

'लेकिन ज़मीन पर रहने के लिए पैर तो ज़मीन पर रहने चाहिए।'

'हाँ', रतन ने पलकें झपकाईं।

बैठक में पेडेस्टल लैम्प के चारों ओर फैलते हलके उजाले में चुप्पी घुलने लगी। नमन चुप था। नूरजहाँ एक ट्रे में चाय और मिठाई लेकर आई।

'रतन, एक बात बताओ,' डॉक्टर ने चाय की चुस्की लेते हुए पूछा।

'जी।'

'आजकल लड़के सड़क पर गाड़ी इतनी तेज़ क्यों चलाते हैं ?'

'वे जल्दी में हैं।'

'क्यों ?'

'जहाँ उन्हें पहुँचना है, वहाँ के लिए देर हो गई है।'

'लेकिन रास्ते पर भीड़ होती है।'

'भीड़ की उन्हें फ़िक्र नहीं।'

'अगर वे शहर की फ़िक्र नहीं करेंगे', नमन ने कहा, 'तो शहर उनकी फ़िक्र क्यों करेगा ?'

'वे शहर को जीत लेंगे।' रतन ने ऊपर देखा।

नमन सोच रहा था कि उसने अक्सर छोटे को बाहर से आकर मोटरसाइकिल टिकाकर बिस्तर पर लेटते हुए देखा है जैसे अब उसके पास कोई काम न हो।

'मकान की शुरुआत एक ईंट से होती है', डॉ. पांडे ने रतन की आँखों में देखा।

'वक़्त कम है,' रतन बोला।

'कहीं घड़ी तो बहुत तेज़ नहीं चल रही ?' नमन मुस्कराया।

'इतनी तेज़ कि सुइयाँ नज़र नहीं आ रहीं', नमन ने यह तब जोड़ा जब रतन बाहर चला गया। इस बीच गेट की घंटी बजी थी।

फिर चुप्पी छा गई।

डॉ. पांडे मुस्कराने लगे। उन्होंने सामने दीवार की ओर देखते हुए कहा कि रतन अपनी पीढ़ी का नौजवान है। वह जल्दी में है। उसे 'फ़ास्ट फूड' की तरह 'फास्ट सक्सेस' चाहिए। वह इन्तज़ार नहीं कर सकता। वह सीधा पहले नम्बर की सीढ़ी पर उछल जाना चाहता है। हालाँकि वह पलकें देर से झपकाता है, मगर उसे लम्बी सीढ़ी नहीं दिख रही। इसीलिए वह बार-बार हवा में पैर डाल देता है और नौकरी छोड़कर घर आ जाता है। नौकरी छोड़कर वह अम्बानी और आमिर के सपने देखता है। सपने तो सपने हैं !

'इलाज क्या है ?' नमन ने यक्ष-प्रश्न किया।

'कोई नियमित काम।'

'क्या वह बीमार है ?'

'शायद।'

'शायद क्यों ?'

'हो सकता है कोई लड़का बिना किसी बीमारी के नौकरी छोड़ दे और सचमुच अम्बानी या आमिर ख़ान बन जाए !'

'क्या इस बीमारी का कोई पक्का टेस्ट नहीं है ?' नमन के माथे पर लकीरें उभर आईं।

'नहीं, सब अटकल है।'

वे चुप हो गए जैसे कुछ कहने को बचा ही न हो। जब सब-कुछ अटकल था, तो अँधेरे में दीवारों को टटोलना ही बचा था। डॉ. पांडे ने ही अन्त में जोड़ा, 'लेकिन अब बाज़ार बहुत जुझारू होता जा रहा है। इन लड़कों को बचाना मुश्किल होगा।'

'बाज़ार से बीमारी का क्या ताल्लुक ?' नूरजहाँ ने पूछा।

'बाज़ार इन्हें भड़काता है', डॉ. पांडे ने कहा, 'हर लड़के को ली वाइस जींस, सेल-फ़ोन, मारुति और उन तीन लड़कियों में से एक लड़की चाहिए जो नए ब्रीफ़ के विज्ञापन में समुद्र की लहरों से दौड़ती हुई लड़के की ओर रोज़ टी.वी. के परदे पर आती हैं।'

'तीन में से एक ?' नूरजहाँ की भँवें ऊपर उठीं।

'हाँ।'

'कोई भी एक ?'

'हाँ', डॉ. पांडे मुस्कराए।

इस मुस्कान और उस उदासी में कोई अन्तर नहीं था, जो अब नूरजहाँ के चेहरे पर उतर आई थी।

रात को नाइटी पहनकर बिस्तर पर लेटते हुए नूरजहाँ ने कहा—'यह अजीब बात है !'

'कौन-सी बात ?' बग़ल में लेटे नमन ने पूछा।

'रतन की बीमारी।'

'बीमारी ?' नमन ने नूर की ओर देखा, 'अभी डॉक्टर भी नहीं जानता कि यह बीमारी है या नहीं।'

नूर के चेहरे पर धुँधलका था। ज़ीरो पॉवर का बल्ब उसके पीछे जल रहा था।

'नमन', धुँधलके से आवाज़ आई।

'हाँ।'

'मुझे मुन्ना को लेकर फ़िक्र होती है।'

'कैसी फ़िक्र ?'

'वह परसों सोलह सौ रुपयों के जूतों की माँग कर रहा था।'

नमन पहले सकते में आया। फिर हँसा, 'मुन्ना अभी सोलह का भी नहीं हुआ। काफ़ी जल्दी में है।'

'यही फ़िक्र है।'

'हम क्या कर सकते हैं ? उसे सी.एम.एस. से नहीं निकाल सकते, जहाँ रईसों के लड़के पढ़ते हैं। न हम बाज़ार बन्द कर सकते हैं, जहाँ सोलह सौ के जूते बिकते हैं।'

चुप्पी पर एक परत धुँधलका चढ़ गया।

'रतन दो हज़ार के जूते पहनता है !' नूर की आवाज़ थी, 'मुन्ना बता रहा था।'

'वह खुद कमाता है !' रमन हँसा।

'अब तो कमाता भी नहीं।'

'फिर कमाएगा। जूते उसने अपने पैसों से ही ख़रीदे हैं।'

नूर हँसी, 'अपने पैसे वह जूते और शराब पर ही ख़र्च करता है।'

इस बार चुप्पी कुछ और ज़्यादा देर चली। धुँधलके की कुछ और परतें कमरे में तैरने लगीं। दोनों की आँखें खुली थीं। सिर तकियों पर सीधे रखे थे, छत को ताकते हुए।

'नूर', नमन की आवाज़ कहीं दूर से आती लगी, 'रतन मेरा सबसे छोटा भाई है। वह मेरे बड़े बेटे की तरह है।'

'मैं जानती हूँ', नूर की आवाज़ ने नमन की डूबती आवाज़ को छुआ, 'मैंने तुम्हें बताया नहीं। महीने में दो-तीन बार रतन मुझसे दो-तीन सौ रुपए ले लेता है। फिर लौटाता नहीं।'

'इतना पैसा...' नमन का स्वर टूट गया।

'शायद उसे शराब के लिए कम पड़ता है।'

'क्या वह इतनी ज़्यादा पीने लगा है ?'

'मुझे शक है। वह शायद ख़ाली शीशियाँ खुद बाहर फेंक देता है। दो-तीन महीनों से मुझे उसके कमरे में कोई बोतल भी नहीं मिली।'

नमन को अपनी छाती के भीतर कुछ अजीब-सा लगा जैसे दिल कुछ और तेज़ धड़कने लगा हो। उसे इस बात की तसल्ली थी कि उसने अपने छोटे भाइयों को आदमी बना दिया है। उसे पहली बार शक हुआ कि छोटे सिर्फ़ उम्र से आदमी बना है। कोई छब्बीस वर्ष का हो जाए तो क्या यह ज़रूरी है कि वह एक ज़िम्मेदार नागरिक भी हो ? यदि ऐसा हो तो भारत बन्द करके लोगों को जगाने की ज़रूरत ही न हो। उसने आँखें बन्द कर लीं।

'सो गए क्या ?'

'नहीं।'

'सुनो।'

'हाँ।'

'मुझे मुन्ना की फ़िक्र है।'

'तुमने यहीं से बात शुरू की थी।'

वह लुढ़ककर नमन के तकिए पर आ गई। वह तुरन्त उठा और उसने पंखा थोड़ा तेज़ कर दिया। फिर वह वापस आकर अपने तकिए पर लेट गया जहाँ नूर का सिर भी था।

'बोलो।' उसने कहा।

'नमन, मैं नहीं चाहती कि मुन्ना अब उसी कमरे में सोए।'

'क्यों ?'

'मुझे शक है कि रतन अक्सर शराब पीकर घर लौटता है। वह सपने में बोलता भी है, मुन्ना बता रहा था।'

एक पल फिर गहरा धुँधलका। तेज़ हवा।

'नूर', नमन ने तकिए पर उसकी ओर देखा, 'हम रतन से बैठक में सोने को नहीं कह सकते।'

'हम मुन्ना से ज़रूर कह सकते हैं।'

नमन ने कुछ नहीं कहा।

बिस्तर पर नूर के अपने तकिए पर लौटने की आहट हुई। फिर उसने उठकर बत्ती बुझा दी और वापस अँधेरे में अपनी जगह आ गई। अँधेरे में अपनी जगह लौटने में कोई दिक़्क़त नहीं हुई।

अगली रात से मुन्ना बैठक में सोने लगा। नूर ने रतन और मुन्ना से कहा कि कभी-कभी रतन को रात में देर हो जाती है और मुन्ना आधी नींद में जाग जाता है—यह ठीक नहीं है, उसे अगली सुबह स्कूल के लिए जल्दी उठना होता है।

रतन अब अकेले कमरे में था। मुन्ना की चारपाई ख़ाली थी। उस पर एक दरी पड़ी थी। मुन्ना का बिस्तर हॉल में सेटी पर लगा दिया गया था, जहाँ वह अब सो रहा था। सोने से पहले मुन्ना हमेशा रतन से कुछ बातें करता था यदि रतन कमरे में हो। रतन अपने कमरे में था और मुन्ना हॉल में बिना उससे बात किए सो गया था। हो सकता है, यह उसका शक ही हो। लेकिन उसे इधर लगा था कि नूर भाभी भी उससे पहले की तरह बात नहीं करतीं। बड़े की नज़रें भी कुछ बदली-बदली-सी लगती थीं जैसे उन पर कोई परदा गिर गया हो।

कमरे में मेज़ पर टेबल-लैम्प जल रहा था, जिसके प्रकाश का गोल वृत्त मेज़ पर ही पड़ता था। सामने की ओर वृत्त टूट रहा था और रोशनी का एक टुकड़ा

चाँद की टूटी कोर की तरह फ़र्श पर पड़ा था। प्रकाश-वृत्त के चारों ओर धुँधलके के परदे गहरा रहे थे। दीवारों पर कुछ अँधेरे के परदों का भ्रम होता था। रतन ने कमरा बन्द कर लिया था। उसकी नज़र दीवारों के परदों में उलझने लगी, जिनमें कभी दादा, कभी भाभी, कभी मुन्ना के चेहरे झाँकते। मुन्ना का चेहरा बार-बार। मुस्कराता हुआ। जैसे वह कोई स्कूल की कहानी सुना रहा है या पूछ रहा है :

'चाचा, अलका रस्तोगी बार-बार क्लास में मेरी ओर देखती है। कभी-कभी मेरी आँखें उसकी आँखों में क्यों उलझ जाती हैं ?'

'वह तुम्हें नहीं देखती, मुन्ना।'

'फिर ?'

'तुम उसे देखते हो...हा...हा।'

'चाऽ चाऽऽ', मुन्ना का ठुनकना।

रतन को एकाएक महसूस हुआ कि कमरे में कोई नहीं है। सिर्फ़ कुछ टूटे चाँद-सी रोशनी है और अँधेरे के झिलमिलाते परदे हैं जो दीवारों में डूब रहे हैं। वह ख़ुद भी नहीं है। वह झाँसी चला गया है। उसे ताज्जुब है, वह सपना को इतने दिन कैसे भूला रहा। सपना...सपना...वह सपने में चीख़ रहा था। चीख़ से उसकी आँख खुल गई। उसे झपकी आ गई थी।

उस रात उसे देर तक नींद नहीं आई। न कमरे में मुन्ना था न सपने में सपना थी। सपना ही नहीं था। कोई सपना नहीं था। निजी उद्यम का सपना देखा था। उसके लिए पूँजी की दरकार थी। मदन भैया ने अमरीकी पूँजी निवेश के लिए मना कर दिया था। वे भी अँधेरे का परदा हो गए थे। जब असली अकेलापन घेरता है तो सब परदा हो जाते हैं। परदे आदमी को और भी अकेला बना देते हैं। आदमी ख़ुद परदा हो जाता है। बियावान हवा में फड़फड़ाता हुआ।

उस रात के अन्तिम पहर में गणेश ने दूध की कटोरी से मुँह उठाकर रतन से कहा—'अरे मूर्ख, जब मेरी मिट्टी की मूरत दूध पी सकती है, गाड़ियों में पेट्रोल डालनेवाला नौजवान अम्बानी हो सकता है और मुम्बई की रेत में खेलनेवाला लड़का आमिर हो सकता है तो तू करोड़पति क्यों नहीं हो सकता ? हाँ, इसके लिए अपना सब-कुछ दाँव पर लगाना पड़ेगा।' फिर गणेश अन्तर्धान हो गए। न वे सपने में दिखे, न सपने के बाहर। रतन ने हड़बड़ाकर आँखें खोलीं। कमरे में अँधेरा था जैसे कोई काले परदों का गोदाम हो।

यद्यपि उसकी नींद अधूरी थी, रतन सुबह ऐसे उठा जैसे उसे काम पर जाना हो। उसी तरह वह तैयार हुआ। मुन्ना के जाने के बाद उसने अपनी हीरो होंडा स्टार्ट की और घर से बाहर निकल पड़ा। नमन और नूर तब अन्दर तैयार हो रहे

थे। उन्होंने हीरो होंडा की गड़गड़ाहट सुनी। नमन ख़ुश हुआ कि शायद रतन नौकरी की तलाश में सुबह-सुबह घर से निकल रहा है। रतन सीधा हज़रतगंज सेंट्रल बैंक में पहुँचा। वह पहला ग्राहक था। उसने काउंटर पर अपनी एकाउंट बुक देकर उसे अपडेट करने को कहा। फिर पूछा कि कितने रुपए एकाउंट में छोड़ना ज़रूरी है। सौ रुपए छोड़कर उसने बाईस हज़ार तैंतीस रुपए निकाल लिए। फिर उसने पेट्रोल पम्प जाकर गाड़ी की टंकी भरवा ली। गाड़ी को पार्किंग में छोड़ा और हज़रतगंज के गलियारों में कूद पड़ा। दुकानें खुल गई थीं। गलियारों में भी। लव-लेन में जब उसे पहला लॉटरीवाला नज़र आया, तो वह उसके सामने ठमठमाकर रुक गया। पहला लॉटरीवाला एक कमसिन लड़का था जो आँखें नीची किए अपनी दुकान सजा रहा था। रतन के थमे पैर देखकर उसने आँखें ऊपर उठाईं। आँखों में पहले ग्राहक की ख़ुशी से ज़्यादा दुकान न सज पाने की उलझन थी।

'क्या चाहिए ?' लड़के के मुँह से निकला।

'जो तुम बेच रहे हो,' रतन हँसा।

लड़के का सिर लॉटरी के थाल से ऊपर था, जो एक काठ के स्टैंड पर रखा था। उसकी मूँछें नहीं आई थीं। आँखें कुछ बड़ी थीं। रंग साँवला था। थाल पर दुकान सजाता उसका चेहरा कुछ-कुछ लड़की का चेहरा लगता था। उसकी पीली टी-शर्ट का कॉलर कुछ गंदा और फटा था। बाल उलझे थे जैसे नींद से उठकर सीधा लव-लेन में आ गया हो।

थाल में रंग-बिरंगे टिकट सजे थे जैसे फूलों का कोई विराट् गुलदस्ता हो। रतन को क्षण-भर लगा कि भाग्य ही उसके सामने गुलदस्ता लिए खड़ा है। उसने पहला टिकट नागालैंड का एक करोड़ इनाम वाला ख़रीदा, जिसमें नाचती हुई नागा सुन्दरी का नीले रंग का चित्र था। उसने अगले नौ टिकट भी उसी 'ड्रा' से लिए—अलग-अलग गड्डियों से या गड्डियों को फेंटकर बीच-बीच में से। साले भाग्य, कहाँ जाओगे मुझसे बचकर ? वह बुदबुदाया।

'क्या ?' लड़के ने फिर आँखें ऊपर उठाईं। अब उसकी आँखों में ख़ुशी थी। दुकान लगाते ही उसके दस टिकट बिक गए थे।

'कुछ नहीं', रतन लड़के के उलझे बाल देख रहा था।

सौ रुपए का नोट थमाकर जब वह पीछे मुड़ा तो उसके मन में एक इच्छा ने सिर उठाया कि वह एक और टिकट ख़रीदकर लड़के को दे दे और उसका भाग्य सँवार दे। लेकिन तभी उसे कुछ भूख-सी महसूस हुई और वह आगे बढ़ गया। बरामदे के बाहर रेलिंग से लगे कपड़ों के कुछ ठेले थे। चाटवाले ठेले अभी नहीं

आए थे। उनकी जगह ख़ाली थी। ख़ाली जगह कुछ अजीब लगी। रतन को अपना पेट फिर कुछ ख़ाली लगा। तभी धूप चली गई। उसने ऊपर देखा। कुछ बादल थे। बारिश बीत चुकी थी। ये बादल कैसे लौट आए थे ? जैसे बादल उसकी कमीज़ में घुस गए हों, रतन को अचानक उमस महसूस हुई। वह आगे बढ़ा। अगले बरामदे में अभी लॉटरी की लाल फ़ीते में भेंट-सी लिपटी मारुति नहीं थी जो दिवाली के साथ आएगी। वह उस अनुपस्थित मारुति की ख़ाली जगह पर क़दम रखता हुआ आगे बढ़ा। बरामदे में अभी भीड़ नहीं थी। फिर भी सामने से आता हुआ उसी की उम्र का एक युवक उसी की ओर बढ़ा और उसके कन्धे से टकरा गया। रतन ने फ़ौरन पीछे मुड़कर देखा। दूसरा लड़का उसकी जींस की जेब की ओर हाथ बढ़ा रहा था। उसने बढ़ा हाथ थामकर एक ज़ोरदार तमाचा लड़के के गाल पर जड़ दिया। वह चीख़े बिना भागा। जब रतन फिर पीछे मुड़ा तो उसे पहलेवाला युवक कहीं नज़र नहीं आया जो उससे टकराया था। बाज़ार में सुबह से ही जुआ और चोरी शुरू हो गए थे।

रतन ने पर्स पीछे की जेब से निकालकर आगे की जेब में रख लिया। पर्स भरा था। उसने बाईं ओर खादी एम्पोरियम के अन्दर काँच की दीवारों के पार झाँका। प्रदर्शन-खिड़की में आकृतियाँ स्थिर थीं, अन्दर वे चल-फिर रही थीं। सामने नीचे मैदान में गाड़ियाँ थीं और गाड़ियों से घिरा थाना था। यदि उसका पर्स चोरी हो जाता तो वह थाने में जाता। क्या उसे पर्स वापस मिलता ? उसे मालूम था कि चोर सिपाहियों को हफ़्ता देते थे और सिपाही गाड़ियों से घिरे थाने में बैठते थे।

वह कॉफ़ी हाउस में घुसा। दरवाज़े के अन्दर खड़े होकर उसने चारों ओर झाँका। सिर्फ़ एक मेज़ पर जगह थी। उस पर कोई बूढ़ा अकेला बैठा था और दीवार की ओर ताक रहा था। उसका आधा चेहरा नज़र आता था जो सफ़ेद दाढ़ी से घिरा था। रतन को पहली नज़र में शक हुआ कि वे कहीं पापा तो नहीं हैं ! खादी के कुर्ते-पाजामे और दाढ़ी की सफ़ेदी से यह सन्देह हुआ था। यह जादू कैसे हो सकता था ? बाँके बिहारी एक क्षण में झाँसी से लखनऊ कॉफ़ी हाउस में कैसे आ सकते थे ? रतन आगे बढ़ा। जब वह मेज़ के सामने खड़ा हुआ तो वृद्ध ने अपनी नज़रें उसकी ओर घुमाईं। आँखें ख़ाली थीं।

'क्या मैं बैठ सकता हूँ ?' रतन ने पूछा।

'बैठो', वृद्ध हँसा, 'इस समय कॉफ़ी हाउस होटल हो गया है।' वह फिर हँसा, 'हरा-भरा होटल।'

उसके बैठते ही बैरा आकर खड़ा हुआ। रतन ने डोसा-कॉफ़ी का ऑर्डर

दिया। फिर उसने पानी का गिलास मुँह से लगाया, जो बैरे ने अभी रखा था। वृद्ध दीवार की जगह रतन को देख रहा था जैसे वह बीच में आ गया हो।

'पढ़ते हो ?' वृद्ध ने पूछा।

'नहीं।' रतन ने कहा।

'नौकरी करते हो ?'

'नहीं।'

'बिज़नेस ?'

'नहीं।'

वृद्ध ने इतनी ज़ोर का ठहाका लगाया कि आस-पास के लोगों ने उनकी ओर देखा। वह कह रहा था—'तुम मेरी तरह हो। मुझे खुद नहीं मालूम कि मैं क्या करता हूँ।'

रतन चुप था।

'जब मैं तुम्हारी उम्र का था', उसने फिर कहा, 'तो मैं समझता था कि मैं नया भारत बनाने में नेहरू की मदद कर रहा हूँ। अब मुझे शक होता है...हर चीज़ पर।'

उसका चेहरा सपाट था।

रतन को ऐसा लगा जैसे वृद्ध उसके जिस्म के पार दीवार देख रहा है। वह बाँके बिहारी नहीं था। लेकिन बातें उन्हीं की तरह करते थे—जो कभी-कभी रतन को किसी और दुनिया की बातें लगती थीं। नेहरू रतन के पैदा होने के पहले ही मर गए थे। उसने नेहरू की तस्वीरें देखी थीं जैसे गणेश, शंकर-पार्वती की। गणेश उसके सपनों में ज़रूर आते थे।

बैरा रतन के सामने डोसा रख गया था। वह काँटा-छुरी चलाते हुए खा रहा था। उसने मुँह का कौर ख़त्म करके पूछा :

'क्या आप लेखक-पत्रकार हैं ?'

'हाँ, मैं पत्रकार हूँ', वृद्ध बोला, 'तुमने कैसे जाना ?'

'मेरे पिता पत्रकार हैं। वे भी ऐसी ही बातें करते हैं।'

वृद्ध मुस्कराया।

'तुम क्या करते हो ?' वृद्ध ने फिर पूछा, 'तुमने बताया नहीं।'

'काम ढूँढ़ रहा हूँ', रतन ने डोसे का टुकड़ा मुँह में डालते हुए कहा।

'कैसा काम ?'

'जो मेरे लायक हो।' रतन गम्भीर था।

वृद्ध हँसा, 'कोई काम उसी के लायक होता है जो उसे करता है।'

'मैं कॉफ़ी की ट्रे किचन से हॉल में ला सकता हूँ', रतन ने कुछ चिढ़कर कहा, 'तो क्या मुझे बैरा हो जाना चाहिए ?'

'हाँ', वृद्ध मुस्करा रहा था, 'हर काम जो कोई कर सके, उसके लायक है।'

'मेरे पास इतना धीरज नहीं है', उसने कुछ हारकर कहा।

एकाएक बिजली चली गई। रतन ने कॉफ़ी का एक घूँट लिया था। उसे गर्मी लगी। उसने ऊपर पंखे की ओर देखा।

'चलता हूँ', कहते हुए वृद्ध उठा और बाहर चला गया। उसकी चाल भी कुछ-कुछ बाँके बिहारी से मिलती थी। या शायद यह रतन का भ्रम था। उसे ख़ुद पता नहीं था।

जिस दरवाज़े से वृद्ध बाहर गया था, उसी दरवाज़े से एक लड़का अन्दर आया और रतन की मेज़ के सामने खड़े होकर बोला :

'सर जी, क्या मैं यहाँ बैठ जाऊँ ?'

'हाँ।'

रतन कॉफ़ी पीते हुए इधर-उधर हॉल में और दरवाज़े के बाहर चालू सड़क को देख रहा था जहाँ आदमी पैदल कम थे, वाहनों में ज़्यादा लदे थे। हॉल में अभी भी सारी मेज़ें भरी थीं। बिजली फिर आ गई थी। पंखे चालू हो गए थे। यह लोगों के चेहरे से पता चलता था।

जैसे रतन की नज़र बार-बार दाईं ओर मेज़ पर बैठी लड़की के चेहरे की ओर फिसल जाती, उसी तरह उसकी मेज़ पर बैठा लड़का उसका चेहरा ताक रहा था।

'सर जी', लड़के ने अचानक कहा, 'एक बात पूछूँ ?'

'पूछो।'

'आप बुरा तो नहीं मानेंगे ?'

'नहीं।'

'क्या आप आमिर ख़ान के भाई हैं ?'

'नहीं।' रतन मुस्कराया।

क्षण-भर बाद उसने पूछा—'तुमने क्यों पूछा ?'

वह जवाब सुनने को तरसा।

'दूर से आपको देखकर आमिर ख़ान का धोखा होता है', लड़के ने कहा, 'मैं दरवाज़े से खिंचा हुआ आपकी तरफ़ चला आया।'

रतन बिल चुकाकर उठा, उसने मुस्कराते हुए लड़के से हाथ मिलाया और बाहर गलियारे में चला आया। गलियारे में भीड़ बढ़ रही थी। वह बाईं ओर फ़र्श पर फैली पत्रिकाओं के चिकने कवर निहारता आगे बढ़ा और चौराहे पर

खड़ा हो गया। हरी बत्ती होने पर उसने सड़क पार की और दाहिने मुड़ गया। अब बरामदों में बाज़ार पूरी तरह लग गया था। गले में एक ट्रे लटकाए खम्भे के पास खड़े एक अधेड़ को रतन ने दूर से देखा और उसी ओर बढ़ा। वह अधेड़ भी उसी की ओर देख रहा था। रतन ने पास पहुँचकर देखा कि ट्रे में लॉटरी के टिकट थे।

'भूखा हूँ,' अधेड़ ने अपनी कीचड़-सनी आँखें फैलाकर कहा, 'टिकट ले लीजिए। आन्ध्र की लॉटरी कल ही खुलने वाली है।'

जब रतन ट्रे को ताकता निश्चल खड़ा रहा, तो अधेड़ ने फिर कहा, 'आपको कल करोड़ मिलेगा। मुझे अभी रोटी मिल जाएगी।'

अधेड़ चौधरी स्वीट हाउस के सामने खड़ा था। बरामदे की हवा में जलेबी की ताज़ा गन्ध थी।

रतन ने ट्रे से टिकट चुने जैसे कोई क्यारी से फूल चुनता है। फिर वह पैसे चुकाकर आगे बढ़ा। वह अगले लॉटरीवाले को ढूँढ़ रहा था जैसे जंगल में शिकारी हिरन, चीते या शेर को ढूँढ़ता है। जनपथ की ओर मुड़ने से पहले उसे एक लॉटरीवाला और नज़र आया जिससे उसने टिकट ख़रीदे। फिर दस टिकट ! उसे लगा, दस उसका लकी नम्बर है।

जनपथ में उसे पाँच लॉटरीवाले नज़र आए। फिर वह हज़रतगंज में लौट आया और मेफ़ेयर की ओर बढ़ा। मेफ़ेयर तक पहुँचते-पहुँचते उसे दो लॉटरी की दुकानें और मिल गईं। दस दुकानों से दस-दस टिकट लेकर वह स्टैंड की ओर गया। वह एक बाज़ार में दस दुकानों से ऊपर टिकट नहीं लेना चाहता था। उसकी हीरो होंडा लाल बाग़ की ओर बढ़ी। लाल बाग़ की दस दुकानों से दस-दस टिकट लेकर वह कैसरबाग़ की ओर बढ़ा। कैसरबाग़ की दस दुकानों की परिक्रमा के बाद वह बाज़ार की पतली सड़क से दस दुकानों पर रुकता हुआ अमीनाबाद पहुँचा। अमीनाबाद बाज़ारों का बाज़ार था। वह हर ओर बाज़ार की गली में घुसता और दस दुकानों की परिक्रमा के बाद बीच में चौड़ी सड़क पर आ जाता। वह फिर दूसरी पतली गली में घुसता। जब सारी गलियाँ ख़त्म हो गईं तो वह थक गया और उसने आइसक्रीम के साथ फ़ालूदा खाया। फिर वह चौक के बाज़ारों की ओर बढ़ा। चौक के बाद वह नखास तक गया। लौटते हुए वह निशातगंज के बाज़ार में रुका। भूतनाथ से लॉटरी की अन्तिम किस्त लेकर जब वह रात को घर पहुँचा तो उसकी जेब में सार्वजनिक क्षेत्र और निजी क्षेत्र—दोनों की लॉटरियों के टिकट थे। दस करोड़ इनाम के दस टिकट मिले थे। दस का आँकड़ा उसका भाग्य बदलने वाला था ! अन्यथा दस के इतने संयोग एक-साथ कैसे घटित होते ?

दस करोड़ से किसी उद्योग का शुभारम्भ हो सकता था। वह यही सोचते हुए उस रात सोया।

उसके पर्स में सात रुपए पचास पैसे बचे थे।

2.5

पैसा नहीं था।

जब से मुन्ना का बिस्तर उसके कमरे से निकला था, रतन के दिल में कोई दरार पड़ गई थी। पहले जिस इत्मीनान से वह भाभी से रुपए ले लेता था और वापस करना भूल जाता था, वह इत्मीनान उसी दिल की दरार में खो गया। लेकिन कोई चारा नहीं था। जेब ख़ाली थी। ख़ाली जेब से शहर में जीना मुमकिन नहीं था। ख़ाली पेट का सवाल उसके सामने अभी तक नहीं आया था—सिवाय बाज़ार में कुछ भिखारियों के मुँह से, जो अपना एक हाथ खोलकर उसके सामने फैला देते और दूसरा हाथ ख़ाली पेट पर फेरते। उसका सवाल ख़ाली जेब का सवाल था। आस-पास कोई और नहीं था जिसके सामने वह हाथ फैलाता। उसने शाम को नमन से कहा—'मुझे पाँच सौ रुपए चाहिए। कम्पनी ने अभी हिसाब नहीं किया। मिलते ही वापस कर दूँगा।' वह जानता था कि वह झूठ बोल रहा है। एक नहीं, दो। पहला, कम्पनी से हिसाब मिल चुका था। दूसरा, रुपए लौटाने का उसका कोई इरादा नहीं था। या शायद अभी जो कैफ़ियत थी, उसमें सच और झूठ के बीच सीमा-रेखा लगातार धुँधली हो रही थी। उसने दिन में मदन को एक चिट्ठी अमरीका डाल दी थी। शुरुआत मदन के उसी वायदे से थी जो उसने भारत छोड़ते वक़्त रतन को गले लगाकर किया था—'कोई ज़रूरत हो तो ज़रूर बताना।' अमरीकी निवेश तकनीकी कारणों से भारत में सम्भव नहीं था, अमरीकी सहायता तो सम्भव थी। रतन ने लिखा कि वह अमरीकी बैंक की सहायता पर ब्याज देने को तैयार है, मगर सहायता उसे तुरन्त चाहिए। पूँजी का अकाल था।

उस शाम नमन ने उसे पाँच सौ रुपए दे दिए। अगले दिन से जीवन सामान्य हो गया। उसकी हीरो होंडा नमन और नूरजहाँ के निकलने के पहले गड़गड़ाने लगी। उसने बता दिया था कि वह नमन और मदन की सलाह के मुताबिक नई नौकरी की तलाश कर रहा है। तलाश अख़बारों से शुरू होकर इंटरनेट और सड़कों पर हीरो होंडा के साथ चलती। हीरो होंडा अक्सर फ़ैजाबाद रोड पर बाईं ओर मुड़ जाती, जहाँ गोमतीनगर के साइबर कैफ़े से बिलियर्ड टेबल जुड़ी थी। कभी-कभी हीरो होंडा जल्दी घर लौट आती जहाँ ताला पड़ा होता। ताला खोलकर

रतन अपने कमरे में चला जाता। इस वक़्त उसे अपना कमरा क़िले की तरह लगता जिसे वह बन्द कर लेता। पंखा खोल देता। गर्मियों के दिन थे। धूप चढ़ते ही बस्ती में सन्नाटा छाने लगता जिसे कोई फेरीवाला या फटफटवाला ही तोड़ता। उस दोपहर रतन नंगे बदन अपने कमरे में चहलक़दमी कर रहा था। अचानक उसके कानों में स्त्री-कंठ की चीख़ें गूँजीं, 'बचाओ...बचाओ !' वह दरवाज़ा खोलकर बाहर भागा। जैसे ही वह बाहर निकला एक फटफटिया फट-फट करती हुई तेज़ भागी। सड़क पर एक औरत रोती हुई खड़ी थी और रोते-रोते कह रही थी, 'मेरी सोने की चेन लेकर भाग गया।' वह अपने ख़ाली गले पर हाथ फेरती जा रही थी और रोती जा रही थी। आस-पास घरों के दरवाज़े खोलकर औरतें निकल आई थीं। मर्द अकेला रतन था जो चड्डी पहने खड़ा था। जब पड़ोसिन ने उसे चोर का पीछा करने को कहा तो वह अन्दर भागा, फिर कुर्ता-पाजमा पहनकर उसने अपनी मोटरसाइकिल स्टार्ट की। वह बाज़ार तक जाकर लौट आया। चोर का कहीं पता नहीं था।

वह गेट बन्द करता, फिर अपना कमरा बन्द करता। तब अपने कपड़े खोलता। हीरो होंडा की हवा के बावजूद बनियान कुछ गीली रहती। उसे निकालकर जिस्म फुरफुराने लगता जब रोयों के बीच से पसीना पंखे की हवा में सूखता। वह फ़र्श पर नंगे पैर टहल रहा था। वह अचानक मेज़ की ओर बढ़ा। उसने मेज़ का सामान कुर्सी पर रख दिया और मेज़पोश हटाकर बिस्तर पर डाल दिया। नंगी मेज़ पर रंग-बिरंगे लॉटरी के टिकट शतरंज की तरह सजे थे। शतरंज कमरे में ऐसे चमकी जैसे बादलों में इन्द्रधनुष प्रकट हो गया हो। इन्द्रधनुष मन में आह्लाद पैदा करता था जैसे आकाश बहुत अपना-अपना हो, बिलकुल अपना...और सात रंगों से आसमान भर गया हो। कुछ पल देखते रहने पर इन्द्रधनुष जादू की तरह लगता जो आहिस्ता-आहिस्ता बिखरने लगता। लेकिन मेज़ पर इन्द्रधनुष बिखरता नहीं था। यह शाश्वत इन्द्रधनुष था, जिसके रंग स्थायी थे। इन रंगों में हिमालय, गंगा और सागर से लेकर कुतुबमीनार, ताजमहल, कोणार्क, खजुराहो, मीनाक्षीपुरम, राम-मन्दिर और महाभारत तक सब-कुछ था। भारत का इतिहास और भूगोल लॉटरी के टिकटों में समा गए थे। बल्कि भविष्य भी। क्योंकि एक लॉटरी के टिकट पर जिस राम-मन्दिर का चित्र था, वह अभी भारत में था नहीं—उसे अयोध्या में होना था ! अभी अयोध्या थी, अयोध्या के बाद काशी और मथुरा को होना था। अभी उत्तर था, फिर दक्षिण, पूर्व और पश्चिम को भी होना था। लॉटरी जुआ थी। भूत-भविष्य-वर्तमान को जुए में ही होना था।

मेज़ पर सजे छोटे-छोटे चमकीले टिकट कितने निरीह, भोले और तस्वीरनुमा

लगते थे। ये रतन का भविष्य थे, यह कोई नहीं जानता था। वह उन्हें ऐसे छूता जैसे झाड़ी में फुदकते ख़रगोश को छू रहा हो। जैसे वे जीवित हों—और अभी उसके कमरे में हिमालय पिघलेगा, गंगा बहेगी और समुद्र धरती को घेर लेगा। क्या पता टिकट का राम-मन्दिर भी उछलकर टिकट से बाहर आ जाए ? ताजमहल, कुतुबमीनार, कोणार्क, खजुराहो—कुछ भी उछलकर बाहर उसकी हथेली पर आ सकता था, बीयर का एक और बड़ा घूँट भरते हुए रतन ने सोचा। यह बाज़ार का ज़माना था। कुछ भी बेचा जा सकता था।

रतन स्वदेशी पूँजी की फ़िराक में था। वह अपने उद्यम का आधार थी। नौकरी बहुत हो गई। नौकरी से हीरो होंडा और शराब चल सकती थी। नौकरी का मतलब पहली तारीख़ से तीस तारीख़ था। अन्तिम सप्ताह में ही उधारी की ज़रूरत पड़ जाती। जेब ख़ाली। पहली को जेब भरती थी। पूँजी खड़ी होने की कोई सूरत नहीं थी। नौकरी रोज़ कुआँ खोदने की तरह थी। बीयर की दूसरी बोतल का आख़िरी घूँट पीकर रतन ने धीरूभाई अम्बानी की तस्वीर आमिर ख़ान की बग़ल में टाँग दी। फ्रेम एक ही नाप का था। मगर अम्बानी अधबूढ़े थे, जबकि आमिर हरी-भरी जवानी में हँस रहा था। रतन ने अम्बानी की जवानी की तस्वीर की बहुत खोज की थी। जवान अम्बानी मिले ही नहीं। जो मिले अधेड़ थे, जिनके बाल सफ़ेद हो रहे थे। अम्बानी की जवानी कहाँ गई ? क्या पूँजी खड़ी करने में बीत गई ? रतन ने कहीं पढ़ा था कि अम्बानी ने किसी खाड़ी-देश में शुरू-शुरू में पेट्रोल पम्प पर काम किया था। क्या वह भी इन्दिरानगर के किसी पेट्रोल पम्प पर जाकर रबर का पाइप थाम ले ? उसे हँसी आ गई। हर समय अपने साथ नई तकनीक लाता था। चूँकि मदन सिलिकन वैली में ख़ुद नौकरी करते थे, इसलिए पूँजी बनाने की नई तकनीकों पर उनका ध्यान ही नहीं गया था।

रतन ने टिकटों पर छपी रकमों पर अपनी नज़र दौड़ाई : दस करोड़ से दस लाख तक के आँकड़े थे। उद्योग की शुरुआत के लिए काफ़ी था।

लॉटरी खुलने की हर तारीख़ के पहले की रात रतन के लिए क़त्ल की रात होती। उस रात या तो वह अद्धा पीकर बेहोश हो जाता या सारी रात आँखों में कटती। खुली आँखों में कभी रात का अँधेरा होता, कभी चाँद-सितारे। चाँद-सितारों की स्थिति बदलती रहती। चाँद कभी दूज का चाँद होता, कभी पूर्णमासी का पूरी रोटी का चाँद—जिसे उसके साथ शहर के भूखे लोग भी देखते। रतन भी भूखा था। उसके पेट से 'रुपया-रुपया' की आवाज़ें आतीं जैसे भूखे के पेट से 'रोटी-रोटी' की आवाज़ें। जैसे चाँद भूखे के लिए रोटी था, रतन के लिए चाँद रुपया था। शहर में कुछ प्रेमी भी थे जिन्हें चाँद में अपनी प्रेमिका की सूरत

दिखाई देती थी। रतन ने एक बार चाँद में सपना को देखा : धीरे-धीरे उसकी नाक बड़ी होने लगी, आँखें छोटी होने लगीं और कान खो गए। वह चीख़ा : 'सपना...सपना...!' मगर सपना चाँद की अँधेरी गुफ़ाओं में डूब गई।

चाँद फिर सोने का सिक्का हो गया।

चाँद-सितारों और सूरज के प्रताप से जो लॉटरी के नतीजे आते, वे रतन के लिए नहीं होते थे। हर बार नतीजे को देखकर लगता कि उसके ग्रहों पर सनातन अँधेरा छाया है। एक बार उसे सौ रुपए मिले, जिनसे वह एक बोतल शराब भी नहीं ख़रीद सकता था। इस नतीजे से एक सवाल और भी खड़ा हुआ कि क्या वह शराब पीने के लिए जुआ खेल रहा था ? उसका पावन उद्देश्य तो अपना व्यवसाय खड़ा करना था—ताकि नौकरी की गुलामी से मुक्ति मिले। पैसे की ज़रूरत से तंग आकर एक दिन नमन की सिफ़ारिश से वह एल.आई.सी. का एजेंट बन गया। यह मज़ेदार काम था जिसमें उसे लोगों को जीवन की सुरक्षा की ज़रूरत और उसकी क्षणभंगुरता की कैफ़ियत की द्वन्द्वात्मक गुत्थी के बारे में बताना था। अक्सर वह अपनी बात कहीं पढ़े टैगोर के उद्धरण से शुरू करता कि जीवन कमल के पत्ते पर ओस की बूँद की तरह है। फिर वह कहता कि एक बार आप कमल का पत्ता छूकर देखिए, छू नहीं पाएँगे, उँगली फिसल जाएगी। उसी उँगली पर ओस की बूँद रख दीजिए, रखने के पहले बूँद फिसल जाएगी। हर रोज़ हम ऐसे रपटीले जीवन पर विश्वास करते हैं ! इस विश्वास में विष मिला है। जीवन बीमा उसी की दवा है।

आहिस्ता-आहिस्ता अलग-अलग लोगों से एक ही बात करते हुए उसे ऊब होने लगी। ऊब से ज़्यादा यह खीज थी। अपने पर। दूसरों पर। दूसरे धीरे-धीरे उसे परे हटते हुए लगने लगे। फिर उसे लगा कि वह ख़ुद ही दूसरों से दूर हो रहा है। वह कहीं दूर भाग जाना चाहता था।

रात को बिस्तर पर लेटे हुए कभी-कभी उसे कमल के पत्ते पर अटकी ओस की बूँद याद आ जाती और वही बूँद उसकी आँखों से दोनों ओर बाहर निकलकर बहने लगती जैसे कोई नदी हो। उसे लगता, वह बूँद की तरह अकेला है। इसी तरह अपने भाग्य पर बिसूरते हुए उसने एक गर्मी, बरसात और जाड़े निकाल दिए। जब फिर गर्मी शुरू हुई तो उसकी बेचैनी बढ़ने लगी। यह शायद इस बार पड़ी कुछ ज़्यादा गर्मी की वजह से भी था। उसे लगा कि उसकी ज़िन्दगी इसी तरह ओस की बूँदों के बारे में बातें करते हुए गर्मी, बरसात और जाड़े से बार-बार गुज़रती हुई अचानक बीत जाएगी और उसे बसंत ऋतु का पता ही नहीं चलेगा। क्या वह एल.आई.सी. की पॉलिसी बेचने के लिए पैदा हुआ था ?

कौन बनेगा अम्बानी ?

वह अब रोज़ बहुत पहले की तरह ही निकलता और पहले की तरह सीधा बिलियर्ड टेबल की ओर चला जाता या वापस घर लौट आता। उजड़े दयार में जी नहीं लगता था। बीयर की बोतलें रोज़-रोज़ ख़रीदना झंझट लगने लगा। जिन की बोतल ख़रीदना ज़्यादा सुविधाजनक था। पैसे की सिर्फ़ निकासी थी। आवक का द्वार बन्द था। किसी को पता नहीं था। रतन ने फिर अमरीका चिट्ठी लिखी और सहायता की दूसरी किस्त की माँग की।

यह अजीब इत्तफ़ाक था कि जिस दिन अमरीकी सहायता रतन को मिली उसी ग्यारह मई के जलते दिन पोखरन-2 का नाभिकीय विस्फोट हुआ और भारत एक महाशक्ति हो गया। दिन-भर गर्म हवाएँ चलीं और रात में शरीर बेचैन रहे। नूरजहाँ को कुछ ज़्यादा ही गर्मी लग रही थी हालाँकि उसने मलमल की नाइटी पहनी थी। जब वह यह पारदर्शी नाइटी पहनकर बिस्तर पर आई तो नमन ने उसे दोनों हाथों से अपनी ओर खींचकर चूमा था। पर अगले ही क्षण वह पलटकर अपने तकिए पर यह कहती हुई लौट गई, 'आज कैसी गर्मी है !' 'कल जैसी ही है', नमन ने हँसते हुए कहा। नूर ने कोई जवाब नहीं दिया। उसे अपने अब्बा का ख़्याल आ गया था जैसे किसी माँ को परदेस में पड़े अपने अकेले बेटे का ख़्याल अचानक आ जाता है।

नूर के अब्बा पिछली साल पचहत्तर के हो गए थे। वे न्यू हैदराबाद के अपने फ़्लैट में अकेले रहते थे। नौकरानी मेहरुन्निसा दिन में आकर घर का काम करती थी और खाना बनाती थी। कोई तकलीफ़ नहीं थी। पैसे की भी नहीं। पेंशन उनकी ज़रूरतों से ज़्यादा थी। सेहत भी ठीक-ठाक थी। यदि पचहत्तर की उम्र में सिर्फ़ रक्तचाप की गोली खानी पड़े तो सेहत को उम्दा ही कहा जाएगा। अलबत्ता उनके सारे बाल सन-से सफ़ेद हो गए थे। जिस्म पर कोई काला बाल ढूँढ़ने से भी नहीं मिलता था। नूर को मालूम नहीं था, उसके अब्बा कभी-कभी गुसलख़ाने में आदमजात नंगे हो जाते और आँखों पर ऐनक चढ़ाकर अपने जिस्म पर एक काला बाल ढूँढ़ते—जो मिलता नहीं था। वे हँसकर ऐनक उतारते और उसे एक ओर रखकर नहाने लगते। यह प्रयोग पाँच वर्ष पहले शुरू हुआ था जैसे कोई पंचवर्षीय योजना हो। इसकी शुरुआत जनवरी '93 में हुई थी, जब वे क़रीब एक माह नखखास में बन्ने मियाँ के घर बिताकर न्यू हैदराबाद अपने फ़्लैट में लौटे थे। बन्ने मियाँ उन्हें ज़बर्दस्ती अपने घर ले गए थे जब पहली बार बाबरी मस्जिद ध्वंस के बाद शहर में हिन्दू-मुस्लिम दंगे का अंदेशा हुआ। नूर एक हफ़्ते बाद उनसे नखखास में मिलने गई थी और पहली नज़र में उन्हें पहचान नहीं सकी थी क्योंकि

उनकी दाढ़ी कब पूरी तरह सफ़ेद हुई उन्हें खुद पता नहीं चला था। वह एक क्षण की आँख-मिचौनी थी जिसमें नूर अब्बा को नहीं पहचान पा रही थी और अब्बा यह देखकर हैरान थे कि वह क्यों नहीं पहचान रही।

वे दिन में पाँच बार नमाज़ और दो बार अख़बार पढ़ते थे—एक अंग्रेज़ी का 'टाइम्स ऑफ इंडिया' और दूसरा उर्दू का 'इन दिनों'। रात को वे टी.वी. के समाचार चैनलों पर समाचार देखते-सुनते-गुनते थे जैसे उन्हें ही सारी दुनिया की फ़िक्र हो और कोई भी पत्ता खड़कने से पहले उनसे पूछता हो। नूर हँसते हुए उनसे यही कहती। वे भी हँसने लगते और हँसते हुए कहते, 'इसके सिवा अब मेरे पास और काम ही क्या है ?' शाम को उनका फ़ोन आया था—

'बेटी, तुमने सुना ?' उनकी आवाज़ उत्तेजित थी।

'क्या अब्बा ?'

'पोखरन का धमाका !'

'दुनिया सुन रही है, अब्बा', वह हँसी।

'नहीं, यहाँ तो मेरे कान फटते हैं !' वे कुछ ज़ोर से बोले।

'अब्बा, टी.वी. की आवाज़ कुछ कम कीजिए। गूँज रही है।'

उन्होंने फ़ोन रख दिया। दूसरी ओर सारी आवाज़ें ख़त्म हो गईं। नूर ने सोचा कि वह फिर नम्बर घुमाए। लेकिन अगले क्षण उसने इरादा बदल दिया और अन्दर की ओर घूम गई। अब बहुत देर हो गई है, बिस्तर पर अँधेरे में आँखें खोले उसने सोचा। उस रात उसने सन्नाटे का सपना देखा जिसमें अब्बा अपनी सफ़ेद दाढ़ी लहराते हुए मुन्ना की तरह एक जंगल की ओर दौड़ रहे थे और कहीं कोई आवाज़ नहीं थी। कोई चिड़िया भी नहीं बोल रही थी। समय का पता नहीं चलता था। जंगल में न सूरज था, न चाँद, न अँधेरा था, न उजाला—जैसे किसी शाम का समय हो।

उसी तरह दो हफ़्ते बाद अट्ठाईस मई की शाम को फिर उनका फ़ोन आया—

'बेटी, तुमने सुना ?'

'क्या अब्बा ?'

'आज पाकिस्तान में भी धमाका हो गया।'

'हाँ, अब्बा', नूर ने कुछ चिढ़कर कहा, 'आप क्यों दुनिया के लिए परेशान हैं ? रात हो गई। सो जाइए।'

'ये धमाके सोने नहीं देंगे।'

उन्होंने अचानक फ़ोन रख दिया जैसे पिछली बार रखा था।

अगली शाम बैंक से लौटते हुए नूरजहाँ और नमन उनसे मिलने गए। वे

नमाज़ अदा करके उठे थे। ख़ुश थे। जैसे उन्हें दीन-दुनिया की न कोई ख़बर हो, न फ़िक्र हो। उन्होंने मुस्कराते हुए दरवाज़ा खोला था। नमन ने उनसे बी.पी. के बारे में पूछा। उन्होंने बताया कि आज सुबह ही नमाज़ के बाद चेक कराया था। ठीक था। कितना ? 85-130। नूरजहाँ ने गहरी साँस ली। उसने कहा, 'अब्बा, कुछ दिन के लिए हमारे घर क्यों नहीं चलते ?' 'तुम्हारे ही शहर में रहते हैं, बेटा।' कहकर वे हँसे।

शहर में भीड़ बढ़ती जा रही थी। सड़कों पर स्कूटर चलाने में दिक़्क़त होती थी। दिक़्क़त का एक कारण नई-नवेली गाड़ियों की तेज़ रफ़्तार थी। वे चुपचाप दौड़ती थीं जैसे हवा में उड़ रही हों। ख़ासकर कोई नौजवान यदि चलानेवाला हो। चलानेवाले ज़्यादातर नौजवान ही होते थे। यह नौजवानों का ज़माना था। फिर भी नवाबों की इस पुरानी राजधानी में अभी थोड़ी-बहुत बुज़ुर्गों की जगह बची थी। थोड़ी-सी। ज़्यादा नहीं। और अब्बा के लिए कितनी ? नूर एकाएक फिर उदास हो गई। वह स्कूटर की पिछली सीट पर बैठी थी। स्कूटर निशातगंज की ओर दौड़ा जा रहा था। निशातगंज में भीड़ और ज़्यादा थी। यह शाम की भीड़ थी। शहर दिन-भर की गर्मी और लू के बाद घरों और दफ़्तरों से बाहर निकल आया था, फिर घरों में लौटने के लिए।

स्कूटर सड़क-पुल के नीचे रुका। फिर दूसरे चौराहे के पहले सड़क पर तीन बार ब्रेक लगाना पड़ा। नूर को हर बार झटका खाकर नमन के कन्धे को थामना पड़ता। एक बार तो वह लुढ़कते-लुढ़कते बची। पिछली साल जब वह पहली बार सड़क पर लुढ़की थी तो उसने पहली बार मारुति के बारे में सोचा था। घर पहुँचकर चोटिल घुटने पर स्प्रिट लगाते हुए उसने नमन से कहा भी था। नमन ने हँसकर उड़ा दिया था, 'क्या कहती हो ? शहर में कितने लोग रोज़ स्कूटर से गिरते हैं ! क्या सभी घुटने से ख़ून टपकाते हुए मारुति लेने चले जाते हैं ?'

निशातगंज के अगले छोर पर बाईं ओर पुरानी बिकाऊ मारुतियों की क़तारों को देखकर फिर नूर ने मारुति के बारे में सोचा। नाले का पुल पार करते हुए उसने यह भी सोचा कि बैंक से सस्ता ऋण तुरन्त मिल जाएगा और दो वेतनों से एक किस्त निकालना मुश्किल नहीं होगा—फिर स्कूटर का ख़र्चा उससे घटा दें तो मारुति काफ़ी सस्ती पड़ेगी। उस रात उसने नमन को कागज़ पर पूरा गणित समझाया और जोड़ा—'यह अब्बा और मुन्ना के लिए भी ज़रूरी है।'

'कैसे ?' नमन भौचक्का रह गया।

'अब्बा को हम कभी-कभी घर लाकर कुछ घंटे बाद आराम से वापस भेज सकेंगे। अभी वे रिक्शे की तकलीफ़ की वजह से भी नहीं निकलते। मुन्ना की बस

निकल जाती है तो उसे स्कूल पहुँचने में बड़ी दिक़्क़त होती है। फिर हम उसे गाड़ी से भेज देंगे।' नूर ने ऐसे कहा जैसे कुछ रटा हुआ बोल रही हो।

नमन चुप रहा। मारुति से परिवार-कल्याण भी जुड़ गया था। वह हतप्रभ था। उसे एक शंका थी कि इस परिवार-कल्याण में रतन शामिल नहीं था। रतन की हालत समझ में नहीं आती थी। उसने बहुत दिनों से जीवन बीमा का भी कोई काम नहीं किया था। कल एल.आई.सी. के हरिहरन बैंक आए थे। उन्होंने यही बताया था। तब से नमन की चिन्ता और बढ़ गई थी। चूँकि इधर उसने रुपए नहीं माँगे थे, इसलिए नमन कुछ निश्चिन्त था। उसे एकाएक खटका हुआ। वह तुरन्त फ़ोन की ओर बढ़ा। उसने पहले बम्बई पवन से बात की। फिर अमरीका मदन से। मदन ने बताया कि रतन की चिट्ठी आई थी। उसने पाँच सौ डॉलर रतन को भेजे हैं। फिर मदन ने पूछा कि रतन के क्या हाल हैं, वह क्या कर रहा है ?

यह यक्ष-प्रश्न था।

उसने फ़ोन रख दिया और माथा थामकर बैठ गया।

वह उसी तरह माथा थामे बैठा था जब नूर मुस्कराती हुई हॉल में दाख़िल हुई और उसने कहा : 'क्या माथा थामे बैठे हो ? मुन्ना आई.आई.टी. में इस साल नहीं तो अगले साल आ जाएगा। मुझे भरोसा है।'

'मुझे भी भरोसा है,' नमन ने नज़रें उठाकर कहा।

नूर सामने बैठ गई थी। उसने नमन की आँखों में आँखें डालकर कहा—'एक बात ज़रूर है।'

'क्या ?'

'अगर मुन्ना इस साल न चुना गया तो हमें उसकी मेज़ अपने कमरे में लानी होगी।'

'क्यों ?'

'क्योंकि उसकी मेज़ पर मेज़पोश के नीचे रतन ने जुए की बिसात बिछा दी है।'

'क्या कह रही हो ?' नमन ने त्यौरियाँ चढ़ाईं।

'मेज़पोश के नीचे लॉटरी के टिकट बिछे हैं।'

'किस लॉटरी के ?'

'हिन्दुस्तान-भर की लॉटरी के।'

नमन की आँखें फिर अपने कोटरों में वापस लौट गईं। नूर कुछ क्षण बाद फिर बोली :

'रतन बाहर वही है, अन्दर बदल रहा है।'

नमन की आँखें फिर बाहर निकल आईं जैसे नूर को पूरी तरह सुन लेना चाहती हों। जैसे नूर के शब्द उसकी समझ में न आए हों, उसने पूछा :

'क्या बदल रहा है ?'

'वह ज़्यादा पीता है। बाथरूम में सुबह शराब की गन्ध होती है जब उसके बाद मैं बाथरूम में जाती हूँ।'

काम की जगह जुआ...और शराब ! नमन का माथा घूमा—जिसे उसने फिर थाम लिया। उसे याद आया कि एक-दो बार रात को वह रतन के कमरे में गया था, और उसे शराब की गन्ध का शक हुआ था जिसे उसने शक मानकर दिमाग़ से निकाल दिया था। नूर को भ्रम नहीं था। उसने बाथरूम में शिनाख़्त कर ली थी।

क्या छोटे की पहचान अब उसकी टट्टी-पेशाब में है ? नमन ने माथा पकड़े सोचा।

2.6

पूस की रात थी।

नूरजहाँ कॉर्डिगन उतारकर रजाई में घुसने की तैयारी कर रही थी जब उसे ख़्याल आया कि उसे अब्बा को फ़ोन कर लेना चाहिए था। एक तो सर्दी अपने जोम पर थी। दूसरे, शाम को टी.वी. पर ग्राहम स्टेंस और उसके दोनों बच्चों के उड़ीसा के एक गाँव में जीप में सोए हुए ज़िन्दा जलाए जाने की ख़बर थी। टी.वी. के परदे पर उस जली जीप के कंकाल के बिम्ब छपे थे जिसमें तीनों रात को सोए और सवेरे नहीं उठे थे। स्टेंस के ज़िन्दा जलाए जाने के कल्पित चलचित्रों से नूर को 1984 में अमरीक सिंह का कानपुर की सड़क पर दौड़ता-चीख़ता जिस्म याद आ गया था। वह सिहर गई थी। शायद उसे आशंका थी कि अब्बा फ़ोन करेंगे। उनका फ़ोन न आने से कुछ तसल्ली हुई थी : शायद उन्होंने टी.वी. के परदे पर जली जीप के बिम्ब देखे ही न हों और उन्हें ग्राहम स्टेंस और उसके बच्चों की हत्या का पता ही न चला हो ! यदि ऐसा था तो उन्हें फ़ोन करके परेशान करने का कोई तुक नहीं था। लेकिन अभी रजाई में प्रवेश करते हुए उसने फिर सोचा कि फ़ोन कर लेती तो बेहतर था। अब देर हो गई थी।

अगले दिन सुबह नौ बजे धूप निकली थी जब न्यू हैदराबाद से मेहरुन्निसा का फ़ोन आया। उसने बताया कि वह अब्बा के फ़्लैट की घंटी बजाकर हार गई। कोई खोलता नहीं। रोज़ उसे दरवाज़ा खुला मिलता था और अब्बा हुक्का पीते

हुए। नूर और नमन फ़ौरन शॉल ओढ़कर निकले और उनकी मारुति अब्बा के घर की ओर दौड़ी। दरवाज़ा तोड़ा गया। अब्बा रजाई ओढ़े बिस्तर पर बैठे थे। उनकी आँखें खुली थीं। सामने टी.वी. खुला था : पर्दे पर कोई फ़िल्मी नाच-गाना चल रहा था। अब्बा की साँस नहीं चल रही थी। नमन ने पहले टी.वी. बन्द किया। फिर अब्बा की आँखें बन्द कीं। दोनों ने मिलकर पहले उनके घुटने सीधे किए, फिर कमर। तब अब्बा लेटे। वे क़यामत तक बैठकर आँखें खोले इन्तज़ार नहीं कर सकते थे।

अब्बा टी.वी. के पर्दे पर क्या देख रहे थे जब वे रतन की तरह आँख झपकना भूल गए ?

उनके दिल ने पर्दे की किस छवि के बाद धड़कने से इनकार कर दिया ? क्या पचहत्तर बरस हर साँस चलते हुए दिल अचानक पैरों की तरह थक गया था ? उन्हें दिल की कोई बीमारी नहीं थी। फिर एकाएक दिल इतना मज़बूर कैसे हो गया ? क्या यह दिल का दौरा था ? नूरजहाँ के मन में यह बहस ज़िन्दगी-भर चलेगी।

माघ शुरू हो गया। सर्दी कम नहीं हुई। आसमान में बादल घिरने लगे। कभी-कभी बूँदाबाँदी हो जाती। अब बरसते आसमान के नीचे ठंड में ऑफ़िस जाना तकलीफ़देह नहीं था। मारुति सड़क पर खुले सिरों को चिढ़ाती हुई दौड़ती। नूरजहाँ सूखे कपड़े और सूखे बाल लिये बैंक में मुस्कराती हुई घुसती। कभी-कभी वह मुन्ना को भी कॉलेज छोड़ती हुई बैंक जाती। रतन घर में सामने पड़ता तो उससे भी वह पूछती कि तुम्हें हज़रतगंज जाना हो तो हमारे साथ चलो। वह साथ चलता नहीं था। ऐसा लगता कि वह साथ चलने से कतराता है। नमन उससे गाड़ी में साथ चलने को कभी नहीं पूछता था। जिस दिन मारुति घर आई, उसी रात रतन कुछ देर से लौटा था। उसने हॉल में टी.वी. के सामने बैठे नमन से घर में खड़ी सफ़ेद मारुति के बारे में पूछा था। जब नमन ने 'अपनी' कहा तो रतन मुस्कराया था। वह यह कहते हुए अपने कमरे में लड़खड़ाता हुआ गया था :

'क्या अब मारुति में बैठकर क्रान्ति करेंगे, दादा ?'

रतन पिए था। नमन जानता था। लेकिन उसकी बात शराब के अँधेरे से निकलकर नमन के दिल के अँधेरे से टकरा गई थी।

जिस दिन हज़रतगंज में साम्प्रदायिकता-विरोधी जुलूस निकला, उस दिन धूप भी निकली थी। ख़ुशनुमा मौसम था। जुलूस की दो क़तारें थीं। लोग रंग-बिरंगे ऊनी कपड़े पहने थे जैसे किसी पिकनिक में आए हों। एक सफ़ेद बालों वाले बुज़ुर्ग काला कोट-पेंट पहने थे जैसे लिबास से भी विरोध ज़ाहिर कर रहे हों। अलबत्ता

ख़रगोश-सा सफ़ेद ऊनी मफ़लर उनके गले में लहरा रहा था। लोगों के चेहरों पर कुछ तनाव या इन्तज़ार नज़र आता था। नारे लगाते हुए उनके होंठ खुलते। कुछ मुट्ठियाँ हवा में तन जातीं। दोनों क़तारों में सौ-सौ लोग थे। सड़क पर दोनों ओर और बरामदों में चलते हुए लोग उनकी ओर देख रहे थे। दर्शकों की नज़रों में कौतूहल था। यह जुलूस वामपन्थी पार्टियों और कुछ संगठनों द्वारा आहूत था क्योंकि विश्व हिन्दू परिषद ने फिर रामनवमी के दिन रामभक्तों से अयोध्या पहुँचने का आह्वान किया था। चुनाव होनेवाले थे। पोस्टर और नारों में इसी ओर ध्यान खींचा गया था कि अयोध्या और चुनावों का एक-साथ गरमाना कोई संयोग नहीं था। मन्दिर के हल्ले की धूल में भूख और बेरोज़गारी और महँगाई छिप जाती थीं।

जुलूस के पहले मीटिंग में एक दाढ़ी बढ़ाए युवक ने एक नारे का प्रस्ताव रखा था : 'धर्म हटाओ, देश बचाओ !' नमन ने अपनी कुछ सफ़ेद होती दाढ़ी हिलाते हुए इसका विरोध किया था। उसका कहना था कि अधिकांश लोग किसी निजी धर्म के बिना नहीं रह सकते; हमें असली जन-समस्याओं पर एकाग्र होना चाहिए जिन्हें मौजूदा तंत्र धर्म की धुन्ध में ढँक रहा था। इसी सिक्के का दूसरा पहलू सत्ता के खेल में धार्मिक रूपकों और प्रतीकों का दोहन था। अयोध्या में यही हो रहा था। इस दोहन का पर्दाफ़ाश ज़रूरी था। उसने कहा कि सन् 1949 में जो रामलला बाबरी मस्जिद में अवतरित हुए और जिनकी अध्यक्षता में 1992 में मस्जिद गिरी, वे तुलसी के राम नहीं थे। राम दिल्ली की कुर्सी का पायदान नहीं हो सकते।

जुलूस हज़रतगंज के चौराहे से राज्यपाल के आवास की ओर बढ़ा। यह तय हुआ था कि राज्यपाल को एक ज्ञापन दिया जाएगा। पहले मुख्य द्वार पर रोका गया। फिर अन्दर घास पर बैठकर प्रतीक्षा करने को कहा गया। तब कुछ देर बाद बूढ़े राज्यपाल मुस्कराते हुए आए और पुरस्कार की तरह ज्ञापन लेकर लौट गए। जुलूस तितर-बितर होकर राज्यपाल आवास से बाहर आया। लोग गेट से बाहर निकलकर गुच्छों में इधर-उधर सड़क पर चलने लगे। एक अकेले युवक के सड़क पर पड़ते क़दम लड़खड़ा रहे थे। नमन की ओर उसकी पीठ थी। उसने तेज़ क़दमों से आगे बढ़कर युवक का चेहरा देखा। वह रतन नहीं था।

रतन इस समय हज़रतगंज के गलियारों में घूम रहा था। बल्कि ठीक-ठीक कहें तो वह इस क्षण 'लव-लेन' से निकलकर खुली जगह में आ गया था और एक ठेले के सामने खड़ा हुआ गोलगप्पे खा रहा था। 'लव-लेन' तो अब मछली बाज़ार हो गई थी जिसमें सदा भीड़ नज़र आती थी। रतन ने नमन को जुलूस की अगुआई करते और नारे लगाते हनुमानजी के मन्दिर के सामने खड़े होकर

देखा था। वह लगातार मुस्करा रहा था जैसे कोई प्रहसन देख रहा हो। असल में वह आज सुबह से ही उदास था। आज सुबह उसने मेज़पोश के नीचे से लॉटरी का आख़िरी टिकट निकालकर फाड़ा था। लॉटरी का नम्बर फिर नहीं लगा था। उसे मालूम नहीं था कि यह आख़िरी टिकट है। आख़िरी टिकट निकालकर उसने मेज़पोश के नीचे अँधेरे में उँगलियों से मेज़ की सतह टटोली थी : सतह चिकनी और ख़ाली थी। यह कहना मुश्किल था कि रतन की उदासी का उत्स मेज़ की ख़ाली सतह थी या लॉटरी का नम्बर न आना। यह मुमकिन है कि वह अपने बड़े भाई का नारे में उठा हाथ देखकर इसलिए मुस्कराया हो कि भीतर बहुत उदासी थी। वह अभी गोलगप्पे शायद इसीलिए खा रहा था।

गोलगप्पे खाकर वह आगे बढ़ा। भीड़ में रास्ता भूलभुलैया की तरह था। गलियारे में प्रवेश करने पर रतन ने उसी भव्य दुकान के अन्दर झाँका जिसके सामने हर दिवाली पर एक सफ़ेद मारुति बतौर इनाम सजाई जाती थी जो दिवाली के बाद भी अपनी जगह खड़ी रहती थी। यह दुकान की दिवाली-लॉटरी का इनाम था, जिसे सदा अपने विजेता का इन्तज़ार रहता था। एक लाल रिबन में भेंट की तरह बँधी सफ़ेद मारुति को देखकर रतन ने अपनी लॉटरी के इनाम का तसव्वुर किया—जो कहीं इन्तज़ार कर रहा था। लेकिन अब उसके पास टिकट नहीं था।

क्या दादा-भाभी को बिना टिकट के इनाम मिल गया था ? उनकी मारुति इस मारुति की सगी बहन लगती थी। या सब मारुतियाँ एक-दूसरे की सगी बहन थीं और उनके मालिक एक-दूसरे के सगे भाई ? जो शहर की हर सड़क पर एक-दूसरे के पीछे बेतहाशा भागते नज़र आते थे। जैसे कोई दौड़ चल रही हो। क्या इसीलिए रतन दादा की मारुति देखकर हँसा था : 'क्या अब मारुति में बैठकर क्रान्ति करेंगे दादा ?'

गलियारे के ख़त्म होने पर सामने साहू टाकीज़ था जहाँ आमिर ख़ान की फ़िल्म लगी थी। साहू के सामने आदमियों और वाहनों की भीड़ थी—बीच-बीच में लड़कियाँ नज़र आती थीं। दुपहियों की क़तारें उदास खड़ी थीं। जैसे एक-दूसरे की बाँहों में बाँहें डाले आमिर ख़ान की फ़िल्म देखने का इन्तज़ार कर रही हों ! अभी घंटी बजेगी और वे एक-दूसरे के पीछे हॉल में घुसकर सीटों पर बैठ जाएँगी।

रतन आगे बढ़ा जहाँ मन्दिर था। मन्दिर के सामने भीड़ थी। भीड़ के बाहर एक भक्त खड़ा हाथ फैलाए प्रार्थना गा रहा था। रतन उसे बरसों से देख रहा था। सड़क पर प्रार्थना गाता हुआ वह बूढ़ा हो गया था। क्या मैं भी सड़क पर इसी तरह चलता हुआ बूढ़ा हो जाऊँगा ? रतन एकाएक चौंका। उसे लगा, वह लौटकर आमिर ख़ान की फ़िल्म का टिकट ख़रीद ले। मगर यह फ़िल्म वह ग्यारह

बार देख चुका था जिसमें एक हज़ार मुश्किलें पार करके आमिर अपनी प्रेमिका को पा लेता है क्योंकि उसके जीने का यही लक्ष्य था ! बाक़ी उसके पास भगवान का दिया सब-कुछ था। कैसी विडम्बना थी कि रतन के पास भगवान का दिया कुछ नहीं था, केवल प्रेमिका थी—जिसे उसे अभी पाना था। उसे पता नहीं चला कि वह कब हनुमानजी के सामने आँखें मूँदे हाथ बाँधे प्रार्थना करने वाले बूढ़े के बग़ल में खड़ा हो गया।

अगले दिन नूरजहाँ बैंक से दोपहर में लौट आई। उसके सिर में दर्द था। सिर फटा जाता था। सिर में दर्द रात से ही शुरू हो गया था जब नमन बिस्तर पर बहस अधूरी छोड़कर खर्राटे लेने लगा। बहस का विषय छोटे का इधर रोज़-रोज़ लड़खड़ाते क़दमों से घर लौटना था। रोज़-रोज़ ? नमन को ताज्जुब हुआ था। नूरजहाँ ने निरीक्षण और आकलन को और आगे बढ़ाया। वह मदन के डॉलर शराब में उड़ा रहा था। पैसा कमाना उसने कब से छोड़ दिया था। शायद वह इसे ज़रूरी नहीं समझता। उसने कमरे में अम्बानी और आमिर की तस्वीरें लगा रखी थीं। उसके कमरे में मेज़पोश के नीचे लॉटरी के टिकट थे। क्या कोई लॉटरी से अम्बानी या आमिर हो सकता था ? क्या एक नौजवान का सबसे पहला फ़र्ज़ अपनी रोटी कमाना नहीं था ? क्या वह ज़िन्दगी-भर भाइयों के पैसों से दारू पिएगा ? क्या तुमने जवानी आने के साथ अपनी रोटी नहीं कमाई ? या मैंने ? और मैं तो लड़की थी ! लड़की नहीं, नमन ने टोका, ख़ूबसूरत लड़की। नूर झुँझला गई। फिर वह सीधी अपनी मूल बात पर आई। मुझे मुन्ना की फ़िक्र है, उसने कहा। वह पिछली साल किसी कम्पटीशन में नहीं आया। घर का क्या माहौल था ?

जब नूरजहाँ ने जाड़ों की दोपहर की नर्म धूप में अपना गेट खोला तो उसे अन्दर से तैरती आती मुन्ना की स्निग्ध खिलखिलाहट सुनाई दी। उसने घड़ी देखी : डेढ़ बजा था। यह उसके कॉलेज से लौटने का वक़्त नहीं था। वह घर में कैसे था ? और ऐसे क्यों हँस रहा था ? वह बेआवाज़ अन्दर घुसी। रतन का कमरा खुला था। मेज़ पर दो बीयर के गिलास रखे थे जिन पर झाग उठ रहा था। झाग के पीछे आमने-सामने रतन और मुन्ना विराजे थे। रतन मुस्करा रहा था, मुन्ना हँसे जा रहा था। नूरजहाँ मूर्तिवत् खड़ी रह गई। फिर उसने धूप का चश्मा उतारकर दृश्य देखा जैसे चश्मा उतार देने से दृश्य बदल जाएगा। काला चश्मा कोई जादू नहीं था। उसका पूरा चेहरा लाल था।

एकाएक नूरजहाँ पेट से चीख़ी, 'मुन्ना ऽ ऽ !'

फिर वह फ़र्श पर ढह गई गोया किसी विस्फोट से कोई इमारत गिरी हो।

कुछ क्षण बाद उठकर उसने ख़ुद ही बताया कि मुझे चक्कर आ गया था

और वह रोते हुए मुन्ना से लिपट गई। रतन अपनी मोटरसाइकिल स्टार्ट करके बिना कुछ कहे बाहर चला गया।

घर में नूर का रोना बचा।

धूप चली गई। साए ग़ायब हो गए। रोशनी पहले साँवली हुई, फिर काली हो गई जैसे जल गई हो। घरों में घबराकर बत्तियाँ जलने लगीं। सड़कों पर अँधेरा बरकरार रहा। बिजली के खम्भे नहीं जले। रतन नहीं लौटा। नौ-दस बजे उसके लौटने का वक़्त था। कभी-कभी ग्यारह हो जाते थे। बारह हो गए। वह नहीं लौटा। नमन को नींद नहीं आ रही थी। उसने थाने में एफ़.आई.आर. दर्ज कराने की भी सोची थी। उसे किसी दुर्घटना का ख़तरा लगता था। वह दोपहर में बीयर पीकर बिना खाना खाए हीरो होंडा पर धड़धड़ाते हुए घर से निकला था जब नूर चीख़कर बेहोश हुई और फिर होश में आई। मुन्ना ने यह बताया कि छोटे चाचा ने उसे बीयर नहीं दी थी, उसने ही माँगी थी क्योंकि उसने हॉस्टल में कुछ लड़कों को बीयर पीते देखा था। मगर इस बात की सम्भावना थी कि नूर की चीख़ के लिए रतन ने अपने को ही ज़िम्मेदार माना हो। घर से पीकर मोटरसाइकिल पर निकले छोटे भाई की थाने में रपट लिखाने में यह ख़तरा भी था कि उसका ख़तरा और बढ़ जाए। नूर का मत था कि उन्हें कम-से-कम एक रात इन्तज़ार करना चाहिए। जवान आदमी था, पैसा जेब में था, कहीं भी जा सकता था।

सुबह आठ बजे हज़रतगंज थाने से फ़ोन आया। थानेदार ने बताया कि रतन सक्सेना पिछली रात एक चकले के 'रेड' में पकड़ा गया था। थाने में बन्द है। वह कहता है कि वह आपका भाई है। अगर वह आपका भाई है तो उसे आकर छुड़ा ले जाइए। नमन अपनी मारुति में छोटे को छुड़ा लाया। उसने घर के सामने गाड़ी रोकी और छोटे से पहला वाक्य बोला, 'तुम अन्दर जाकर नहाओ-धोओ, खाना खाओ, मैं अभी आता हूँ।' नमन सीधे डॉ. पांडे के घर गए, जो गोमतीनगर में रहते थे। डॉ. पांडे ने लाल बाग़ में नूर मंज़िल फ़ोन किया, फिर दोनों ने चाय पी और नूर मंज़िल गए। नूर मंज़िल में सारा हाल सुनकर डॉ. वाजपेयी ने कहा कि रतन को शाम को ले आइए, उसे शायद दो सप्ताह के लिए यहाँ रखना होगा।

शाम को मारुति में अपने बेग के साथ बैठते हुए रतन ने मुन्ना की ओर मुस्कराते हुए इस तरह हाथ उठाया जैसे वह चाँद पर जा रहा हो। उसने नूर की ओर नहीं देखा और गाड़ी का दरवाज़ा बन्द कर लिया। दूसरी ओर से नमन झट से बैठा और उसने तुरन्त गाड़ी स्टार्ट कर दी।

'छोटे', सड़क पर दौड़ती गाड़ी में सामने देखते हुए नमन ने कहा, 'अपने को सँभालो।'

छोटे कुछ बुदबुदाया। सड़क पर शोर बहुत था।

नूर मंज़िल में डॉ. वाजपेयी ने छोटे की आँखों में देखते हुए कहा, 'नौजवान, क्या तुम अपने को नहीं सँभालना चाहते ?'

'कौन अपने को नहीं सँभालना चाहता, डॉक्टर ?' छोटे कुछ झुँझला गया।

'हम तुम्हारी मदद करेंगे।' डॉक्टर बोला।

कौन किसकी मदद करता है ? रतन के चेहरे पर कुछ ऐसा ही भाव था।

नूर मंज़िल का भवन-समूह शान्त, सौम्य और भव्य था। कमरों में ए.सी. लगे नज़र आते थे जैसे कोई पाँच सितारा अस्पताल हो। सामने पेड़-पौधे और घास करीने से लगे थे। दाहिनी ओर पेड़ छतरी की तरह उगा था जिसके नीचे पत्थर की बेंच थी। रतन यही पत्थर की बेंच देखता अन्दर घुसा था, जहाँ उसकी डॉ. वाजपेयी से बात हुई। फिर वह एक युवा डॉक्टर और नमन के साथ अन्दर एक बरामदे में गया, जिसके दाईं ओर मैदान था और बाईं ओर दरवाज़े थे जो बड़े-बड़े कमरों में खुलते थे। डॉक्टर आख़िरी दरवाज़े में घुसा। उसके पीछे नमन था। तीन आदमियों की यह क़तार एक कोने की ओर बढ़ी जहाँ पलंग ख़ाली था। रतन को वहाँ बिठाकर और तसल्ली देकर पहले डॉक्टर ने पीठ मोड़ी, फिर नमन ने। रतन अपने पलंग पर निपट अकेला था। कौन किसकी मदद करता है ?

उसने अपनी नज़र हर ओर दौड़ाई। कमरा बड़ा था—किसी छोटे हॉल की तरह। उसमें छह पलंग थे। सब पर आदमी बैठे थे। दूसरे सब उसकी जानिब घूर रहे थे। वे देख उसी की तरफ़ रहे थे, लेकिन कहीं और देखते हुए लगते थे जैसे उनकी आँखें केन्द्रित न हों, फिसल-फिसल जाती हों। जैसे रतन सक्सेना कोई फिसल-पट्टी हो जिस पर आँख रखते ही फिसल जाने का डर हो। क्या उसका चेहरा एक ही दिन में ऐसा रपटीला हो गया था ? वह अपना चेहरा देखना चाहता था। उसने हताश कमरे में अपनी नज़र दौड़ाई। कोई आईना नहीं था।

उसे अचानक लगा वह कुछ देर से अपनी पलकें झपकाना भूल गया है। उसने आँखें मूँद लीं। फिर आँखें खोलीं। चारों ओर देखा। एक-एक चेहरे को ढूँढ़ा। एक के बाद एक हर चेहरा रपटीला था। यह दुख नहीं था। यह भूल-भुलैया में खो जाना था। धुँधलके में हाथ-पाँव मारना था। यद्यपि कमरे में उजाले की कमी नहीं थी। वे आँखें फाड़े उसकी ओर देख रहे थे जैसे वह किसी अजायबघर से आया हो। उन्हें पता नहीं था कि वह भी उन्हें ऐसी ही नज़र से देख रहा है।

रतन हैरान था।

यदि वह थाने से छूटा कोई पागल होता तो बड़े की मारुति में घर छोड़े जाने के बाद नहा-धोकर, नाश्ता करके हज़रतगंज क्यों भागता जहाँ उसने अपनी हीरो

होंडा कल दिन में स्टैंड पर पार्क की थी। बीयर की लहर में उसने हज़रतगंज का एक चक्कर लगाया था। गंज में गुनगुनी धूप थी और रंग-बिरंगे कपड़ों से सजी इठलाती लड़कियाँ थीं जैसे सारी धूप उन्हीं के लिए हो। वह कुछ क़दम किसी लड़की के पीछे चलता तो उसे लगता वह धूप में किसी छाया का पीछा कर रहा है, जो सड़क पर उससे दूर भाग रही थी। हज़रतगंज सायों का मेला था जो धूप की कनात के नीचे लगा था। सड़क पर मेले में लड़कियाँ, लड़के, गाड़ियाँ, हनुमानजी और कुछ कुत्ते थे जिन पर बाज़ार छाया हुआ था। जब रतन साहू के सामने पहुँचा तो चिहुँककर अन्दर मुड़ गया और टिकट लेकर हॉल के अँधेरे में दाख़िल हो गया जहाँ पर्दे पर आमिर की छाया अपनी प्रेमिका की छाया के पीछे भाग रही थी।

आमिर को उसकी महबूबा दिलाकर रतन जब बाहर आया तो धूप अपने सायों को समेटकर जा चुकी थी। हज़रतगंज में अँधेरा उतर रहा था और बाज़ार की रोशनियाँ चौंक-चौंककर जल रही थीं। वह हनुमान मन्दिर की ओर बढ़ा। सामने से मोहन अपनी चोंच-दाढ़ी हिलाता हुआ आ रहा था। उसी ने पहले रतन को देखा और गले लगाकर कहा, 'यार, सर्दी बहुत है, चलो बार चलते हैं।' रतन इस वक़्त कहीं भी जा सकता था। साहू से अँधेरे में निकलकर उसे लगा था कि उसके पास लौटने को घर नहीं है। लोग शहर की सड़कों पर इसीलिए दिन-भर घूमते थे कि उनके पास लौटने को घर था।

रतन को मोहन की गाड़ी में क्लार्क्स के बार में घुसना याद था। जब वे अन्दर घुसे तो अँधेरा था और जब वे बाहर निकले तो अँधेरा था। मोहन ने उसे साहू के सामने छोड़ा था जहाँ उसकी हीरो होंडा पार्किंग में थी। वह उसी ओर बढ़ रहा था जब अचानक आख़िरी शो ख़त्म हुआ और लोग बाहर आने लगे। लोगों के आगे एक लड़की थी। वह आमिर ख़ान की प्रेमिका का लिबास पहने थी। जब वह कुछ और नज़दीक आई तो रतन को लगा कि वह पर्दे की नायिका ही थी जो शो ख़त्म होने पर बाहर निकल आई थी। वह दाहिनी ओर मुड़ गई जहाँ से रतन आ रहा था। उसका शरीर स्वायत्त हो गया और वह पलटकर लड़की के पीछे चलने लगा। उसके पैर सीधे नहीं पड़ रहे थे। गंज में अँधेरा था, सड़क ख़ाली थी—जिसके दोनों ओर कुछ रोशनियाँ थीं। आकाश में तारे निकल आए थे।

किसी ने उसके कन्धों पर हाथ रखा और पूछा—'पाँच सौ रुपए हैं ?' 'हाँ', रतन ने कहा। तभी वह लड़की पीछे मुड़ी और सड़क पर एक तिपहिया रुका। उस आदमी ने रतन को तिपहिए में बिठाया और ख़ुद भी बैठ गया। दूसरी ओर

से वही लड़की आकर बैठ गई थी। उसका गुदाज़ नितम्ब रतन के नितम्ब को दबा रहा था।

'खाना !'

अस्पताल का कर्मचारी थाली लिये खड़ा था। उसने एक छोटी टेबल रतन के सामने रख दी और टेबल पर खाना रख दिया। वह अंतिम था। कमरे के सारे पलंगों के सामने थालियाँ रख दी गई थीं। वे एक-साथ खाने लगे जैसे हर पलंग पर एक ही आदमी खा रहा हो। फिर उसने बाथरूम में जाकर हाथ धोए, पेशाब किया और आईने के सामने खड़ा हो गया। वह पहली नज़र में अपने को पहचान नहीं सका। फिर उसने धीरे-धीरे अपने को पहचाना जैसे कोई पुराना दोस्त बहुत दिनों बाद मिला हो। यह शायद दवाओं का असर था या शायद बहुत रातों के बाद यह ऐसी रात थी जब उसने शराब नहीं पी थी। बाल उलझे थे। दाढ़ी बढ़ी थी। आँखें ख़ाली थीं। इतनी ख़ाली आँखें उसने कभी नहीं देखी थीं। जैसे घर के सब दरवाज़े बन्द हों। अन्दर सिर्फ़ एक चीख़ थी।

चीख़ सुनाई नहीं दी। उसने बहुत कोशिश की। कान खड़े थे। कानों में किवाड़ पर दस्तक हुई। यह किवाड़ अन्दर नहीं था। बाहर था। बाथरूम के बाहर। फिर लगातार किवाड़ पर घूँसे पड़ने लगे। रतन ने घबराकर दरवाज़ा खोल दिया।

'क्या कर रहे थे ?' कोई चीख़ा।

'अपना चेहरा ढूँढ़ रहा था', रतन के मुँह से निकला।

'मिल गया ?'

'नहीं।'

'जिसके पास चेहरा होता है, वह यहाँ नहीं आता।'

वह काला आदमी जिसका सामने का दाँत टूटा था, हँसा। फिर रतन को एक ओर ठेलते हुए वह तेज़ी से अन्दर घुस गया। रतन वापस अपने बिस्तर पर लौट आया। वापस लौटकर उसने हॉल के बाक़ी आदमियों की ओर देखा, जो उसी की जानिब देख रहे थे। इस देखने और न देखने में कोई फ़र्क नहीं था। तभी बाथरूम के दरवाज़े के खुलने और बन्द होने की आवाज़ आई और काला आदमी बाहर आया। काले आदमी के बाल भी काले थे। बाल खड़े थे। उसके नथुने फड़फड़ा रहे थे। वह रतन को घूरते हुए अपने बिस्तर की ओर गया।

यह अजीब इत्तफ़ाक था कि अगली सुबह जब वह बाथरूम में नहा रहा था तो तीन बार दरवाज़े पर दस्तक हुई और दरवाज़ा खुलने पर काला आदमी ही मुस्कराता नज़र आया जिसका एक दाँत टूटा था। फिर ऐसी आँख-मिचौनी शुरू

हुई कि जब वह किसी पत्रिका से नज़रें उठाता या दूध का गिलास मेज़ पर वापस रखता तो उसे ही अपनी तरफ़ ताकते हुए पाता। टी.वी. देखते हुए वह बग़ल में बैठा मिलता। ताश या कैरम खेलते हुए वह उसका पार्टनर हो जाता। प्रार्थना के समय भी वह उसकी बग़ल में या पीछे होता। तब रतन अपनी प्रार्थना में एक प्रार्थना और जोड़ता कि हे ईश्वर, मुझे इस आदमी से बचाओ !

शाम को मैदान में बैडमिंटन खेलते हुए रतन देखता कि वह आदमी सामने नेट के दूसरी ओर है या उसकी बग़ल में उसका डबल्स का पार्टनर। नूर मंज़िल में अपना पार्टनर चुनने की आज़ादी नहीं थी। जो कोर्ट में हो उसी के साथ खेलना था। पहली ही शाम मुन्ना ने उसे मुस्कराते हुए अपने पार्टनर के लिए बधाई दी थी।

'उसके खेल के लिए ?' रतन ने पूछा।

'खेल और टूटे दाँत, दोनों के लिए', मुन्ना हँसा।

वह नमन और नूर के साथ उससे मिलने आया था। वह पहली शाम आया। फिर नहीं आया। नूर ने पहले कहा कि उसकी तबियत ठीक नहीं, फिर कहा कि उसके इम्तिहान सिर पर हैं, वह पढ़ रहा है। बेशक नूर और नमन हर शाम आते और उससे कहते कि तुम आज कल से बेहतर लग रहे हो। डॉक्टर भी हर सुबह यही कहता था। रतन को कोई फ़र्क महसूस नहीं होता था। फ़र्क सिर्फ़ सुबह, दोपहर, शाम और रात का था, जो रोज़ दुहराए जाते थे। उसने अपनी कलाई की घड़ी उतारकर तकिए के नीचे रख दी। उसे पता नहीं चला। उसने अस्पताल में लगी घड़ियों की ओर देखना भी छोड़ दिया था जैसे घड़ी न हो, दीवार का ही हिस्सा हो। जैसे वह उस समय में पहुँच गया हो जब समय घड़ी में क़ैद नहीं था—बल्कि अँधेरे-उजाले में फैला था।

थोड़ा उजाला कम होता तो काले आदमी की आँखें गोल-गोल उल्लू की आँखों जैसी लगतीं। वे कुछ ज़्यादा चमकने लगतीं जैसे पूरा अँधेरा हो। वह मुँह खोलता तो उसके दाँत भालू के दाँत हो जाते—एक दाँत टूटे होने के बावजूद। आख़िरी रात रतन यही सोचता हुआ सोया था। कमरे में उस रात कोई तीसरा नहीं था। आधी रात उसे लगा कि कोई उसकी पीठ पर सवार है और हाँफ रहा है। उसके नथुनों में तम्बाकू की वही गन्ध भर गई जो काले आदमी के आस-पास होने पर उसे महसूस होती थी। गन्ध के साथ चीख़ भी शरीर में गूँजी जैसे वह पहली शाम की तरह आईने के सामने खड़ा हो।

रतन कभी नहीं जानेगा कि यह सपना था या सपना नहीं था। वह चीख़ उसके गले से बाहर ज़रूर आई थी। उसके बाद नर्स का उसे पकड़ना और डॉक्टर द्वारा इंजेक्शन दिया जाना याद रहेगा।

तीन

3.1

रतन दो साल पहले लखनऊ से लौटा था। दो साल बाद मुम्बई जा रहा था।

उसे फिर झाँसी छोड़कर जाना होगा, यह बाँके बिहारी ने नहीं सोचा था। पिछले वर्ष सरस्वती पाठशाला की नौकरी छूट जाने के बाद रतन ने फिर पीना शुरू कर दिया था। एक-डेढ़ साल उसका शराब को हाथ न लगाना एक चमत्कार था। बल्कि इस दौरान उसने खंडेराव गेट के बाहर एक जिम में जाना शुरू कर दिया था। जब उसने जिम में जाना शुरू किया तो बाँके बिहारी ने कहा कुछ नहीं, वे मन-ही-मन हँसे थे। वे हँसे इसलिए थे कि खंडेराव गेट के बाहर दूसरी सड़क पर ही व्यायामशाला थी जिसमें वे अपनी किशोर उम्र में जाते थे। व्यायामशाला में भी हाथ-पैर की कसरत होती थी और दम फूलता था। यही जिम में होता था। जिम में आधुनिक पश्चिमी तकनीक थी और उसमें फ़ीस लगती थी। शहर के अमीर लड़कों में इसका रिवाज़ था। चूँकि पैसे रतन की अपनी कमाई के थे, इसलिए कुछ कहने की ज़रूरत नहीं थी। रतन की अनुपस्थिति में बाँके बिहारी जब पहली बार इस बार अटारी में घुसे तो वे आमिर और अम्बानी की तस्वीरें देखकर भी चौंके थे।

नौकरी छूट गई। जिम नहीं छूटा। शराब फिर शुरू हो गई। पहले पता नहीं चला। फिर एक रात जब बाँके बिहारी ने दरवाज़ा खोला और रतन पौर में अन्दर घुसा तो एक तीखी गन्ध के साथ घुसा जो देर रात तक बाँके बिहारी के नथुनों में अटकी रही। कहने को तो उसने जीवन बीमा का काम फिर शुरू कर दिया था। लेकिन सचमुच कितना काम करता था, यह वही जानता था। या शायद वह भी नहीं जानता था। यदि वह जानता होता तो उसे रोज़ शराब पीना क्यों ज़रूरी होता, जिसके लिए पिछले माह उसने अपनी माँ की सोने की अँगूठी चुराई थी। गायत्री को अपनी अँगूठी खोने का इतना दुख नहीं था जितना इस बात का कि उसका बेटा अपने ही घर में चोरी करे ! इसका मतलब अब यह उसका घर नहीं था। वह पराया था। घर में घर का बेटा पराया हो गया था। मेडिकल कॉलेज

के डॉ. चौधरी ने सलाह दी थी कि यदि सम्भव हो तो रतन का माहौल बदल देना चाहिए। इसीलिए वह मुम्बई जा रहा था।

ट्रेन एक घंटे लेट थी।

वे दोनों प्लेटफ़ॉर्म की एक बेंच पर बैठे थे। ऊपर छाया थी। पटरियों पर और पटरियों के परे शुरू मार्च की धूप फैली थी। बाँके बिहारी पचहत्तर पार कर चुके थे। लेकिन अभी भी उन्हें इस धूप में पेड़ से झरती पत्तियों और परीक्षाओं की गन्ध आती थी जैसे घर के आँगन का पेड़ हर साल उनकी परीक्षा लेता हो। यह धूप अजीब थी जो कभी ठंडी लगती, कभी गर्म।

'चाय', चायवाला सामने खड़ा था।

दोनों ने एक-एक कप लिया और सुड़कने लगे।

रतन की आँखें चाय के कप पर थीं। बाँके बिहारी अपनी सफ़ेद दाढ़ी हिलाते हुए इधर-उधर देख रहे थे। बेंच के सामने आधे प्लेटफ़ॉर्म पर धूप थी, जिसमें लोग दोनों ओर चल रहे थे। बाँके बिहारी लोगों को देखकर भी नहीं देख रहे थे। उनके दिमाग़ में सोने की अँगूठी चल रही थी। यह सिर्फ़ अँगूठी-चोरी की बात नहीं थी। इसकी तह में रतन का काठ होता दिल था। उसे मालूम था कि उसका पत्रकार पिता पचहत्तर के पार है। उसे मालूम था कि उसकी कोई ख़ास आमदनी नहीं है। उसे मालूम था कि उसे अपने बेटों से पैसा लेना पसन्द नहीं है। उसे मालूम था कि उसकी अपनी उम्र अट्ठाईस है। उसे यह भी मालूम था कि अट्ठाईस वर्ष के पुरुष को सिर्फ़ अपनी ही रोटी नहीं कमानी चाहिए, बल्कि अपने माता-पिता का भी ख़्याल रखना चाहिए। या क्या उसे अब कुछ भी मालूम नहीं था ? क्या उसका दिल काठ हो गया था ? क्या उसने अपनी माँ की अँगूठी शराब के लिए इसलिए चुराई थी कि उसका रोटी-शराब का पारिवारिक बीमा है ? मगर वह बीमार था ! यह बात अलग थी कि कोई भी डॉक्टर यह पक्की तौर पर कहने को तैयार नहीं था कि उसे शिज़ोफ्रेनिया है क्योंकि ऐसा कोई टेस्ट अभी ईजाद नहीं हुआ था। यह मामूली व्यक्तित्व-विपर्यय भी हो सकता था। या सिर्फ़ दारू की लत भी हो सकती थी—जिसके लिए लखनऊ की नूर मंज़िल में उसका इलाज हुआ था। दारू की लत रतन की पीढ़ी में उसी तरह सामान्य थी जैसे बीड़ी-सिगरेट की लत बाँके बिहारी की पीढ़ी में थी। क्या यह एक युवा पीढ़ी का जुनून था ? क्या शराब के लिए माँ की अँगूठी चुराना एक पीढ़ी का मिज़ाज हो सकता था ?

फ़ोन तीनों बेटों के आते थे। अलबत्ता नमन के फ़ोन कुछ कम हो गए थे। वह पैसे भेजने की बात ज़रूर करता था। गायत्री ने पवन को जब यह बताया कि रतन फिर शराब पीने लगा है और डॉक्टर ने उसे हवा बदलने की सलाह दी

है तो पवन ने कहा कि अम्माँ, उसे यहाँ भेज दो। पवन ने बताया कि उसने एक फ़ैक्टरी डाली है, रतन को उसी में लगा लेगा। बाँके बिहारी और गायत्री ने तय किया था कि अँगूठी-चोरी की बात किसी बेटे को नहीं बतानी है। जैसे यह उनकी निजी शर्म थी। जैसे यदि वह बीमार भी था तो उन्हीं की ग़लती थी। आख़िरकार वे माँ-बाप थे। उन्होंने उसे पाल-पोसकर बड़ा किया था।

'रतन', बाँके बिहारी का स्वर धीमा था।

प्लेटफ़ॉर्म पर शोर था। रतन चाय ख़त्म करके सामने देख रहा था। एकटक। उसकी सिर्फ़ आँखें खुली थीं। कान बन्द थे।

'रतन', पिता ने फिर पुकारा।

'हाँ', रतन ने कहा जैसे कहीं से लौटने की थकान हो। मगर उसका स्वर तेज़ था। कुछ खीजा हुआ।

गायत्री ने यह बात पहले पकड़ी थी। रतन अब जल्दी खीज जाता था। बाँके बिहारी का ध्यान कुछ बाद में गया। जब तक उनका ध्यान गया उसकी आवाज़ की तुर्शी कुछ और बढ़ गई थी।

'बेटा', बाँके बिहारी की आवाज़ रुक गई। उसकी जगह प्लेटफ़ॉर्म का शोर आ गया। उन्होंने फिर कहा, 'बेटा, अँगूठी की बात पवन को मत बताना।'

रतन कुछ नहीं बोला। पिता की जानिब देखता रहा।

जब ट्रेन आई और रतन डिब्बे में अपनी बर्थ पर बैठ गया तो बाँके बिहारी 'अपना ख़्याल रखना' कहकर नीचे प्लेटफ़ॉर्म पर आ गए। रतन को उनके पैर छूना याद न रहा। बाँके बिहारी को बेटे का पैर न छूना याद रहा।

रेल का पटरी पर दौड़ता हुआ डिब्बा था। डिब्बे में एक बर्थ के कोने में रतन बैठा था। उसकी एक बाँह खिड़की पर रखी थी। खिड़की की तीन सलाखों के बाहर पेड़, पहाड़ियाँ और बियाबान थे जहाँ धूप फैली थी। जब तक धूप फैली रही, रतन एक ही मुद्रा में बैठा रहा जैसे धूप का एक समय हो जिसमें रतन बैठा हो। खिड़की के इस ओर रतन सीधा बैठा था जैसे किसी निशाने पर बैठा हो। उसके पैर और पीठ सीधे थे। आँखें सामने थीं। कभी वह आँखें बाईं ओर बियाबान में घुमा देता। फिर कुछ देर बाद आँखें अपने आप डिब्बे में लौट आतीं जहाँ ख़ूब चहल-पहल थी। यही क्रम चला जब तक धूप चली जैसे खिड़की पर कोई आदमी नहीं, कोई स्वचालित रोबोट बैठा हो। खिड़की के पार धूप और छाया का हर पल बदलता हुआ संसार था।

उसे लगा, समय खिड़की के बाहर बह रहा है।

वह खिड़की पर बैठा था जैसे किसी ख़ाली नदी के किनारे बैठा हो। जब तक

धूप रही, कोई ख़्याल उसके दिमाग़ में नहीं आया। कुछ रेत-सी दिमाग़ में उड़ती रही। कोई बियाबान छाया रहा। इस बियाबान में सिर्फ़ साए थे, कोई चेहरा नहीं था। रतन का भी चेहरा नहीं था। न आमिर था, न अम्बानी था। दो वर्ष किसी गुफ़ा में गुज़र गए थे, जिसमें कोई रोशनी नहीं थी।

अँधेरे में ऊपर की बर्थ पर लेटे हुए उसने आँखें मूँद लीं। बग़ल के कूपे से एक बच्चे के रोने की आवाज़ आई। जिस तरह वह अचानक रोया था, उसी तरह अचानक चुप हो गया। रतन को लगा यह वही शिशु है जो कभी-कभी उसके भीतर एकाएक रोने लगता था। जब वह चुप हो गया तो आहिस्ता-आहिस्ता एक चेहरा अँधेरे में उभरा। कोई शक नहीं था। यह सपना थी। सरस्वती पाठशाला में रोज़-रोज़ पढ़ाते हुए वह शायद उसे भूल गया था। वह जब बी.एड. का सत्र ख़त्म करके लौटी तो रतन की नौकरी फिर छूट गई थी। वह उस शाम जीवन साह के चौराहे पर टैम्पो के इन्तज़ार में खड़ी थी जब रतन हीरो होंडा पर आया और उसके सामने रुक गया। जो चेहरा उसकी ओर पलटा, वह अब अँधेरे में उसके सामने था। वह मुस्कराई थी। जब रतन ने उसे पीछे बैठने को कहा तो उसने कहा कि मैं कभी मोटरसाइकिल पर नहीं बैठी। पीछे बैठकर उसने रतन की कमीज़ एक बच्चे की तरह पकड़ी। फिर बाँह रतन की कमर में डाल दी। और उससे लिपट गई। रतन ने गाड़ी की गति बढ़ा दी थी। धूप अभी-अभी गई थी। सड़क पर ख़ूब उजाला था। दोनों ओर रेत और पत्थर थे। दाईं ओर कुछ ऊबड़-खाबड़ और गहरी घाटी थी, जिसके परे तालाब था जो अभी अदृश्य था—बाक़ी दुनिया की तरह। जब रतन ने एकाएक गाड़ी रोकी, सपना उससे चिपक गई। उसे अपनी पीठ पर सपना के वक्ष का दबाव महसूस हुआ था, रतन को अँधेरे में याद आया।

वे एक गर्म चट्टान पर एक-दूसरे की ओर देखते हुए बैठे थे। चारों ओर हवा कुछ गर्म थी। क़िला पीछे पहाड़ी पर गुमसुम बैठा था जैसे धूप की याद में खो गया हो।

गर्म चट्टान पर सपना से क्या बातें हुईं, यह रतन को याद नहीं था। यह याद था कि कुछ दिनों बाद सपना बालिका महाविद्यालय में नौकरी करने लगी थी। रतन बेकार था। सपना को उम्दा नौकरी मिलना ख़ुशी की बात थी। इस ख़ुशी का उत्सव ज़रूरी था। पैसे नहीं थे। मगर ख़ुशी का एकल समारोह बहुत ज़रूरी था। अम्माँ की अँगूठी काम आई। वह चोरी नहीं थी। घर की एक चीज़ का घर के लिए इस्तेमाल था। क्या रतन घर का बेटा नहीं था ? क्या रतन अम्माँ का बेटा नहीं था जैसे अँगूठी अम्माँ का ज़ेवर थी ?

रतन की कुछ समझ में नहीं आया जब सोने के एक टुकड़े का मूल्य बेटे

से ज़्यादा आँका गया। उसने अम्माँ से पूछा। अम्माँ पहले हँसीं, फिर चुप हो गईं। आहिस्ता-आहिस्ता उनकी आँखों से आँसू बहने लगे...जैसे कोई मर गया हो। कौन मरा ?

सपना, बताओ, कौन मरा ?

'आदमी !'

दादर के प्लेटफ़ॉर्म पर उतरकर रतन फुसफुसाया। प्लेटफ़ॉर्म पर आदमी ही आदमी थे। आदमियों के परे ख़ाली रेलवे लाइन थी। रेलवे लाइन के दूसरी ओर रतन को आदमी अलग-अलग नज़र नहीं आए। ऐसा लगा कि पूरे प्लेटफ़ॉर्म पर एक सिरे से दूसरे सिरे तक एक ही आदमी खड़ा है जिसके हज़ारों सिर और दुगुने पैर हैं। रतन ने ऐसा आदमी अभी तक नहीं देखा था।

'आदमी !' वह चीख़ा।

'क्या हुआ ?' पवन ने उसकी ओर नज़र घुमाई।

जब रतन ने उसकी ओर देखा तो कोई उसके पीछे उससे टकरा गया। फिर उसने रतन को आगे की ओर ठेला। रतन ने आँखें फिर सामने मोड़ीं और आगे चलने लगा। पवन का सवाल हवा में टँगा रहा, क्या हुआ ?

भीड़ सिर्फ़ प्लेटफ़ॉर्म पर ही नहीं थी। जब वे स्टेशन से बाहर आए तो चारों ओर भीड़ थी जैसे मुम्बई भीड़ में रहती हो। सामने चौराहे पर भीड़ थी, सड़कों पर भीड़ थी, स्टेशन के बाहर भीड़ थी जैसे स्टेशन के अन्दर भीड़ थी। लोग हुजूमों में जी रहे थे और जुलूसों में चल रहे थे जैसे चीटियाँ हों।

'आदमी !' रतन ने फिर कहा जैसे वह कुछ ढूँढ़ रहा हो।

किसी ने कुछ नहीं सुना। धूप और हवा में आदमियों का शोर था। यह कुछ अजीब कोलाहल था जिसमें आदमी की आवाज़ें मोटरों और बसों की चीख़ों में समा रही थीं जैसे वे उन्हीं की आवाज़ें हों। सामने एक इमारत की मुँडेरों पर कबूतरों की बस्ती थी। मगर हवा में कबूतरों की भी कोई आवाज़ नहीं थी। वे धूप में ख़ाली चोंचें खोल रहे थे जैसे अपनी गुटुरगूँ ढूँढ़ रहे हों।

'आदमी', आवाज़ धीमी थी जैसे कोई फुसफुसा रहा हो।

गाड़ी चलाते पवन ने कुछ नहीं कहा। केवल बग़ल में बैठे छोटे को क्षण-भर ग़ौर से देखा। फिर वह सामने देखने लगा।

'सफ़र कैसा रहा ?' पवन ने पूछा।

'ठीक।'

छोटे को पवन फिर बड़े के विलोम लगे। बड़े की भरी-पूरी दाढ़ी थी और सिर के बाल भी छोटे नहीं थे। पवन का चेहरा और सिर सफ़ाचट थे। दाढ़ी और बालों

में नज़र उलझती थी। सफ़ाचट चेहरे पर फिसल जाती थी जैसे कोई ढलान हो। जब पवन पिछले साल झाँसी आए थे तो उनका सिर नहीं घुटा था। तब वे मुम्बई में डिप्टी कमिश्नर, आयकर थे। अब उन्होंने नौकरी छोड़ दी थी और कुछ व्यवसाय शुरू किया था। रतन ने यही सुना था। उसने यह भी सुना था कि पवन ने एक करोड़ रिश्वत लेकर नौकरी छोड़ दी है। यही पैसा उसका स्वदेशी पूँजी-निवेश था, जो उद्योग का आधार था। बहरहाल, ये शहर की अफ़वाहें थीं, जिनका उत्स पत्रकार बाँके बिहारी के सफल पुत्रों के लिए ईर्ष्या हो सकती थी। लोगों को जलन इसलिए भी थी कि एक क़स्बाई पत्रकार के बेटे इतने लायक निकले थे जबकि पत्रकार जीवन-भर शहर में चप्पल चटकाता घूमता रहा। न उसने कभी अपने किसी पुत्र के लिए कोई सिफ़ारिश ढूँढ़ी, न कोई जुगाड़ भिड़ाई—बल्कि शहर के बाहर कोई आर्थिक सहायता भी नहीं दी। बाँके बिहारी का कहना था कि प्राणी-जगत् में मनुष्य ही इतना अहमक है कि बच्चों के वयस्क होने पर भी वह उनकी टाँगों के नीचे सीढ़ी लगाता घूमता है। बेटों ने ही घर की दीवारों की तरह एक-दूसरे को सहारा दिया था।

रतन जानता था कि पवन भैया की पूँजी का स्रोत उनकी ससुराल भी हो सकती थी—जिनका कानपुर में एक कारख़ाना था। जब उसने एक-दो बार यह बात शहर की अफ़वाहों के जवाब में कही तो लोग मुस्कराने लगे। रतन चुप हो गया जैसे वह अभी चुप था जब पवन भैया बग़ल में बैठे मुम्बई की सड़कों पर अपनी शानदार गाड़ी चला रहे थे। उन्होंने खिड़कियों के काँच बन्द करके ए.सी. चला दिया था। गाड़ी के अन्दर अनुपम ठंडक थी जैसे काश्मीर की वादियों की हवाएँ बह रही हों। अलबत्ता बाहर सड़क पर गर्म धूप में लिपटी गाड़ियाँ थीं और सड़क के दोनों ओर हाहाकार करता शहर था : कहीं बदरंग झोपड़पट्टियाँ थीं, कहीं अधनंगे लोग थे, कहीं भूख हाथ पसारे खड़ी थी।

विशाल द्वार पर व्हिस्परिंग पाम्स, लोखंडवाला का बोर्ड था और द्वार के पार इक्के-दुक्के लोग थे जैसे भीड़ के जहन्नुम के बीच आदमी की जन्नत की तामीर हुई हो। सामने ही आकाश को छूती इमारत शुरू होती थी, जिसमें फ़्लैटों की खिड़कियाँ नज़र आती थीं। बाईं ओर एक विशाल पार्क था, जिसके बीच बनी झील अभी नज़रों से ओझल थी। गाड़ी नीचे रुकने की बजाय इमारत की चढ़ाई पर बनी सड़क पर ऊपर चढ़ने लगी। रतन ने आँखें फाड़कर पूछा—'क्या गाड़ी घर के दरवाज़े पर ही रुकेगी ?'

'नहीं', पवन हँसा, 'पहली तीन मंज़िलें गाड़ियों के लिए हैं, बाक़ी पच्चीस आदमियों के लिए।'

रतन मुम्बई में पहली बार खिलखिलाया, 'वाह, इस इमारत में आदमी और गाड़ियाँ एक-साथ रहती हैं।'

'हाँ', पवन मुस्कराता रहा।

गाड़ी चक्कर खाती हुई तीसरी मंज़िल पर रुकी। सामने दीवार थी। दोनों दाएँ-बाएँ बाहर आए। बाहर पेड़ों के सिरे और आकाश नज़र आते थे। मुम्बई के पेड़ ज़्यादा हरे और आसमान ज़्यादा गहरा था। बाईसवीं मंज़िल पर फ़्लैट का दरवाज़ा खोलते ही सामने काँच की दीवार के दूसरी ओर दूर पहाड़ी नज़र आई। रतन खिड़की की ओर खिंचता चला गया। दूर पहाड़ी की कमर तक झोपड़पट्टियों की छतें नज़र आती थीं। झोपड़पट्टियाँ धूप में चमक रही थीं। नीचे बस्ती थी जो पहाड़ी तक फैली थी। ऐसा लगता था जैसे झोपड़पट्टियाँ ज़मीन ढूँढ़ती हुई पहाड़ी पर चढ़ गई हों।

'रतन', पवन ने पुकारा।

'हाँ।'

वह दीवार से लौट आया। पवन उसे गलियारे में पहले कमरे में ले गया और बोला, 'यह तुम्हारा कमरा है। तुम नहा-धोकर फ़्रिज से खाना लेकर खा लेना। आज तुम आराम करो। मैं काम से जा रहा हूँ। शाम को आऊँगा। किशोरी तीन-चार बजे तक आ जाएगी।' जब पवन बाहर गया तो दरवाज़ा बन्द करके उसने टेबल पर एक चिट देखी, जिस पर नीचे किशोरी लिखा था और लिखा था कि मैं 'किटी' में जा रही हूँ। जैसे ही नज़र पलटी, उसकी नज़र दीवार पर टँगी एक तस्वीर पर पड़ी। वह ठगा-सा खड़ा रह गया। वह किसी स्त्री के गोरे पैरों—केवल पैरों—की तस्वीर थी जिसमें दोनों पैरों में सोने की पायलें पड़ी थीं और अँगूठों में सोने के बिछुए थे। तस्वीर में और कुछ नहीं था। केवल पैर थे और पैरों में सोने के दमकते हुए आभूषण थे। ये किसके पैर थे ? क्या ये किशोरी भाभी के पैर थे ? न ये पत्थर के पैर थे, न पीतल के पैर थे। ये किसके ज़िन्दा पैर थे ?

उसने ऐसी तस्वीर कभी नहीं देखी थी।

जब घंटी बजी, तो रतन हड़बड़ाकर उठा। वह तुरन्त अपनी चप्पलें घसीटता हुआ हॉल में आया और उसने लैच खोला। दरवाज़ा खोलने पर उसने देखा कि भाभी सामने खड़ी थीं। वे अन्दर आईं। रतन नीचे उनके पैरों की ओर देख रहा था। वे रतन का चेहरा देख रही थीं।

'सो रहे थे', वे मुस्कराईं, 'खाना खा लिया ?'

'जी', उसने आँखें एक क्षण को ऊपर उठाईं और फिर नीचे देखने लगा।

'क्या देख रहे हो ?'

'आपके पैर।'

'क्यों ?' वे हँसीं।

'मैं आपके पैर मिला रहा हूँ।'

'किससे ?'

'उस तस्वीर से', रतन ने तस्वीर की ओर इंगित किया।

किशोरी खिलखिलाई।

'वे मेरे पैर नहीं हैं', उसने कहा।

'फिर किसके पैर हैं, भाभी ?' रतन की भँवें ऊपर उठ गईं।

'ये कौशल्या मैया के चरण हैं', किशोरी का चेहरा गम्भीर था।

रतन ने आँखें फाड़ीं, 'मैया कौन ?'

'ओह', किशोरी ने रतन को ऐसी नज़र से देखा जैसे वह बच्चा हो, 'मैया मेरी गुरु-मैया हैं। इन्हें सब लोग कौशल्या मैया कहते हैं। इनका असली नाम श्रीमती कौशल्या वर्मा है। इनके पति आई.ए.एस. हैं।'

रतन ने फिर चरणों के चित्र को देखा : वे युवा चरण लगते थे। उसने जिज्ञासा की : 'भाभी, क्या मैया जवान हैं ?'

'मैया बूढ़ी नहीं हैं', किशोरी ने कहा, 'यह तस्वीर कुछ पुरानी है।'

तभी फ़ोन की घंटी बजी। रिसीवर उठाकर किशोरी ने कहा, 'जय कौशल्या मैया।' फिर उसकी फ़ोन पर सहेली से बात शुरू हुई, जो चलती रही। रतन की आँखों में नींद थी। उसके पैर अपने कमरे की ओर बढ़े। वह लेटकर फिर सो गया।

उस शाम पवन भैया के आने के पहले किशोरी भाभी ने उसे बताया कि भैया के नौकरी के संकट की वजह से वह मैया की शरण में गई थी। संकटमोचन हुआ। राज़ी-ख़ुशी नौकरी छोड़ी। नए कारख़ाने की शुरुआत हुई। अब तुम भी आ गए हो। नए काम में भैया का हाथ बँटाओ। यह कहकर किशोरी रतन की ओर देखते हुए मुस्कराईं। पवन देर से आए। वे कारख़ाने से सीधे जिम चले गए थे, उन्होंने बताया।

'जिम कहाँ है ?' रतन ने पूछा।

'इस कॉलोनी में भी है', पवन ने कहा। फिर पूछा, 'क्यों ?'

'मैं झाँसी में जाता था।'

'तुम यहाँ भी जा सकते हो', पवन मुस्कराया।

काँच की दीवार पर परदा नहीं था। अँधेरा था। अँधेरे में न पहाड़ी नज़र आती थी, न बस्ती। अलबत्ता कुछ रोशनियाँ ज़रूर थीं जो बस्ती में अपनी जगह

जुगनुओं-सी बैठी थीं। बस्ती की छतों का ऊबड़-खाबड़पन अँधेरे में छिप गया था। केवल नीचे घाटी में बैठे चमकीले जुगनू बचे थे। हाथ में शराब का गिलास लिए पवन ने रतन से कहा कि तुम बिलकुल ठीक हो, मेरा मन कहता है। दो-एक दिन में मुम्बई के चोटी के विशेषज्ञ डॉ. मुखर्जी से एप्वाइंटमेंट लेता हूँ। उनसे सलाह लेकर मैं तुम्हें अपने साथ रोज़ फ़ैक्टरी ले जाऊँगा। तुम काम में मेरी मदद करना। चाहो तो दो-चार दिन मुम्बई घूम लो।

पवन बगुले-सी सफ़ेद निकर और टी-शर्ट पहने था। उसके चेहरे पर बालों का नमूना सिर्फ़ भौंहें थीं। भौंहों के ऊपर गोल खोपड़ी थी जो घूमती हुई लगती थी। उसके आने और जाने में कोई फ़र्क नहीं था। पता ही नहीं चलता था कि वह आ रहा है या जा रहा है।

रतन अँधेरे काँच के पास खड़ा कभी नीचे बस्ती को देखता, कभी पवन की खल्वाट खोपड़ी को।

3.2

अजीब शहर है !

समुद्र में सोना बरस रहा है और लोग उसकी तरफ़ पीठ किए बैठे हैं—रतन ने लोगों के सामने खड़े हुए सोचा। वह गेटवे ऑफ़ इंडिया पर खड़ा था, जहाँ उसे अभी पवन ने छोड़ा था। पवन को ताज होटल में किसी से मिलना था, उसने कहा था, उसे देर हो जाएगी। उसने रतन को पचास का एक नोट देकर लौटने का रास्ता बता दिया था। उसने कहा था कि तुम पहली बार मुम्बई आए हो, तुम्हें अपने-आप शहर देखना चाहिए।

उसके सामने रेलिंग से सटी बेंचों पर कुछ बुज़ुर्ग पारसी जोड़े और कुछ थके हुए पर्यटक बैठे थे। उनकी पीठ समुद्र की ओर थी और चेहरे शहर की भीड़ की ओर—जो फ़व्वारे, गाड़ियों और सड़कों के इर्द-गिर्द फैली थी। रेलिंग के परे समुद्र था जिसकी सोचती सतह पर डूबता हुआ सूर्य सोने की खेती कर रहा था। पानी पर सूर्य की सुनहरी किरणें काँपतीं जैसे खेत में सोने की बालियाँ झूम रही हों। समुद्र पश्चिम दिशा में फैलता गया था जहाँ से अंग्रेज़ भारत में आए थे और सोना लेकर लौट गए थे।

नीचे समुद्र में किनारे पर कुछ नावें लंगर डाले खड़ी थीं। उधर सीढ़ियों के नीचे भी कुछ फ़ेरी थीं जो एलीफ़ेंटा से लौटी थीं और कल सुबह जिन्हें फिर एलीफ़ेंटा जाना था। समुद्र के भीतर कुछ दूरी पर प्रकाश-स्तम्भ था। सोना उसके

चारों ओर भी चमक रहा था। समुद्र की सतह पर सोना जगमगा रहा था और लोग थके हुए शहर की भीड़ देख रहे थे। फ़व्वारे के इर्द-गिर्द ज़रूर कुछ चमकते हुए चेहरे थे जो अभी वातानुकूलित गाड़ियों से निकले थे और फिर उन्हीं गाड़ियों में लौट जाएँगे : ये चेहरे सोने के चेहरे लगते थे। इन्हें घेरे हुए लोगों का सैलाब था जो मांस और हड्डियों के साँचे में ढला था।

एकाएक समुद्र से सोना गायब हो गया। सूर्य समुद्र की पश्चिमी ढलान पर अचानक लुढ़क गया था। वह सोने का जाल लपेट ले गया था। आसमान का पश्चिमी कोना समुद्र की तरह सूना था। कोई स्लेटी रंग समुद्र और आकाश पर छाने लगा था जैसे कोई अँधेरे को हवा में घोल रहा हो।

अँधेरे में धरती की रोशनियाँ जगमगाने लगी थीं। गेटवे ऑफ़ इंडिया की इबारत को पढ़ा जा सकता था। काला समुद्र उसके परे था। इस ओर फ़व्वारे में उछलता हुआ पानी उजला था, लेकिन उसमें सोना नहीं था। उसके इर्द-गिर्द चेहरों पर उसी पानी की रोशनी थी। सड़क पर कुछ दूर ताज इंटरकांटीनेंटल की रोशनियाँ जल गई थीं गोया अँधेरे में कोई अलग नगरी हो जो आसमान में उठ रही हो।

समुद्र अँधेरा था। जंगल की तरह। ख़ौफ़नाक। क्षितिज भी खो गया था। ऐसा लगता था जैसे समुद्र ही पलटकर ऊपर तन गया है। आसमान में तारे नहीं थे। समुद्र पर प्रकाश-स्तम्भ की रोशनी टिमटिमा रही थी जैसे जंगल में किसी बुढ़िया की झोपड़ी में दीया जल रहा हो। अभी कोई डाकू आएगा और उसे मारकर चला जाएगा ! रतन ने अपना सिर झकझोरा, जिसमें फिर ऊलजलूल ख़्याल आने लगे थे। वह भव्य द्वार को पार कर सीढ़ियाँ उतरने लगा जो समुद्र में प्रवेश करती थीं जैसे अंग्रेज़ समुद्र पर पैदल आए हों और सीढ़ियों पर चढ़कर अपने देश में घुसे हों। किनारे से कुछ दूर समुद्र में दो जहाज़ थे जिनकी रोशनियाँ दिपू-दिपू कर रहीं थीं। जहाज़ों के परे अँधेरा था।

रतन आख़िरी सीढ़ी पर खड़ा हो गया। सीढ़ियाँ अन्दर समुद्र में चली गई थीं। लहरें सीढ़ियों से टकरा रही थीं। ऊपर खड़े हुए उनकी बेचैनी दिखाई नहीं देती थी। वे सीढ़ियों तक छटपटाती हुई आतीं और आखिरी सीढ़ी पर अपना सिर पटक देतीं। उनकी चीख़ आसमान में गूँजती। सीढ़ियों के ऊपर भव्य द्वार की कुछ रोशनी सीढ़ियों तक अँधेरे में छनती हुई आ रही थी। अन्तिम सीढ़ी पर लहरों का फेन चमकता जैसे उनके दाँत हों।

जब एक लहर उसके जूतों को भिगो गई तो वह पीछे मुड़ गया। वह सीढ़ियाँ चढ़ने लगा जैसे समुद्र से ख़ाली हाथ लौट रहा हो। उसने ऊपर भव्य द्वार में एक

हारे राजकुमार की तरह प्रवेश किया। दूसरी ओर वह जगमग रोशनी में बाहर आया जहाँ महानगर शुरू होता था। वह फ़व्वारे के जल और प्रकाश और लोगों को पार करता हुआ सड़क पर पहुँचा जहाँ साँवली रोशनी थी जो तरल थी। यह रोशनी समुद्र किनारे की ठंडी हवा में घुली थी। वह सड़क देखता हुआ बाईं ओर निकल गया और गलियारे में दूसरे लोगों के साथ चलने लगा। गलियारे में रोशनी कुछ और कम थी। दुकानें बन्द हो गई थीं। लोग समुद्र और दुकानों से लौटकर अपने घर जा रहे थे। मुम्बई में घर शहर से इतनी दूर थे जैसे परदेस हों। लोग घर परदेस की तरह जाते थे और दिन-भर दफ़्तरों या रेलगाड़ियों में रहते थे।

उसने अचानक दाईं ओर देखा : सड़क के बीचोबीच एक घोड़ा टाँग उठाए खड़ा था। घोड़ा एक मंच की ऊँचाई पर था। यह काला घोड़ा था, यह रतन को मालूम नहीं था। लेकिन इससे कोई फ़र्क नहीं पड़ता था। काला घोड़ा अपनी जगह खड़ा था, जिसमें यह धुँधला समय शामिल था। रतन की नज़र काले घोड़े के पुट्ठों से फिसलकर एकाएक सामने धुँधलके में दो सुडौल, जुम्बिश खाते नितम्बों पर पड़ी जो गलियारे में आगे जा रहे थे। लड़की के बाल खुले थे और वह जींस पहने थी। बाल नितम्बों को छूते और छिटक-छिटक जाते। लेकिन पीछे से वे फिर झूमते हुए आगे बढ़ते और जींस को चूमकर फिर दूर भाग जाते। रतन ने हताश अपने साथ चलते लड़के की ओर देखा और कहा :

'क्या तुम जानते हो कि आमिर ख़ान कहाँ रहता है ?'

'नहीं', लड़का मुस्कराया, 'मैं जानता हूँ कि यह लड़की कहाँ रहती है।'

रतन चुप था। सामने देख रहा था।

'माँगता ?' लड़के ने पूछा।

चुप्पी में समुद्री हवा का एक झोंका।

'पाँच सौ रुपए। कमरा तुम्हारा।'

फिर चुप्पी।

लड़का आगे बढ़ गया। लड़की की चाल भी तेज़ हो गई। सड़क से गाड़ियों की सरसराहट और हॉर्न की आवाज़ें आने लगीं। बसों की आवाजें अलग थीं। एक बस गलियारे से लगे स्टॉप पर रुकी और फिर चली। दोनों बार घंटियों की आवाज़ें हुईं। दो लोग उतरे। कोई नहीं चढ़ा। रतन गलियारे में चलता रहा जहाँ धुँधलका था। कभी-कभी उजाला लगता। फिर अँधेरा हो जाता। अँधेरे से फिर परछाइयाँ निकलने लगतीं, परछाइयाँ लम्बी होने लगतीं। इन्हीं परछाइयों में रतन की परछाईं होती, जिसे वह ढूँढ़ता। चौराहे पर रोशनी थी जैसे दिन हो। चारों ओर दौड़ती गाड़ियों को अपनी बत्तियाँ जलाने की ज़रूरत नहीं थी। रतन ने यह पहली

बार देखा। सड़कों पर घने बादलों के दिन की रोशनी थी जैसे शहर के केन्द्र में दिन और रात में कोई फ़र्क न हो। केन्द्र में फ़व्वारा था, जिसकी पतली-पतली धारें रोशनी में चमक रही थीं। गर्मियों के दिन थे। दुकानें बन्द हो गई थीं। समुद्र से दूर चलते हुए बदन में पसीना आ रहा था। इसीलिए फ़व्वारे के चमकते पानी को देखना अच्छा लगता था।

वह बाएँ मुड़ा और फुटपाथ पर चलने लगा जो ऊपर चारों ओर खुला था जहाँ आकाश था। आकाश में कुछ तारे निकल आए थे। फुटपाथ पर लोग थे, चर्चगेट की ओर जाते हुए। वह सीढ़ियों से ज़मीन के भीतर उतरा और प्रकाशमान खोह से होता हुआ ऊपर स्टेशन में पहुँच गया जो ख़ुद एक खोह की तरह था। स्टेशन काफ़ी चौड़ा था और गहमागहमी से भरा था। बाईं ओर टिकटघर के एक क्यू में वह खड़ा हो गया। यह क्यू लखनऊ के क्यू की तरह नहीं था, जो कछुए की चाल चलता और कभी-कभी रुक जाता। यह क्यू हाँफते कुत्ते की तरह चल रहा था।

टिकट लेकर जब रतन प्लेटफ़ॉर्म की ओर बढ़ा तो उसकी नज़र ऊपर गाड़ियों के छूटने के टाइम-टेबल पर पड़ी : नौ तेरह, नौ सत्रह, नौ तेईस ! गाड़ियों के छूटने के समय ऐसे थे जैसे अन्तरिक्ष में उपग्रह छूटने के समय हों। वह प्लेटफ़ॉर्म पर पंखे के नीचे खड़े कुछ लोगों के साथ खड़ा हो गया। उमस से कुछ निजात मिली। बनियान अभी भी जिस्म से चिपकी थी। जब गाड़ी आई और वह पंखे के नीचे खड़े लोगों के साथ एक डिब्बे में घुसकर उनके साथ एक बेंच पर बैठा तो उसे लगा कि बेंच पर बैठे सारे लोग एक ही बनियान के अन्दर बैठे हैं। बेंचों के सामने खड़े हुए लोग ठसाठस भरे थे। उनके हाथ ऊपर कुन्दों में फँसे थे और पैर फ़र्श पर अँधेरे में दूसरे पैरों के साथ खो गए थे। रतन को एकबारगी लगा कि उसके पैर भी इसी हज़ारों पैरों वाले जन्तु के पैरों में फँसे हैं जो हर डिब्बे में एक ही बनियान पहने बैठा है।

गाड़ी चली। मगर हवा नहीं चली। या शायद डिब्बे में हवा के लिए जगह नहीं थी। वह डिब्बे के बाहर तेज़ी से पीछे की ओर चल रही थी। अन्दर से आ रही आवाज़ के लिए जगह की दरकार नहीं थी। किन्तु यह आवाज़ कहाँ से आ रही थी ? चेहरे सन्न थे। मुँह बन्द थे। एकाएक डिब्बे के गलियारे से किसी के गाने की आवाज़ आई : 'चोली के पीछे क्या है...चोली के पीछे ?' यह एक लड़के की आवाज़ थी। रतन ने दाएँ-बाएँ देखा। गर्दन हिलाने की जगह नहीं थी। लेकिन दूसरे चेहरे निस्पन्द थे जैसे वह आवाज़ ट्रेन की ही कोई खटर-पटर हो।

खट-खट...खटर-पटर...

ट्रेन फिर रुकी। कोई स्टेशन था। बेंच से एक आदमी उठकर गया था। उसकी जगह दूसरा उछलकर बैठा था। रतन ने उसी से पूछा—'कौन-सा स्टेशन है ?' 'माटुंगा', उसने कहा। 'कान्दिवली कितनी दूर है ?' रतन ने पूछा। 'अभी दूर है', उसने कहा। गानेवाला लड़का गाते हुए इसी ओर आ गया था। सहसा एक खुली हथेली रतन के सामने फैल गई, जो गा रही थी। रतन ने गाती हुई हथेली पर पचास पैसे रख दिए। हथेली ने सिक्का उसे वापस कर दिया और गाने के बीच में कहा—'एक रुपया।' चोली के पीछे एक रुपया आ गया था। गाती हुई हथेली ग़ायब हुई और फिर रेल की खटर-पटर शुरू हो गई। रेल की खटर-पटर पर तैरती हुई कोई तीखी, कसैली गन्ध डिब्बे में घुसी और नथुनों में भर गई। यह मछली की बासी गन्ध थी। तेज़ होती हुई। कोई नाक नहीं ढँकी। सबको आदत थी। सब रोज़ आते-जाते दो बार यहाँ से गुज़रते थे।

यह बाँदरा की खाड़ी थी।

कुछ देर बाद पड़ोसी ने बताया कि यह मलाड है, अगला स्टेशन कान्दिवली है, तुम उठकर गलियारे में चले जाओ और जिस ओर लोग बाहर की तरफ़ मुँह किए खड़े हों, तुम भी उसी ओर खड़े हो जाना, ट्रेन रुके तो बाहर जाते रेले के साथ उतर जाना, तुम्हें सिर्फ़ अपने पैर दूसरे पैरों के साथ चलाने होंगे। जब गाड़ी रुकी तो रेला नहीं चला। रतन चीख़ा, 'मुझे कान्दिवली उतरना है।' आगे खड़े दोनों लड़के एक-साथ बोले—'यह विरार की गाड़ी है, कान्दिवली की भीड़ क्यों बढ़ाते हो ? अब विरार पर उतरना।' उनके साथ आगे दो लड़के और भी थे। उन्होंने रतन को रास्ता नहीं दिया। गाड़ी चल दी। चारों लड़के ठहाका मारकर हँसे। रतन की निरीह नज़रें चारों ओर घूमीं। कोई नज़र नहीं मिली—जैसे वहाँ कोई और नहीं था।

लड़के देर तक हँसते रहे।

विरार पर उतरकर रतन सामने खड़ी गाड़ी में घुसा और उसने सामने खड़े तीन लड़कों से पूछा, 'यह कान्दिवली जाएगी ?' 'जाएगी', एक ने कहा। रतन वहीं खड़ा रहा। शायद कुन्दा पकड़े हुए ठंडी हवा में उसकी आँख झपक गई थी। यह खड़े हुए सोना था—जो ज़िन्दगी में पहली बार उसके साथ हो रहा था, हालाँकि उसे यह मालूम नहीं था। जब आँख खुली तो उसने प्लेटफ़ॉर्म पर कान्दिवली का बोर्ड देखा, जिस पर गाड़ी दौड़ रही थी। उसने पास खड़े लड़के से कहा—'तुमने तो कहा था कि यह कान्दिवली जाती है ?' 'जा रही है', वह हँसा, 'तुमने यह नहीं पूछा था कि यह कान्दिवली रुकेगी ?' उसके मुँह से फिर दारू का भभका बाहर आया। रतन अँधेरी पर उतरा। उसने एक बुज़ुर्ग आदमी से पूछा। उसने कहा, 'मैं कान्दिवली जा रहा हूँ। मेरे साथ चलो।'

वह उस रात बारह बजे घर पहुँचा।

अगली सुबह डॉ. मुखर्जी से बॉम्बे हॉस्पिटल में मिलना था। रतन पिछली सीट पर पवन के साथ वातानुकूलित गाड़ी में बैठा था, जिसे ड्राइवर चला रहा था। वे चर्चगेट की ओर जा रहे थे जहाँ से पिछली रात रतन अकेला तीन घंटे में ट्रेन से लौटा था। ठंडी गाड़ी में उन्हें एक घंटा भी नहीं लगा। न पसीना आया। वे अपनी-अपनी बनियानों के अन्दर बैठे रहे। अपनी-अपनी बनियानों में ही वे डॉ. मुखर्जी के कमरे में पहुँचे, जो वातानुकूलित था। पवन ने रतन की उपस्थिति में रतन की कैफ़ियत बयान की, जिसमें सोने की अँगूठी की चोरी शामिल नहीं थी। डॉक्टर ने रतन की आँखें देखीं और पूछा कि क्या तुम कभी-कभी पलक झपकाना भूल जाते हो ?

'क्या आपको याद रहता है ?' रतन ने डॉक्टर की ओर देखा।

डॉक्टर मुस्कराया। उसने बताया कि यह व्यक्तित्व-विक्षेप है, जो सँभाला जा सकता है। उसने दवाएँ लिखीं और कहा कि रतन को काम ज़रूर करना चाहिए—न कम, न ज़्यादा। शराब और पैसे से दूर रहना चाहिए !

जब वे डॉक्टर के कमरे से बाहर आए तो पवन ने गलियारे में बेंचों पर बैठे कुछ युवकों के चेहरे ग़ौर से देखे। वह पहचान नहीं सका कि कौन रोगी है और कौन रोगी नहीं है। क्या हवा इस क़दर बदल गई थी ? जैसा कि डॉ. मुखर्जी ने बताया, शिज़ोफ़्रेनिया की कोई निश्चयात्मक जाँच नहीं थी। अटकल थे। अनुमान थे। जैसे कोई अँधेरे में कुछ टटोल रहा हो।

पहले रतन सुबह नीली और रात को हरी गोली खाता था। अब रंग बदल गए। सुबह का रंग सफ़ेद था। रात का काला। डॉक्टर की सलाह के मुताबिक पवन उसे अपने साथ काम पर ले जाने लगा। उसका पी.वी.सी. पाइप का कारख़ाना दहिसर में था। सफ़ेद गोली खाकर वह काम पर जाता। लौटते हुए अँधेरा हो जाता। फिर वह टी.वी. देखता, खाना खाता और काली गोली खाकर सो जाता। कुछ सोचने का वक़्त नहीं था। सफ़ेद और काली गोलियों के बीच जिस्म कारख़ाने में काम करता और रात को थककर सो जाता।

रात को उसे सपने बहुत आते थे। सपनों में आँकड़े आते जिन्हें वह दिन-भर कम्प्यूटर में बन्द करता और खोलता था। ये माल ख़रीदने और बेचने के आँकड़े थे। ख़रीदने और बेचने की दरों के आँकड़े थे। क्रय-विक्रय के आँकड़े थे। जमा-ख़र्च के आँकड़े थे। बैंक-स्टेटमेंट से मिलान के आँकड़े थे। कभी-कभी वह कारख़ाने के अन्दर भी जाता था जहाँ एक ओर कच्चा माल एक्सट्रूडर में डाला जाता और दूसरी ओर गर्म साँचे से पी.वी.सी. पाइप गोल-गोल घूमते हुए निकलते

और पानी में डूब जाते। कारख़ाना साफ़-सुथरा था। फ़्लोर पर अक्सर दस-बारह मज़दूर होते थे। सुपरवाइज़र उसे देखकर खड़ा हो जाता जैसे वह सचमुच मालिक हो।

'अपने को मालिक ही समझो', पवन ने पहले ही दिन कारख़ाने के फ़्लोर पर खड़े हुए कहा था।

'हाँ', रतन के मुँह से निकला।

रतन का काम एक कम्प्यूटर असिस्टेंट का काम था, जो पहले मुनीम करते थे। पहले का ज़माना होता तो वह मुनीम होता। क्या कभी घर के लोग पहले मुनीम होते थे ? जब उसे यह ख़्याल आया तो उसने कम्प्यूटर बन्द कर दिया और चाय मँगाई। चाय पीकर वह बाहर आ गया, जहाँ दूरियों में पेड़ फैले थे। सपने में पेड़ भी बहुत आते थे, जिनके पीछे पहाड़ी होती और पहाड़ी पर झोपड़पट्टियों की खल्वाट छतें—जो असल में रतन की खिड़की के बाहर शहर की घाटी के पार थीं। छतों के ऊपर पहाड़ी की चोटी तक पेड़ ही पेड़ थे जैसे दौड़कर ऊपर चढ़ गए हों। रतन पहाड़ी की चोटी तक दौड़ता हुआ चढ़ता था और हाँफ़ता नहीं था।

यह सपने में ही हो सकता था।

पवन ने उससे शुरू में कहा था कि जब भी पैसे की ज़रूरत हो तो वह माँग ले। रोज़ दहिसर आना-जाना, खाना-पीना पवन के साथ होता था। लौटकर कहीं जाने को समय नहीं था। हर इतवार पवन उसे सौ का एक नोट देता और कहता, 'जाओ, कहीं घूम आओ।' एक बार कुनमुनाकर जब रतन ने कहा कि सौ का नोट अब दस का नोट हो गया है, तो पवन बोला, 'यह पैसे की बात नहीं है। यह डॉक्टर की सलाह की बात है। तुम्हें पैसे से दूर रहना है।'

पैसे से दूर और काम के पास !

जब काम का पहला महीना ख़त्म हुआ तो बरसात शुरू हो गई। रतन को यह उम्मीद थी कि उसे बतौर वेतन नहीं तो बतौर जेब-ख़र्च कुछ एकमुश्त रकम मिलेगी। एक हफ़्ता बीत गया। कोई ज़िक्र नहीं हुआ। तब रतन ने ही प्रस्ताव रखा। डॉक्टर की क़सम देकर यह रियायत मिली कि हर सप्ताह के बीच में भी उसे सौ का नोट मिलेगा। खाना-रहना तो मुफ़्त था ही। कपड़े की अभी ज़रूरत नहीं थी।

तब भी महीने के एक हज़ार रुपए नहीं होते थे।

मगर बहस की कोई गुंजाइश नहीं थी क्योंकि मल्लिका पाइप्स आख़िरकार रतन की ही कम्पनी थी। रतन से पवन और किशोरी बार-बार यही कहते थे। किशोरी यह कहते हुए मुस्कराती थी। वह यह भी नहीं कह सकता था कि

मल्लिका पाइप्स तो पवन की बेटी के नाम पर है और वे ही इसे चलाते हैं। रतन तो सिर्फ़ एक कम्प्यूटर चलाता था। अम्बानी-स्वप्न का यही अंजाम था ! रतन अपने कमरे में काँच की खिड़की के सामने खड़ा यही सोच रहा था। यह शनिवार की रात थी। वह खाना और काली गोली खाकर खिड़की के सामने खड़ा था। बारिश आज दिन-भर थमी नहीं थी। कभी-कभी पानी उचाट ज़रूर हो जाता, लेकिन फिर एकदम बरसने लगता गोया कभी रुका ही न हो। एक-दो बार धूप भी निकली थी। मगर लगता यही था कि बारिश कभी थमी नहीं, न थमेगी। यह कुछ-कुछ आदिकाल की बारिश लगती थी जब धरती समुद्र से डरकर जंगल में छिप जाती थी।

रतन अचानक पीछे मुड़ा। उसने अपनी अटैची से दोनों तस्वीरें निकालीं, जो वह लखनऊ से झाँसी और झाँसी से मुम्बई लाया था। उसने अम्बानी की तस्वीर फ्रेम से निकाली और उसके टुकड़ों के टुकड़े करने लगा।

3.3

इतवार का दिन था।

धूप अचानक निकल आई थी। कमरे में भरी रोशनी की वजह से रतन की नज़र काँच की खिड़की की ओर मुड़ी जहाँ नीचे घाटी में पेड़ों के सिरों और मकानों की छत पर धूप चमक रही थी, जिसके पीछे झिलमिल पहाड़ी ऊँची दीवार की तरह फैली थी। वह बिस्तर से उठकर फ़र्श पर खड़ा हुआ था और उजली खिड़की की ओर देखते हुए ख़ुशी से भर गया था। जब वह नीली जींस और पीली टी-शर्ट पहने फ़्लैट से बाहर आकर लिफ़्ट के सामने खड़ा हुआ तो वह मुस्करा रहा था। वह अकेला था।

गलियारे में और कोई नहीं था।

न लिफ़्ट में कोई और था। सिर्फ़ जलती हुई रोशनी उसके साथ अँधेरे में जा रही थी। पैरों के नीचे अँधेरे में जाते हुए सुबह पहली बार उसने सोचा कि आज वह पहली बार आमिर ख़ान को जीता-जागता सदेह देखेगा। यह परदे का आमिर ख़ान नहीं होगा जो रोशनी के साथ पैदा होता है और उसी के साथ ग़ायब हो जाता है। यह आमिर ख़ान की छाया नहीं होगी जिसे कुछ देर को सच समझने की मजबूरी हो। एक ही क्षण में वह दुनिया-भर के परदों पर होता था और लोग अँधेरे में उसे सच समझते थे। लोग उसके साथ हँसते, रोते, प्रेम करते और धोखा खाते थे।

जब लिफ़्ट का दरवाज़ा खुला तो सुरक्षाकर्मी अपनी वर्दी में सामने खड़ा था। आमिर ख़ान इसी तरह थोड़ी देर बाद आज की तारीख़ में सामने खड़ा होगा। रतन लिफ़्ट से बाहर आया और बाएँ मुड़ा। बरामदे से बाहर आते हुए उसकी नज़र सामने पार्क के बीच में रेस्टॉरेंट की इमारत पर पड़ी, जिसके नीचे जिम था। जिम जाने के लिए पवन ने पहले दिन कहा ज़रूर था। फिर नहीं कहा। रतन का मन भी कहने को नहीं हुआ। असल में दिन-भर कम्प्यूटर पर काम करते हुए वह शाम तक इतना थक जाता था कि टी.वी. देखने के अलावा और कुछ करने का मन ही नहीं करता था। परदे के सामने मन कुंडली मारकर अपनी जगह जम जाता। हाथ-पैर हिलाने के लिए मन का चलना ज़रूरी था।

वह बाएँ सड़क पर मुड़कर चलने लगा। सड़क सूनी थी जैसे वह भी इतवार की धूप में ऊँघ रही हो। उसने दाईं ओर पार्क की झाड़ियों के परे पेड़ों और लॉन और लॉन को घेरे नहर की ओर देखा, जो यहाँ से नज़र नहीं आती थी। नहर में तीन-चार मोटर-बोटें थीं जिनमें बच्चे अपने अभिभावकों के साथ घूमते थे—उनके रास्ते में तीन गुफ़ाएँ थीं। ये गुफ़ाएँ कृत्रिम थीं। लेकिन मोटर-बोट में बैठे बच्चे जब किसी गुफ़ा के अँधेरे में पहुँचते, तो उन्हें गुफ़ा असली लगती। असल में यह अँधेरे की गुफ़ा थी। थोड़ी देर में बच्चे नहर में घूमने पहुँचेंगे। सड़क पर चलते हुए तरण-ताल की ऊँची दीवार नज़र आती थी, जिस पर एक युवती स्विमिंग-सूट पहने खड़ी थी। सूट उसकी देह से चिपका था। वह पानी में कूदकर आई थी और फिर पानी में कूदने वाली थी। पानी उसकी प्रतीक्षा कर रहा था। ताड़ के पेड़ दूर आकाश में हामी में अपना सिर हिला रहे थे।

व्हिस्परिंग पॉम्स से बाहर निकलकर रतन सड़क के किनारे बस-स्टॉप पर खड़ा हो गया था। न जाने कहाँ से एकाएक बादल आ गए जिनका पता कुछ बूँदों से चला। रतन ने ऊपर देखा। उसने पीछे भी देखा। व्हिस्परिंग पॉम्स में धूप थी जैसे धूप वहाँ रहने वाले लोगों और गाड़ियों के लिए ही हो। जैसे बारिश शुरू हुई थी, उसी तरह बस आ गई। रतन फुर्ती से चढ़ा और एक सीट पर बैठ गया। वह ख़ुश था कि बस बारिश के साथ आ गई थी और वह भीगने से बच गया था। उसने नीचे अपनी जींस और टी-शर्ट की ओर देखा : कुछ बूँदें ही पड़ी थीं। तब उसने उस लड़की को देखा जो उसकी बग़ल में खिड़की से लगी बैठी थी। शायद कुछ बूँदें खिड़की से उछलकर उस पर गिरीं। वह खिड़की से दूर उसके पास कुछ खिसकी। उसके साँवले चेहरे पर वही तरल लुनाई थी जो समुद्र अपनी बेटियों को देता है। जब वह पास खिसकी तो रतन ने घूमकर उसे ग़ौर से देखा। उसे अचानक सपना की याद आई।

कान्दिवली का पुराना क़स्बाई बाज़ार खदबदा रहा था जिसमें डबल-डेकर बस हाथी की तरह चली जा रही थी। वह हॉर्न भी दे रही थी जैसे हाथी के गले में घंटी बँधी हो। क़स्बाई बाज़ार में मुम्बई की भीड़ थी। लोग, दुपहिए, तिपहिए, चौपहिए—सब आपस में गुँथे आगे और पीछे एक-साथ जा रहे थे। बस में बैठे हुए रतन को लगा जैसे वह साँवली लड़की के साथ कहीं अकेला जा रहा है। उसका ध्यान दाईं ओर एक जिम ने तोड़ा, जिसमें कुछ लड़कों के जिस्म चमक रहे थे। ऐसा लगा जैसे यह भी मुम्बई के बाज़ार की कोई दुकान है।

बाहर बारिश थी।

पुल के नीचे से गुज़रने के बाद बारिश ग़ायब हो गई और धूप निकल आई जैसे पुल धूल और पानी को बाँट रहा हो। पुल के आगे सड़क भी सूखी थी। कुछ और आगे बाज़ार में भीड़ के बीच स्टॉप पर बस रुकी। रतन की बग़ल में बैठी लड़की उसके घुटनों को छूती हुई बाहर चली गई। उसने लड़की को चलती बस से दूर बाज़ार में जाते हुए देखा। उसे पता ही नहीं चला कि कब बाज़ार ने उसे अचानक लील लिया। बस अचानक बाईं ओर बस्ती में मुड़ी और फिर एक बार और मुड़कर खुले टर्मिनल पर पहुँचकर रुक गई। लोग ऐसे उतरे जैसे बस से क़ैदी छूटकर भाग रहे हों। वे एक ही ओर जा रहे थे। वे जिस ओर जा रहे थे, उसी ओर रेलवे स्टेशन था। लाख ख़्याल करो, किसी कन्धे से कन्धा टकरा जाता या कोई पीछे से थोड़ा धक्का ही दे देता। ऐसा लगता जैसे महानगर में न कोई अकेला चलता है, न अकेला जीता है। लोग भीड़ में साँस ले रहे थे गोया किसी अँधेरी गुफ़ा में बन्द हों।

भीड़ पर धूप चमक रही थी।

रतन स्टेशन पर टिकट लेने के लिए क्यू में खड़ा हो गया। यह एकरेखीय भीड़ थी जो खिड़की पर टूटती और पूँछ की ओर बढ़ती जाती। आगे निरन्तर टूटते रहने के बावजूद इसका आकार सुरसा के मुँह की तरह था। सिर्फ़ आकार ही अन्तहीन था। क्यू के चेहरे सपाट थे जैसे लोग जाने के लिए जा रहे हों और इसलिए लौटेंगे क्योंकि जा रहे हैं। एक क्यू को दूसरे क्यू से बदल सकते थे। सब एक-से लगते थे।

जब वह खिड़की से टिकट लेकर पीछे मुड़ा तो सड़क पर उसने उसी साँवली लड़की को देखा जो बस में उसकी बग़ल में बैठी थी। तभी अचानक आसमान से पानी गिरा। पानी की धारों के नीचे भागती हुई लड़की सामने पुल की सीढ़ियों पर चढ़ गई। रतन सीढ़ियों की ओर भागा। पानी तेज़ था। इस समुद्री शहर में कभी-कभी इसी तरह बारिश होती थी जैसे कोई अचानक चीख़ने लगे और फिर

एकाएक चुप हो जाए। तब आसमान फोड़कर धूप निकल आती थी।

सीढ़ियों पर शेड के नीचे रतन साँवली लड़की के पीछे पहुँच गया। उसने चाल धीमी की। वह लड़की के पीछे-पीछे जा रहा था। लड़की के गले और बाँहों पर पानी की बूँदें थीं जिनमें उसका साँवला रंग घुल रहा था। सीढ़ियों पर भीड़ चढ़-उतर रही थी। वे पुल पार करके दूसरी ओर सीढ़ियों पर उतरने लगे। नीचे उतरकर लड़की लड़कियों के एक झुंड में खड़ी हो गई। प्लेटफ़ॉर्म पर एक ओर यह झुंड खड़ा था जिसके सामने लोकल के महिलाओं के डिब्बे को रुकना था। लड़की झुंड के किनारे पर खड़ी थी। रतन उसके पास पुरुषों के झुंड में खड़ा हो गया। प्लेटफ़ॉर्म पर शेड के नीचे लोगों और बारिश की आवाज़ें थीं, जो आपस में घुल-मिल रही थीं। पानी और भीड़ के शोर के बीच लड़की अचानक उसकी ओर मुड़ी और बोली :

'हे।'

'हाँ', रतन ने मुँह मोड़कर कहा।

'तुम मेरा पीछा क्यों कर रहे हो ?'

'तुम्हारे गले पर बारिश देख रहा था।'

प्लेटफ़ॉर्म पर लोकल बे-आवाज़ आकर रुक गई। लड़की मुस्कराती हुई डिब्बे की ओर चली गई। वह उसे देखता हुआ अपने डिब्बे में चढ़ा। उसे एक खिड़की के पास जगह मिल गई। शायद छुट्टी की वजह से भीड़ कुछ कम थी। वह खिड़की के बाहर देख रहा था जहाँ दृश्य लगातार पीछे की ओर जा रहा था गोया कान्दिवली बोरिवली की ओर जा रही हो। अलबत्ता रतन गोरेगाँव जा रहा था जहाँ से बस पकड़कर उसे फ़िल्म सिटी जाना था जहाँ आज आमिर ख़ान की शूटिंग थी। चलती रेल की खिड़की के बाहर पहले बस्ती चली, फिर झोपड़पट्टियाँ, फिर कुछ दूर झाड़-झंखाड़, फिर सूनी धरती...फिर कुछ नारियल के पेड़।

मुँगड़ा ऽऽ ओ मुँगड़ा मैं गुड़ की डली
माँगता है तो आ जा रसिया
ये मैं...मायके...चली

दस-ग्यारह साल की एक लड़की की आवाज़ थी जो खंजड़ी बजा रही थी जैसे कोई भजन गा रही हो...मँगता है तो आ जा रसिया ! लड़की के चेहरे पर ऐसा ही भाव था जैसे वह कोई भजन गा रही हो। डिब्बे के लोग जब उसे देखते मुस्कराने लगते, वह नहीं मुस्कराती थी। आँखें बन्द किए हुए खंजड़ी बजाती हुई वह भजन गा रही थी।

रेल की खिड़की के बाहर क़तारों में बँधी भैंसों का एक समूह नज़र आया, जिसके ऊपर छप्पर था और सामने भैंसों के आगे हौदियों में चारा भरा था। भैंसें गाड़ी की आवाज़ से बेख़बर थीं। वे चारा खा रही थीं या शून्य में ताक रही थीं। एक-दो भैंसों ने ज़रूर इत्तफ़ाकन गाड़ी की ओर देखा। तभी गाड़ी में खंजड़ी की आवाज़ बन्द हो गई और लड़की ने लोगों के सामने अपना हाथ पसारा। उसके पीछे एक उससे छोटा लड़का था। लड़का लड़की का हाथ थामे था। लड़की की आँखें अभी भी बन्द थीं जैसे वे भजन में डूबी हों।

एक क्षण को लड़की की पलकें खुलीं जब रतन ने आँखें झपकाईं।

लड़की अन्धी थी।

आमिर ख़ान की बारात का दृश्य था। आमिर दूल्हा बना घोड़े पर बैठा था। घोड़े के सामने चार लड़के और चार लड़कियाँ घेरा बनाए नाच रहे थे। वे नाच रहे थे और गा रहे थे। संगीतमय गीत की पंक्ति बार-बार बजाई जाती और बार-बार नाच शुरू होता, फिर 'कट' की आवाज़ आती और दृश्य थम जाता। घोड़े के पीछे चलते बाराती और आगे चलता बैंड भी रुक जाते। बत्तियाँ गुल हो जातीं। अँधेरा छा जाता। जैसे सचमुच रात हो। यह फ़िल्म सिटी के भीतर का अँधेरा था, बाहर धूप निकल आई थी। रतन फिल्म सिटी में पवन के एक दोस्त—शंकर शेट्टी—की सिफ़ारिश से घुसा था। वह एक तरफ़ एक झुंड में खड़ा शूटिंग देख रहा था। इस बार जब बत्तियाँ जलीं और 'एक्शन' की आवाज़ आई तो रतन को लगा कि आमिर ख़ान एक भैंसे पर बैठा है, जिसने तबेले से चलती गाड़ी में रतन की ओर मुँह उठाकर देखा था। नृत्य और संगीत पूर्ववत् चल रहा था। गीत का स्थायी इस प्रकार था :

छैला आया ब्याहने लैला...

हर बार स्थायी के अन्त के बाद लड़कों की तर्जनियाँ ऊपर हवा में उठ जातीं और लड़कियों के लहँगे घेरे बनाने लगते। मगर आमिर भैंसे पर बैठा था, जो धीरे-धीरे घोड़े की तरह आगे बढ़ रहा था। तबेले का भैंसा आमिर की टाँगों के नीचे कैसे आ गया था ? और घोड़ा कहाँ गया ? क्या घोड़ा बाहर मैदान में घास खा रहा था ? जब शक शुरू हुआ तो आमिर ख़ान तक पहुँचा। भैंसे पर जो व्यक्ति सूट पहने बैठा था, उसके चेहरे पर सफ़ेद फूलों की लड़ियाँ थीं। चेहरा फूलों के पीछे छिपा था। कोई ज़रूरी नहीं था कि यह आमिर ख़ान का ही चेहरा हो।

और फ़िल्मों में तो 'डबल' का बहुत रिवाज़ है, रतन ने सोचा। यदि घोड़ा भैंसा हो गया था तो आमिर ख़ान अपना 'डबल' भी हो सकता था ! फिर यह आमिर ख़ान की सच्ची शादी नहीं थी। यह झूठी कहानी का झूठा शॉट था, जो परदे पर असली लगता था।

स्टूडियो में चारों ओर रोशनियों और कैमरे को देखते हुए रतन को अचानक परदे के झूठ का तीखा अहसास हुआ, जिसे लोग सिनेमा हॉल के अँधेरे में यथार्थ समझते थे। परदे पर केवल मांसल छायाएँ थीं। क्या परदे पर भी 'डबल' और भैंसे के चेहरे नज़र आ सकते थे ?

आमिर ख़ान असली था।

यही देखने के लिए रतन दूसरी ओर बैठे आमिर ख़ान की ओर बढ़ा था जब वह शॉट ख़त्म हो जाने के बाद अपने चेहरे से श्वेत पुष्पों की लड़ियाँ हटाकर एक कुर्सी पर बैठा। उसका सूट आकाश की तरह नीला था, टाई लाल थी और कमीज़ पर नीली धारियाँ थीं—अलबत्ता कमीज़ का कॉलर सफ़ेद था। उसके चेहरे पर न मुस्कान थी, न उदासी थी। उसके चेहरे पर कुछ नहीं था। रतन को इतने ख़ालीपन की उम्मीद नहीं थी। जैसे कोई साँस लेता पुतला बैठा हो। जो अगले शॉट में ज़रूरत के मुताबिक भाव अपने चेहरे में भर देगा जैसे कोई चित्रकार ख़ाली कैनवस पर रंग भरता है।

आमिर ने सहसा आँखें मूँद लीं। तब पता चला कि उसकी आँखें खुली थीं। वह कुर्सी पर पसर गया।

यह संयोग ही था कि रतन की जींस और आमिर ख़ान के सूट के रंग एक थे। केश-विन्यास एक-सा था। चेहरे उन्नीस-बीस होंगे—रतन आईने में देखा अपना चेहरा याद करता हुआ सिर्फ़ आमिर का चेहरा देख सकता था। वह आमिर से कुछ दुबला था। रंग भी कुछ साँवला था। वह आमिर का 'डबल' ज़रूर हो सकता था। मगर 'डबल' होने की अलग ज़िम्मेदारियाँ थीं। आमिर के सारे जोखिम रतन के जोखिम थे। रतन को पहाड़ी से कूदना था, नाले को फाँदना था, पागल घोड़े को दौड़ाना था और नायिका को जलती हवेली से बाहर निकालकर आमिर के हाथों में थमाना था ताकि आमिर अपना 'क्लोज़-अप' दे सके। रतन 'क्लोज़-अप' में कहीं नहीं था। वह केवल धुँधलाते लाँग शॉट में था—जैसे अपने जिस्म को धुआँ करके आमिर ख़ान के चेहरे पर रोशनी बिखेर देगा।

रतन को लगा कि उसकी यही 'डबल' नियति है।

वह आमिर की कुर्सी की ओर बढ़ा। जब वह कुर्सी तक पहुँचा, आमिर आँखें खोलकर बग़ल में बैठी प्रीति ज़िंटा से हँस-हँसकर बातें कर रहा था। यह वही

आमिर नहीं था जो ख़ाली चेहरा लिए अभी कुर्सी पर अधलेटा था। यह हँसता हुआ आमिर था जो प्रीति ज़िंटा के गालों पर बार-बार गड्ढे पैदा कर रहा था।

एकाएक आमिर के हाथ से रूमाल छूटकर नीचे गिर पड़ा। इससे पहले कि वह झुककर रूमाल उठाए, रतन ने 'डबल' की तरह उछलकर रूमाल उठाया और उसे आमिर के हाथ में थमा दिया। रूमाल देते हुए रतन का हाथ आमिर के हाथ से छुआ।

'थैंक्स', आमिर ने कहा।

रतन ने हाथ आगे बढ़ाया। आमिर का हाथ उसके हाथ में था। रतन अपना हाथ देख रहा था। वह यह हाथ कभी नहीं भूलेगा।

स्टूडियो के बाहर लम्बे साए थे, बची-खुची धूप थी और क्षितिज पर पहाड़ियाँ थीं। रतन कुछ देर दाईं ओर चला। सामने एक विराट्, भव्य सेट लगा था। जब एक व्यक्ति ने उसे बताया कि यह 'देवदास' का सेट है तो वह चौंका। उसने टी.वी. पर विमल राय की 'देवदास' देखी थी। वह किसी दूसरे समय और जहान की कहानी लगती थी। उस हताश और हारे हुए देवदास के लिए ऐसा जगमग सेट विस्मयकारी था। रतन के लिए देवदास का पात्र ही अबूझ था। भला ऐसी भी क्या पर्दादारी कि अपनी प्रेमिका को गाँव में एक बूढ़े से बँधने के लिए छोड़कर आदमी शहर भाग जाए ? फ़िल्म देखते हुए और उसके बाद उसे लगता रहा था कि कोई उसके कानों में फुसफुसा रहा है, 'कुछ करो, कुछ करो।'

कोई कुछ करता क्यों नहीं ?

देवदास को फिर से फ़िल्माने के लिए सेट को विराट् और भव्य बना दिया था। इसमें करोड़ों लगे थे, रतन ने कहीं पढ़ा था। यदि यह देवदास का घर था तो राजमहल की तरह था जिसमें दमकते हुए झाड़-फ़ानूस थे, जगमग दीवारें थीं और आईने ही आईने थे। सीढ़ियाँ आईनों से निकलकर आईनों में खो जाती थीं। फ़र्श छत पर चमकता। छत आईनों में घुलती हुई लगती। आईनों की एक विराट् भूलभुलैया थी, जिसमें आदमी की चरम पीड़ा का नाटक फिर खेला जाएगा। नाटक का अन्त आईनों के फ़र्श पर होगा :

'कौन कम्बख़्त बर्दाश्त करने के लिए पीता है ?' देवदास फिर कराहेगा, 'मैं तो इसलिए पीता हूँ कि साँस ले सकूँ।'

ख़ाली, बियाबान सेट के सामने खड़े हुए रतन को दिलीप कुमार का वह रुँधा चेहरा और अधखुली आँखें याद आईं जिन्हें लिये वह पारो को गाँव में छोड़कर शहर भागता है। उसके चेहरे पर कोई भीतरी बाधा छलक आई थी, जो लगातार

फ़िल्म के अन्तिम दृश्य तक गहराती रही जब तक कि मौत का सन्नाटा चेहरे पर नहीं उतरा। पारो और चन्द्रमुखी के बीच भागता हताश देवदास एक बाधित आत्मा थी, जो न जी पाती थी न मर पाती थी। ज़माना अपने ही बच्चों से कैसा बदला ले रहा था !

रतन को अचानक लगा कि विराट् सेट पर दूर बरामदे में दिलीप कुमार अकेला लड़खड़ाता हुआ चला जा रहा है...वहाँ और कोई नहीं था...न कोई आदमी, न कैमरा, न ट्रॉली, न लाइट... जैसे यह कोई फ़िल्म का सेट न हो, शहर का कोई हिस्सा हो। वह उसी ओर भागा ताकि फ़र्श पर गिरते हुए देवदास को सहारा दे सके। इसके पहले कि वह सेट की सीढ़ियों पर पैर रखे, दो सुरक्षाकर्मियों ने दौड़कर उसे पकड़ लिया और गेट की ओर ले चले।

'मैं अपने नायक का डबल हूँ', रतन सड़क पर यही बुदबुदाता चला जा रहा था जैसे वह खुद रतन न हो, रतन की छाया हो। यद्यपि अब छाया के लिए कोई जगह नहीं थी। सूरज सारी छायाएँ अपने जाल में बटोरकर पहाड़ियों के पीछे चला गया था। सुरमई अँधेरा पहाड़ियों में उगता लगता था जो सड़क पर उतरकर दूर-दूर तक फैल रहा था। उसी गहराती सुरमई शाम में रतन बुदबुदाता हुआ चल रहा था...यदि आमिर लड़खड़ाते देवदास को न सँभाले तो उसका 'डबल' कैसे सँभालेगा ? भला कोई 'डबल' अपना 'डबल' कैसे हो सकता था ? वह सदा किसी और का 'डबल' होगा। देवदास की समस्या उल्टी थी। उसका कोई 'डबल' नहीं था। कोई उसका 'डबल' होता तो उसका जोखिम अपने सिर पर ले लेता। उसका जोखिम उसके भीतर था : उसकी बाधाग्रस्त आत्मा ! जो अपने ज़माने की परछाईं थी।

क्या मैं भी अपने ज़माने की परछाईं हूँ ? रतन ने सड़क पर मुड़कर सोचा। उसके सामने पहाड़ी पर अँधेरा छा गया था। कोई प्रकाश नहीं था। प्रकाश सड़क पर था, जहाँ रतन अपनी छाया की तरह चल रहा था। न वह अम्बानी हो सकता था, न आमिर हो सकता था। अलबत्ता वह आमिर का 'डबल' हो सकता था। उसकी ज़िन्दगी एक चालू कम्प्यूटर की ज़िन्दगी थी जिससे वह मल्लिका पाइप्स पहुँचते ही उसी कम्प्यूटर के आख़िरी पुर्जे की तरह जुड़ जाता था। और क्या बचा था उसकी ज़िन्दगी में ? शहर में थोड़ा-सा समुद्र था, ठंडी हवाएँ थीं, ताड़ के पेड़ थे और कुछ लड़कियाँ थीं—जिनमें वह हमेशा सपना को ढूँढ़ता था।

सपना का चेहरा इस तरह एकाएक सामने आ गया जैसे वह कोई छाया न हो, सचमुच सपना हो। अब सड़क पर रोशनी नहीं थी। अचानक एक लड़की सफ़ेद साड़ी पहने सामने से आई थी और उसी साड़ी की रोशनी में उसका चेहरा

चमका था, जो सपना का चेहरा था। रतन के क़दम अँधेरी सड़क पर अपनी जगह थम गए थे : वह सपना का चेहरा देख रहा था ! उसने चाहा कि उसे पुकारे। मगर तभी उसका हाथ अपने गले पर चला गया क्योंकि उसे लगा कि उसके गले में कोई आवाज़ नहीं है...क्योंकि वह रतन नहीं है, रतन की छाया है।

'सपना ऽऽ', वह सहसा अँधेरे में चीख़ा।

फिर वह सड़क पर दौड़ने लगा। जब वह रोशनी में आता, उसकी छाया उससे जुड़ जाती। फिर छाया दूर कहीं पहाड़ियों की ओर चली जाती, जहाँ अब अँधेरे की पहाड़ियाँ थीं। सड़क पर एकाएक इतना अँधेरा हो गया कि उसने आँखें बन्द कर लीं। क्योंकि आँखें खोलने और बन्द करने में कोई फ़र्क नहीं था। वह हाँफ़ता हुआ दौड़ रहा था। उसकी साँसें धीरे-धीरे लम्बी हुई थीं। फिर साँस की लम्बाई स्थिर हो गई। लम्बी साँसों के बीच हाँफना था। उसका मुँह अपने-आप खुल गया। कुत्ते की तरह।

उसने आँखें खोलीं। रोशनी कुछ दूर थी। दूर रोशनी ज़्यादा थी जैसे कोई बाज़ार हो। वह दौड़ता रहा। एकाएक गोबर की गन्ध हवा में तैरी। रतन के पैर धीमे होने लगे। उसने सड़क पर चलते हुए चारों ओर देखा। भैंसों के तबेले कहीं नज़र नहीं आए। वह आगे रोशनी की ओर बढ़ता रहा। तभी हवा में कॉफ़ी की गन्ध आई। वह बाज़ार में प्रवेश कर रहा था। दोनों ओर दुकानें थीं। दुकानों के अन्दर रोशनी थी। दुकानों के बाहर रोशनी थी। सड़क पर लोग कम थे। वह आगे बढ़ता रहा। सहसा पानी गिरा जैसे किसी ने आकाश के झरने का ढक्कन हटा दिया हो। धारें मोटी थीं। सड़क पर पता नहीं कहाँ से छाते आ गए। रतन के पास छाता नहीं था। वह बाईं ओर मुड़कर सड़क के किनारे सीढ़ियों पर खड़ा हो गया जहाँ ऊपर छत थी। सीढ़ियों के ऊपर एक चौड़ा दरवाज़ा था, जो बन्द था। दरवाज़े के बाहर नीली वर्दी पहने दरबान खड़ा था। उसने रतन को सीढ़ियों पर खड़ा देखकर बाएँ हाथ से दरवाज़ा खोला और दाएँ हाथ से उसे अन्दर जाने का इशारा किया जैसे ही उनकी नज़रें मिलीं। जैसे कोई अपने घर में बुला रहा हो, वह अन्दर चला गया।

पहली नज़र में रतन की आँखें फटी रह गईं। यह कोई तिलिस्मी संसार था। हॉल में दूसरी ओर एक गोल मंच था जो आहिस्ता-आहिस्ता अपनी धुरी पर चारों ओर घूम रहा था जैसे धरती हर क्षण घूमती है और हमें पता नहीं चलता। गोल मंच पर पाँच अप्सराएँ थिरक रही थीं। हॉल में चारों ओर मेज़ें लगी थीं जिनको कुर्सियाँ घेरे थीं और कुर्सियों पर लोग बैठे थे जो घूमते मंच की ओर घूर रहे थे।

'क्या आप अकेले हैं ?' एक वर्दीधारी वेटर ने पूछा।

'हाँ।'

'इस तरफ़ आइए।'

वह वेटर के पीछे चला। कोने में एक मेज़ ख़ाली थी। वह गोल घूमते मंच की ओर मुँह करके बैठ गया। तब उसने वह गाना सुना जो अप्सराओं के होंठों से निकलता लगता था। पहले वह हॉल का संगीतमय शोर था। जैसे ही रतन मेज़ पर बैठा और उसने घूमते मंच की ओर देखा, शोर एक दिलकश गीत में बदल गया :

आप जैसा कोई मेरी ज़िन्दगी में आएऽ
तो बात बन जाएऽ
हाँ-हाँ-हाँ ऽऽ
बात बन जाएऽ

ज़ोर बात बन जाने पर था। मगर रतन को लगा कि असली ज़ोर 'आप जैसा कोई' पर है, जिसे होंठों से हवा में फेंकते हुए अप्सराएँ जिस ओर निहारतीं उसी ओर आदमियों की नज़रें फँसी रह जातीं। हॉल के जिस कोने में रतन की मेज़ थी, उस कोने और मंच के बीच चार मेज़ें थीं जिन पर चार-चार लोग बैठे थे। जब कोई अप्सरा उस ओर देखती तो दूसरी ओर बत्तीस और दो आँखें तन जातीं। 'आप जैसा कोई' की अनन्त सम्भावनाएँ थीं, जो सिगरेटों के धुएँ और चारों ओर लगे आईनों में नाच रही थीं। मेज़ों पर भरे-अधभरे गिलास रखे थे और झपझपाती आँखें थीं। कभी-कभी आँखें झपकना भी भूल जाती थीं। रतन के साथ यह पहली बार पहला पेग ख़त्म करने पर हुआ।

आप जैसा कोई मेरी ज़िन्दगी में आएऽ

रोशनी गोल घूमते मंच पर थी जहाँ अप्सराएँ नाच रही थीं। मेज़ों पर रुपहला अँधेरा था। आदमियों की आँखें ऐसे चमक रही थीं जैसे अँधेरे में जानवरों की आँखें चमकती हैं। रतन को एकाएक लगा कि किसी जंगल के अँधेरे में जानवरों की आँखें बिल्लौरों-सी चमक रही हैं...गोल-गोल...प्रकाश-पुंजों की तरह। उसे लगा जैसे जंगल में कोई गा रहा है...आप जैसा कोई...। अँधेरे में जानवरों की चमकती आँखें गाने की ओर देख रही थीं जैसे मन्त्रबिद्ध हों। उनकी छायाएँ हिलती-डुलती थीं। कभी-कभी उनके दाँत चमकने लगते। जंगल में अँधेरे के पेड़ थे और घात लगाए बैठे जानवरों के दाँत थे। जानवर चुप थे। जंगल में उनकी कोई आवाज़ नहीं थी। जंगल में सिर्फ़ गाना था। सिर्फ़ गाने की आवाज़ पेड़ों और पत्तियों में घूम रही थी। कभी-कभी पत्तियाँ हिलतीं और डालें आपस में टकरा जातीं।

रतन का बायाँ हाथ सहसा मेज़ पर रखे ख़ाली गिलास से टकराया। गिलास फ़र्श पर गिरकर टूट गया। काँच के बिखरने की आवाज़ एक क्षण संगीत पर छा गई। उसी क्षण रतन ने जाना कि वह एक बार में बैठा था जिसमें कुछ लड़कियाँ मंच पर नाच रही थीं। लड़कियाँ जवान थीं। हसीन थीं। उनके आधे जिस्म ढँके थे। उनकी आँखें अपने शरीर के घोंसले से निकलकर हॉल में घूमने लगतीं और फिर एकाएक पलटकर अपने घोंसलों में लौट जातीं। जब कोई ग्राहक बड़ा नोट हाथ में झंडी की तरह उठाता तो कोई लड़की मंच से उतरकर उस झंडी तक पहुँच जाती। झंडी हाथ में देते हुए मर्द का हाथ लड़की के हाथ को टटोलता। कभी लड़की मुस्कराती। कभी वह नहीं मुस्कराती। उस क्षण वह पलटकर मंच की ओर लौटती। लोग आस-पास सिर्फ़ उसके जुम्बिश खाते नितम्बों को लौटते हुए देखते जैसे वे जंगल की हवा में स्वायत्त उड़ रहे हों। एक बार एक युवक ने मेज़ से उठकर लौटते नितम्बों का पीछा करने की कोशिश की। मगर उसके लड़खड़ाते पैरों ने उसका साथ नहीं दिया। वह तीन-चार क़दम चलकर फ़र्श पर ढेर हो गया। रतन अपनी कुर्सी से उठकर उसे उठाने की सोच रहा था। तभी दो आदमी कहीं से आए और उसे उठाकर दरवाज़े की ओर ले गए। दोनों आदमियों के हाथों में टँगे उस युवक ने दरवाज़े के दूसरी ओर जाने के पहले आख़िरी बार मंच की ओर देखा। उसकी आँखें अँधेरे में चमकीं और खो गईं।

रतन फिर अपने पास लौट आया। अपने पास कुछ नहीं था। सपना का ख़्याल भी नहीं था। यह ख़्याल भी नहीं था कि सपना का ख़्याल नहीं है। सिर्फ़ अपना जिस्म था : एक पेंट और कमीज़ में लिपटा हुआ, जो दो जूतों पर चलता था। सामने मेज़ पर आधा भरा शराब का गिलास था। उसने अन्दर घुसते हुए सोचा था कि वह एक पेग लेगा, कुछ सुस्ताएगा और चला जाएगा। मगर यह चौथा पेग था। उसे यह भी ख़्याल नहीं था कि यह चौथा पेग है। उसकी मेज़ को घेरे एक अँधेरे-उजाले का संसार था। वह यह भी भूल गया था कि यह संसार कुछ देर पहले नहीं था और कुछ देर बाद नहीं होगा। वह इस क्षण मेज़ पर इस तरह बैठा था जैसे सृष्टि के आरम्भ से बैठा हो और अन्त तक बैठा रहेगा। मेज़ पर अँधेरा था। कुछ दूर गोल मंच रोशनी में गोल-गोल नाच रहा था और उस पर अपने हाथ-पैर और आँखें चलातीं पाँच लड़कियाँ नाच रही थीं।

रतन की आँखें मंच पर थीं : कभी किसी लड़की की ब्रा खोलती हुई या कभी किसी लड़की के नाड़े से खेलती हुई, जो अदृश्य था।

क्या यह किसी 'डबल' की हरकत थी ? उसने किसी को मंच पर जाते नहीं देखा था। क्या 'डबल' नाड़े की तरह अदृश्य था ? रतन सहसा मेज़ से उठा और

मंच की ओर बढ़ा। मंच अपनी जगह गोल घूम रहा था। कोई सीढ़ी नहीं थी। वह घूमते मंच के पास खड़ा हो गया। अगले क्षण कोई आया और उसने पूछा—

'क्या चाहिए ?'

'कुछ नहीं।'

'इधर क्यों आए ?' अजनबी पहलवान-सा लगता था।

'क्या तुमने देखा ?' रतन ने आँखें फाड़ीं।

'क्या ?'

'कोई मंच पर नाड़े से खेल रहा है।'

'मंच पर नाड़ा नहीं खुलेगा', पहलवान हँसा, 'तुम अपनी मेज़ पर जाओ।'

'उसे रोकना चाहिए', रतन ने एक पैर मंच की ओर बढ़ाया।

पहलवान का एक हाथ रतन के कन्धे पर था। उसने दूसरा हाथ रतन के दूसरे कन्धे पर रखा और रतन पूरा घूम गया। रतन के पैर नहीं लड़खड़ा रहे थे। वह वापस अपनी मेज़ पर पहुँचकर बैठ गया। पहलवान लौट गया। रतन ने अपना गिलास उठाया जिसमें शराब बाक़ी थी। उसे अपने पास 'डबल' न होने का अफ़सोस था। यदि 'डबल' होता तो वह पहलवान को फ़र्श पर लिटाता और उछलकर मंच पर चढ़ जाता।

पहलवान बिल लेकर आ गया। रतन ने अपना पर्स जेब से निकाला। पर्स में चार सौ रुपए थे और कुछ रेज़गारी थी। फिर उसने बिल हाथ में उठाकर देखा : 699 रु.। उसे हँसी आ गई। हँसी पर्स के और बिल के रुपयों में मिलान न होने पर नहीं आई थी। हँसी बिल की राशि देखकर आई थी।

'क्या यह बिल शराब का है ?' उसने नज़रें उठाकर पहलवान से पूछा।

'हाँ', पहलवान ने कहा।

रतन मुस्करा रहा था।

'हँस क्यों रहे हो ?' पहलवान ने पूछा।

'टोटल बाटा के बिल का है', यह कहते हुए रतन ने चार सौ रुपए बिल की ट्रे में रख दिए।

'बाक़ी ?' पहलवान कुछ कड़का।

'नहीं हैं।'

'मेरे साथ आओ', पहलवान ने कहा।

काउंटर पर रतन अपना बायाँ हाथ रखे सफ़ाई दे रहा था कि वह शहर में नया है और उसे यहाँ के रेट का अन्दाज़ा नहीं था। उसके बाएँ हाथ में घड़ी का सुनहरा डायल चमक रहा था। पहलवान ने घड़ी उतार ली। वह कल पैसे देकर

घड़ी वापस ले सकता था। उसकी पीठ के पीछे हॉल का कोई गीत फिर शोर में बदल गया था।

देर रात जब वह बाहर आया, उसके पैर लड़खड़ा रहे थे। बारिश ख़त्म हो गई थी। आसमान काला था। हवा ठंडी थी। सड़क पर रोशनियाँ जल रही थीं जिनके बीच में अँधेरा था। जब वह एक खम्भे के नीचे आया तो उसने बाईं कलाई ऊपर उठाकर समय ढूँढ़ने की कोशिश की। कलाई ख़ाली थी। समय नहीं था। उसे सहसा एक नई ख़ुशी ने घेर लिया। वह आज़ाद था।

3.4

अगली सुबह जब रतन कमरे से बाहर आया तो उसने देखा कि हॉल में बेबी खड़ी है। उसका अनुमान ही था कि वह बेबी है। उसने उसे सात-आठ वर्ष पहले लखनऊ में देखा था जब वह गोद में थी। उसे मालूम था कि वह पंचगनी में पढ़ती है। वह ज़रूर किसी छुट्टी में आई होगी। वह हॉल के बीच खड़ी उसे देखती हुई मुस्करा रही थी। वह फक् गोरी थी। उसने नीला नाइट-सूट पहना था और उसके बाल पंखे की हवा में उड़ रहे थे। वह मुस्करा रही थी जैसे कोई परी हो।

'हाय बेबी', रतन ने आगे बढ़कर कहा, 'मुझे पहचाना ?'

वह मुस्कराती रही जैसे कोई परी हो।

किशोरी ने किचन से निकलकर हॉल में आते हुए कहा—'बेबी, ये तुम्हारे छोटे चाचू हैं।'

'छोटे चाचू !' परी हँसी।

बाहर फैली धूप की रोशनी काँच की दीवार से होती हुई हॉल में भर गई थी। आकाश में बादल नहीं थे। नीले आसमान के नीचे ताड़ के पेड़ आहिस्ता-आहिस्ता हिल रहे थे। रतन की नज़र काँच की दीवार से लौटकर फिर परी के चेहरे पर रुक गई। उसे लगा, परी के कन्धों पर अभी पंख उग रहे हैं।

'तुम कब आईं, परी ?' रतन ने पूछा।

'रोज़', वह हँसी।

'रोज़ ?'

'हाँ, मैं रोज़ घर आती हूँ।'

'चाहे पँचगनी में रहो ?'

'हाँ।'

किशोरी डाइनिंग टेबल साफ़ करते हुए हँसी। फिर उसने मेज़ पर दूध का

गिलास बेबी की ओर खिसकाते हुए कहा—'चलो, दूध पिओ।'

जब बेबी ने दूध का गिलास मुँह से लगाया तो पवन भी हॉल में आ गया और उसने चाय पीते रतन से कहा कि ज़रा जल्दी तैयार होना, आज थोड़ा जल्दी निकलेंगे। रास्ते में पवन ने रतन को याद दिलाया कि डॉक्टर की राय के मुताबिक उसे शराब से दूर रहना चाहिए। रतन गाड़ी में पवन की बग़ल में बैठा सामने सड़क की चालू भीड़ को देखता रहा जैसे पवन ने किसी और को सलाह दी हो या उसके साथ बैठा व्यक्ति रतन न हो, कोई और हो। क्या रतन का कोई 'डबल' हो सकता था ? 'डबल' हर तकलीफ़ में एवजी करता था। क्या कोई उसकी बाधा ले सकता था ? सामने आधी सड़क सीधी बह रही थी, आधी उल्टी बह रही थी जैसे कोई आदमियों की नदी हो। लेकिन क्या कोई नदी आधी सीधी, आधी उल्टी बह सकती थी ? रतन के दिमाग़ में ऐसे ही उल्टे-सीधे ख़्याल आते रहे जब तक वे फ़ैक्टरी नहीं पहुँचे और वह कम्प्यूटर के सामने नहीं बैठा। कम्प्यूटर के सामने बैठते ही उसके दिमाग़ के परदे पर कम्प्यूटर के परदे की तरह आँकड़े उभरने लगे। परदे पर आँकड़ों के सिवा कुछ नहीं था। परदे पर कब घंटा दुगुना हो जाता था, कब चौगुना—पता ही नहीं चलता था।

एकाएक दोपहर में गर्मी बढ़ गई और चारों ओर कारख़ानों में कुछ शोर-सा उठा। पवन अपने केबिन से निकलकर बाहर गया। लौटकर उसने टी.वी. चला दिया। परदे पर दो गगनचुम्बी मीनारें शनैः-शनैः ढहती हुई नज़र आईं। ये वायुयानों की टक्कर से खंडित हुई थीं। टक्कर भी बार-बार दिखाई जा रही थी। टक्कर के बाद मीनारें टूटतीं और ढहने लगतीं जैसे रेत की बनी हों। गिरती मीनारों के साथ भागते हुए आदमियों और औरतों की तस्वीरें थीं जिनके चेहरे भय के चेहरे थे। उनके चेहरों पर वही डर था जो किसी सोते आदमी के चेहरे पर अचानक खिंच आता है जब वह आँखें खोलता है और अपने को अपने ही बिस्तर पर घिरा हुआ पाता है। यह बादशाह का बिस्तर था। यह अमेरिका था।

केबिन में फड़फड़ाते कैलेंडर पर 11 सितम्बर, 2001 की तारीख़ थी। टी.वी. पर न्यूयार्क के वर्ल्ड ट्रेड सेंटर की जुड़वाँ मीनारें बार-बार गिर रही थीं। मलबा ज़मीन पर गिरता था और आसमान काला हो जाता था। लोग सड़कों पर भाग रहे थे जैसे धरती से दूर भाग जाएँगे।

डर की लहरें अमेरिका से निकलकर सात समुद्रों से होती हुई दुनिया-भर में फैल गई थीं। मुम्बई समुद्र के किनारे थी, जिसमें पोली ज़मीन के नीचे समुद्र से घिरे सात द्वीप थे। सातों द्वीपों का डर अकेला था। यदि बादशाह के बिस्तर पर विस्फोट हुआ था, तो कहीं कुछ भी हो सकता था।

दुनिया सन्न थी।

पवन ने मदन को फ़ोन किया। वह सकुशल था। न्यूयार्क नहीं गया था। पवन ने तुरन्त झाँसी फ़ोन किया और अम्माँ-पापा को मदन की ख़ैरियत की ख़बर दी। बाँके बिहारी ने छोटे के बारे में पूछा। पवन ने कहा कि रतन ठीक है, मैं उसे फ़ोन देता हूँ, आप खुद बात कर लें। रतन ने पापा और अम्माँ से बात की। उसने दोनों से कहा कि मैं बिलकुल ठीक हूँ, आप कोई चिन्ता न करें। वह सबके साथ हॉल में टी.वी. के सामने बैठा था। उसके बाद अम्माँ-पापा ने बेबी से बात की।

रात हो गई थी।

फ़ोन रखकर टी.वी. के परदे की ओर देखते हुए बेबी ने पूछा :

'कितनी मीनारें गिरीं ?'

'दो', पवन ने कहा।

'दो कैसे ?'

'क्यों ?'

'बीस तो मैं ही गिन चुकी हूँ।'

पवन हँसा। रतन मुस्कराया।

'दो ही हैं', पवन ने कहा, 'तुमने दस बार दोनों का गिरना देखा।'

'लोग भाग क्यों रहे हैं ?' बेबी ने फिर पूछा।

'ये जान बचाकर भागते हुए लोग हैं', रतन ने कहा, 'ये धरती के पार चले जाएँगे।'

'धरती के पार !' बेबी चौंकी।

'हाँ', रतन ने कहा, 'जान बचाने के लिए।'

बेबी ने एक क्षण सोचा। फिर पूछा—'दोनों मीनारों पर हमला करने वाले दोनों जहाज़ क्या ऑटोमेटिक हैं ?'

'नहीं।'

'तो क्या चालकों को जान प्यारी नहीं ?'

'नहीं।'

'कोई पागल ही अपनी जान इस तरह ले सकता है', बेबी ने रतन की ओर नज़रें घुमाते हुए कहा।

'दूसरे उन्हें पागल ही कहते हैं। वे कहते हैं कि बादशाह पागल है और वे बादशाह को जगा रहे हैं।'

'लोगों को मारकर !' बेबी की आँखें ऊपर उठ गईं।

चुप्पी छा गई।

पवन और किशोरी के चेहरों पर भी चुप्पी थी। वे दोनों बेबी के चेहरे को देख रहे थे। रतन इन दिनों फ़िल्म सिटी की सैर के बाद आमिर और देवदास के बारे में बहुत सोचता था। ख़ासकर देवदास की भीतरी बाधा के बारे में—जो अपने ज़माने का आईना थी। गिरती मीनारों से उठता धुआँ देखते हुए रतन को आत्महत्या के बहुत-से दृश्य याद आए जैसे पंखे से लटका हुआ प्रेमी या बीसवीं मंज़िल से छलाँग लगाता हुआ बूढ़ा या नदी में कूदती हुई लड़की। क्या यह लड़की सपना थी ? वह बाद में जानेगा कि एक चालक ने सिर्फ़ विमान उड़ाने का प्रशिक्षण लिया था, विमान उतारने का नहीं। वही चालक अभी परदे पर मीनार को बार-बार जहाज़ से ठोकर मार रहा था।

बेबी ने रिमोट हाथ में लेकर कोई संगीत का चैनल लगा दिया जिसमें माइकेल जैक्सन मंच पर नाचते हुए गा रहा था। या वह गाते हुए नाच रहा था ?

पवन की खल्वाट खोपड़ी रात की रोशनी में चमक रही थी। बाल सिर्फ़ उसकी भौंहों की जगह थे। बाक़ी चेहरा सपाट था। चेहरा भावहीन था। टी.वी. के परदे पर टिकी आँखें जड़ थीं। यदि आँखें खुली न होतीं तो शक हो सकता था कि पवन परदे के सामने नहीं, परदे के पीछे बैठा है। असल में इस समय वह डायना के बारे में सोच रहा था जिससे कल दोपहर कोलाबा के उसके फ़्लैट में मिलना तय था। वह डायना को उस ज़माने से जानता था जब वह आयकर विभाग में था। वह पहली बार उससे क्लब में मिला था। डायना भरी-पूरी औरत थी, जिसके जिस्म में समुद्र और आँखों में ज्वार-भाटा था। दूसरी बार जब वह उससे मिलने गया तो वह केवल नाइटी पहने थी, जो उसने फ़्लैट का दरवाज़ा बन्द करके यह कहते हुए उतार दी थी, 'अभी रात नहीं हुई।' जब पवन उसके फ़्लैट से बाहर आया, उस वक़्त आधी रात थी। पवन को लगा था जैसे वह अपना शरीर अन्दर पलंग पर छोड़ आया है...या हॉल के फ़र्श पर...या किचन में, जहाँ डायना ऑमलेट बना रही थी।

इस बार पवन ने जब परदे की जानिब देखा तो परदे पर डायना की नंगी देह मुस्कराती हुई अँगड़ाई ले रही थी। उसके काले बाल हवा में उड़ रहे थे। अगले क्षण काले बाल आसमान में धुएँ के बादल हो गए और नीचे धरती पर दोनों मीनारें धँसकने लगीं गोया डायना की जाँघें हों।

किशोरी काँच की दीवार के ऊपर कौशल्या मैया के चरणों की ओर कातर निगाहों से देख रही थी जो सोने की पायलों से घिरे थे। काँच की दीवार के परे अँधेरा था। टी.वी. के परदे पर फिर मीनारें गिर रही थीं। गगनचुम्बी मीनारों के बार-बार ज़मींदोज़ होने के साथ दिल काँपता। फिर दिल सुन्न हो जाता था जैसे

उसमें ख़ून की जगह पानी भर गया हो। सहसा फ़ोन की घंटी बजी। किशोरी ने फ़ोन उठाया और उसके मुँह से निकला, 'जय कौशल्या मैया !'

किशोरी के मुँह से बार-बार 'जय कौशल्या मैया' निकलने के पीछे सिर्फ़ परदे पर मीनारों का गिरना नहीं था। उसके पीछे डायना भी थी जिसका नाम कभी अंजली हो जाता, कभी सुनयना और कभी कुछ और। किशोरी को पता चल जाता था। कभी पवन के बदन की पराई गन्ध से, कभी किसी फ़ोन से और कभी गाड़ी के फ़र्श पर सीट के नीचे गिरे कंडोम के छिलके से। जब ऐसा कुछ होता तो किशोरी की आँख से एक आँसू गिरता और उसके मुँह से निकलता 'जय कौशल्या मैया'। इस समय उसके मन में अपनी सहेली वर्षा की फ़ोर्ड आइकॉन थी जो उसने किशोरी की तरह अपने पास ज़ेन होने के बावजूद ख़रीदी थी। यह वर्षा की दूसरी ए.सी. गाड़ी थी। किशोरी के पास केवल एक थी जो पवन को बिठाए डायना, सुनयना या अंजली का पीछा करती रहती थी। इससे बुरा भाग्य किसी और का क्या होगा ?

यों तो संकट की कभी कोई कमी नहीं थी। कभी उसके पास नई डिज़ाइन की साड़ी नहीं थी, कभी कोई नई डिज़ाइन की ड्रेस नहीं थी, कभी कोई हार या अँगूठी जो वर्षा या नीला के पास थी, उसके पास नहीं थी। मगर इस बार तो हद हो गई थी। उसे सहसा एक हादसे की तरह एहसास हुआ था कि उसके पास गांधीजी की छड़ी की तरह एक इकलौती गाड़ी है। इसीलिए फ़ोन पर अचानक एक आह की तरह उसके मुँह से निकला था : 'जय कौशल्या मैया !'

वह अँधेरी काँच की दीवार के ऊपर कौशल्या मैया के स्वर्णमंडित चरणों को निहार रही थी जब पवन ने टी.वी. के रिमोट का बटन दबाते हुए कहा—'बहुत रात हो गई।' बेबी पहले ही 'गुड नाइट' बोलकर अपने कमरे में चली गई थी, जहाँ खिड़की के परे दूर अँधेरी पहाड़ियाँ थीं जो सूर्य की रोशनी में हरी हो जाती थीं। बेबी सोने से पहले पहाड़ियों पर पर्दा डाल देती थी। रतन अपने कमरे की खिड़की के पर्दे रात को खोल देता था क्योंकि रात में अचानक आँख खुलने पर उसे आकाश में दमकते सितारे या धरती पर अँधेरी पहाड़ियाँ देखना अच्छा लगता था। उसे लगता था कि वह कमरे में अकेला नहीं है।

किशोरी ने अपने कमरे को भीतर से बन्द करते हुए पवन से कहा—'वर्षा के घर आज फ़ोर्ड आइकॉन आई है।'

'तुमने उसे बधाई दी ?' पवन ने मुस्कराते हुए कहा।

'हाँ', किशोरी बोली, 'मगर बधाई देते हुए दिल बेचैन हो गया।'

'क्यों ?'

'मैंने फ़ोर्ड आइकॉन का तसव्वुर किया—जो मेरे पास नहीं है।'

'तुम्हारे पास ज़ेन है।'

'ज़ेन तो उसके पास भी है। ज़ेन में वो बात कहाँ ?'

'मुझे तो नहीं लगता', पवन ने बिस्तर पर चित लेटते हुए कहा।

'ज़ेन से तुम्हारी सारी ज़रूरतें पूरी हो जाती हैं।' किशोरी ने पवन को तेज़ निगाहों से देखा। वह नाइटी पहन रही थी।

'और तुम्हारी ज़रूरतें ?' पवन ने उसकी ओर नज़रें मोड़ीं।

पल-भर की चुप्पी के बाद किशोरी ने घोषणा की—'फ़ोर्ड आइकॉन मेरी ज़रूरत है।'

'कैसे ?' पवन बिस्तर पर उठकर बैठते हुए बोला, 'बेबी तो यहाँ रहती नहीं !'

'मैं तो रहती हूँ। जहाँ जाती हूँ, भर्र-भर्र करते ऑटो से जाती हूँ।' उसने आँखें सिकोड़ीं।

'ऐसे कहाँ-कहाँ जाती हो, डॉर्लिंग ?'

'कौशल्या मैया के सत्संग। किटी पार्टी। शॉपिंग। फ्रेंड्स के घर या उनके साथ फ़िल्म...वगैरह, वगैरह..।'

'वगैरह ? वगैरह ?' पवन हँसा।

'यह तुम्हारा वगैरह-वगैरह नहीं है', किशोरी तीखी आवाज़ में बोली।

पवन चुप हो गया। तीर निशाने पर लगा था। वह हथियार डालते हुए नर्म स्वर में बोला, 'लेकिन पैसे कहाँ हैं ?'

वह हँसी।

फिर उसने कहा, 'पिछले माह ही तुमने कम्प्यूटर असिस्टेंट जोशी की छुट्टी की है क्योंकि उसका काम रतन कर रहा है। उसकी तनख़्वाह क्या थी ?'

'सात हज़ार।'

'क़रीब इतना ही ई.एम.आई. बैंक लोन पर बनेगा। मैंने पता कर लिया है।'

पवन को लगा कि उसके पास कहने को कुछ नहीं बचा। उसने बाईं ओर करवट ली जहाँ किशोरी आकर लेट गई थी। उसने सिरहाने रखे लैम्प का स्विच बन्द कर दिया था। कमरे में अँधेरा था। कुछ देर बाद अँधेरे में तेज़ साँसों की आवाज़ें गूँजने लगीं जैसे पलंग पर दो जानवर क़ैद हों। फिर कोई आह निकली...पवन...पवन...।

आधी रात को किशोरी अचानक बिस्तर पर उठकर औचक बैठ गई। वह बार-बार अँधेरे में आँखें फाड़कर कमरे में चारों ओर देख रही थी मानो अपने को

भरोसा दे रही हो कि सपना टूट गया है। यह ऐसा सपना था जो वह बार-बार देखती थी। वह ख़ुद भूल गई थी कि यह किसी वास्तविक घटना की पुनरावृत्ति है या कोई दिल में जड़ जमाए बैठी आशंका है ! सपने में दोपहर का वक़्त था। वह घर से अकेली किटी पार्टी में जाने के लिए घर बन्द करके बाहर आती है। वर्षा अपने घर पर बताती है कि पार्टी स्थगित हो गई है। किशोरी को अचानक तेज़ सिर-दर्द होता है और वह लौटकर अपने फ़्लैट के ताले में चाबी घुमाती है। वह किवाड़ खोलकर अन्दर जाती है। फिर वह हॉल में दाईं ओर मुड़कर अपने कमरे की ओर बढ़ती है। रास्ते में दूसरा कमरा है, जिससे हँसने की आवाज़ आती है। कोई औरत हँस रही है ! किशोरी बन्द दरवाज़ा अन्दर की तरफ़ ठेलती है। पलंग पर चित लेटी एक नंगी औरत हँस रही है। पवन फ़र्श पर तिरछा उसके पास नंगा खड़ा है। किशोरी ने उसे इतना बंजर कभी नहीं देखा : न चेहरे पर बाल हैं, न शरीर पर—सिर्फ़ नाक के दोनों ओर भँवों पर बाल हैं। किशोरी को देखकर उसका चेहरा फक् हो जाता है। बिस्तर पर लेटी नंगी औरत की हँसी रुक गई है। किशोरी पवन की आँखों में देख रही है, जो झपक नहीं रहीं—जैसे कभी-कभी रतन की आँखें झपकना भूल जाती हैं।

पलंग पर लेटी नंगी औरत शायद मुस्कराती है।

किशोरी उल्टे पाँव पीछे लौटती है और दरवाज़े को ज़ोर से बन्द करते हुए अपने कमरे की ओर बढ़ जाती है।

कमरे के अँधेरे में किशोरी ने बिस्तर पर लेटे पवन को देखा और फिर ख़ुद उसी अँधेरे में लेट गई। उसे कुछ तसल्ली-सी महसूस हुई कि यह दूसरा कमरा नहीं है—जिसमें अभी रतन सो रहा था।

3.5

आँख खुलते ही खिड़की के काँच में उजाला देखकर रतन कमरे से बाहर आया। गैलरी में उसे बाईं ओर से बेबी के कमरे से कोई आता हुआ लगा। बेबी का कमरा बन्द था—वह कब से पँचगनी लौट गई थी। बन्द कमरे से कौन बाहर आ रहा था ? रतन ने बाईं ओर नज़रें मोड़ीं : उसे लगा मानो वह ख़ुद बेबी के कमरे से बाहर आ रहा है ! क़द-काठी नाक-नक़्श वही थे। गैलरी के धुँधलके में रंग ठीक से नज़र नहीं आ रहा था। सफ़ाचट चेहरा और सिर पर बाल ही बाल थे। यह पवन नहीं हो सकता था। जब वह कुछ और नज़दीक आया तो उसका मुस्कराता चेहरा नज़र आया।

'मदन भैया !' रतन के मुँह से निकला।

वह मदन के पैरों की ओर झुका। मदन ने उसे सीने से लगा लिया।

मदन आधी रात मुम्बई आया था। वह अपनी कम्पनी के काम से अचानक आ गया था। पवन और किशोरी उसे सान्ताक्रुज़ लेने गए थे। पवन ने जान-बूझकर रतन को पिछली रात नहीं बताया था ताकि वह रात में एयरपोर्ट आकर परेशान न हो। सुबह उसे 'सरप्राइज़' भी मिलेगा ! पवन ने हॉल में चाय पीते हुए यह बताया।

मदन और रतन आमने-सामने बैठे थे। रतन का पहली नज़र का अचरज ख़त्म हो गया था। उस विस्मय का कारण गैलरी का अँधेरा भी था। मदन का रंग ज़्यादा साफ़ हो गया था—वह गोरों के देश में रहता था। उसके चेहरे पर गोरों के देश का पानी झलक रहा था। उसकी निकर और टी-शर्ट अमरीकी थे। उसकी मुस्कान अमरीकी थी। वह रतन को धोखा अँधेरे में ही दे सकता था क्योंकि उनकी उम्र में ज़्यादा फ़र्क नहीं था। रतन अपने सामने बैठे बड़े भाई को उसके सवालों के जवाब देते हुए बार-बार चाय के कप से नज़रें उठाकर देख रहा था। मदन अपने देश के सफलतम युवकों में से था जो अमरीका जाकर बसते थे। अमरीका की धरती पर उसका अपना घर था, जहाँ दो गाड़ियाँ खड़ी थीं। वह दूसरे अप्रवासी भारतीय युवकों से एक क़दम आगे था। उसने एक अमरीकी लड़की से शादी की थी, जिसका नाम ज़ेन था। ज़ेन अभी तक भारत नहीं आई थी। मदन ने कहा, वह अगली बार ज़रूर आएगी। अलबत्ता उसकी तस्वीरें ज़रूर भारत आई थीं। रतन को उसकी तस्वीरें हॉलीवुड की किसी अभिनेत्री की तस्वीरें लगती थीं। इस समय मदन को देखते हुए उसे ज़ेन की तस्वीर याद आई।

चाय का कप मेज़ पर रखकर, पवन ने मदन से पूछा, 'दिन में कहीं जाना है ?'

'आज कहीं नहीं।'

'फिर ?'

'नहाकर सो जाऊँगा।'

'मेरी नींद भी अधूरी है', पवन ने कहा, 'मैं भी सोऊँगा। दोपहर में उठकर बीयर पिएँगे। आज फ़ैक्टरी में भी कुछ ख़ास काम नहीं।' फिर वह रतन की ओर देखते हुए मुस्कराया और बोला, 'और असली मालिक तो वहाँ रहेंगे ही। रतन, एक ट्रक माल कल्यान जाना है। मैंने ट्रांसपोर्टर को बोल दिया है। देख लेना।'

'ठीक है,' कहते हुए रतन कुर्सी से उठकर बाथरूम की ओर चला। उसे लगा, उससे यही अपेक्षित है।

बाथरूम में कपड़े उतारते हुए उसे यह तकलीफ़ हुई कि वह कुछ देर और मदन भैया के साथ क्यों नहीं बैठ सका। पवन ने तो एकदम उठ जाने के लिए नहीं कहा था। उसे ऐसा क्यों लगा कि वे अनकहे यही कह रहे हैं ? यदि वे कह भी रहे थे, तो क्या यह आज्ञा थी ? क्या इस आज्ञा का पालन उसकी मजबूरी थी ? यदि सचमुच ऐसा था, तो वह नौकर था ! असली मालिक तो पवन ही थे। तो क्या वे उसे असली मालिक कहकर चिढ़ा रहे थे ? वह नंगा शावर के नीचे खड़ा हो गया। पानी धारों में उसके शरीर पर गिरने लगा। उसने आँखें बन्द कर लीं। पानी उसके सिर से पैर तक लुढ़कता हुआ इस तरह बहने लगा जैसे वह पानी के नीचे खड़ी कोई पत्थर की मूर्ति हो।

वह मूर्ति की तरह अपने कमरे से कपड़े पहनकर बाहर आया और डाइनिंग टेबल पर बैठ गया। हॉल में पवन बैठा अख़बार पढ़ रहा था। मदन अन्दर चला गया था। पवन अख़बार पढ़ता रहा। रतन पराँठा खाता रहा। यह आलू का पराँठा था, जो मदन को पसन्द था। पराँठा खाकर, हाथ धोकर जब वह बाहर जाने लगा तो पवन ने अख़बार से नज़रें उठाकर मुस्कराते हुए कहा—'मालिक, अपनी फ़ैक्टरी का ख़्याल रखना।'

रतन ने पलटकर एक बार देखा।

रोज़ की तरह वह आज वातानुकूलित गाड़ी से नहीं जा रहा था। वह अभी बस से कान्दिवली स्टेशन जाएगा और लोकल के सेकंड क्लास में धक्के खाएगा। धक्के खाते हुए वह दहिसर पहुँचेगा और फिर फ़ैक्टरी। फ़ैक्टरी का मालिक धक्के खाते हुए फ़ैक्टरी पहुंचेगा। जब वह कम्प्यूटर सहायक होता था तो आरामदेह वातानूकूलित गाड़ी में जाता था जिसे कभी-कभी मालिक भी चलाता था। गाड़ी में दोपहर का भोजन भी होता था। आज वह दोपहर में चाय की मदद से समोसे खाएगा।

दोपहर में कल्यान का ट्रक लोड होते हुए पाँच नग कम पड़ गए। रतन ने कहा कि चालान में पाँच कम दिखाकर ट्रक भेज दो। स्टोरकीपर चन्द्रकान्त ने घर पवन से बात किए बिना चालान नहीं बनाया। ऊपर से उसने यही कहा, 'सेठ, बुरा मत मानना। कोई ग़लती हो गई तो बड़ा सेठ मुझे नौकरी से निकाल देगा।' यह कहने की बात थी। असल बात यह थी कि चन्द्रकान्त को रतन पर भरोसा नहीं था क्योंकि वह जानता था कि पवन को भी रतन पर भरोसा नहीं है। फ़ैक्टरी के कर्मचारियों की नज़र में वह कम्प्यूटर सहायक ही था। भ्रम की कोई गुंजाइश नहीं थी। उसका चेहरा उसी तरह कोरा हो गया जैसे आँकड़ों के बिना कम्प्यूटर होता है।

उस शाम शरीर में लोकल के धक्के ही धक्के लिए जब उसने फ़्लैट की घंटी बजाई तो अँधेरा हो गया था। दरवाज़ा हँसते हुए मदन ने खोला। मेज़ पर स्कॉच की बोतल रखी थी। बोतल के दोनों ओर दो भरे गिलास थे और दोनों बड़े भाई हँस रहे थे। दोनों के बीच कोई मज़ाक हुआ था।

'आओ छोटे', मदन ने कहा।

मदन हँसते हुए बोला था। पवन अब भी हँस रहा था। रतन हँसी के फ़व्वारे में भीगता हुआ अन्दर आया और कुर्सी पर बैठ गया।

'कैसा रहा दिन ?' पवन ने पूछा।

'ठीक।'

'कोई ख़ास बात ?'

'कल्यान का ट्रक ही था। चला गया। चन्द्रकान्त ने आपसे पूछ ही लिया था।'

संक्षिप्त सन्नाटे के बाद पवन ने कहा—'उसने मुझसे क्यों पूछा ? तुम ही बता देते।'

'मैंने तो वही कहा था', रतन बोला, 'जो आपने कहा। चन्द्रकान्त ने नहीं माना।'

एक और संक्षिप्त सन्नाटे के बाद पवन ने फिर कहा, 'मैं कल उससे बात करूँगा।'

रतन कुछ नहीं बोला। वह जानता था कि चन्द्रकान्त से कोई बात नहीं होगी।

मदन स्वर्णमंडित पैरों की तस्वीर के नीचे बैठा था। गिलास से एक घूँट लेकर उसने कहा—'मैं तुम्हें देखकर बहुत ख़ुश हूँ, रतन।'

रतन हैरान था।

'मैं बहुत ख़ुश हूँ', मदन ने फिर कहा 'कि 'तुम्हारा अपना काम करने का सपना पूरा हुआ।' फिर कुछ रुककर, 'तुम्हें पूरी मेहनत और लगन से काम करना चाहिए। मुम्बई में समुद्र ही सीमा है। यहाँ आदमी एक दिन में फ़ुटपाथ से मालाबार हिल पहुँच जाता है।'

रतन के कान खुले थे और आँखें बन्द थीं जैसे वह कोई प्रवचन सुन रहा हो। जब प्रवचन बन्द हो गया तो उसने मुस्कराते हुए कहा, 'मैं तो अभी भी लोखंडवाला की बाईसवीं मंज़िल पर हूँ।'

दोनों बड़े भाई हँसे।

मेज़ पर तीसरा गिलास नहीं था। डॉक्टर ने मना किया था, रतन को याद आया। पवन ने मदन को ज़रूर बता दिया था। दोनों उसे दुधमुँहा छोटा भाई मान

रहे थे। यह बात अलग थी कि वह फ़ैक्ट्री का असली मालिक था !

वह कुर्सी से काठ-सा मुँह लिये उठा और थोड़ी देर बाद काली गोली खाकर सो गया। उसने खाने के लिए मना कर दिया था। उसे भूख नहीं थी।

किशोरी को रतन का खाने के लिए मना करना बुरा नहीं लगा, क्योंकि जवाब में पहले उसने कुछ नहीं कहा—जैसा कि वह हमेशा ऐसे मौके पर कहती थीं, औपचारिकतावश ही। फिर जैसे उसे कुछ याद आया हो, उसने मुड़ते हुए रतन से कहा, 'अच्छा।' रतन ने सुना नहीं था। सुनता भी तो फिर से मुड़ने की ज़रूरत नहीं थीं। रतन के अपना कमरा बन्द कर लेने के बाद किशोरी किचन से बाहर निकल आई। उसने हॉल में प्रवेश करने के पहले रतन के कमरे का दरवाज़ा आहिस्ता से ठेला—दरवाज़ा अन्दर से बन्द था। वह इत्मीनान से हॉल में घुसी।

'आओ भाभी', मदन ने कहा, 'तुम्हें हमारा साथ देना होगा।'

फिर उसने तीसरे गिलास में स्कॉच डाली और स्कॉच में बर्फ़ और गिलास किशोरी के हाथ में पकड़ा दिया। 'चियर्स !' मदन ने अपना गिलास हवा में उठाया, 'उस नई गाड़ी के लिए जो आप लेने जा रही हैं।'

तीनों हँसे।

फिर चुप्पी छा गई। हॉल में। हॉल के बाहर। काँच की आधी दीवार के परे। जहाँ पेड़ और पहाड़ी और बस्ती अँधेरे में गड्डमड्ड हो रहे थे।

'भाभी', मदन की आवाज़ थी।

'हाँ।'

'क्या आपको रतन अब नॉर्मल लगता है ?' मदन के चेहरे पर चिन्ता थी।

'हाँ, क्यों ?' किशोरी के चेहरे पर कुछ नहीं था।

वह अभी कौशल्या मैया के स्वर्णजड़ित चरणों के नीचे बैठी थी।

'अम्माँ-पापा बहुत चिन्ता करते हैं', मदन ने कहा, 'जब भी मैं उन्हें फ़ोन करता हूँ।'

'मैंने तुमसे कहा न, मदन', पवन तुरन्त बोला, 'कोई फिक्र की बात नहीं है। वह दवा खाता है। काम करता है। और क्या चाहिए ?'

किशोरी को एकाएक लगा कि गैलरी के परदे के पीछे कोई खड़ा है। वह उठकर परदे की ओर गई। परदे के पीछे कोई नहीं था। अलबत्ता परदा कुछ हिल रहा था। क्या यह पंखे की हवा की वजह से था ? लेकिन पंखा तो शाम से चल रहा था। परदा अभी क्यों हिला ? उसने रतन के कमरे के दरवाज़े को हल्का-सा धक्का दिया। दरवाज़ा पहले की तरह बन्द था। परदा भी रुक गया था जैसे कभी हिला ही न हो। क्या परदा सचमुच हिला था ? या यह किशोरी के दिमाग़ का

ख़लल था ?

किशोरी वापस अपनी जगह पर आकर बैठ गई जहाँ कौशल्या मैया के चरणों की छाया थी। यहाँ किसी शक की कोई गुंजाइश नहीं थी।

'मदन', एकाएक किशोरी चहकी।

'हाँ।'

'तुम्हारी गाड़ी का रंग क्या है ?'

'सफ़ेद।'

'और ज़ेन की गाड़ी का ?'

'नीला।'

किशोरी ने ऊपर एक नज़र कौशल्या मैया की तस्वीर पर डाली, फिर पवन से कहा—'फ़ोर्ड आइकॉन नीले रंग की लेंगे।'

'ज़ेन तो सफ़ेद है ही', पवन हँसा।

मदन हँसा।

किशोरी हँसी।

ऐसा लगा जैसे कौशल्या मैया के सोने के पैर भी हँसे।

हॉल की हँसी का समवेत कोलाहल बग़ल में रतन के कमरे की खुली खिड़की से अन्दर उसके कानों में पहुँचा और वह हड़बड़ाकर उठ बैठा। तब उसे लगा कि उसे पेशाब लगा है। जब वह गैलरी के अँधेरे में दाख़िल हुआ तो हॉल में हँसी की जगह बातें शुरू हो गई थीं। उसने बाथरूम में फ़्लश नहीं किया क्योंकि हॉल की बातें साफ़ सुनाई दे रही थीं।

'आपकी पाइप फ़ैक्टरी परिवार के लिए शुभ है।' मदन की आवाज़ थी, 'आप फ़ोर्ड आइकॉन ले रहे हैं, छोटे का सपना पूरा हुआ।'

यह सुनते ही रतन का पेशाब बन्द हो गया। वह बाथरूम के बाहर आकर कुछ पल गैलरी के अँधेरे में खड़ा रहा। कोई आवाज़ नहीं हुई थी। न पर्दा हिला। किसी को शक नहीं हुआ। वह अँधेरे में खड़ा हुआ छोटे के सपने के बारे में सोचता रहा जो अब पूरा हो गया था और जिसके पूरे होने की ख़ुशी में हॉल में तीनों लोग फिर हँसने लगे थे। इस बार हँसी कुछ ज़्यादा तीखी थी। शायद स्कॉच का नशा भी शामिल हो गया था। पवन का स्वर सबसे ऊँचा था।...उसे अलग करके सुनते हुए रतन को लगा कि उसके कान फट जाएँगे। उसने दोनों कानों पर हाथ रख लिए। फिर वह चुपचाप अपने कमरे की ओर बढ़ा जैसे कोई बम फटा हो और उसे अपने कमरे में जाकर फ़र्श पर लेट जाना हो। उसने चुपचाप अपना कमरा बन्द किया और बिस्तर पर लेट गया जैसे फ़र्श पर लेट रहा हो।

जब रतन आमिर का सपना देख रहा था तो मदन भैया-भाभी को बता रहा था कि वह हर इतवार अमरीका में राम-मन्दिर जाता है। और ज़ेन ? किशोरी ने पूछा। ज़ेन भी जाती है, मदन ने कहा, और आरती की लौ की आँच हथेलियों में लेकर आँखों से लगाती है। यह ज़रूर है कि उसके हाथ सीधे नहीं चलते जैसे शुरू में मदन के हाथ नहीं चलते थे, क्योंकि अमरीका पहुँचकर मदन को याद नहीं आया था कि उसने पिछली बार भारत में आरती कब ली थी। अमरीका पहुँचकर भारत बहुत याद आता था—बल्कि झाँसी की गलियाँ, सरस्वती शिशुमन्दिर और शिवजी का मन्दिर जिसके ऊपर पीपल की पत्तियाँ धूप और हवा और पानी में डोलती रहती थीं। शुरू-शुरू में जब वह थका-हारा रात को अपने कमरे में आता तो अक्सर उसे अपना घर, शहर और अम्माँ याद आतीं। दो-चार बार तो उसकी आँखों में आँसू भी आ गए। एक बार आँखों में आए आँसू रुके नहीं। बहने लगे। बहते रहे। तब उसने जाना कि वह रो रहा है। उसी सप्ताह वह इतवार को मन्दिर गया था। फिर हर इतवार जाने लगा था जैसे हर इतवार एक सी.डी. लाकर वह एक बम्बइया फ़िल्म देखता था।

कोई बॉलीबुड फ़िल्म और राम-मन्दिर !

मन्दिर की बात तब चली जब मदन ने किशोरी से दीवार पर टँगी सोने की पायलों से सजी पैरों की तस्वीर के बारे में पूछा। मदन ने बताया कि विश्व हिन्दू परिषद का ऑफ़िस मन्दिर में ही है।

'ऐसा दृश्य दुनिया में कहीं नहीं है !'

मदन ने मालाबार हिल के रेस्तराँ की दूसरी मंज़िल की छत पर बैठे हुए कहा। मेज़ पर एक ओर पवन था, दूसरी ओर मदन और सामने किशोरी बैठी थी। सूर्य समुद्र के आख़िरी सिरे पर डूब चुका था। अँधेरा शायद वहीं से निकलकर समुद्र और मुम्बई और मुम्बई के आसमान पर छा गया था। अँधेरे के नीचे मुम्बई की जगर-मगर रोशनियाँ थीं, जिनके समुद्री सिरे पर मैरीन ड्राइव की रोशनियों की माला थी। रोशनियों की माला के बाईं ओर शहर था, दाईं ओर समुद्र का साँस लेता हुआ अँधेरा था जो दूर क्षितिज में कहाँ आसमान में तब्दील हो जाता था, कुछ पता ही नहीं चलता था।

मालाबार हिल से नीचे रोशनियों की माला को देखते हुए लगता था जैसे आसमान की किसी खिड़की में बैठे हों।

एकाएक मदन फिर बोला—'मैंने एफ़ील टॉवर से पेरिस देखा, टेम्स के पुल

से लंदन देखा, कुतुबमीनार से दिल्ली देखी—मगर ऐसा नज़ारा कहीं नहीं देखा। लगता है कोई अँधेरे-उजाले का सपना हो !'

सामने बैठी किशोरी मदन का संजीदा चेहरा देखकर मुस्कराने लगी। पवन आलू-बोंडा खा रहा था। उसकी नज़रें चटनी से लिपटे आलू-बोंडा पर थीं। रतन ने अपना चेहरा समुद्र की ओर मोड़ लिया था। उसने मदन के शब्द दुहराए : 'अँधेरे-उजाले का सपना !'

किशोरी हँसी। फिर उसने रतन की तरफ़ आँखें घुमाकर कहा—'रतन, आलू बोंडा खाओ। आलू-बोंडा ठंडा हो रहा है।'

रतन आलू-बोंडा खाने लगा।

छत पर सारी टेबलें भरी थीं। भरी टेबलों पर शोर था। लोग एक-दूसरे को या टेबलों पर फैली प्लेटों को देख रहे थे। टेबलों पर बातें ही बातें थीं। अँधेरा नहीं था। न उजाला था। अँधेरे-उजाले का मिला-जुला रंग छत पर फैला था, जिसमें आवाज़ों का शोर घुल रहा था।

किशोरी की नज़र पहाड़ी के पेड़ों के अँधेरे से गुज़रती हुई मैरीन ड्राइव की सड़क पर फिसलने लगी जहाँ गाड़ियाँ खिलौनों-सी दौड़ रही थीं। वह कुछ देर एकटक सड़क पर फिसलती गाड़ियों को देखती रही जैसे पहली बार देख रही हो। उसे ख़ुद पता नहीं था। वह अँधेरी सड़क पर नीली फ़ोर्ड ढूँढ़ रही थी।

'आलू-बोंडा और लोगी ?' पवन ने पूछा।

'नहीं।'

'चिकन टिक्का ?'

'नहीं।'

'फ़िश-फ़्राइड ?'

'नहीं।'

'कोक या पेप्सी ?'

'फ़ोर्ड आइकॉन', किशोरी के मुँह से निकला।

'क्या ?' पवन हँसा।

'ओह', किशोरी ने झेंपी नज़र मैरीन ड्राइव से वापस टेबल पर खींच ली।

रतन समुद्र के अँधेरे में देख रहा था। मदन ने उसके हाथ पर हाथ रखते हुए एक पर्यटक की तरह कहा, 'क्या नज़ारा है ?' रतन चौंका। मदन का हाथ बर्फ़ की तरह ठंडा था।

एकाएक शहर की सारी बत्तियाँ गुल हो गईं जैसे अँधेरा समुद्र सारे शहर में फैल गया हो और मालाबार हिल कोई अँधेरे का स्तूप हो, जिस पर रतन बैठा हो।

उस रात जब वे घर पहुँचे, पवन ने आदतन टी.वी. खोल दिया। परदे पर दिन में हुए संसद पर हमले की छायाएँ घूम रही थीं। पृष्ठभूमि में संसद की गोल इमारत का कोई टुकड़ा था। कोई संसद की ओर बन्दूक लिए दौड़ रहा था। कई लोग दूसरी ओर से लपक रहे थे। चेहरे डरे हुए थे। अन्ततः हमलावर धराशायी हो गए थे। एक लहूलुहान आतंकवादी का 'क्लोज़-अप' था। संसद पर हमला ! यह सीधे दिल पर हमले की तरह था। मानो कोई बन्दूक तानकर सीधा दिल को छेद दे ! हमलावर रंग-रूप से यहीं का लगता था जैसे कोई अपने ही घर से बन्दूक लिए सामने आ जाए।

तेरह दिसम्बर मुम्बई में—चाहे वह मालाबार हिल की छत पर ही क्यों न हो—कोई ऐसा ठंडा दिन नहीं था। फिर मदन का हाथ मौत की तरह ठंडा क्यों लगा था ? रतन टी.वी. के सामने मूर्तिवत् बैठा यही सोच रहा था।

पर्दे पर तफ़तीश जारी थी।

3.6

मुम्बई में फूल खिले थे।

एक ओर बाँद्रा की खाड़ी की सड़ी मछलियों की गन्ध थी, दूसरी ओर पाली हिल पर हर तरफ़ फूल खिले थे। आमिर ख़ान का निवास ढूँढ़ते हुए वह नरगिस दत्त रोड से गुज़रा। उसने दिलीप कुमार का बँगला देखा...और कुछ देर देखता रहा...फूल खिले थे, देवदास नहीं था। वह आगे बढ़ा। दो बार राहगीरों से पूछना पड़ा। आख़िरकार वह बेला विस्टा अपार्टमेंट्स के सामने खड़ा था, जिसमें ग्यारह नम्बर फ़्लैट में आमिर ख़ान रहता था।

'ग्यारह नम्बर किस माले पर है ?' रतन ने गेट पर खड़े सुरक्षाकर्मी से पूछा।

'क्यों ?'

'उसमें आमिर ख़ान रहता है।'

'तो ?'

'मुझे उससे मिलना है।'

सुरक्षाकर्मी ने रतन को ऊपर से नीचे तक देखा। वह किसी गाड़ी से नहीं उतरा था। उसकी कमीज़ पर लोकल और बस की मुचड़न थी।

'तुम नहीं मिल सकते,' सुरक्षाकर्मी ने अपनी मूँछों के बीच कहा।

'क्यों ?

'वह किसी से नहीं मिलता।'

रतन सन्न रह गया। उसकी कुछ समझ में नहीं आया।

'मैं उससे हाथ मिला चुका हूँ', रतन के मुँह से निकला।

'कहाँ ?'

'फ़िल्म सिटी में।'

'तो फिर वहीं जाकर हाथ मिला लो', मुच्छड़ मुस्कराया।

'क्यों, क्या वह अभी वहीं है ?'

'हाँ', मुच्छड़ हँसा।

रतन मुच्छड़ का झूठ समझकर पीछे मुड़ा और सड़क के दूसरी ओर खड़ा हो गया। हर तरफ़ हर रंग के फूल थे। फूल दिखाई देते थे, सुनाई नहीं देते थे। लगता था, फूलों में गन्ध नहीं है। क्या मुम्बई के फूलों में गन्ध नहीं है, आमिर ? मैंने कल पापा को झाँसी फ़ोन करके बता दिया है। उन्होंने कहा कि झाँसी के आँगन में इन दिनों नीम के फूल झरते हैं, जिनमें नीम की गन्ध है—मैं तुम्हें आकर ले जाता हूँ। न जाने क्यों उन्होंने कहा कि मैं आता हूँ ? मैं अकेला भी लौट सकता था। बल्कि आदमी को अकेला ही लौटना चाहिए। लौटने के लिए अकेला आदमी ठीक होता है। लौटने के लिए अकेला आदमी काफ़ी होता है। क्या मैं अब अपने लिए काफ़ी नहीं रहा, आमिर ?

सड़क के दोनों ओर इमारतें थीं, जहाँ फूल खिले थे। रतन हर तरफ़ देखता हुआ खड़ा था जैसे आमिर किसी ओर से फूलों से निकलकर हवा में उड़ता हुआ आ जाएगा। लेकिन हवा ख़ाली थी। आसमान ख़ाली था। आसमान में दो-चार बादल के टुकड़े थे, जिन पर धूप चमक रही थी जैसे सड़क के दोनों ओर इमारतों और पेड़ों पर। धूप फेंकता हुआ सूरज अपनी खिड़की में इत्मीनान से बैठा था।

देखो आमिर, तुम इसी सड़क पर बचपन में निकर-कमीज़ पहने फुदकते होगे जैसे मैं झाँसी की गलियों में दौड़ता-फिरता था। तुम निकर-कमीज़ पीछे छोड़कर आमिर ख़ान हो गए—जबकि तुम्हारे पहले कोई आमिर ख़ान नहीं था ! शायद यही मंत्र है। मैं इसी को पकड़ नहीं सका। मैंने अम्बानी या आमिर होने की कोशिश की—और मैं रतन भी न हो सका !

मैं रतन होना चाहता हूँ, आमिर !

मैं रतन होना चाहता हूँ !

रतन कौन है ?

जो भी हो, मैं तुमसे एक बार हाथ मिलाना चाहता हूँ। एक बार पहले भी मैंने तुमसे हाथ मिलाया था। एक बार आख़िरी बार मैं तुमसे हाथ मिलाना

चाहता हूँ। तुम्हारे हाथ में मैं अपना नाम छोड़ जाऊँगा। यदि तुम नहीं मिले तो मैं अपना नाम इसी पहाड़ी पर छोड़ दूँगा। इस बार मैं अपने नाम की गठरी मुम्बई में छोड़ जाऊँगा।

अब मुझसे सहा नहीं जाता, आमिर !

तुम हर फ़िल्म में अपना दूसरा नाम कैसे सह लेते हो ? क्या इसीलिए तुम एक बार में एक फ़िल्म करते हो ? एक नाम का बड़ा बोझ होता है, क्यों ?

सूरज समुद्र की ओर छिपने जा रहा था, जब रतन एकाएक आमिर के घर की ओर दौड़ा। वह गेट के अन्दर घुसकर इमारत की ओर जा रहा था जब दोनों ओर से दो सुरक्षाकर्मियों ने उसे पकड़ लिया। उन्होंने उसे बरामदे में एक तरफ़ खड़ा कर दिया। बाँद्रा पुलिस थाने में फ़ोन किया गया कि एक युवक 'आमिर, आमिर' करता हुआ इमारत में ज़बर्दस्ती घुस रहा था। आमिर ख़ान का मामला था। पुलिस की गाड़ी तुरन्त आ गई और रतन को ले गई। थाने में इंस्पेक्टर काले ने पूछताछ शुरू की । जब रतन ने अपना पता लोखंडवाला बताया तो इंस्पेक्टर चौंका। उसने अपने हाथ की खुजली को रोका। वह दो-चार झापड़ रसीद करने के मूड में था।

'पाली हिल किसलिए गए थे ?' उसने अपनी मेज़ से जंगली आँखें उठाकर पूछा।

'आमिर से मिलने', रतन ने मेज़ के सामने कुर्सी के पीछे खड़े हुए कहा।

'आमिर...' इंस्पेक्टर हँसा, 'आमिर ख़ान भी नहीं। क्या वह तुम्हारा दोस्त है ?'

'हाँ।'

'कैसे ?'

'मैं एक बार उससे हाथ मिला चुका हूँ।'

इंस्पेक्टर खिलखिलाकर हँसा। फिर उसने पूछा, 'क्या करोगे उससे मिलकर ?'

'अपने दिल की बात बताऊँगा।'

इंस्पेक्टर मुस्करा रहा था। 'क्या है तुम्हारे दिल की बात ?' उसने पूछा।

'उसे ही बताऊँगा', कहते हुए रतन ने नज़रें नीची कर लीं।

'स्साले...', इंस्पेक्टर ने खड़े होते हुए कहा, 'सब यहाँ हीरो बनने चले आते हैं। बाँद्रा का सबसे बड़ा लफ़ड़ा यही है। सुबह से यह तीसरा है। पहला सलमान ख़ान बनने आया था। दूसरा शाहरुख़ ख़ान बनने। सालों को अपना धर्म भी याद नहीं रहता। सिर्फ़ ख़ानों का माधुरी और ऐश्वर्या के साथ नाचना याद रहता है।'

इंस्पेक्टर काले ने सिपाही को बुलाकर रतन को लॉक-अप में डालने को कहा।

फ़ोन पर लोखंडवाला बात हो गई थी। पवन अपने भाई को लेने आ रहा था। कुछ देर में वह आ गया। लौटते हुए गाड़ी में कोई बात नहीं हुई। रात हो गई थी। पवन ने रतन से यह ज़रूर पूछा कि क्या तुमने पापा को फ़ोन किया था ? जब रतन ने 'हाँ' कहा, तो उसने पल-भर को अपनी नज़र उसकी ओर मोड़ते हुए पूछा, 'क्यों ?' रतन चुप रहा। जब पवन ने नज़रें सीधी कर लीं, तो उसने कहा, 'ऐसे ही।'

'पापा कल आ रहे हैं', पवन ने नज़रें सीधी किए हुए कहा।

घर पहुँचकर रतन ने खाना खाया। जब वह अपने कमरे में जा रहा था तो पवन ने कहा, 'दवा खाकर सो जाना।'

रतन ने काली गोली नहीं खाई। उसने कुछ दिनों से गोलियाँ खाना बन्द कर दिया था।

फूल लोखंडवाला में भी ख़ूब खिले थे। सड़क से लगी क्यारियों में और क्यारियों के परे पार्क में। पार्क में फूलों का मेला लगा था। मेला अन्दर नहर का पुल पार करते ही शुरू हो जाता था। बाँके बिहारी सुबह जब यहाँ घूमने आए तो एक आदमी सफ़ेद निकर-कमीज़ और जूते-मोजे पहने मछलियों को ब्रेड खिला रहा था। वह पुल पर खड़ा था और रोटी के टुकड़े तोड़-तोड़कर नहर के पानी में डाल रहा था जहाँ मछलियाँ इकट्ठी हो गई थीं। मछलियाँ बड़ी और रंग-बिरंगी थीं। हवा ठंडी थी। बाँके बिहारी पुल पर उछलती मछलियों को निहारते खड़े थे।

पुल के नीचे मछलियाँ मुँह खोले पानी में ठहर गई थीं।

गोल नहर के बीच फूलों का उत्सव था। जैसे ही बाँके बिहारी ने नज़रें घुमाईं, वे सन्न रह गए : क्यारियों में फूल दहक रहे थे। लाल गुलाब, पीले डहेलिया, सफ़ेद चमेली, बैंगनी गुलादाउदी...कोई भी रंग किसी ओर नज़र आ जाता था जैसे आदमी की तकलीफ़ की कोई नई रंगत हो। दुख सतरंगा केलिडोस्कोप था, जिसकी तरतीब क्यारियों में फूलों की तरह बदलती रहती थी। दिल आसमान की तरह दुखता था। ताड़ के पेड़ मजबूरी में बार-बार हाथ हिला देते।

बाँके बिहारी पत्थर की पगडंडी पर चल रहे थे, जिसके दोनों ओर फूल थे और कहीं-कहीं पेड़ सिर झुकाए खड़े थे। वे कभी-कभी सामने हवा में देखते, फिर पत्थरों पर सिर झुका देते। उनके क़दम पत्थरों को पीछे ठेलते हुए लगते थे। छोटे ने पिछली रात उन्हें अपनी दिनचर्या और आय बता दी थी। उनका बिस्तर छोटे

के कमरे में ही लगा था यद्यपि बेबी का कमरा ख़ाली था। छोटे दिन-भर कम्प्यूटर के परदे पर काम करता था और रात में घर आकर टी.वी. के परदे पर नाच-गाना देखता था जैसे उसकी साँस की डोर परदे के पीछे बँधी हो। परदे पर काम करने के लिए उसे एक हज़ार भी नहीं मिलता था जबकि कम्प्यूटर असिस्टेंट पहले सात हज़ार लेता था। पवन कहता था कि डॉक्टर ने छोटे को पैसे से दूर रखने को कहा है। यों भी छोटे कोई कर्मचारी नहीं था जो मासिक वेतन ले ! छोटे कारख़ाने का मालिक था। पवन की तरह।

छोटे ने पिछली रात कहा था—'पापा, मैं मालिक नहीं हूँ। मैं ऐसा नौकर हूँ, जिसे वेतन देने की भी ज़रूरत नहीं।...मैं...मैं बँधुआ मज़दूर हूँ !'

यह चक्र था। गोल नहर के चारों ओर गोल-गोल घूमने की तरह। यदि कोई नहर पार न करे, तो सृष्टि के अन्त तक गोल-गोल घूम सकता था। नहर पार करना ज़रूरी था। नहर दिलफ़रेब थी। ऊपर से देखने पर यह गहरी लगती थी। पानी हरा था। पानी में अनगिनत छोटी-बड़ी मछलियाँ थीं। जब कोई मोटर-बोट पानी में चलती तो बच्चों को लगता कि नदी में नाव जा रही है। नदी के कगार ऊँचे थे। दोनों किनारों पर ताड़ के पेड़ थे। एक पेड़ पीपल का था। पेड़ घना था। उसके नीचे अँधेरा-सा छाया रहता। जैसे ही दिन चढ़ता, अँधेरा पानी में कूदने लगता। तीन खोहें थीं जिनमें से नदी गुज़रती थी। खोह के अन्दर ऊबड़-खाबड़ पत्थर थे और अँधेरा था, जिसमें न पानी दिखता था, न बोट दिखती थी और आँखों के बन्द करने या खोलने में कोई फ़र्क नहीं था। सिर्फ़ अपना पानी में बहना महसूस होता था। ऐसा भी नहीं था कि कोई गन्तव्य हो। गोल-गोल घूमने की क्या मंज़िल हो सकती थी ?

नहर पार करना ज़रूरी था।

बाँके बिहारी नहर पार करके छोटे स्विमिंग-पूल के किनारे छतरी के नीचे बैठ गए। और कोई नहीं था। वे अकेले थे। सामने तालाब, फिर लॉन, लॉन को घेरे फूलों की क्यारियाँ और क्यारियों के परे ताड़ के पेड़ थे। दाहिने कोने में छह पेड़ एक-साथ झुंड में खड़े थे। जब हवा चलती तो वे आपस में फुसफुसाते हुए लगते। व्हिस्परिंग पॉम्स ! कोई आदमी नहीं था। कल सुबह जब वे दादर स्टेशन पर उतरे, तो पुल पार करके लोकल के प्लेटफ़ॉर्म पर चलते हुए अचानक बेहोश हो गए थे। पवन ने उन्हें पीछे से थामकर एक बेंच पर बिठा दिया था। कुछ देर में उनकी चेतना लौटी जब उन्होंने स्वीकार कर लिया कि मुम्बई में उतने ही आदमी हैं जितना सागर में पानी। प्लेटफ़ॉर्म पर आदमियों के हुजूम के बीच एक आदमी की साँस घुट गई थी। तब बाँके बिहारी ने कल्पना भी नहीं की थी कि इसी

महानगर में पवन ऐसी बस्ती में रहता होगा जहाँ आदमी नज़र नहीं आएगा !

वे मुस्कराए।

उन्हें अचानक बाईसवीं मंज़िल के फ़्लैट के हॉल में सोने की पायल धारण किए स्त्री-चरणों का चित्र याद आ गया था। यह आठवाँ आश्चर्य था। उन्होंने अभी तक न ऐसी कोई तस्वीर देखी थी, न मूर्ति। गोरे पैरों पर चमचमाते सोने से देवी को पहचानकर उसे बन्द आँखों से मूर्त करना था और उसी मूर्ति की आराधना करनी थी। चरण जीवन्त थे, अमर नहीं थे। दीवार पर लटकती उस तस्वीर को देखकर बाँके बिहारी बेचैन हो गए थे। गायत्री जिन देवी-देवताओं को पूजती थी, वे सब अमर थे। पवन के घर में जिस देवी के चरणों की तस्वीर लगी थी, वह अमर नहीं थी। वह मर जाएगी। उसके सोने में लिपटे मरे पैरों की तस्वीर दीवार पर लटकी रहेगी। पवन और किशोरी उसी को पूजेंगे।

झाँसी का अपना घर होता तो बाँके बिहारी तस्वीर उतारकर नाली में फेंक देते। यहाँ न झाँसी का घर था, न कोई नाली नज़र आती थी। जब आदमियों से भरी इमारतें थीं तो नालियाँ भी ज़रूर होंगी। आदमी नालियों के बिना नहीं जी सकता। नालियाँ इमारतों के फ़र्श और दीवारों में छिपी होंगी और बस्ती की ज़मीन के भीतर पैवस्त होंगी। ज़मीन के ऊपर चमचमाती सड़क और इमारतें और मुस्कराते लोग और क्यारियों में फूल नज़र आते थे। फूलों के ऊपर आसमान में खुभे हुए ताड़ के पेड़ थे, जो आपस में फुसफुसाते थे। धूप क्यारियों से ताड़ों तक तनी थी।

नालियाँ कहीं नहीं नज़र आती थीं।

जब धूप बाँके बिहारी के शरीर पर पड़ी तो उन्हें गर्मी लगने लगी और वे बेंच से उठकर पत्थर की पगडंडी से होते हुए पार्क के बाहर आ गए। सड़क को पार करके जब वे इमारत की ओर मुड़े तो एक ड्राइवर गाड़ी का दरवाज़ा खोले साहब का इन्तज़ार कर रहा था। लिफ़्ट से दो साहब उतरे। बाँके बिहारी ख़ाली लिफ़्ट से ऊपर गए। फ़्लैट की घंटी बजाई। डाइनिंग टेबल पर पवन और रतन तैयार बैठे हुए नाश्ता कर रहे थे। बाँके बिहारी भी टेबल पर बैठ गए। जब किशोरी ने पूछा कि क्या आप भी नाश्ता करेंगे, तो उन्होंने सिर्फ़ एक कप चाय माँगी।

चाय सुड़कते हुए बाँके बिहारी ने कहा—'पवन !'

'जी।'

'मैं तुम्हें कल एक बात बताना भूल गया।'

'क्या ?'

'हमारा अगले इतवार का रिज़र्वेशन है।'

'ऐसी क्या जल्दी है, पापा ? आप यहाँ पहली बार आए हैं।'

'रिज़र्वेशन', बाँके बिहारी ने चाय का एक घूँट लेकर कहा, 'कन्फ़र्म्ड है।'

'ख़ैर, एक हफ़्ते में मैं आपको मुम्बई दिखा दूँगा।'

टेबल पर मौन छा गया। प्लेटों पर चम्मचों की आवाज़ होती रही।

'पवन', बाँके बिहारी ने फिर कहा।

'जी।'

'मैं छोटे को साथ ले जा रहा हूँ।'

'क्क्.. क्यों ?' पवन हकला गया। उसके हाथ से चम्मच छूट गया था। चम्मच के फ़र्श पर गिरने की आवाज़ हुई थी...झन्न ऽ...।

उसी झन्नाटे से चौंककर किशोरी हॉल में आ गई थी जहाँ पवन पिता की ओर देख रहा था, 'क्यों ?'

बाँके बिहारी के सामने पवन था। पीछे किशोरी खड़ी थी। वे बीच में घिर गए थे। उन्होंने पहले पवन को आँखें उठाकर देखा, फिर किशोरी को, आँखें पीछे मोड़कर। फिर वे बोले :

'तुम्हारी अम्माँ यही चाहती हैं।'

'लेकिन...'

'लेकिन क्या ?'

'रतन यहाँ काम कर रहा है और उसका इलाज भी चल रहा है।' पवन ने बोलते हुए रतन की जानिब देखा।

रतन प्लेट में रखे ऑमलेट की ओर ऐसे देख रहा था जैसे किसी और के बारे में बात चल रही हो। उसके मुँह में ऑमलेट था।

'दोनों काम झाँसी में भी हो सकते हैं, पवन', बाँके बिहारी मुस्कराए, 'हवा काफ़ी बदल गई है।'

'हवा...कौन-सी हवा ?'

'जिसे बदलने छोटे यहाँ आया था।'

पवन कुछ समझा नहीं। उसने यह ज़रूर सोचा कि आज फ़ैक्टरी पहुँचकर वह कम्प्यूटर ऑपरेटर को वापस काम पर आने के लिए फ़ोन करेगा। बाँके बिहारी ने इसीलिए उसे तुरन्त बता देना ज़रूरी समझा था। चाय ख़त्म करके जब वे ख़ाली कमरे में घुसे तो उन्होंने अन्दर से सिटकनी चढ़ा दी। वे पलंग पर पहले बैठे, फिर लेट गए। उनकी दोनों आँखों से गालों पर आँसू बह रहे थे जैसे कोई नालियाँ हों।

उस दिन फ़ैक्टरी पहुँचकर पवन ने पहले लखनऊ और फिर अमेरिका फ़ोन

किया। उसने नमन को बताया कि पापा अचानक मुम्बई आ गए हैं और छोटे को झाँसी वापस ले जाना चाहते हैं। 'तो...तो क्या हर्ज है', नमन की आवाज़ थी, 'ले जाने दो।' 'दादा, आप सोचिए', पवन का स्वर उत्तेजित हो गया, 'यहाँ छोटे का इलाज और काम—दोनों चल रहे हैं।' नमन पवन की बौखलाहट नहीं समझा। जब बाँके बिहारी छोटे को लखनऊ से ले गए तो नमन को अफ़सोस और निजात एक-साथ महसूस हुई थी—अफ़सोस में पिता के प्रति अपराधबोध था, निजात घर के द्वन्द्व से थी। क्या पवन के घर में कोई टंटा नहीं होगा ? वह किशोरी को जानता था। उसे अचरज हुआ। इस हैरानी ने उसका अपराधबोध और बढ़ा दिया। यद्यपि फ़ोन पर उसने पवन से कहा कि वह पापा से शाम को फ़ोन पर बात करेगा, पर उसका फ़ोन नहीं आया।

मदन का अमरीका से फ़ोन आया। उसने बाँके बिहारी से कहा कि छोटे को मुम्बई में ही रखना ठीक है—काम और इलाज, दोनों के लिए। उसने यह भी कहा कि मैं छोटे को अमरीका बुला लेता, लेकिन यहाँ बेरोज़गारी बहुत है—अमरीकियों के लिए काम नहीं, तो भारतीयों को कहाँ से मिलेगा ? बाँके बिहारी चुप थे। दूसरी ओर से कुछ तीखी आवाज़ आई, 'पापा, आप सुन रहे हैं न ?' 'हाँ', बाँके बिहारी ने कहा। मदन ने आख़िरी पत्ता फेंका, 'मैंने अम्माँ को रुपयों के लिए लिखा था। उन्होंने कोई जवाब नहीं दिया। ज़रूरत हो तो ज़रूर बताइएगा।'

'ठीक है', कहते हुए बाँके बिहारी ने फ़ोन रख दिया।

पवन सामने बैठा सुन रहा था। 'ठीक है', सुनकर उसे ख़ुशी हुई। उसे लगा कि पापा ने अपना निर्णय बदल दिया है।

'मदन ने क्या कहा ?' पवन ने पूछा।

'वह मुझसे कह रहा था', बाँके बिहारी ने कहा, 'कि मैं एक रिटायर्ड बाप से पूछकर बताऊँ कि क्या उसे अपने छोटे बेटे के इलाज के लिए रुपयों की ज़रूरत है ? यदि बाप माँगेगा, तो बेटा देगा।'

पवन के चेहरे का रंग उड़ गया। उसे अब घर के हर क्षितिज पर कलह नज़र आ रही थी। किशोरी ने पहले ही छोटे को बुलाने के लिए मना किया था। तब पवन ने उससे कहा था कि छोटे कम्प्यूटर प्रोग्रामर की नौकरी कर चुका है, वह फ़ैक्टरी के काम में उसकी मदद करेगा। घर का आदमी है, उसने कहा था, घर में रहेगा—और कारख़ाने में सहायक की तरह काम करेगा। काम नया था। ख़र्चा कम-से-कम करने की ज़रूरत थी। इसी किफ़ायत से फ़ोर्ड आइकॉन का सपना पैदा हुआ था। किशोरी के सपने का क्या होगा ?

रतन टी.वी. पर लगातार चैनल बदल रहा था। संगीत से वह धारावाहिक पर

आ जाता और धारावाहिक से ख़बरों पर—जिनमें प्रधानमंत्री का यह ऐलान था कि दो दशक बाद भारत विश्व-शक्ति बन जाएगा। यह भारत की नियति थी। नियति को कौन बदल सकता था ? रतन ने फिर चैनल बदल दिया। संगीत के चैनल पर 'रीमिक्स' का नया गीत आ रहा था जिसमें त्रासदी तेज़ संगीत के साथ व्यंग्य की तरह लगती थी :

मार कटारी मर जाना
ये अँखियाँ किसी से मिलाना न...
पीछे...पड़ेगा...पछताना...

जब पवन ने उन्हें जुहू-तट पर छोड़ा तो बाँके बिहारी को सामने दुकानें ही दुकानें नज़र आईं। यह शक भी हुआ कि कहीं पवन ने जल्दी में उन्हें ग़लत जगह पर तो नहीं छोड़ दिया। उसे सांताक्रुज़ में ही कोई ज़रूरी काम था। वह डेढ़ घंटे बाद यहीं आएगा, उसने चलते-चलते कहा था। वे गाड़ी से उतरकर दुकानों की ओर बढ़े। दुकानों के ऊपर साफ़ आसमान था : कहीं बहुमंज़िली इमारतों की लाटें नहीं थीं। आसमान का यह सपाटपन समुद्र की उम्मीद जगाता था। बाँके बिहारी ने पहाड़ देखे थे, रेगिस्तान देखा था, समुद्र नहीं देखा था। तभी वह दिखा, दुकानों के बीच झाँकता हुआ जैसे किसी बच्चे की चमकती आँखें दीवार की ओर से ताक रही हों। पहले बच्चे की आँखें नज़र आती हैं, फिर उसका मुस्कराता हुआ चेहरा ओट से बाहर आ जाता है।

सामने समुद्र था। सूर्य की अंतिम किरणें उसकी छलकती सतह पर गिर रही थीं। धूप और पानी का ऐसा मेल बाँके बिहारी ने कभी नहीं देखा था, जो अभी क्षितिज पर पृथ्वी के दूसरी ओर लुढ़कता हुआ लगता था। क्षितिज के छोर से पैरों के आगे तक बेचैन पानी ही पानी था। धरती इसी पानी से घिरी थी। बाँके बिहारी के पैर रेत में धँसे थे। उनकी आँखें पानी पर सूर्य की चमक को खोज रही थीं। पगलाई लहरें मुँह में फेन लिए रेत पर बिखर-बिखर जातीं।

रेत पर दौड़ता हुआ घोड़ा ऐसे निकल गया जैसे सड़क पर दौड़ रहा हो। उस पर एक हँसता हुआ बच्चा बैठा था। फिर सामने से एक गुब्बारे वाला निकला। सींगदाने की टोकरी लिए एक आदमी बाँके बिहारी के सामने खड़ा हो गया, 'सेठ, माँगता ?' सेठ ? वे मुस्कराए और रेत पर आगे बढ़ गए। समुद्र-तट पर काफ़ी भीड़ थी। कुछ लोग सफ़ेद निकर-टी-शर्ट और जूते पहने दौड़ रहे थे। दौड़ते लोग

हर उम्र के थे। लड़के थे। लड़कियाँ थीं। लड़कियों के चेहरों पर छलकता पसीना ऐसा लगता जैसे समुद्र छलक रहा हो।

वे रेत पर आगे बढ़ते रहे। मुम्बई के दिन गर्म होने लगे थे। मगर शाम को जुहू-तट पर ठंडी हवाएँ चल रही थीं जैसे दूर समुद्र की गहराइयों को छूकर आ रही हों। दाईं ओर दीवार के पार बँगले थे, कुछ इमारतें थीं और उनको घेरे ताड़ के पेड़ थे जिनके सिर हिल रहे थे। वे आकाश में हँसते हुए लगते थे। दीवार के पार तब एक होटल का स्विमिंग पूल नज़र आया, जिसका पानी नीला था। पूल की पृष्ठभूमि में भव्य इमारत थी। दो-चार लोग अधनंगे देवी-देवताओं से नीले पानी के इर्द-गिर्द घूम रहे थे। यह कोई मायानगरी लगती थी जिसमें कुछ पेड़ सन्तरियों-से खड़े थे। ऐसा लगता था जैसे अभी रोशनियाँ जलेंगी और पेड़ सलाम करेंगे।

दीवार की ओर धुँधलके में दो आकृतियाँ बैठी थीं जो लिपटकर एक होती-सी लगती थीं। दीवार की छाया में कुछ अँधेरा-सा शुरू हो गया था। अनजाने ही बाँके बिहारी दीवार की ओर बढ़ते हुए आगे चलने लगे। यहाँ लोग कम थे। कभी-कभी रेत पर अपने पैरों की आवाज़ सुनाई देती। एक ओर रेत की आवाज़ थी, दूसरी ओर लहरों का बार-बार तट पर झपटना था। बीच में पानी के निशान थे।

सूर्य क्षितिज की ओर बढ़ रहा था।

बाँके बिहारी की नज़र दीवार से टिके एक जोड़े से फिसलती हुई सामने की ओर धुँधलके में गई जहाँ दूर कुछ रोशनियाँ जल गई थीं। ये धरती की रोशनियाँ थीं। समुद्र पर ढलता सूर्य एक दीए-सा टिमटिमा रहा था। सामने रेत पर अचानक बाँके बिहारी ने दारा सिंह को देखा, जो दौड़ नहीं रहा था। वह उन्हीं की तरह रेत पर टहल रहा था। शायद वे हम-उम्र थे। वह मुस्करा रहा था। उसके कपड़ों में रईसी थी। वह पेंट और कुर्ता पहने था। लेकिन वे बहुत सफ़ेद थे—उसके जूतों की तरह। उसके साथ एक चुस्त वृद्धा थी, जो झक्क सफ़ेद साड़ी पहने थी और गोरी थीं। दारा सिंह की तरह।

बाँके बिहारी कुछ और आगे बढ़े। अब वे रेत पर अकेले थे। एक घोड़ागाड़ी उन्हीं का चक्कर लगाकर लौट पड़ी। उसका चक्कर ख़त्म हो गया था। उसमें एक युवा दम्पति के साथ एक छोटा बच्चा था जो खिलखिला रहा था। जब रेत पर बच्चे की खिलखिलाहट ख़त्म हो गई, तो एक क्षण सन्नाटा छाया रहा। फिर एकाएक समुद्र की गर्जना सुनाई दी। बाँके बिहारी रेत पर रुक गए। उनका मुँह समुद्र की ओर था। सूर्य क्षितिज को छू रहा था। उसका आहिस्ता-आहिस्ता पानी में उतरना महसूस होता था।

उन्हें पता नहीं चला। उनके क़दम उसी ओर बढ़ रहे थे। सूर्य अब असली सूर्य नहीं लगता था। ऐसा लगता था जैसे पीले काग़ज़ का कोई टुकड़ा आकाश के परदे पर चिपका दिया गया हो। जैसे क़ाइनात असली न हो, उसकी कोई झाँकी हो। समुद्र अपनी ही छाया हो गया था जैसे वे अब अपनी छाया थे।

एक खटका हुआ और सूर्य की आख़िरी कोर छिटककर दूर पानी में डूब गई। कोई अँधेरे का पर्दा गिरा।

वे आगे बढ़ते रहे जैसे रेत और पानी में कोई फ़र्क न हो। जैसे पानी में धँसती टाँगें उनकी अपनी न हों। ये टाँगें धरती पर आठ दशक कहाँ-कहाँ घूमी थीं ! सुबह से शाम तक। हर रोज़। यही पैर अब पानी में चल रहे थे। पैरों के नीचे रेत धँसकने लगी। धीरे-धीरे पानी गले तक आ गया। सहसा पैरों से रेत छूट गई। तभी किसी ने उनको कन्धों से पकड़कर पीछे मोड़ दिया। वे हाँफ़ रहे थे। जब उन्हें थामे हुए युवक किनारे की रेत पर पहुँच गया तो उसने पूछा :

'क्या आपको तैरना आता है ?'

'नहीं।'

'फिर आप समुद्र में पैदल क्यों चल रहे थे ?'

'क्या मैं चल रहा था ?'

युवक मुस्कराया। फिर उसने कहा, 'अब आपकी आत्महत्या की उम्र नहीं रही।'

ऊपर से नीचे तक भीगे बाँके बिहारी काँप गए जब ठंडी हवा का थपेड़ा लगा।

वे उस युवक को रेत पर जाता हुआ देखते रहे, जिसका वे चेहरा नहीं देख पाए थे...उसके नंगे बदन से पानी की बूँदें रेत पर गिर रही थीं। एकाएक उन्हें लगा कि वह रतन था। रेत पर उसकी छाया दूर जाती हुई आहिस्ता-आहिस्ता साँवली हवा में घुल गई जहाँ लोग ही लोग थे।

क्या सचमुच कोई था जो उन्हें समुद्र से खींचकर रेत पर छोड़ गया था ?

चार

4.1

शहर के लोगों ने इसे होली का मज़ाक समझा।

वह इतवार की सुबह थी जब कुछ लड़कों ने सपना को थाने में घुसते हुए देखा। नया थाना क़िले की छाँव में खंडेराव गेट की सड़क के किनारे बना था। यह सड़क दिन-रात चालू रहती थी। जिन तीन-चार लड़कों ने सपना को देखा, उनमें से एक लड़का सपना के पीछे थाने में घुसा और कुछ देर बाद लौटकर उसने अपने दोस्तों को बताया कि बालिका महाविद्यालय की सपना बहिन जी ने बलात्कार की एफ.आई.आर. लिखाई है। हवलदार ने उसे इतना ही बताया था। उस लड़के के दोस्त हँसे और उन दोस्तों के दोस्त हँसे जिन्होंने यह ख़बर सुनी। सबने कहा कि हवलदार ने ज़रूर मज़ाक किया है। अगली सुबह दोस्तों के दोस्तों ने यह ख़बर कचहरी, बाज़ार और विद्यालयों में फैला दी जहाँ परीक्षाएँ चल रही थीं। सब हँस दिए। यह पहली अप्रैल थी। मूर्खों का दिन था। कौन किसे मूर्ख साबित कर दे, इसी की होड़ थी। लोग ऊपर से हँस रहे थे, भीतर ही भीतर चौकन्ने थे—कहीं यह ख़बर सच ही न हो ?

दोपहर होते-न-होते शहर में यह ख़बर सनसनी-सी फैली कि सपना के पड़ोसी रतन को पुलिस घर से गिरफ़्तार करके ले गई। जिन लोगों ने रतन को हथकड़ी पहने थाने जाते देखा, उन्होंने ही आँखें फाड़-फाड़कर यह बताया कि हथकड़ी घड़ी की तरह पहने रतन पलक नहीं झपका रहा था। जब लोगों ने यह सुना तो उनका होली और पहली अप्रैल का गणित गड़बड़ा गया। मगर यह बहुमुखी अचम्भा था। लोग जानते थे कि सपना और रतन एक-दूसरे के पड़ोसी थे और उनका एक-दूसरे के घर आना-जाना था। जानकारों ने बताया कि उनकी दोस्ती पन्द्रह बरस पुरानी थी जब रतन सपना को गणित पढ़ाता था और सपना रतन को 'गुरु' कहती थी। लोगों ने उन्हें शहर की सड़कों पर साथ-साथ जाते देखा था। सपना को कई बार इधर रतन की मोटरसाइकिल पर पीछे बैठे देखा गया था जैसे बड़े शहरों में लड़के-लड़कियाँ बैठते हैं। कुछ लोगों ने उन्हें एक-साथ सिनेमाघर में भी देखा था। जीवनसाह के चौराहे पर चाट खाते या इलाइट के रेस्तराँ में चाय पीते भी उन्हें देखा गया था।

जब दोनों की इतनी गहरी दोस्ती थी, तब बीच में बलात्कार कहाँ से आ गया ? ऐसी दोस्ती का अंजाम अब इस छोटे शहर में भी एक अदद सूना कमरा और एक अदद कंडोम हो गए थे—जिसमें परिवार-नियोजन और टी.वी. का भरपूर योगदान था। अब वह ज़माना नहीं था कि लड़के-लड़कियाँ मोहल्लों में छतों से नज़रों के तीर चलाएँ और मन्दिरों में एक-दूसरे से टकरा जाएँ। तब शहर में प्रेमी और प्रेमिका के बीच चुम्बन एक पराक्रम था। अब प्रेमी ने प्रेमिका का बलात्कार किया ! फिर प्रेमिका ने थाने में जाकर उसकी रपट लिखाई !! लोग पहले खिलखिलाकर हँसते, फिर सहम जाते। शहर को क्या हो गया था ?

जब रतन अपने घर से हथकड़ी पहने निकला तो गायत्री देहरी पर पछाड़ खाकर गिरी। यह दूसरी बार था। पहली बार उसने पछाड़ खाई थी जब बाँके बिहारी 'भारत छोड़ो' आन्दोलन में गिरफ़्तार हुए थे। तब उनके विवाह को दो माह हुए थे। ऐसी ही एक सुबह थी। फ़र्क यही था कि तब रिमझिम-रिमझिम पानी बरस रहा था। अभी गायत्री के साथ चबूतरे पर धूप फैली थी, जो सड़क को घेरे थी।

एक फ़र्क और था। तब गायत्री घर की नई-नवेली दुलहिन थी, जिसे गिरते ही घर की स्त्रियों ने सँभाल लिया था। देहरी पर अभी पल-भर बूढ़ी गायत्री अचेत पड़ी रही। तब पड़ोसिन ने पानी का लोटा लाकर उसके मुँह पर छींटे डाले और वह उठी। उठकर उसकी समझ में नहीं आया कि वह क्या करे। उसका मन हुआ कि वह फिर लेट जाए। लेकिन देहरी लेटने की जगह नहीं थी। वह भीतर दालान में चली गई। दालान में अलगनी से तौलिया उठाकर उसने चेहरे से पानी पोंछा जो कमला ने छिड़का था। यह निखालिस पानी था। इसमें किसी आँसू की मिलावट नहीं थी। सुबह का वक़्त था। घर में काम था। कमला चली गई थी।

गायत्री के घर में कोई काम नहीं था। दोनों पुरुष घर के बाहर चले गए थे। बाँके बिहारी कल रात गुजरात चले गए थे। रतन सुबह थाने चला गया था। जब सिपाही ने पौर की साँकल बजाई तो दरवाज़ा गायत्री ने ही खोला था। सिपाही ने जब रतन के बारे में पूछा तो गायत्री ने पूछा, 'क्यों ? क्या काम है ?' 'उसे बुलाओ', सिपाही ने कुछ कड़क आवाज़ में कहा। बाहर पुलिस की जीप खड़ी थी। देहरी के नीचे थानेदार खड़ा था जिसकी डाकुओं जैसी मूँछें थीं। गायत्री ने छोटे को आवाज़ दी। छोटे के पौर में आते ही थानेदार पौर में आ गया और उसने सिपाही से कहा कि रतन को हथकड़ी डाल दे। गायत्री की 'क्यों ?' के जवाब में थानेदार ने बताया कि इसने बलात्कार किया है। गायत्री की 'किससे ?' के जवाब में थानेदार ने कहा—'सपना।' गायत्री को चक्कर आ गया था। रतन को हथकड़ी पड़ चुकी थी।

रतन का देहरी से उतरना और गायत्री का देहरी पर गिरना एक-साथ हुआ।

आँखें खोलकर गायत्री ने सड़क पर फैली धूप में देखा था जैसे अभी वह घर में चारों ओर देख रही थी गोया छोटे किसी अँधेरे कोने में छिप गया हो। छोटे जेल गया था जैसे सन् '42 में बाँके बिहारी जेल गए थे। लेकिन बाँके बिहारी के घर से बाहर पैर रखते ही फूलों की मालाएँ उनके गले में गिरने लगी थीं। मानो आकाश से फूलों की वर्षा हो रही हो। मोहल्ले में नारे गूँजे थे : 'अंग्रेज़ो, भारत छोड़ो !' 'इन्क़लाब ज़िन्दाबाद !' ऐसा लगता था जैसे मोहल्ले में कोई त्योहार मनाया जा रहा हो। रिमझिम-रिमझिम पानी बरस रहा था।

गायत्री ने चबूतरे पर मूर्छा से जागकर जब धूप में चारों ओर आँखें फाड़कर देखा था तो मोहल्ले में केवल सन्नाटा-ही-सन्नाटा था जैसे सुबह से एकाएक दोपहर हो गई हो और सारे दरवाज़े बन्द हों। तभी वह तुरन्त अन्दर चली आई थी और बार-बार घड़ी देख रही थी। जिस आले में ऊपर घड़ी थी, उसी में नीचे मन्दिर था जिसमें मूर्तियाँ रखी थीं। वह आले के सामने बैठ गई। उसकी आँखें आहिस्ता-आहिस्ता अपने-आप मुँद गईं। आँगन में पानी की फुहार पड़ रही थी, जो घूँघट में से भी नज़र आती थी। अलबत्ता एक-दो बार शक ज़रूर हुआ था कि आँगन में पानी कहीं आँखों में पानी की परछाईं तो नहीं है ! गायत्री ने आँसू पोंछकर देखा था। आँगन में पानी की फुहार थी जैसे कोई फ़व्वारा एकाएक अवतरित हो गया हो।

घर की स्त्रियों ने बताया था कि रानीमहल पर तिरंगा फहराने की अगुवाई बाँके बिहारी ने की थी, जिनकी रेख अब मूँछ में बदल रही थी। रानीमहल रानी लक्ष्मीबाई का महल था, जिसे अंग्रेज़ों ने कोतवाली बना दिया था। रानीमहल को मुक्त कराना था। ढाई सौ लोग थे जिन्होंने कोतवाली को घेर लिया था। बाँके बिहारी कुछ और लड़कों के साथ रानीमहल में पीछे से घुस गए थे और उन्होंने महल की छत पर चढ़कर तिरंगा फहरा दिया था। ऐसे ही प्रयास शहर के पोस्ट ऑफ़िस, सदर की कचहरी और सीपरी के रेलवे स्टेशन पर भी हुए थे। लेकिन सचमुच कहाँ यूनियन जैक उतरा और तिरंगा चढ़ा—इसको लेकर शहर में कई किंवदन्तियाँ थीं। शहर में हड़ताल और जुलूस सबने देखे थे। रानीमहल पर फहराता तिरंगा किसने देखा ? यह भी कहा गया कि सरकार ने तुरन्त झंडे बदल दिए थे। इसलिए कोई देख नहीं सका। जिन्होंने झंडे बदले, उन्होंने देखे। साल-भर बाद जब बाँके बिहारी जेल से लौटे तो गायत्री ने उनसे झंडे का सवाल किया था। बाँके बिहारी मुस्कराए थे।

बाँके बिहारी का बेटा बलात्कार के जुर्म में जेल गया था।

गायत्री की आँखें खुल गईं। उन्हें बहुत बेचैनी महसूस हुई। आँगन में धूप और तेज़ हो गई थी। नीम की छाया अभी आँगन में नहीं थी। कोई अकेली पत्ती कभी अपनी छाया के साथ हवा में काँपते हुए आँगन में गिर जाती। आले के मन्दिर के सामने रेहल पर रामायण रखी थी। गायत्री ने सुन्दरकांड खोला और पाठ आरम्भ किया : जामवंत के बचन सुहाए...। यह पाठ संकटमोचक था। जीवन में जब-जब संकट घिरता, गायत्री सुन्दरकांड का पाठ करने बैठ जाती। तब बाँके बिहारी मुस्कराने लगते। मुस्कराते हुए कहते, 'जब सुन्दरकांड है, तो संकट का क्या टोटा ?' लेकिन ऐसा संकट पहली बार आया था और बाँके बिहारी घर पर नहीं थे। गायत्री निपट अकेली थी। उसने लखनऊ फ़ोन कर दिया था। बड़े रात तक आएँगे। बाँके बिहारी कल अहमदाबाद पहुँच गए होंगे। उन्होंने अभी तक फ़ोन नहीं किया। बड़े ने उन्हें कुछ बताने को मना किया था। कहा था, मैं आकर छोटे को छुड़ा लूँगा।

सुरसा का मुँह बढ़ता जाता है, बढ़ता जाता है...पहले योजन भर...फिर सौ योजन...हनुमान सहसा अपने विराट् रूप को लघु रूप में संकुचित करते हैं और सुरसा के शरीर में प्रवेश कर उससे बाहर निकल आते हैं। सुरसा संकट है। हनुमान का रूप बदलना राम की कृपा है। राम की कृपा के बिना कुछ भी सम्भव नहीं है। राम की कृपा से सब-कुछ हो जाता है...जाकी कृपा पंगु गिरि लंघै, अन्धे को सब कछु दरसाईं। तो क्या छोटे थाने से लौटकर नहीं आ सकता ? उसने सुबह सिर्फ़ दूध पिया था।

हनुमान लंका में पहुँचते हैं, जिसके सोने के परकोटे पर मणियाँ चमक रही हैं। समुद्र के बीचोबीच ऐसा भी देश था ! इसी सोने की लंका में राक्षसों का निवास था और यहीं अशोक वाटिका में सीता बन्दी थीं। हनुमान उन्हें देखते हैं...सीता कृशकाय हैं...कृस तनु सीस जटा एक बेनी...और राम का नाम जप रही हैं। गायत्री की आँखें मुँद गईं। उन्होंने अशोक वाटिका में एक वस्त्र धारण किए सीता को एक वृक्ष के नीचे बैठे देखा, जिसकी एक डाल पर हाथ में अँगूठी लिए हनुमान जी बैठे थे। अँगूठी से प्रकाश की किरणें झर रही हैं। यह राम की अँगूठी है। इसी अँगूठी को अभी हनुमान सीता को दिखाएँगे। सीता प्रतीक्षारत बैठी हैं...बैठेहिं बीति जात निसि जामा...बैठे-ही-बैठे रात के चारों पहर बीत जाते हैं...दिन के चारों पहर गायत्री ऐसे ही बैठी रहेगी जब तक बड़े नहीं आएँगे !

गायत्री चुप थी। घर में कोई आवाज़ नहीं थी। आँगन में तेज़ होती धूप की कोई आवाज़ नहीं थी। नीम की पत्तियों में छिपी कोई गौरैया कभी चुपके से चूँ-चूँ करती और चुप हो जाती।

जब गायत्री ने आँखें खोलीं तो मन्दिर के आले में घड़ी टिक्-टिक् कर रही थी। कछुक दिवस जननी धरु धीरा...माता, कुछ दिन...दो-एक दिन और धीरज धरो। अभी हनुमानजी को अशोक वाटिका उजाड़ना है, राक्षसों को छकाना है और अपनी पूँछ से लंका जलाकर सागर में कूदना है। हनुमान जी, राम को सीता का सन्देश ज़रूर देना :

दीन दयाल बिरिदु संभारी। हरहु नाथ मम संकट भारी॥

मेरा संकट भारी है, राम, जल्दी हरो ! रावण के महल में बन्दी सीता रो रही है। उसकी आँखों से झर-झर आँसू गिरते हैं। हनुमान, तुम भी अब जाने की बात करते हो। मैं राक्षसों के शहर में फिर अकेली हो जाऊँगी, फिर दिन के चारों पहर ऐसे ही बैठी रहूँगी जैसे मैं पत्थर की मूरत हूँ और मेरी आँखों से पानी झर रहा है।

गायत्री को आँसुओं का झरना छाती पर पता चला जब धारें ठंडी लगीं। सीता उनकी आँखों से रो रही थी...मेरा संकट विकट है, जल्दी आओ, राम !

जब पाँचवीं बार सीता गायत्री की आँखों से रोईं तो पौर की साँकल बजी। वे उठीं। हर बार जब सुन्दरकांड के अन्त में राम की सेना को रास्ता देने के लिए सागर अपने घर लौट जाता तो गायत्री फिर पहले श्लोक और सुरसा के बढ़ते मुँह पर आ जातीं जैसे सुन्दरकांड की परिक्रमा दे रही हों। हर बार उनके मुँह से 'हरहु नाथ मम संकट भारी' निकलता और हर बार सीताजी उनकी आँखों से रोने लगतीं। आँचल से आँसू पोंछते हुए उन्होंने किवाड़ खोले। चबूतरे पर पाँच लड़के भगवा दुपट्टा सिर पर लपेटे खड़े थे। एक बोला, 'बाई, हम लोग रामनवमी पर अयोध्या जा रहे हैं। जो बन पड़े, राम-मन्दिर के लिए दीजिए।'

गायत्री की आँखों में आँसू सूखे नहीं थे। उन्होंने आँचल में बँधा पचास का नोट खोला और लड़कों को दे दिया। वे उस क्षण भूल गईं कि बाँके बिहारी दस साल से कह रहे हैं कि राम अब अयोध्या के उस मन्दिर में नहीं रहते, जो बाबरी मस्जिद की जगह कुछ लोग बनाना चाहते हैं। अब राम को घर के मन्दिर में ही पूजने का समय है, वे कहते। वे तो यह भी कहते हैं कि अयोध्या के अदृश्य राम मन्दिर का सिंहासन अयोध्या में नहीं है। बल्कि दिल्ली के संसद भवन में रखा है—जिस पर प्रधानमंत्री बैठते हैं। वे यह कहकर हँसते हैं जैसे कोई मज़ाक हो !

क्या सीताजी का रोना कोई मज़ाक है ?

रात के पहले पहर में फिर साँकल बजी। गायत्री फिर रेहल से उठीं। उठते हुए

उन्होंने आले की घड़ी में देखा : दस बजे थे। जब उन्होंने किवाड़ खोले तो एक बार उन्हें बाँके बिहारी का भ्रम हुआ। लेकिन चबूतरे पर खड़ी आकृति की दाढ़ी के बाल काले थे। रोशनी कुछ दूर सड़क पर बिजली के खम्भे से आ रही थी। 'बड़े', उन्होंने कहा। 'हाँ, अम्माँ', कहते हुए बड़े ने गायत्री के पैर छुए। अन्दर आँगन में आकर उसने बताया कि वह शाम को ही आ गया था। मगर सीधा वह श्याम बिहारी निगम वकील के पास गया था, जो उसके दोस्त थे। फिर वे कोतवाली जाकर थानेदार से मिले। कल ज़मानत हो जाएगी। 'मैं छोटे से भी मिल आया हूँ', उसने कहा, 'वह ठीक है। एक रात की तो बात है। कल वह घर आ जाएगा।'

'सच, कल वह घर आ जाएगा ?' गायत्री ने दुहराया।

'हाँ, अम्माँ, वह कल ज़रूर आ जाएगा। कोई फ़िक्र की बात नहीं है।'

बड़े ने आँगन की बत्ती जला दी। उसी उजाले में उसने कनखी से देखा कि चूल्हा ठंडा पड़ा है।

'अम्माँ, मुझे भूख लगी है', बड़े ने कहा।

'क्या छोटे ने खाया ?' गायत्री ने पूछा।

'हाँ, उसे मैं खाना देकर आया हूँ।'

'अच्छा', गायत्री की आवाज़ हल्की हो गई, 'मैं जल्दी से पराँठे बना देती हूँ। तुम हाथ-मुँह धो लो।'

'अच्छा', बड़े ने कहा, 'अम्माँ, तुम अपने लिए भी पराँठे बना लेना।'

पहले बड़े ने पराँठा खाया—आम के अचार के साथ। दोपहर की बची न सब्ज़ी थी, न दाल। दोपहर में खाना नहीं बना था। बड़े का शक सही था। अम्माँ ने दिन-भर कौर मुँह में नहीं डाला था। पता नहीं, पानी पिया था या नहीं। वे कभी-कभी निर्जला उपवास करती थीं। मगर वह मन का उपवास होता था। यह दुख का उपवास था।

'पराँठा अच्छा बना है, अम्माँ। चूल्हे की आँच का है। गैस का खाना खाते-खाते थक गया हूँ।' फिर कुछ रुककर उसने कहा, 'अम्माँ, मैंने थोड़ा श्याम के घर खा लिया था। अब तुम अपने लिए बना लो।'

चौके में बैठा बतियाता बड़े गायत्री को खाता हुआ देखता रहा। गायत्री ने भी एक ही पराँठा खाया। तीसरा पराँठा तवे पर डालने का उसका मन ही नहीं हुआ था। वह नूर और मुन्ना के बारे में पूछती रही। मुन्ना अब आई.आई.टी. कानपुर में पढ़ रहा था—भैया की तरह। 'तो क्या मुन्ना भी भैया की तरह अमरीका जाएगा ?' गायत्री ने पूछा। 'पता नहीं', बड़े मुस्कराए।

'क्या छोटे कोई दवाई खाता था, अम्माँ ?' बड़े ने पूछा।

'कुछ दिनों से छोड़ दी थी', गायत्री ने कहा, 'कहता था, मैं बिलकुल ठीक हूँ। दवा की कोई ज़रूरत नहीं।'

चौके में थोड़ा-सा उजाला था। चूल्हे के ऊपर दीवारों और छत पर धुएँ की कालिख छितरी थी। बड़े को लगा कि वह अम्माँ का चेहरा ठीक से देख नहीं पा रहा। चेहरे पर झुर्रियाँ नज़र आ रही थीं।

'तुमने समझाया नहीं, अम्माँ ?'

'समझाया', वह पहली बार हताश मुस्कराई, 'उसने समझने का बहाना किया। आज सुबह उसके जाने के बाद मैं ऊपर गई। अलमारी के कोने में गोलियाँ पड़ी थीं, जो मैं सुबह-शाम देती थी।'

'डाक्टर को बताया था ?' बड़े ने फिर पूछा।

'तुम्हारे पापा गए थे। डॉक्टर ने कहा कि उसे बहला-फुसलाकर दवा खिलाओ।'

बड़े का मुँह चूल्हे की दीवार की ओर था, जो काली थी। वह उसी ओर देख रहा था।

'बड़े', गायत्री ने कहा।

'हाँ।'

'तुम अब सो जाओ। बहुत थके होगे।'

वह हाथ धोकर ऊपर चला गया। गायत्री उसे ऊपर जाता देखती रही। उसे अंदेशा था कि वह सपना के बारे में कुछ न पूछ बैठे। वह क्या बताएगी ? उसे क्या पता था ?

अगले दिन लौटकर देहरी पार करते हुए रतन की पलकें फिर नहीं झपकीं जैसे एक दिन उसने बिना पलकें गिराए गुज़ार दिया हो। वह अपने घर में ऐसे घुसा जैसे कोई पराए घर में घुसता है। बड़े उसके पीछे आए। उनके चेहरे पर भी कोई भाव नहीं था। गायत्री की आँखें भर आईं। उन आँसुओं के पर्दे के पीछे झुर्रियों में फँसी कोई मुस्कान थी जिसका पता नहीं चलता था। रतन सीधा टट्टी में घुस गया। टट्टी से निकलकर वह स्नानघर में घुसा। जब वह स्नानघर से निकला तो गायत्री ने कहा—'खाना तैयार है।' वह सीधा चौके में आ गया। गायत्री ने उरद की दाल और भरे हुए बैंगन बनाए थे—जो रतन की पसन्द थी। रतन सिर नीचा किए खाता रहा जैसे किसी होटल में बैठा हो जहाँ ऑर्डर करने की ज़रूरत नहीं थी। गायत्री को पता था उसे क्या चाहिए।

'रात को नींद आई थी ?' आख़िरकार गायत्री ने पहला सवाल पूछा।

'आधी।'

'क्यों ?'

'मच्छर थे और दूसरा क़ैदी था जो खर्राटे लेता था। एक कुत्ता भी बार-बार भौंक रहा था जैसे पहरा दे रहा हो।'

कुछ पल बाद गायत्री ने पूछा—

'एक रोटी और दूँ ?'

'नहीं।'

गायत्री जानती थी, वह पाँचवीं रोटी नहीं लेगा, भात लेगा। गायत्री ने चूल्हे से उठकर तीन चमचे भात छोटे की थाली में परोसा।

रतन ने नज़रें नहीं उठाईं। वह भात खाकर उठा और हाथ धोकर ऊपर चला गया। सीढ़ियों पर ऊपर जाते हुए उसने अपना दाहिना हाथ दीवार पर रखा था जो उसकी कमर तक आती थी। गायत्री उसे चौके से ऊपर जाते देखती रही।

जब रतन अटारी में चला गया तो आँगन में खड़े बड़े ने कहा :

'दीवार खड़ी करके तुमने ठीक किया, अम्माँ !'

'हाँ', चौके से आवाज़ आई।

बड़े सीढ़ियों की ओर देख रहे थे जहाँ नीम की शाखें और पत्तियाँ और उनकी छाया थी। धूप की बूँदें और धारें पेड़ से छनकर सीढ़ियों और सीढ़ियों की दीवार पर गिर रही थीं। बड़े की आँखों में वही धूप चमक रही थी।

'हम लोग जब बड़े हुए', बड़े ने कहा, 'हमें दीवार का न होना पता ही नहीं चला। जैसे पेड़ ही दीवार हो।'

गायत्री चुप रही। बड़े आँगन में टहलते रहे।

'बड़े', गायत्री ने कहा।

'हाँ।'

'अहमदाबाद से फ़ोन आया।'

'आ जाएगा, अम्माँ', बड़े ने कहा, 'क्यों फ़िक्र करती हो ?'

'मैं पापा की फ़िक्र नहीं करती।'

'फिर ?'

'छोटे...' गायत्री का स्वर टूट गया।

बड़े आँगन में रसोई की ओर मुँह करके रुक गए। गायत्री चूल्हे में रोटी सेंक रही थी। उसका मुँह आग की ओर था।

'अम्माँ', बड़े बोले, 'छोटे की फ़िक्र मत करो। मैं हूँ न ?'

'हाँ', चूल्हे की आग से आवाज़ आई।

'श्याम मुझे फ़ोन कर देगा जब तारीख़ पड़ेगी।' बड़े ने कहा, 'मैं आ जाऊँगा।'

'अच्छा...'

दिन-भर नमन का मन ऊपर जाने का नहीं हुआ जहाँ रतन सो रहा था। वह पौर में लेटा रहा। कभी झपकी आ जाती। झपकी टूटती तो वह फिर अख़बार पढ़ने लगता। गुजरात अभी शान्त नहीं हुआ था। अहमदाबाद के कुछ भागों में कर्फ़्यू लगता था जहाँ बाँके बिहारी गए थे। चूँकि बाँके बिहारी अहमदाबाद गए थे, उसने अहमदाबाद की ख़बरों को शब्द-शब्द पढ़ा।

धूप जा चुकी थी जब रतन पौर में आया।

'बैठो', नमन ने उससे सामने बैठने को हाथ से इशारा किया।

रतन सामने बैठ गया। पौर में सन्नाटा गहराने लगा।

'छोटे', बड़े के गले से आवाज़ निकली जैसे चट्टान टूटी हो।

'हाँ', छोटे ने बड़े की ओर देखा।

'यह सब कैसे हुआ ?'

'दादा...' छोटे रुका जैसे हकला रहा हो, 'मैं उसे प्यार करता हूँ।'

बड़े एकटक उसके चेहरे को देखते रहे।

4.2

पहली रात खाना खाकर बाँके बिहारी और श्याम सुन्दर प्रोफ़ेसर्स कॉलोनी से बाहर आए और दाहिनी ओर मुड़ गए। सड़क पर और दोनों ओर कोठियों में रोशनियाँ थीं, जिनके बीच कहीं-कहीं पेड़ों में अँधेरे ने अपनी चादर फैला दी थी। अप्रैल का आसमान साफ़ था। तारे इच्छा की तरह निकल आए थे और नीचे धरती की ओर ताक रहे थे। थोड़ा चलने के बाद चौड़ी सड़क नज़र आई, जिस पर दोनों ओर गाड़ियाँ दौड़ रही थीं। दाईं ओर मुड़कर वे आगे बढ़े और विजय चौक पर पहुँचकर रुक गए। यह नए शहर का एक गुलज़ार चौराहा था, जो किसी दूसरे शहर का भी हो सकता था।

'यह चौराहा', बाँके बिहारी ने कहा, 'पुणे या लखनऊ में भी हो सकता है।'

श्याम सुन्दर हँसे। वे बोले, 'यह चौराहा एक साल पहले या एक साल बाद भी हो सकता है।'

विजय चौराहा जगमग था। नई चमाचम गाड़ियाँ सड़क पर मछलियों-सी दौड़ रही थीं। दुकानें खुली थीं। लोग बाज़ार में घूम रहे थे। लड़कियाँ बिजली की रोशनी में हँस रही थीं।

जन-जीवन सामान्य था।

बाँके बिहारी यह सोचकर हैरान थे कि उन्हें शायद आशंका थी कि वे शहर की सड़कों पर पिछले माह हुए क़त्लेआम की छायाएँ देखेंगे। उनकी आँखों के सामने अभी एक दुकान के सामने खड़ी दो लड़कियाँ आइसक्रीम खाते हुए हँस रही थीं।

'क्यों हँस रहे हो ?' श्याम सुन्दर ने पूछा।

'क्या तुम्हें यह चौराहा हँसता हुआ नहीं लगता ?' बाँके बिहारी ने पूछा।

श्याम सुन्दर भी मुस्कराने लगे।

वे पीछे मुड़कर सड़क पर दूर तक सीधे चले गए जहाँ पेड़ कुछ घने हो गए थे और रोशनी कुछ कम थी। पेड़ों का अँधेरा भी घना था। लौटकर जब वे प्रोफ़ेसर्स कॉलोनी के अन्दर घुसे तो बाँके बिहारी ने देखा कि इमारतों के सामने मैदान में स्कूटर खड़े थे। दस बज रहा था। क्या ये इसी तरह खड़े रहेंगे ? बाँके बिहारी के सवाल के जवाब में श्याम सुन्दर ने कहा, 'हाँ, यहाँ यही चलन है।' 'झाँसी में तो लोग इन्हें घरों में छिपा लेते', बाँके बिहारी बोले, 'या कुत्तों की तरह इन्हें ज़ंजीर से बाँध देते।'

वे श्याम सुन्दर के साले मोहन के पास रुके थे, जो गुजरात विश्वविद्यालय में पढ़ाते थे। उनका फ़्लैट तीसरी मंज़िल पर था, जिसके ऊपर छत थी। मोहन के फ़्लैट के सामने के फ़्लैट में ताला लगा था। मोहन ने बताया था कि नवरंगपुरा में मुसलमानों के घर उसी तरह चिह्नित थे जैसे नाज़ी जर्मनी में यहूदियों के। जब शहर भड़कता, मुसलमान पुराने शहर में अपनी बस्तियों में भाग जाते।

'क्या अभी यहाँ ख़तरा है ?' बाँके बिहारी ने पूछा।

'हिन्दुओं को कोई ख़तरा नहीं', मोहन ने कहा, 'मेरी बेटी दूरदर्शन में काम करती है। कभी-कभी वह बारह बजे रात को अकेली लौटती है।'

'लखनऊ में यह सम्भव नहीं', बाँके बिहारी ने कहा, 'झाँसी की तो बात ही छोड़िए।'

'यह गांधी का शहर है', श्याम सुन्दर बोले।

फ़्लैट की घंटी बजी। दरवाज़ा मोहन ने खोला। एक साँवली छरहरी लम्बी लड़की नीली साड़ी पहने अन्दर आई और उसने मुस्कराते हुए दोनों अतिथियों को हाथ जोड़कर 'नमस्कार' किया।

'माधुरी', मोहन बाँके बिहारी की ओर देखते हुए बोले, 'मेरी बेटी।'

'कैसे हैं, फूफाजी ?' माधुरी ने श्याम सुन्दर से पूछा।

'अच्छा हूँ', श्याम सुन्दर ने कहा, 'दूरदर्शन से आ रही हो ?'

'हाँ', वह मुस्कराई।

बाँके बिहारी को पता नहीं चला था। वे लगातार मुस्करा रहे थे। उनकी आँखें माधुरी के चेहरे पर टिकी थीं। माधुरी के चेहरे पर कोई तरल स्निग्धता थी, जो नए खिले फूल में होती है। यह वही कोमलता थी जिसे देखकर उन्हें अक्सर अफ़सोस होता कि उनकी कोई बेटी नहीं है। फिर उन्हें यह ख़्याल आता कि उनका एक लड़का अनब्याहा है। क्या इस लड़की की शादी उससे होकर वह उनके आँगन में आ सकती है जैसे कोई चिड़िया आँगन में उड़ती है ? जैसे ही यह ख़्याल ज़ेहन में आया, उनकी मुस्कान और चौड़ी हो गई।

'अंकल', माधुरी ने बाँके बिहारी की ओर देखते हुए कहा, 'क्यों मुस्करा रहे हैं ?'

'तुम्हें देखकर।'

'लव एट फ़र्स्ट साइट', वह हँसी।

सब मुस्कराए।

उसकी हँसी और नज़र में एक ख़ास तरह की कोमलता थी जो लड़कियाँ अक्सर बूढ़ों के लिए महसूस करती हैं। यह खिलते फूल की झरते फूल के लिए करुणा भी हो सकती है। बाँके बिहारी का चेहरा हर तरफ़ सफ़ेद बालों से घिरा था जैसे कोई ऋषि सामने खड़ा हो जिसके हाथ का कमंडल खो गया हो। लेकिन ऋषि कुर्ता-पाजामा नहीं पहनते। अलबत्ता उनके वस्त्र का रंग अब सिर्फ़ गेरुआ नहीं रहा था। ऋषि टी.वी. के परदे पर सफ़ेद लिबास में भी नज़र आते थे।

जब श्याम सुन्दर ने बताया कि बाँके बिहारी उनके पुराने दोस्त हैं, तो माधुरी ने उनकी ओर देखकर कहा कि आपकी दाढ़ी से आपकी उम्र का पता नहीं चलता, सिर्फ़ दाढ़ी का पता चलता है जैसे कोई किसी दूसरे युग से अचानक आ गया हो।

फिर वह कॉफ़ी बनाने अन्दर चली गई।

अगले दिन वे सबसे पहले वली दकनी की मज़ार की ओर चले। मोहन की मारुति में उसके साथ आगे श्याम सुन्दर बैठे थे। पीछे बाँके बिहारी के साथ मोहन का एक शिष्य था, जिसका नाम अमृत था—वह कविताएँ लिखता था। धूप तेज़ हो चली थी। सड़कों पर आदमी और वाहन थे। सर्राती मारुति में बैठे हुए बाँके बिहारी को लगा जैसे वे किसी सैर पर जा रहे हों। वे खिड़की के बाहर दोनों ओर सड़कों और उनके परे इमारतों को देख रहे थे। इमारतें हर बड़े शहर में ऐसी ही होती थीं और ऐसे ही पेड़ थे जो इमारतों के बीच नज़र आते थे, आकाश में अपने

हाथ हिलाते हुए। एकाएक मारुति रुकी। सड़क के किनारे जहाँ वे उतरे वहाँ एक मन्दिर था जिसमें हनुमान की मूर्ति थी। हनुमान मन्दिर नया लगता था जिसमें मूर्ति कुछ ज़्यादा रौद्र लग रही थी। यह एक तिराहा था। तिराहे से लगा हुआ पुलिस मुख्यालय और पुलिस कमिश्नर का ऑफ़िस था, जिनके साए में वली दकनी की मज़ार थी—जो अब नहीं थी। बाँके बिहारी तिराहे पर खड़े चारों ओर देख रहे थे। जैसे मज़ार कहीं किसी तरफ़ हवा में ठिठकी खड़ी हो।

'मज़ार कहाँ थी ?' श्याम सुन्दर ने पूछा।

'जहाँ आप खड़े हैं', मोहन ने कहा।

बाँके बिहारी थोड़ा हटकर सड़क के किनारे बजरी पर खड़े थे। वे बोले—'मैंने बाबरी मस्ज़िद का मलबा देखा है। यहाँ कोई मलबा भी नहीं।'

'मलबा है', अमृत ने कहा।

'कहाँ ?'

'मेरे पैरों के नीचे', अमृत डामर की सड़क पर खड़ा था।

'डामर को ग़ौर से देखिए', मोहन ने कहा।

डामर धूप में चमक रहा था।

'यह ताज़ा डामर है', श्याम सुन्दर ने कहा, 'ऐसा लगता है जैसे यहाँ इमर्जेंसी का बुलडोज़र चला हो और फिर नई सड़क बनी हो।'

मोहन ने बताया कि यहीं तिराहे के बीचोबीच वली दकनी की भरी-पूरी मज़ार थी, जिस पर आदमी से ऊँची छतरी थी। तिराहे से गुज़रनेवाला हर आदमी इस आदमी से ऊँची छतरी की परिक्रमा देता हुआ लगता था। गोधराकांड के अगले दिन यह ज़मींदोज़ हुई थी जब शहर पगलाया था।

'ताज़े डामर को ग़ौर से देखिए', अमृत ने कहा, 'यह सड़क से तीन सूत ऊपर उठा है। यही तीन सूत मज़ार का मलबा सड़क के नीचे क़ैद है, जिसे कुचलते हुए शहर के लोग अब रोज़ इधर-उधर भागते हैं।'

तिराहे पर दुपहिया, तिपहिया और चौपहिया वाहन दौड़ रहे थे। कोई आदमी नहीं था। कोई भक्त नव-निर्मित हनुमान मन्दिर में भी नहीं था। न कोई पुजारी। केवल गेरुए हनुमान क्रुद्ध मुद्रा में गदा उठाए अकेले खड़े थे। उनका एक पैर आगे था, एक पीछे था...जैसे कहीं भाग रहे हों। उनका मुँह तिराहे से विपरीत दिशा में था। बालू पर खड़े छोटे-से मन्दिर के चारों ओर धूप झिलमिला रही थी। डामर को छूकर धूप कुछ और तेज़ हो जाती थी और हवा कुछ और गर्म। बाँके बिहारी एक नज़र मन्दिर पर डालते, फिर सूने डामर को देखने लगते। आहिस्ता-आहिस्ता डामर की वीरानी उनकी आँखों में भरने लगी जैसे वे किसी रेगिस्तान में खड़े हों।

रेत हवा में उड़ रही थी। उसी बवंडर की रेत में दूर टँगी एक क़ब्र उन्होंने अचानक देखी, जो लगातार उनके पास आ रही थी। जब वह कुछ और पास आई तो उन्होंने उसे पहचाना : वह मगहर से आई कबीर की क़ब्र थी, जिसे उन्होंने मगहर में देखा था और जो यहाँ-वहाँ टूटी थी। उन्होंने वली दकनी की क़ब्र नहीं देखी थी। यह वली दकनी की क़ब्र भी हो सकती थी, जिसे वे कबीर की क़ब्र समझ रहे थे। अयोध्या से मगहर उतना ही दूर था जितना गोधरा से अहमदाबाद !

'जब किसी आदमी के पैर इस मलबे पर पड़ते हैं', अमृत आकाश की जानिब देखते हुए कह रहा था, 'तो तीन सूत मलबे से कोई आवाज़ आती है, जो आकाश में गूँजती है।'

अमृत तीन सूत मलबे पर खड़ा था। वह मौन आकाश की ओर देख रहा था, जहाँ सिर्फ़ धूप थी।

एक आदमी कहीं से आकर तिराहे पर घूमा।

'सुनिए', अमृत अचानक बोला, 'ग़ौर से सुनिए।'

तीनों बुज़ुर्गों ने अनायास ऊपर की ओर देखा जैसे सचमुच वहाँ कोई आवाज़ हो। आसमान में तेज़ धूप थी। उन्होंने नज़रें वापस अमृत के चेहरे पर टिका दीं।

अमृत की निगाहें आसमान में टिकी थीं।

चुप्पी छा गई। सड़क सूनी थी। कोई आदमी नहीं था। न कोई आवाज़ थी।

धरती से आसमान तक सन्नाटा था।

अमृत ख़ुद अपने आँसू पोंछ रहा था।

वली दकनी की मज़ार से गुलबर्ग सोसाइटी दूर थी, पर ज़्यादा दूर नहीं थी। सड़क से दाएँ सोसाइटी के गेट में मुड़ने से पहले कुछ सँकरा और बहुत भरा बाज़ार था, जिसकी सड़क पर भीड़ थी। गाड़ी एक ओर लगाकर वे आगे बढ़े। भरे बाज़ार से कुछ क़दम दाईं ओर क़ब्रिस्तान-सी वीरान बस्ती होगी—यह बस्ती में घुसने से पहले कोई सोच भी नहीं सकता था। पहली नज़र में वहाँ कोई परिन्दा भी नज़र नहीं आया। ऐसा लगा जैसे यह कोई सृष्टि के बाहर की जगह हो ! वे बस्ती के बीचोबीच खड़े हो गए। चारों ओर भाँय-भाँय करते दुमंज़िले-तिमंज़िले मकान थे, जिनके कुछ हिस्से जले हुए नज़र आते थे। उन्होंने आँखें फाड़कर चारों ओर देखा। कहीं धुआँ नहीं था। एक ओर मस्जिद थी, जो और ज़्यादा सुनसान नज़र आती थी।

एकाएक एक मकान से एक आदमी बाहर निकला जैसे कोई भूत हो। चारों ओर धूप फैली थी और ऊपर सूर्य चमक रहा था। अहाते में मकानों के साए एक-दूसरे में गुँथे थे जैसे एक-दूसरे को सहारा दे रहे हों। वह आदमी साए-सा

आहिस्ता-आहिस्ता मैदान के बीच में आया और चारों आगन्तुकों को घूरने लगा।

'यहाँ अब लूटने को कुछ नहीं बचा', उसने कहा।

वे चारों उसे देख रहे थे।

'न मारने को आदमी', वह हँसा, 'मैं ज़रूर हूँ—अगर मुझे इस लायक समझो।'

'हम आपसे मिलने आए हैं', श्याम सुन्दर ने कहा।

वह ठहाका मारकर हँसा। फिर बोला—'मुझसे मिलकर आपको क्या मिलेगा ? मेरे पास कुछ नहीं है। मेरा सब लुट गया।'

फिर वह एक माह पहले की वह दोपहर बयान करने लगा जब दंगाई इस बस्ती में एक सैलाब की तरह घुसे थे और उन्होंने उन्नीसों मकानों को घेर लिया था। गेट से लगा मकान एहसान जाफ़री का था जो सुबह से ही फ़ोन पर दिल्ली दरबार तक बस्ती की फ़रियाद ले गए थे। उन्हें अहाते में घसीटकर इस तरह ज़िन्दा मारा गया जैसे जानवर को ज़िबह करते हैं। सारे मकान घिर गए थे जैसे युद्ध में कोई निहत्था दुश्मनों से घिर जाता है। बस्ती के पीछे रेल की पटरी से पत्थरों की बौछार हो रही थी। घरों में विस्फोट हुए और आग लगी और घरों के अन्दर बच्चे और औरतें और मर्द इस तरह मरे जैसे बिल में ज़हर से चींटियों का दम घुट जाता है।

'चार चींटियाँ मेरी थीं', वह आदमी रो रहा था, 'एक मेरी बीवी और तीन बच्चे।'

फिर उसने ख़ुद अपनी गन्दी कमीज़ से अपने आँसू पोंछते हुए कहा—'मैं अपनी बीवी और बच्चों के लिए नहीं रो रहा हूँ। मैं इसलिए रो रहा हूँ कि उस दोपहर मैं अकेला छत पर पीछे रेलवे लाइन की तरफ़ से आते पत्थरों का जवाब देने क्यों चला गया था।' एक क्षण की चुप्पी के बाद फिर उसका हताश स्वर सन्नाटे में गूँजा, 'दंगाई भी छत पर नहीं आए।'

जब उस आदमी ने चार चींटियों की बात कही तो बाँके बिहारी अपने को रोक न सके। वे पीछे मुड़कर चलते गए जहाँ एहसान जाफ़री का घर था। उनके आँसू रुकते न थे। वे बार-बार अपना चश्मा पोंछ रहे थे। वे अकेले एहसान जाफ़री के घर में घुस गए। घर ख़ाली था। उसकी दीवारें जली थीं। फ़र्श पर कूड़ा-करकट पड़ा था। वे सामने के बरामदे में आगे बढ़ते गए। आख़िरी सिरे पर कोई बेडौल हथेली-भर का टुकड़ा पड़ा था। बाँके बिहारी ने वह टुकड़ा हाथ में उठा लिया। वह कुछ जीवन्त और जला हुआ लगा। ऐसा लगा जैसे जले मांस से मढ़ा कोई हड्डी का टुकड़ा हो ! वे उसे नाक के पास ले गए। उसमें चिरायँध थी।

क्या यह आदमी का मांस था ?

वे उस हथेली-भर के टुकड़े को अपनी हथेली में लिये पहली मंज़िल पर गए। पहली मंज़िल पर वीरान कमरों में अधजली दीवारें थीं। भीतरी कमरे में कुछ अँधेरा था। बाँके बिहारी ने उस अँधेरे में झाँका। यह कुएँ जैसा अँधेरा था जिसमें कुछ भी डूब सकता था। उनका दिल काँपा। वे धुर ऊपर छत पर चढ़ गए जहाँ खड़ी स्त्रियाँ उस दोपहर नीचे एहसान जाफ़री को अहाते में बदहवास दौड़ता देख रही थीं। जाफ़री को घेरे दंगाइयों की चीख़ती भीड़ थी। वे अचानक चीख़े जैसे एहसान जाफ़री की आवाज़ गूँजी हो :

'मुझे मार दो ! सबको छोड़ दो !'

अहाते में खड़े चारों लोगों ने ऊपर छत की ओर देखा और बाँके बिहारी को नीचे आने का इशारा किया। वे बेजान रोबोट की तरह पीछे मुड़े और सीढ़ियों की ओर बढ़े। अब उनकी आँखों में आँसू नहीं थे। हाथ में मांस का जला टुकड़ा था। वे एक बार अपनी खुली हथेली को देखते, फिर अगली सीढ़ी को जो नीचे जा रही थी। उन्हें ऐसा ही लगा जैसे सीढ़ी अपने आप नीचे जा रही है और वे अपनी खुली हथेली को देख रहे हैं जिसमें मृत्यु-गन्ध है। छत और सीढ़ियों पर धूप थी। भीतर अँधेरा था। अँधेरे में कोई बच्चा बार-बार चीख़ रहा था, कोई औरत सिसक रही थी ! वे नीचे बरामदे में एक क्षण रुके। कहीं कोई आवाज़ नहीं थी। उनके कान सन्नाटे में भन्ना रहे थे।

बाँके बिहारी अपनी हथेली में हथेली-भर जला टुकड़ा लिये उसी ओर बढ़े जहाँ चारों लोग खड़े थे। वे अपनी हथेली हवा में उठाए थे। गुलबर्ग सोसाइटी का अन्तिम नागरिक बाँके बिहारी की खुली हथेली को घूर रहा था। जब वे पास आ गए तो उस अधेड़ ने जिसके सिर और दाढ़ी के काले-सफ़ेद बाल उलझे हुए थे और जिसके पाजामा-कमीज़ गन्दे थे, पूछा :

'यह तुम्हें कहाँ मिला ?'

'घर के बरामदे में।'

सबकी नज़रें हथेली पर थीं।

'यह क्या है ?' श्याम सुन्दर ने पूछा।

शायद चिरायँध हवा में फैलकर गुम हो गई थी।

'यह मेरी बच्ची की हथेली है', अधेड़ ने कहा, 'जब मैं उस दोपहर अपनी छत से नीचे पहुँचा तो सिर्फ़ यही निशानी मुझे अपने घर में मिली।'

सन्नाटा।

'लेकिन यह जाफ़री साहब के घर में कैसे पहुँची ?' कोई बुदबुदाया जैसे

अधेड़ पर यक़ीन न हो।

'मैं ही इसे वहाँ रख आया था।' अन्तिम नागरिक बोला।

'क्यों ?'

'जिस दिन गोधरा हुआ, उसी रात मैं जाफ़री साहब के घर गया था। मैंने उनसे पूछा, क्या हम भाग जाएँ ? वे बोले, नहीं, मैं भी तो नहीं भाग रहा। कुछ नहीं होगा।...पहले वे मारे गए, फिर मेरे बीवी-बच्चे। मैं अपनी आख़िरी निशानी उन्हीं के घर छोड़ आया था।'

उसने अपनी आँखें नीची कर लीं।

ऐसा सन्नाटा पृथ्वी पर पहले नहीं हुआ था।

नरोडा-पाटिया पहुँचने से पहले अमृत ने अपनी जेब से एक भगवा दुपट्टा निकाला और अपने सिर पर बाँध लिया। बग़ल में बैठे बाँके बिहारी उसे हैरत से देखते रहे। इस बार उन्होंने गाड़ी में बैठकर सीट की पीठ से अपनी पीठ नहीं टिकाई थी जब से वे गुलबर्ग सोसाइटी से बाहर आए। वे काठ-से बैठे थे जैसे उनकी पीठ सीट पर रखी हो। वे बार-बार अपनी ख़ाली हथेली अपनी आँखों के सामने फैला देते थे।

'अब मैं उन्हीं में से एक हो गया', अमृत ने बाँके बिहारी से कहा, 'जिनके बारे में आप जानना चाहते हैं।'

मुख्य सड़क पर जहाँ मोहन ने गाड़ी रोकी, वहीं से थोड़ा-सा आगे एक चाय की दुकान थी। वे उसी ओर बढ़े। दुकान के सामने दो बेंचें पड़ी थीं, जिन पर दो-तीन लोग बैठे थे। बेंचों पर एक पेड़ की छाया थी। वे चारों दोनों बेंचों पर आमने-सामने बैठ गए। अमृत चाय के लिए कह आया था। बैठने से पहले चारों सड़क के किनारे कुछ देर सड़क के दोनों ओर देखते हुए खड़े रहे थे। सड़क और उसके दोनों ओर दूर खड़े मकान आम लग रहे थे जैसे सब-कुछ सामान्य हो। वे यही बात कर रहे थे। अमृत की बग़ल में उसी की उम्र का एक लड़का बैठा था जिसकी ठाकुरों जैसी मूँछें थीं और गले में भगवा दुपट्टा पड़ा था। मूँछें फड़कीं। उसने अमृत के सिर पर बँधे भगवा दुपट्टे को देखते हुए कहा :

'सब-कुछ ठीक नहीं है।'

'फिर ?' अमृत ने उसकी ओर देखा।

'सड़क के दोनों तरफ़ सब ठीक कर दिया गया है', उसने मुस्कराते हुए कहा, 'बस्ती में अन्दर घुसो तो तुम्हें कुछ टूटी दीवारें नज़र आएँगी। घरों के अन्दर दीवारें जली मिलेंगी।'

तभी वह एकाएक रुक गया। उसने अमृत से पूछा—'तुम लोग कहाँ से आए

हो ?'

'कानपुर से। मैं इन लोगों को यहाँ दिखाने लाया हूँ।' अमृत ने कुछ उम्मीद से उसकी ओर देखा।

'अब देखने को क्या बचा है ?' वह हँसा, 'सब जल गया।' उसने अपने हाथ ऊपर हवा में फेंके जैसे उन्हीं हाथों ने सब-कुछ जलाया हो।

अमृत और श्याम सुन्दर और मोहन और बाँके बिहारी उसी युवक की ओर देख रहे थे, जो अचानक चुप हो गया था। सड़क पर आते-जाते वाहन थे और लोग थे जिनके चेहरे धूप में चमक रहे थे।

'अगर मूँछें हटा दें', अमृत ने उस युवक से कहा, 'तो तुम आमिर ख़ान लगते हो।'

वह मुस्कराया। फिर उसने कहा, 'कुछ लोग यही कहते हैं।...लेकिन एक बात मेरी समझ में नहीं आती।'

'क्या ?'

'जब यूसुफ़ ख़ान से दिलीप कुमार हो गया, तो आमिर ख़ान से राम कुमार क्यों नहीं हुआ ?'

'तुम्हारा नाम क्या है ?'

'राम कुमार।'

वह हँसा। अमृत ने तुरन्त उसका साथ दिया और उसकी हथेली पर ताली मारी जैसे उसका पुराना दोस्त हो। राम कुमार ने उसका हाथ नीचे आता देख अपनी हथेली सीधी कर दी थी। उसकी हँसी पहले ख़त्म हुई। अमृत तब रुका।

'यार, एक बात बताओ', अमृत ने पूछा।

'क्या ?'

'मैं इन बुज़ुर्गों को यहाँ का सच्चा हाल दिखाने कहाँ ले जाऊँ ?'

उसने एक बार अपने चारों ओर देखा। आस-पास कोई नहीं था। बेंचों पर अमृत के साथ आए तीन बुज़ुर्ग बचे थे। फिर उसने मुँह खोला :

'मैंने तुमसे कहा न, कि अब सिर्फ़ जली दीवारें बची हैं। वे गैस सिलिंडर नहीं हैं जो घरों में फूटे। न वे तेल के डिब्बे हैं जिन्हें आदमियों पर उँडेला गया और आग लगाई गई। वह आग भी नहीं है। न वह पानी है जिसमें बिजली चलाकर लोगों को आख़िरी बार नहलाया गया। न वे त्रिशूल और तलवारें हैं जिनसे पेट चिरे और सिर कटे। जलते हुए टायर भी नहीं हैं। शरीर कोई नहीं बचा। और...और...।' वह रुक गया। नीचे मिट्टी में देखने लगा।

'और क्या ?' अमृत ने पूछा। तीनों बुज़ुर्गों की आँखें और कान पूरे खुले थे।

'और सलमा की देह भी नहीं बची।' राम कुमार ने आँखें सीधी कीं।

'सलमा कौन ?'

'मैं उसे उतना ही चाहता था जितना आमिर प्रीति ज़िंटा को 'दिल चाहता है' में चाहता है। मैं उसे सड़क पर स्कूल जाते देखता था जहाँ वह पढ़ाती थी। मैं सड़क से स्कूल और उसके घर उसके पीछे-पीछे चला जाता था। कभी उससे बात नहीं कर सका। दंगे की दोपहर हम हाथ में तलवार लिए उसके घर में घुस गए। जो सामने आया, मरा। जब आख़िरी कमरा बचा तो उसके अन्दर घुसकर मैंने सिटकनी चढ़ा दी। अन्दर सलमा थी। मैं पागल हो गया था। जब तलवार फेंककर मैंने उसे दबोचा, वह चीख़ी। आख़िरी बार भी मैंने सिर्फ़ उसकी चीख़ सुनी—कोई आवाज़ नहीं।...कुछ देर बाद मेरे साथियों ने किवाड़ तोड़ दिए और कमरे के साथ सलमा को भी जला दिया।'

बाँके बिहारी लगातार उस युवक पर आँखें गड़ाए थे जैसे कुछ ढूँढ़ने की कोशिश कर रहे हों। क्या उसका चेहरा रतन से मिलता था ?

जब वे साबरमती आश्रम पहुँचे धूप जा चुकी थी। साँवला उजाला पेड़ों से नदी तक छाया था। आसमान कुछ ज़्यादा उजला था जैसे वहाँ सूर्य की स्मृति चमक रही हो। आश्रम के मैदान में पेड़ों तले गांधी की छवियाँ घूमती थीं। वे घास में मुस्कराते थे और हवाओं में हँसते थे। गहराते पेड़ों में उनकी प्रार्थनाएँ थीं। नदी सूख रही थी। नदी में बालू-ही-बालू नज़र आती थी। दूर एक मोटी धार थी। वे आश्रम की अन्तिम दीवार के पास खड़े थे, जिसके परे नीचे रेत शुरू होती थी, फिर पानी और आसमान था। उन्होंने गांधी के अजायबघर का एक चक्कर लगा लिया था, जिसमें दक्षिण अफ्रीका से लेकर उनकी अन्तिम प्रार्थना-सभा तक की झलकियाँ थीं। दंगों के दौरान उनके नोआखली और कलकत्ता के चित्र थे। बाँके बिहारी उन चित्रों में गांधीजी का चेहरा देखते रहे थे।

जिस शहर में एक ओर गुलबर्ग सोसाइटी थी और दूसरी ओर नरोडा-पाटिया था, उसी शहर में गांधी-आश्रम अब सचमुच एक अजायबघर ही था। गुलबर्ग सोसाइटी के अहाते में एक दोपहर दंगाइयों की भीड़ से घिरा जो आदमी 'मुझे मार दो, सबको छोड़ दो !' चीख़ रहा था, क्या वह गांधी नहीं था ? क्या एहसान जाफ़री के उजाड़ बरामदे में जो जली हथेली रखी थी, वह गांधी की हथेली नहीं थी ? बाँके बिहारी ने अजायबघर के चित्रों में उस हथेली की छाप ढूँढ़ने की कोशिश की थी। उन्होंने अजायबघर में उस युवक का चेहरा भी खोजा था जो सलमा का प्रेमी था।

दूर आकाश में सूर्य की स्मृति घुल रही थी। अँधेरा घिरने लगा। नदी और

साँवली हुई। रेत धीरे-धीरे चलने लगी। तभी पीछे पेड़ों से आवाज़ आई और गांधी का प्रकाश और ध्वनि का खेल शुरू हो गया। वे चारों पीछे मुड़कर आगे बढ़े और कुर्सियों पर बैठ गए। गांधी की कहानी एक अजीब कहानी थी जैसे कोई सपने को सच मानकर जीने लगे और दुनिया आहिस्ता-आहिस्ता उस सपने में ढलती जाए। सपने की उठान पर जलियाँवाला कांड था, जिसमें सैकड़ों लोग गोलियों से भून दिए गए थे। 'ब्लैक होल' अंग्रेज़ी राज का षड्यंत्र था। नरोडा-पाटिया जनतंत्र का षड्यंत्र था ! 'ब्लैक होल' में आदमी जानवरों की तरह मारे गए थे। नरोडा-पाटिया में आदमियों को आदमी की तरह ज़िन्दा जलाया गया, औरतों को औरतों की तरह रेप किया गया और बच्चों को बच्चों की तरह हवा में उछालकर संगीन पर छेदा गया ! 'ब्लैक होल' में लाशें बची थीं। नरोडा-पाटिया में लाशें नहीं थीं—ताकि कोई सनद न रहे जो वक़्त पर काम आए। बाँके बिहारी अपनी कुर्सी से उठकर पीछे चहारदीवारी के पास खड़े हो गए, जहाँ दूर काली नदी बह रही थी।

रात काली थी। आसमान में तारे नहीं थे। धरती का कालापन आकाश को छू रहा था जब बाँके बिहारी और श्याम सुन्दर रात को प्रोफ़ेसर्स कॉलोनी के बाहर घूमने निकले। जब बाँके बिहारी ने श्याम सुन्दर से पूछा कि मोहन के फ़्लैट में भीतर के कमरे में दो-दो टी.वी. खुले कैसे रखे हैं, तो श्याम सुन्दर ने बताया कि वह लूट का माल है जो मोहन की बेटी की मारुति में आया था। 'लूट का माल ?' बाँके बिहारी ने हैरत से श्याम सुन्दर की ओर सड़क की रोशनी में देखा। 'हाँ', श्याम सुन्दर ने कहा, 'वही मुस्लिम दुकानों की लूट जो महीने-भर पहले दंगे में हुई थी और जिसमें हिन्दू मारुतियों ने खुलकर हिस्सा लिया था।' बाँके बिहारी चलते-चलते रुक गए। उनका हाथ दिल की ओर उठा जैसे कोई धक्का लगा हो। उनकी आँखों में माधुरी की भोली सूरत डोलने लगी...लव एट फ़र्स्ट साइट ! उन्हें अपने आँगन में उड़ती चिड़िया का भी ख़्याल आया। क्या चिड़िया डाका डाल सकती थी ? जब बाँके बिहारी ने यही पूछा तो श्याम सुन्दर हँसने लगे। वे शायद कुछ ज़्यादा ज़ोर से हँसे थे क्योंकि आगे जाते जोड़े ने घूमकर उनकी ओर देखा। जोड़ा जवान था। युवती माधुरी की तरह साँवली और छरहरी थी। क्या इसने भी बाज़ार की लूट में भाग लिया होगा ? बाँके बिहारी ने कई बार सोचा।

पिछली रात वे नवरंगपुरा के विजय चौराहे से लौट गए थे। इस रात वे विजय चौराहा पार करके दूसरी ओर निकले और बाज़ार में टहलते रहे जहाँ ख़ूब रोशनी थी और लड़कियाँ आइसक्रीम खा रही थीं और हँस रही थीं। बाँके बिहारी हर चेहरे को देखते और उनके मन में यक्ष-प्रश्न सिर उठाने लगता : क्या यह सुन्दर,

सामान्य लड़की भी हिन्दू लूट में शामिल हो सकती थी ? इसका चेहरा कितना मासूम है, यह फूल की तरह निष्कलंक लग रही है ! क्या यह किसी दुकान में घुसकर लुटेरे की भूमिका निभा सकती है ? क्या वह गाल पर गड्ढे वाली लड़की किसी दुकान से हाथों में साड़ियाँ चपेटे भाग सकती है ? और वह फ्रॉक पहने कमसिन छोरी ! क्या वह भी ?'

सड़क पर दो लड़के तेज़ मोटरसाइकिलें भगाते निकले। क्या ये मोटरसाइकिलें लूटकर भाग रहे थे ? पकड़ो पकड़ो...बाँके बिहारी बुदबुदाए।

एक क्षण साथ चलते बाँके बिहारी के चेहरे को श्याम सुन्दर ने देखा। बाँके बिहारी सीधे देख रहे थे, जहाँ सड़क रात में चली जाती थी। उनका चेहरा ख़ाली था।

फिर वे लौट पड़े।

4.3

इतवार था।

यों अवकाश-प्राप्त शिक्षक के.सी. चन्द्रा के लिए हर दिन इतवार था। फ़र्क यही था कि इतवार को घर में बेटी और मोहल्ले में पड़ोसी बाहर नहीं जाते थे। मोहल्ले के लोग अक्सर उस दिन देर से उठते थे और दाढ़ी नहीं बनाते थे। चन्द्रा उस दिन ज़रूर दाढ़ी बनाते थे। जब वे दाढ़ी बनाते थे तो सपना अक्सर पीछे की अटारी से नीचे उतरती थी। आज वह नहीं उतरी। दाढ़ी बनाकर उन्होंने रसोई में बैठी पत्नी से पूछा :

'सपना क्या अभी सो रही है ?'

'नहीं।'

'फिर कहाँ है ?'

'सुबह-सुबह कहीं चली गई है।'

'कहाँ ?'

'बताया नहीं।'

नौकरी-पेशा बेटी के बारे में चिन्ता करना उन्होंने कब का छोड़ दिया था। वे स्नानघर में घुस गए। नहाते हुए उन्होंने दो-तीन बार गुनगुनाया, 'देखी ज़माने की यारी...'। फिर बाहर निकलकर एक पराँठे और दही का नाश्ता किया। नाश्ता करते हुए इतवार का अख़बार उनके हाथ में था, जो नाश्ते के बाद भी बना रहा। वे देर तक अख़बार पढ़ते रहे। जब अख़बार ख़त्म हो गया तो वे तख़्त पर लेट

गए और उन्होंने आँखें मूँद लीं। उन्हें पता नहीं चला कब उनकी आँख लग गई।

दालान में सपना की आवाज़ से उनकी आँख खुली। सपना सेंडिल खोल रही थी। उन्होंने पूछा, 'कहाँ गई थी सुबह-सुबह ?'

'थाने', सपना की ठंडी आवाज़ थी।

चन्द्रा तख़्त पर उछलकर बैठ गए, 'थाने !'

'हाँ।'

'क्यों ?'

'एफ़.आई.आर. लिखाने।'

'किस की एफ़.आई.आर. ?'

'रेप की।'

सपना की माँ भी दालान में आकर खड़ी हो गई थी। सपना ने दोनों को बताया कि कल दोपहर में जब वह रतन के घर गई थी तो रतन ने उससे बलात्कार किया। उसी की रपट उसने थाने में लिखाई थी।

चन्द्रा तख़्त से उतरकर फ़र्श पर खड़े हो गए थे जैसे अचानक किसी भँवर में फँस गए हों। सपना की माँ उनकी बग़ल में खड़ी थी। सपना दोनों के सामने खड़ी थी। उसकी दोनों आँखें माँ-बाप की चारों आँखों का सामना कर रही थीं।

'क्या मुझे कुछ बताने की ज़रूरत नहीं थी ?' पिता की निरीह चीख़ दालान में गूँजी।

'बता रही हूँ, पापा।' सपना की नज़रें सीधी थीं।

'मैं एफ़.आई.आर. के पहले की बात कर रहा हूँ।'

'यह मेरा निजी मामला है।'

'अब यह निजी कहाँ रहा, बेटा ?' चन्द्रा के मुँह से शब्द फूटे, 'अब यह शहर का मामला हो गया है।'

सपना कुछ नहीं बोली। तीनों एक-दूसरे की ओर देखते रहे। फिर सपना ने कहा—'माँ, मुझे भूख लगी है।'

दोनों स्त्रियाँ रसोई की ओर चली गईं। चन्द्रा जैसे खड़े थे वैसे ही खड़े रहे गोया वे बैठना भूल गए हों।

सपना रसोई में ही पटे पर बैठ गई। उसने दो पराँठे खाए, एक गिलास पानी पिया और यह कहते हुए ऊपर चली गई कि मैं बहुत थक गई हूँ, सोऊँगी, मुझे जगाना मत। चन्द्रा उसे सीढ़ियों पर अपनी अटारी में जाता हुआ देखते रहे। जब वह ऊपर चली गई और पत्नी दालान में आई तो उन्होंने उससे पूछा—'क्या कह रही थी ?'

'कह रही थी कि मैं थक गई हूँ, सोऊँगी, मुझे जगाना मत।'

चन्द्रा खीज गए, 'मैं सोने के बारे में नहीं पूछ रहा।'

'फिर ?'

'एफ़.आई.आर. के बारे में।'

'एफ़.आई.आर. के बारे में उसने कुछ नहीं कहा।'

'तुमने पूछा नहीं ?'

'क्या पूछती मैं ?'

प्रश्न कुछ देर हवा में टँगा रहा। फिर उल्टा डूब गया।

'अब क्या होगा ?' पत्नी ने पूछा।

'धीरे-धीरे बात शहर-भर में फैल जाएगी।' चन्द्रा बोले।

वे तख़्त पर बैठ गए थे। पत्नी सामने बैठी थी। वह पति की ओर देख रही थी। वे नीचे ख़ाली तख़्त की ओर देख रहे थे जैसे वहाँ कुछ लिखा हो। असल में वे बात के शहर में फैलने की कल्पना कर रहे थे। पहले अफ़वाह उठेगी, फिर ख़बर बनेगी। शहर-भर में लोग उसे मज़े से चुभलेंगे। ख़बर का केन्द्र सपना होगी, जो युवा और सुन्दर और अविवाहित है। जितनी चन्द्रा की कल्पना आगे बढ़ती, उतनी ही उनकी तकलीफ़ बढ़ती जाती। सपना उनकी इकलौती बेटी थी।

'बात बिरादरी में फैली', पत्नी ने नीचे देखते हुए कहा, 'तो उससे ब्याह कौन करेगा ?'

पिछले दिनों चन्द्रा ने आईने में अपने बढ़ते हुए सफ़ेद बाल देखकर यहाँ तक सोचा था कि अगली बार सपना के विवाह की बात मारुति पर अटकी तो वे यह मकान बेच देंगे और सपना का ब्याह करके अपने गाँव के घर बड़ागाँव चले जाएँगे। बाक़ी ज़िन्दगी पेंशन के सहारे गाँव की साफ़ हवा में कट जाएगी। उन्होंने यह भी सोचा था कि अगली बार ब्याह की बात वे अकेले करेंगे, सपना वहाँ नहीं होगी। वह अपने को रानी लक्ष्मीबाई समझती है ! और अपने ब्याह में तो लक्ष्मीबाई ने भी पेंच नहीं डाला था।

'सब तुम्हारी ग़लती है', चन्द्रा पत्नी की ओर देखते हुए बोले।

'क्यों ?'

'जब वह बड़ी हो गई, तब भी रतन के घर जाती रही। तुमने रोका नहीं !'

'जब वह बड़ी हो गई तो अकेली आगरा पढ़ने गई। तुमने क्या रोका ?'

दालान में सन्नाटा छा गया। अप्रैल की दोपहर का सन्नाटा था। आँगन की धूप भाँय-भाँय कर रही थी। चन्द्रा आँगन की ओर देख रहे थे जहाँ कोई नहीं था।

सपना की माँ फिर बोली, 'अब क्या होगा ?'

उसका स्वर कातर था।

'कचहरी में मुकदमा चलेगा', वे छत की ओर देखते हुए बोले, 'सपना को कटघरे में खड़ा करके वकील उससे सवाल-जवाब करेंगे। शायद अख़बार में भी छपे।'

उसने अपनी आँखें नीची कीं और आँचल से पोंछी।

चन्द्रा छत की जानिब देख रहे थे। उन्हें लगा जैसे वे फिर नदी के भँवर में फँस गए हैं जैसे एक बार लड़कपन में फँसे थे—और उन्हें तैरना नहीं आता।

सपना उस समय ऊपर अटारी में सपना देख रही थी। सपने में कभी वह किताब पढ़ती थी, कभी क्लास में भाषण देती थी, इस समय वह फ़िल्म देख रही थी। परदे पर पीले और लाल और नीले और सफ़ेद फूलों की घाटी फैली थी। पृष्ठभूमि में बर्फ़ीले पहाड़ थे। यह घाटी कश्मीर के पहलगाँव या स्विट्ज़रलैंड के किसी गाँव में हो सकती थी। सपना को मालूम नहीं था। न उसे जानने की ज़रूरत थी। परदे पर फूलों की घाटी चादर-सी फैली थी। तब फूलों के बीच में हँसती नायिका का क्लोज़-अप परदे पर उभरा जैसे कोई फूल अचानक हँस पड़ा हो। नायक उसी की ओर टकटकी लगाए देख रहा था। दोनों बहुत जवान और बहुत ख़ूबसूरत थे गोया किसी दूसरे ग्रह से आए हों। सहसा दृश्य बदल गया। यह टूटी, दरकी, ऊबड़-खाबड़ ज़मीन थी जैसी सपना ने पत्र-पत्रिकाओं में चाँद की तस्वीरों में देखी थी। प्रेमी-प्रेमिका अब फूलों की घाटी से चाँद पर आ गए थे, जिसकी ज़मीन टूटी और ऊबड़-खाबड़ थी। वे चाँद पर हाथ में हाथ लिए दौड़ रहे थे। उनके पैर नंगे थे। चाँद का आसमान वैसा ही था जैसा धरती का आसमान था। मगर ज़मीन टूटी थी। चाँद पर दौड़ते हुए अचानक प्रेमिका का पैर टूटी ज़मीन पर टेढ़ा हो जाता है। उसका हाथ प्रेमी के हाथ से छूट जाता है। लेकिन प्रेमी को पता नहीं चलता। वह अपना ख़ाली हाथ चाँद पर झुलाता हुआ आगे दौड़ता जाता है जैसे उसके हाथ में प्रेमिका का हाथ हो।

प्रेमिका चाँद की टूटी ज़मीन पर फँस गई है।

नायिका का क्लोज़-अप चेहरा सपना का चेहरा है, साँवला ! क्या वह इतनी सुन्दर है ? लाँग शॉट में नायक ख़ाली हाथ फेंकता हुआ दूर भागा जा रहा है।

यह चाँद होना ज़रूरी नहीं है। यह धरती का कोई टुकड़ा भी हो सकता है। यह ओरछा दरवाज़े के बाहर कोई खेत भी हो सकता है, जिसकी रबी की फ़सल कट चुकी हो।

ओरछा की सड़क बेतवा नदी तक जाती है, जिसमें पत्थर की चट्टानें हैं। नदी

में पानी नहीं है, चट्टानें हैं। क्या इसे अब भी नदी कहेंगे ?

दोनों किनारों पर पेड़ खड़े हाथ हिला रहे हैं जैसे उस पानी को अलविदा कह रहे हों जो अब नहीं है।

परदे पर बिना पानी की नदी से वह डर गई। यह कुछ ऐसा ही था जैसे बिना आदमी की धरती हो। उसने हड़बड़ाकर आँखें खोलीं। फिर वह बिस्तर पर बैठ गई। उसे पसीना आ गया था गोकि छत का पंखा चल रहा था। उसने उठकर पंखा तेज़ किया और बिस्तर पर लौट आई। उसने अपना सपना याद करने की कोशिश की। वह कल रात सोई नहीं थी। सुबह एफ़.आई.आर. दर्ज कराने के बाद उसे नींद आई। वह जानती थी कि एफ़.आई.आर. दर्ज कराने का मतलब शहर में रुसवाई है। स्कूल, बाज़ार और मोहल्ले में चलना दूभर हो जाएगा। लोगों की नज़रें कीचड़ की तरह उछलेंगी। लड़के हँसेंगे, ठहाके लगाएँगे। तिपहिए से स्कूल जाना मुश्किल हो जाएगा। पता नहीं कौन बग़ल में या सामने बैठ जाए और क्या-क्या कहे ? वह किस-किस से लड़ेगी ? कौन जाने शहर का उपद्रव देखकर स्कूलवाले भी जवाब दे दें ! लेकिन यह सब दूसरे करेंगे, उनका मामला होगा। उसकी अपनी ज़िम्मेदारी अपने प्रति यही थी कि वह अगली सुबह थाने जाए ! रात-भर छत पर चक्कर लगाते हुए उसने यही सोचा था। आसमान में सप्तऋषि आहिस्ता-आहिस्ता अपने रास्ते पर चल रहे थे।

जैसे सप्तऋषि की गति आकाश में थी, उसकी गति सुबह थाने की ओर थी। तभी थानेदार ने कहा था—'यह शहर में अपनी तरह की पहली मिसाल है। आप ख़ुद अकेली रेप की एफ़.आई.आर. लिखाने आ गईं।'

'यह मेरा मामला है।'

थानेदार ने कुछ नहीं कहा। उसने सपना की डॉक्टरी जाँच का इन्तज़ाम कर दिया। सपना ने जानबूझकर नहाया नहीं था।

बिस्तर से उठकर सपना आईने के सामने बैठ गई और अपने चेहरे को उस चेहरे से मिलाने लगी जो उसने सपने में देखा था। अप्रैल का महीना स्कूल में पूरा करना होगा। फिर गर्मी की छुट्टियाँ हो जाएँगी। अगले साल वह आगरा न्यू आगरा के स्कूल में चली जाएगी, जहाँ उसकी सहेली उषा की माँ प्रिंसिपल है—उन्होंने उसे पहले भी बुलाया था। पराए शहर में अपने परिवार से दूर वह शायद अपने से भी दूर चली जाएगी। अपने से दूर चला जाना मुक्ति होगी, सपना ने आईने में देखते हुए सोचा।

अगली सुबह जब वह स्कूल के लिए कुछ जल्दी तैयार होकर सायबान में खड़ी थी तो उसने देखा कि पुलिस की गाड़ी रतन के घर के सामने रुकी। पुलिस

घर में घुसी। कुछ देर बाद रतन अपने दोनों बँधे हाथ सामने लिए घर से निकला। सपना ने उसे नीली कमीज़ से पहचाना, जो उसने होली की दोपहर को पहनी थी जब सपना उससे ऊपर अटारी में मिलने गई। जब पुलिस की गाड़ी चली तो वह सायबान से अन्दर लौट गई और फिर आँगन में उतरकर पीछे अपने कमरे में ऊपर चली गई। उसने अपने कमरे में भीतर की साँकल चढ़ा ली और पलटकर औंधी पलंग पर लेट गई। आँसू धीरे-धीरे चादर पर गिरने लगे।

उस दिन वह स्कूल नहीं गई। लोगों ने समझा कि वह एफ.आई.आर. की वजह से बाहर नहीं निकली। अगली सुबह वह इस तरह देहरी से नीचे उतरी जैसे रोज़ सुबह स्कूल जाने के लिए उतरती थी। मोहल्ले की सड़क पर रोज़ की तरह धूप, छाँव, गाय, कुत्ते, बच्चे और लोग थे। चबूतरों पर कुछ स्त्रियों के चेहरे नज़र आते थे। सपना को लगा जैसे स्त्रियाँ उसे देखने को बाहर निकली हैं और सड़क पर पुरुष उसे कनखियों से देख रहे हैं। पुरुष काम पर जा रहे थे, स्त्रियाँ घरों में लौट रही थीं। कुछ देर में सड़क पर धूप, छाँव, गाएँ, कुत्ते और बच्चे रह जाएँगे।

मानिक चौक के बाज़ार में चलना मुश्किल था। इस समय रोज़ ऐसी ही भीड़ होती थी। लोग भीड़ में अपने पैरों के लिए जगह ढूँढ़ते थे। उन्हें दूसरों को देखने की फुर्सत नहीं थी। बाज़ार खुल गया था। भीड़ जुलूस की तरह जा रही थी। यह बहुमुखी जुलूस था, जिसमें लोग गलियों से शामिल होते थे और दोनों ओर आगे-पीछे जाते थे। यह बाज़ार का जुलूस था, जिसमें खो जाना आसान था। यहाँ कोई किसी को नहीं देखता था। सपना तिराहे पर आकर एक टैम्पो में बैठ गई, जो सदर की ओर जाता था। टैम्पो में उसके अलावा दो लड़कियाँ और पाँच लड़के थे। वह किसी को नहीं जानती थी। सब उसे जानते थे। दो लड़कों और दोनों लड़कियों ने उससे 'नमस्ते' की। वे मुस्करा रहे थे। खुलती धूप में उनकी मुस्कान सहज भी हो सकती थी। लेकिन क्या कोई लगातार पन्द्रह मिनट मुस्करा सकता है ?

बाज़ार की तरह विद्यालय की चहल-पहल सामान्य थी। लड़कियाँ इधर-उधर भाग रही थीं। शिक्षिकाएँ कक्षाओं की ओर जा रही थीं। सपना क्लास में लड़कियों के सामने उनके साथ दूसरी दुनिया में पहुँच जाती। उसे हल्कापन महसूस होता जैसे वह धुपैले आकाश में पेड़ों की पत्तियों से गुज़र रही हो। इंटरवल की घंटी के बाद जब वह स्टाफ़रूम में घुसी तो उसे लगा कि अब वह ज़मीन पर है जहाँ दूसरी स्त्रियाँ दरवाज़े में उसकी ओर ताक रही हैं। वह रोज़ की तरह कमरे के बीच में रखी लम्बी मेज़ पर बैठ गई जिस पर दूसरी स्त्रियाँ अपने टिफ़न खोले बैठी थीं। वे हँस रही थीं और खा रही थीं। सपना ने भी अपना कटोरदान खोल

लिया।

होली और मौसम की छिटपुट चर्चा के बाद श्रीमती वर्मा ने कहा—'आज पेपर में पहले पेज पर आडवाणी का रेप पर बयान है।'

'क्या ?' सामने बैठी श्रीमती तिवारी ने पूछा।

सपना की आँखें बारी-बारी दोनों चेहरों की तरफ़ घूमीं।

'आडवाणी कहते हैं', श्रीमती वर्मा बोली 'कि बलात्कार की सज़ा मृत्यु दंड होनी चाहिए।'

'तब सज़ाएँ और भी कम हो जाएँगी', श्रीमती तिवारी ने कहा और पराँठे का एक कौर अपने मुँह में डाल लिया।

एक घूँट पानी पीकर श्रीमती वर्मा ने पूछा—'क्यों ?'

'न्यायपालिका के रुख़ का सवाल है', श्रीमती तिवारी ने निवाला चबाते हुए कहा, 'निन्यानबे प्रतिशत न्यायाधीश पुरुष होते हैं।'

'अभी कितनों को सज़ा होती है ?' श्रीमती तिवारी की बग़ल में बैठीं श्रीमती मिश्रा ने पूछा।

'चार प्रतिशत', श्रीमती तिवारी कहकर मुस्कराईं।

तीनों वार्ताकारों ने अभी तक सपना की ओर न देखा था, न उससे कुछ पूछा था। फिर भी उसे लगा कि उसका मत मेज़ पर आना ज़रूरी है।

'मृत्युदंड की ज़रूरत नहीं है', सपना ने कहा, 'दंड की ज़रूरत है।'

सबने उसकी ओर देखा। सपना को लगा कि सब निगाहें उस पर टिकी हैं। निगाहें टिकी हैं और हटती नहीं। उसने सिर नीचे झुका लिया और कटोरदान से एक कौर तोड़कर मुँह में डाला। उसके चेहरे पर कोई भाव नहीं था। मन में जिज्ञासा थी। क्या सबको मालूम है ?

'सही सज़ा के लिए', श्रीमती वर्मा ने कहा, 'रेप का केस महिला न्यायाधीश की अदालत में होना चाहिए।'

'क्यों ?' कहीं से आवाज़ आई।

'क्योंकि रेप में क़ानून से ज़्यादा नारी-स्वभाव की समझ ज़रूरी है।'

जिस ओर से यह आवाज़ आई थी, सबने उसी ओर देखा। यह सपना की सपाट आवाज़ थी।

टिफ़न ख़ाली हो गए थे। मेज़ पर चाय के प्याले थे। सब चाय पीने लगीं।

'असली मुद्दा मर्ज़ी का है', मेज़ के एक सिरे से मिस सिंह बोलीं, जो अभी तक चुप रही थीं। मिस सिंह पाँच फीट छह इंच की हृष्ट-पुष्ट हरियाणवी युवती थीं, जो अविवाहित थीं।

कोई और कुछ नहीं बोली। सब चाय सुड़कती रहीं।

'यदि आदमी-औरत अकेले हों', मिस सिंह फिर बोलीं, 'तो अकेला आदमी कुछ नहीं कर सकता।'

'मगर औरत तुम्हारी तरह होनी चाहिए !' श्रीमती वर्मा ने मिस सिंह की ओर देखते हुए कहा और मुस्कराईं।

सब हँसीं। सिंह भी।

'सिंह !' श्रीमती तिवारी ने कहा, 'सिंह तो खुद भी रेप कर सकती हैं।'

श्रीमती मिश्रा हँसीं, 'इसके लिए भी क़ानून बनाने की बात चल रही है।'

मृत्युदंड ! जब सपना स्टॉफ़-रूम से निकलकर क्लास की ओर जा रही थी तो उसके दिमाग़ में यही शब्द गूँज रहे थे। नहीं, नहीं, उसकी छाती धड़की। वह रतन की जान नहीं लेना चाहती। वह रतन की जान नहीं ले सकती ! ख़ुद ज़िन्दा रहने के लिए रतन को मारना ज़रूरी नहीं है। ख़ुद ज़िन्दा रहने के लिए एफ़.आई.आर. दर्ज कराना ज़रूरी था !

मृत्युदंड ! ऐसी ही प्रतिध्वनियाँ उसके भीतर एक सिरे से दूसरे सिरे तक गूँजती रही, जब सपना क्लास ले रही थी। सामने बैठी मासूम लड़कियों की आँखों में उसे श्रीमती वर्मा, श्रीमती मिश्रा, श्रीमती तिवारी और मिस सिंह की आँखें तैरती हुई नज़र आतीं। आँखें मुस्कराती हुई लगती थीं। ख़ासकर मिस सिंह की आँखें, जो हँस रही थीं जैसे दोहरा रही हों : यदि आदमी-औरत अकेले हों, तो अकेला आदमी कुछ नहीं कर सकता ! सपना की आँखें सिंह की हँसती आँखों को देख रही थीं और उसके भीतर दीवारों से मृत्युदंड की अनुगूँजें टकरा रही थीं। उसके होंठों से कभी इतिहास निकलता, कभी समाजशास्त्र और कभी कविता जैसे ज़ुबान आँखों और देह से अलग हो गई हो। उसने अनजाने अपने कानों को अलग रख दिया था।

सूरज ढले जब वह घर लौटी तो उसे पसीना आ रहा था। उमस देह की तह तक महसूस हो रही थी—दिल तक। वह दालान में मूढ़े पर पंखे के नीचे बैठ गई। तख़्त पर चन्द्रा गोल तकिए पर अधलेटे थे। माँ रसोई से चाय का प्याला लेकर आई और उसने चाय सपना के हाथ में पकड़ा दी। सपना चाय सुड़कने लगी। चन्द्रा ने अपनी पसीना-पसीना होती बेटी की ओर देखते हुए कहा :

'गर्मी बहुत है, बेटा', वे तख़्त पर बैठ गए थे।

'हाँ', सपना ने कहा और होंठ प्याले से लगा दिए।

माँ दालान के खम्भे से टिकी खड़ी थी। धूप आँगन से जा चुकी थी। सुबह

सपना के जाने के बाद चन्द्रा बाहर निकले थे और मानिक चौक तक टूथपेस्ट लेने गए थे। आते-जाते दस लोगों ने एफ़.आई.आर. के बारे में पूछा था जैसे उन्हें और कोई काम न हो। शहर के लोगों को एक ज़रूरी काम मिल गया था। चन्द्रा ने भुगत लिया था। पता नहीं क्या-क्या भुगता था ! लेकिन उम्र के इस आख़िरी पड़ाव पर यह ऐसा मुकाम था, जिसकी उन्होंने कभी कल्पना भी नहीं की थी। कहीं बेहतर होता यदि सपना रतन के साथ शहर छोड़कर भाग जाती ! कुछ दिन लोग पूछते, कुछ पता चला ? फिर सब भूल जाते। या शहर में कोई और बड़ी दुर्घटना हो जाती। इस एफ़.आई.आर. से ज़्यादा मज़ेदार दुर्घटना जल्दी नहीं होगी और फिर अदालत में मुकदमा चलेगा। चन्द्रा का कलेजा काँप गया। वे चाय पीती सपना को देख रहे थे। नन्ही-सी जान ! कैसे झेलेगी ?

'बेटा !' दो दिन की सफ़ेद दाढ़ी के बीच चन्द्रा के मुँह से जो आवाज़ आई, वह कुछ काँपी।

सपना ने चौंककर मुँह उठाया, 'जी, पापा !'

'तुम...तुम ठीक हो न ?'

'जी, पापा !' उसकी आँखें पिता पर टिकी थीं।

माँ दोनों को देख रही थी।

'बेटा, तुम घर में अकेली लड़के की तरह बड़ी हुईं', चन्द्रा बोले, 'मैंने कभी नहीं सोचा था कि...' उनकी आवाज़ ठहर गई।

'मुझे अफ़सोस है, पापा', सपना की आँखें नीचीं और स्वर संजीदा था, 'कि मैं आपको और माँ को ऐसी तकलीफ़ दे रही हूँ।'

कोई आवाज़ नहीं। कहीं कोई गौरैया बोली।

जैसे काले बादलों को चीरकर सूर्य की कुछ किरणें निकलती हैं, चन्द्रा मुस्कराए, 'हमारी तकलीफ़ की बात नहीं है, बेटा। हम तो वैसे भी तुम्हारे ब्याह के बाद अपने गाँव जाने की सोच रहे थे। आदमी जहाँ पैदा हो, अन्त में उसी ज़मीन पर लौटने की सोचता है।'

'आप लोग गाँव जाइए, पापा।'

'तुम्हें यहाँ अकेला छोड़कर ?' वे हँसे।

'नहीं, 'सपना ने कहा, 'मैं आगरा में नौकरी करूँगी।'

'नौकरी मिल जाएगी ?' चन्द्रा ने पूछा।

'मेरी फ़ोन पर बात हो गई है।'

चुप्पी।

'जब मुकदमे की तारीख़ पड़ेगी,' सपना ने कहा जैसे किसी और का मुकदमा

हो, 'तो मैं आगरा से आ जाऊँगी, आप गाँव से आ जाना।'

चन्द्रा अपनी बेटी को हैरत से देख रहे थे।

सपना की माँ खम्भे से लगी खड़ी थीं और रो रही थीं।

4.4

जब तिपहिया दरवाज़े पर रुका तो अँधेरा घिरने लगा था। मगर इतनी रात नहीं हुई थी कि दरवाज़ा बन्द हो। बाँके बिहारी ने घड़ी देखी : साढ़े सात बजे थे। वे बैग हाथ में लिए चबूतरे पर चढ़े और उन्होंने साँकल बजाई। गायत्री ने दरवाज़ा खोला। चबूतरे पर खड़े हुए बाँके बिहारी ने कहा—

'इतनी जल्दी दरवाज़ा बन्द कर लिया ?'

'मुझे लगा तुम्हारी गाड़ी लेट हो गई।'

'ज़्यादा लेट नहीं थी।' बाँके बिहारी चबूतरे पर ही खड़े थे।

'अन्दर आओ', गायत्री ने कहा।

आँगन में आकर बाँके बिहारी ने पूछा, 'छोटे कहाँ है ?'

'ऊपर।'

'इतनी जल्दी ऊपर चला गया ?'

'वह शाम को बाहर नहीं निकला।'

'क्यों ?'

सवाल के जवाब में गायत्री ने सवाल पूछा—'रोटी खाओगे ?'

'थोड़ी देर में।'

तब गायत्री ने आँगन के पीछे ख़ाली ज़ीने को देखकर कहा—'बैठ जाओ।'

वह एक गिलास पानी ले आई। जब पानी पीकर बाँके बिहारी ने मुँह पोंछ लिया तो गायत्री ने उन्हें सपना की एफ़.आई.आर., छोटे की गिरफ़्तारी और बड़े की छोटे की ज़मानत कराने की बात ब्यौरेवार बताई। वे दालान में तख़्त पर सिर नीचा किए बैठे थे। बीच-बीच में वे सिर उठाते, फिर सिर नीचा कर लेते। सिर की कोई और स्थिति नहीं हो सकती थी। उन्हें इसका अफ़सोस था। उन्हें अफ़सोस था कि वे अपने सिर को हाथ में लेकर घुमा नहीं सकते थे।

'तुमने मुझे कुछ नहीं बताया जब मैंने अहमदाबाद से फ़ोन किया ?' उन्होंने पूछा।

'बड़े ने मना किया था', गायत्री ने कहा, 'और छोटे घर आ गए थे।' छोटे

घर में थे। छोटे घर में थे, इसीलिए घर बन्द था। घर बन्द होने का कारण बाँके बिहारी की गाड़ी का लेट होना नहीं था। जब कुछ देर उन्होंने अपना सिर ऊपर नहीं उठाया तो गायत्री ने पूछा, 'क्या सोच रहे हो ?'

'कोई अच्छा वकील देखना होगा।'

'बड़े ने देख लिया है। उसका दोस्त है। तारीख़ पर बड़े भी आएँगे।'

बाँके बिहारी तुरन्त कुछ करना चाहते थे। उन्होंने ख़ुद ऊपर जाने या छोटे को नीचे बुलाने की बात सोची। मगर छोटे से क्या बात हो सकती थी ? उसे एफ़.आई.आर. के बाद देखना ज़रूर था। वह सुबह भी हो सकता था। अभी क्या-क्या देखना बाक़ी था ? उन्होंने होली की दोपहर ऊपर बन्द अटारी में खिड़की के छेद से सपना और रतन को एक खाट पर लेटे देखा था और वे नीचे आँगन में लौट आए थे। फिर वे अहमदाबाद चले गए थे जहाँ उन्होंने गांधी के आश्रम से साबरमती नदी देखी थी जिसमें पानी नहीं था। लौटकर एफ़.आई.आर. देख रहे हैं ! जैसे साबरमती नदी में पानी न होने की प्राथमिकी झाँसी में दर्ज हुई हो।

अगले दिन सुबह बाँके बिहारी ने जो गुजरात-किस्त अपने अख़बार के लिए लिखी, वह नरोडा-पाटिया पर थी। उसका आरम्भ सूखी साबरमती नदी से होता था, जो उस शाम उन्होंने साबरमती आश्रम में देखी थी। बिना पानी की नदी के बाद जलियाँवाला बाग़ का ज़िक्र था, जो गांधी के विराट् असहयोग आन्दोलन का उत्स था। 13 अप्रैल, 1919 को बैसाखी के दिन जलियाँवाला बाग़ में कुछ हज़ार लोग एक प्रतिबन्धित सभा के लिए इकट्ठे हुए थे। सारे रास्ते बन्द करके अंग्रेज़ी सेना ने मैदान की भीड़ पर दस मिनट गोलियाँ चलाई थीं। सैकड़ों मारे गए। सरकार के अनुसार 379। कुछ लोगों ने भागकर मैदान के चारों ओर दीवारों पर चढ़ने की कोशिश की, कुछ सूखे कुएँ में कूद गए। बाँके बिहारी ने अपनी रपट में इस ऐतिहासिक हादसे के बरक्स 2002 के गुजरात नरसंहार को रखा।

जलियाँवाला बाग़ की 379 हत्याओं के लिए जनरल डायर पर इंग्लैंड में मुकदमा चला था। गुजरात के नरसंहार के लिए जिसमें क़रीब तीन हज़ार जानें गईं, कहाँ मुकदमा चलेगा ?

मृतकों की संख्या महत्त्वपूर्ण नहीं थी। एक मनुष्य की हत्या का दुख ही बार-बार संख्या के आईनों में उसी पीड़ा को दुहराता था। एक आदमी की हत्या दुनिया की हत्या थी। नरोडा-पाटिया के नरसंहार की संख्या से कहीं ज़्यादा अहम उसकी तकनीक थी, जिसके बरक्स जलियाँवाला बाग़ एक क्रूर खेल लगता था। ज़रा तसव्वुर कीजिए, एक गर्भवती स्त्री से सार्वजनिक सामूहिक बलात्कार, फिर

उसका पेट चीरकर शिशु को निकालना और हवा में उछालना। जब नवजात शिशु हवा में नीचे उतरता है तो धरती से पहले उसे एक संगीन की नोक धारण कर लेती है। नवजात शिशु चीख़ भी नहीं पाता। जीवन की पहली चीख़ भी मयस्सर नहीं ! उसकी माता सार्वजनिक बलात्कार के दौरान पहले चीख़ती है, फिर बेहोश हो जाती है। उसे दूसरी नंगी औरतों के साथ पेट्रोल डालकर जला दिया जाता है। कोई नामोनिशान नहीं।

नरोडा-पाटिया में कुछ नहीं हुआ।

एक घर के आँगन में पानी भर दिया गया। घर के सब लोग उसी आँगन में खदेड़ दिए गए हैं : आदमी, औरतें और बच्चे। एक बिजली का तार पानी में लोगों की तरह भीग रहा है। सहसा तार में बिजली दौड़ती है और आँगन के लोग लाशों में बदल जाते हैं !

किसी को चीख़ने का अवकाश नहीं मिलता। उस दस साल के रफ़ीक को भी नहीं जिसके मुँह में मिट्टी का तेल डालकर उसे जला दिया जाता है ! जलियाँवाला बाग़ की चीख़ें सदी के पार हमारे कानों में गूँजती हैं। गुजरात की चुप्पी कब तक गूँजेगी ?

अन्त में बाँके बिहारी ने एक नवयुवक का उल्लेख किया जिसका नाम राम कुमार था और जिसे वे नरोडा-पाटिया की मुख्य सड़क पर एक चाय की दुकान पर मिले थे। राम कुमार नरोडा-पाटिया की एक गली में रहता था। उसी मोहल्ले में उसके घर से कुछ घर दूर सलमा रहती थी, जिसे वह उतना ही प्यार करता था जितना आमिर ख़ान 'दिल चाहता है' में प्रीति ज़िंटा से करता है। वे कभी-कभी नरोडा-पाटिया से बाहर शहर में मिलते थे और बाग़ों में घूमते थे या सिनेमाघर के अँधेरे कोने में फ़िल्म देखते थे। फिर वह दोपहर आई जब तलवारें और त्रिशूल लेकर कुछ लोगों ने सलमा के घर पर हमला बोल दिया। राम कुमार भी माथे पर दुपट्टा बाँधे भीड़ में था। जब वह आक्रमणकारी भीड़ को रोक न सका तो सबसे आगे पहुँच गया। उसने सलमा को एक कमरे में बन्द कर लिया और अन्दर से सिटकनी लगा ली। कुछ देर बाद उस कमरे के किवाड़ तोड़ दिए गए। सलमा का घर गैस सिलिंडर फोड़कर जला दिया गया, जिसमें सलमा भी थी।

बाँके बिहारी के आलेख का अन्तिम वाक्य था : राम कुमार अब किसी औरत से प्यार नहीं करेगा। उन्हें पता नहीं था। वे इस रपट में कथाकार हो गए थे। पिछले दशक में कई बार उनके मन में अपने जीवन पर आधारित एक उपन्यास लिखने का विचार उठा था। बस, अन्त क्या हो ? यही समझ में नहीं आता था। यों नायक को किसी भी मोड़ या चट्टान पर मारकर अन्त किया जा सकता था। लेकिन वह

लेखक का अन्त होगा, उपन्यास का अन्त नहीं होगा। उपन्यास में नायक स्वतः अपनी नियति की खोज करता है। मेरी नियति क्या है ? बाँके बिहारी सोचते। सन् '42 में जब एक छरहरे लड़के ने कोतवाली पर लपककर झंडा फहराया था, तो वह उस नियति का आरम्भ था। फिर पत्रकारिता का लम्बा दौर था, इस दौर में निजी जीवन की ज़िम्मेदारियाँ सीमित थीं। ये सीमाएँ बाँके बिहारी ने खुद बाँधी थीं। उनका कहना था कि सृष्टि में आदमी ही ऐसा जानवर है जो अपने बच्चों के पिता की भूमिका तब तक अदा करना चाहता है जब तक बच्चा ख़ुद ही उलटकर उसके विरुद्ध खड़ा न हो जाए। अपने बच्चों के लिए अपने शहर में स्नातक तक की पढ़ाई की ज़िम्मेदारी उन्होंने स्वीकार की थी। इसके बाद वयस्कता का दौर शुरू होता था, जिसका सामना पुत्रों को स्वयं करना था। यह बात अलग थी कि बड़े ने अपना घर भाइयों की उच्च शिक्षा का मंच बना दिया था और पवन ने मदन का आई.आई.टी. का ख़र्चा उठाया था। यह उनका आपसी सहकार था। इस सहकारिता की सीमा छोटे के द्वारा पता चली। पहले लखनऊ में। फिर मुम्बई में। मुम्बई में तो हद हो गई ! तब अपनी नियति का भान हुआ। इस उम्र में ! बाँके बिहारी पौर के चबूतरे पर चौकी से आँखें उठाकर मुस्कराए। नरोडा-पाटिया की रपट पूरी हो गई थी। यदि छोटे को मुम्बई से वापस लाने की ज़रूरत न होती, तो न वे फिर लखनऊ फ़ोन करते, न फिर काम शुरू करते। न फिर यह नरोडा-पाटिया की रपट लिखी जाती। क्या नरोडा-पाटिया की रपट का उत्स रतन की बीमारी थी, जिसका कोई निश्चित अन्तिम सबूत नहीं था ? यह बीमारी हो भी सकती थी, नहीं भी हो सकती थी। यह रतन का बिगड़ा हुआ मिज़ाज भी हो सकता था। बाँके बिहारी बाहर ख़ाली सड़क पर धूप के टुकड़े को देख रहे थे।

धूप के टुकड़े को देखते हुए उन्हें यह सोचकर हैरानी हुई कि वे जीवन-भर देश और दुनिया की चिन्ता करना ही अपना काम समझते रहे जैसे इसी काम से उनके सारे काम सर जाएँगे। अब अचानक सामने सपना की एफ़.आई.आर. थी और ज़मानत पर छूटे हुए छोटे थे। छोटे झाँसी के थाने में भी रात काट आए थे। लखनऊ में वे एक रात थाने में रहे थे। मुम्बई में मँझले उसे थाने से छुड़ाकर लाए थे। सन् '42 में वे ख़ुद हाथों में हथकड़ियाँ डालकर घर से ले जाए गए थे। उन्होंने कभी नहीं सोचा था कि उनका बेटा बलात्कार के आरोप में गिरफ़्तार होगा। लखनऊ में वह रंडीबाज़ी में पकड़ा गया था। मुम्बई में लफ़ंगई करते हुए। अपने शहर में उसकी प्रेमिका ने उस पर बलात्कार का आरोप लगाया था !

धूप काँपी। धूप में कुछ छायाएँ तैर गईं। बाँके बिहारी ने ऐनक उतारकर धोती के छोर से अपनी आँखें पोंछी। उन्होंने फिर सोचा : उपन्यास का अन्त क्या

होगा ?

जैसे सफल उपन्यासों में मृत्यु-पूर्व घटित होता है, उन्हें अपने बचपन का गाँव याद आने लगा। उन्हें ऊख के खेत में या जंगली ऊँची घास में खो जाना अच्छा लगता था। कभी-कभी उन्हें लगता कि वे घास की तरह ही बड़े हुए। वे आहिस्ता-आहिस्ता लम्बे हुए थे और उन्हें पता ही नहीं चला था क्योंकि ऊख या लम्बी घास उन्हें हमेशा अपने भीतर छिपा लेती थी। जब वे बड़े हो रहे थे तो इसी घास में एक दोपहर दूसरी दिशा से गोरी, गदराई सावित्री आ गई थी जिसे पौर के अँधेरे में हड़बड़ाकर दो बार उन्होंने अपने दोनों हाथों के बीच भींच लिया था। अपने से बड़ी घास के बीच भी बाँके बिहारी ने यही किया था और दोनों गुत्थमगुत्था घास में गिर गए थे। घास हवा में हिलती रही थी। फिर सावित्री का ब्याह हो गया था और अगली साल बाँके बिहारी का। मगर लम्बी घास में खो जाने की तमन्ना हरदम बनी रही। कभी-कभी उन्हें लगता कि वे अनजाने किसी दिन किसी लम्बी घास में घुसेंगे और फिर बाहर नहीं आएँगे। वे धरती पर उगी घास में पत्ती बन जाएँगे जो दूसरी पत्तियों में खो जाएगी। उन्हें ख़ुशी होती कि उस पत्ती को कोई ढूँढ़ नहीं सकेगा।

पौर में अचानक आँगन से रतन आ गया और बोला, 'पापा, आप कब आए ?'

'कल रात', बाँके बिहारी ने उसे अपनी नज़र में भरते हुए कहा।

'आपकी ट्रिप कैसी रही ?' उसका स्वर सामान्य था।

'ठीक', उन्होंने मुश्किल से कहा।

'क्या अब गुजरात ठीक हो गया है ?' उसने लापरवाही से पूछा।

'मैं यही देखने गया था।'

'क्या देखा आपने ?' उसने ऐसे मुस्कराते हुए पूछा जैसे बाँके बिहारी किसी पहाड़ की सैर से लौटे हों।

हिमालय की किसी चोटी की तरह, गुजरात रतन के लिए बहुत दूर था। उसे कोई मतलब नहीं था। न उसे उस क्षण उस व्यक्ति से कोई मतलब था जिस पर रेप का आरोप था और जो अभी एक रात थाने में गुज़ारकर आया था। बाँके बिहारी स्तब्ध थे।

जब वे कुछ नहीं बोले, तो वह आँगन में लौट गया। पौर के ख़ालीपन को देखते हुए उनके मन में वह अदृश्य परदा काँपा जो रतन के चेहरे पर था। यही परदा पहली बार उन्होंने दस बरस पहले रतन के चेहरे पर देखा था, जिसे अभी पहचाना। वह इतवार का दिन था। रतन रात को घर लौटा। जब बाँके बिहारी

ने दरवाज़ा खोला, तो रतन के मुँह से पहली बार शराब की गन्ध आई। वे फ़ौरन पलटकर आँगन की ओर बढ़े और दालान में मुड़ गए। रतन आँगन में खड़ा हो गया। उसने दालान की तरफ़ मुँह करके पूछा :

'पापा, एक बात बताइए।'

'क्या ?' वे फिर पलटे।

'अब शहर में किले की क्या ज़रूरत है ?'

'क्यों ?' वे भौचक्के थे।

'अगर अब बाबरी मस्जिद की ज़रूरत नहीं, तो क़िले की क्या ज़रूरत है ?' उसकी ज़बान लड़खड़ाई, 'पहाड़ी पर कोई होटल होना चाहिए, जिसकी रोशनियाँ रात में चमकें। क़िले के अँधेरे में क्या रखा है ?'

बाँके बिहारी बेटे के चेहरे की जानिब देखते हुए खड़े थे। तब वे यह समझे थे कि यह पहली शराब का परदा है। उन्हें क्या पता था कि यह परदा दस बरस में गाढ़ा होता हुआ एक दिन गुजरात पर छा जाएगा ! तब रसोई से गायत्री की आवाज़ आई थी और छोटे रसोई में चले गए थे। बाँके बिहारी पौर में चबूतरे पर लौट गए थे और इसी तरह एक ख़ाली बोरे से रीते बैठे थे। बाबरी मस्जिद गिरने की ख़बर उन्हें उसी दिन तीसरे पहर फ़ोन पर मिली थी। यह एक दुःस्वप्न के सच होने की तरह था। फ़ोन रखकर उनका मन हुआ था कि शहर के बाहर कहीं चले जाएँ जहाँ लम्बी घास हो। उन्हें रतन की उम्र के एक लड़के का हाथ में तिरंगा लिए कोतवाली की ओर बढ़ते हुए बार-बार चीख़ना याद आ रहा था, 'अंग्रेज़ो, भारत छोड़ो !' वह जुलूस में आगे था। उस वक़्त उस लड़के को लगता था कि यह सचमुच 'करो या मरो' का समय है। और इस बार यदि कोतवाली पर झंडा फहरा दिया तो अंग्रेज़ सात समुद्र पार चले जाएँगे और हम अपने घर के मालिक होंगे। मगर यह कैसा घर था ? पहले मस्जिद टूटी, फिर गुजरात में आग लगी। हर जगह दंगे का ख़तरा था। लखनऊ अयोध्या से ज़्यादा दूर नहीं था : लखनऊ में नूर और मुन्ना थे ! क्या अब ऐसे परिवार नहीं होंगे ? क्या लड़के लड़की से उसका धर्म पूछकर उसे चाहेंगे ? जिन्होंने नहीं पूछा, दस साल बाद अहमदाबाद में उन्हें मार दिया गया। बाँके बिहारी अहमदाबाद में एक ऐसे हिन्दू पति से मिले थे जिसकी मुस्लिम पत्नी को इन्हीं दंगों में मार दिया गया था। फिर एक ऐसी हिन्दू पत्नी मिली जिसका मुसलमान डॉक्टर पति उन्हीं दिनों एक रात मरीज़ देखने गया और घर नहीं लौटा—न उसकी लाश लौटी। दोनों घरों में आधे मुसलमान बच्चे थे। मुन्ना का क्या होगा ?

उस रात रतन के ऊपर चले जाने के बाद बाँके बिहारी और गायत्री पौर की

साँकल लगाकर चबूतरे पर आमने-सामने बैठ गए। रोशनी मद्धिम थी।

'क्या छोटे ने होली के दिन की कोई बात तुमसे की ?' बाँके बिहारी ने पूछा।

'नहीं', गायत्री ने पूछा, 'क्या तुमने कुछ नहीं पूछा ?'

'वही मुझसे गुजरात के बारे में पूछ रहा था', वे मुस्कराए। मुस्कराते होंठों के चारों तरफ़ और आँखों में तल्खी थी।

'जब से वह थाने से लौटा है', गायत्री ने कहा, 'मुझसे कोई बात नहीं करता। हर शाम दो अंडे उबालने की बात करता है।'

'दो अंडे !' बाँके बिहारी ने नज़र ऊपर उठाई, 'दो अंडों का क्या करता है ?'

'अंडे ऊपर ले जाता है', गायत्री बोली, 'कुछ देर बाद नीचे आता है और खाकर फिर ऊपर चला जाता है।'

'उसके मुँह से कोई गन्ध नहीं आती ?'

'देखूँगी', गायत्री ने पति की ओर देखते हुए कहा, 'अब क्या होगा ?'

'मुकदमे की तारीख़ पड़ेगी', बाँके बिहारी का स्वर ठंडा था।

चुप्पी।

'फिर रतन और सपना आमने-सामने होंगे। बयान होंगे। जिरह होगी। तब जज फ़ैसला सुनाएगा कि जुर्म हुआ या नहीं हुआ।'

'पता नहीं', गायत्री ने जैसे आँखें बन्द करते हुए कहा, 'होली के दिन क्या हुआ। मैं घर में नहीं थी। तुम तो थे। तुम्हें कुछ नहीं मालूम ?'

'नहीं।'

'तुमने कुछ नहीं देखा ?'

'मैंने हमेशा की तरह सपना को ऊपर जाते देखा। जब वह लौटी तो मैं अन्दर के कमरे में था।'

बाँके बिहारी नीचे देख रहे थे।

'तुमने उसका चेहरा नहीं देखा ?'

'नहीं', उन्होंने कहा, 'ऊपर जाने के पहले देखा था। वह हमेशा की तरह हँस रही थी। उसके चेहरे पर गुलाल का हल्का लाल रंग था, जो छूटा नहीं था। लाल रंग के बीच उसके सफ़ेद दाँत और ज़्यादा चमकते थे।'

गायत्री सहसा चीख़ी, 'मेरे बेटे का क्या होगा ?'

'यह अदालत नहीं है', बाँके बिहारी का स्वर संयत था।

गायत्री की आँखों में आँसू तैरे। बाँके बिहारी ने अपनी धोती के छोर से गायत्री के आँसू पोंछते हुए कहा :

'आँसू सिर्फ पोंछने के काम आते हैं, गायत्री। रो मत !'

गायत्री का मुँह आँगन में खुलते दरवाज़े की ओर था, जहाँ अँधेरा था। आँसुओं की परत आँखों से हट जाने पर जैसे ही उसने आँखें खोलीं, उसे लगा कि दरवाज़े पर कोई खड़ा है। 'कौन ?' उसने कहा। उसकी आवाज़ पौर में गूँजी। दरवाज़े में कोई छाया हिली और ग़ायब हो गई। दरवाज़े पर अँधेरा बचा।

'कौन है ?' बाँके बिहारी ने पूछा।

'अँधेरा।'

'अँधेरा ?'

'मुझे लगा', गायत्री ने कहा, 'छोटे खड़े हैं !'

'छोटे...छोटे...,' कहते हुए बाँके बिहारी उठे और आँगन में चले गए। अँधेरे आँगन में नीम का पेड़ चुप खड़ा था। सीढ़ियाँ सूनी थीं। कोई नहीं था। पेड़ के परे आकाश में तारे टिमटिमा रहे थे। चाँद भी कहीं होगा। नज़र नहीं आता था। तारों भरे आकाश के नीचे आँगन के अँधेरे में नीम का पेड़ चुपचाप खड़ा था।

बाँके बिहारी पलटकर पौर में लौट गए जहाँ गायत्री मूर्तिवत् बैठी थी। वे बैठते हुए बोले–

'कोई नहीं था।'

'मुझे धोखा हुआ होगा।'

'तुम्हें लगा कि छोटे तुम्हारे आँसू पोंछने आया है !'

'हाँ।'

दोनों के बीच ऐसा सन्नाटा था जैसे श्मशान फैला हो।

4.5

कोई बड़ा मैदान है जिसमें एक हज़ार औरतें बैठी हैं। एक हज़ार औरतें बैठी हैं और एक-साथ रो रही हैं जैसे प्रार्थना कर रही हों। वे चुप हैं, सिर्फ़ आँसू उनकी आँखों से बह रहे हैं। फिर वे बिसूरने लगती हैं। उनके होंठों से कराह निकलती है। यह मैदान की पहली आवाज़ है। मैदान में सिर्फ़ औरतें हैं। मैदान में चिड़ियाँ नहीं हैं। मैदान में धूप है। धूप और औरतों की पहली आवाज़ एक कराह है। यह एक हज़ार औरतों की कराह है जो असल में एक औरत की कराह है। मैदान की औरतों के मुँह से एकाएक चीख़ निकलने लगती है। सारी चीख़ें फिर एक समवेत चीख़ में गुँथने लगती हैं जैसे समूची धरती चीख़ रही हो।

यह कोई सपना नहीं था।

अख़बार में ख़बर थी कि अहमदाबाद में एक दिन एक मैदान में एक हज़ार

मुस्लिम औरतें इकट्ठी हुईं और दहाड़ मारकर रोईं। इन औरतों ने इसी साल के शुरू के भीषण नरसंहार में अपनी बेटियाँ, बहनें, बच्चे और आदमी खोए थे। वे मैदान में अपने-अपने दुख लेकर आई थीं। वे बिलख-बिलखकर एक-दूसरे को ढाढ़स बँधा रही थीं। रोते-रोते उनके अपने दुख आँसुओं में घुल गए थे। सिर्फ़ दुख बचा था। यह धरती का दुख था।

बाँके बिहारी को सहसा लगा कि उनके कानों में एक लम्बी चीख़ गूँज रही है। यह आर्त चीख़ जिस औरत के गले से निकल रही थी, वह नरोडा-पाटिया की सलमा की माँ थी जो मैदान के बीचोबीच बैठी थी। बाँके बिहारी ने उस चीख़ में सलमा के नाम से सलमा की माँ को पहचाना। वे हड़बड़ाकर उठे और बैठ गए। अख़बार उनकी छाती से नीचे गिर गया, जिसे वे अभी पढ़ रहे थे। यह जाड़े की सुबह थी। उन्होंने चश्मा लगाकर चबूतरे पर धूप की ओर देखा जैसे वहाँ राम कुमार खड़ा हो : वहाँ अंडे हाथ में लिए रतन पौर में घुस रहा था।

जब रतन अन्दर चला गया तो बाँके बिहारी बाहर आकर चबूतरे पर धूप में टहलने लगे। एक ओर बाज़ार था, दूसरी ओर मोहल्ला था। बाज़ार खुल रहा था, मोहल्ला जाग रहा था। सड़क पर एक कुत्ते ने अँगड़ाई ली और आगे बाज़ार की ओर बढ़ा। उसके पीछे एक धोती में लिपटे काँपते हुए जगदीश कुमार जैन किसी मंत्र का जाप करते हुए आए। वे मन्दिर जा रहे थे। सड़क के जिस हिस्से में धूप थी, बच्चे वहीं इकट्ठे थे। उधर ही एक गाय बैठी थी। अँगड़ाई लेकर जो कुत्ता बाज़ार की ओर बढ़ा था, वह भी लौटकर गाय के पास धूप में बैठ गया। तभी एक तिपहिया दूर सड़क पर विपरीत दिशा से आकर रुका और कोई लड़की उतरी। उसके बाल खुले थे। इसीलिए इतनी दूर से वह पहचानी गई क्योंकि वह जींस पहने थी। बाँके बिहारी ने सपना का घर पहचाना जिसके सामने तिपहिया रुका था। क्या वह सपना ही थी ?

सपना ने एक बैग हाथ में लिए अपने घर में घुसने से पहले दूर चबूतरे पर टहलते हुए बाँके बिहारी को देखा। उसके होंठ एक मुस्कान में फैल गए और दूसरा हाथ स्वचालित-सा ऊपर उठ गया। फिर तुरन्त उसने अपना हाथ नीचे किया और नज़रें सीधी करके घर में घुस गई। चन्द्रा आँगन की धूप में अख़बार लिए बैठे थे। सपना के आँगन में आते ही माँ भी रसोई से बाहर निकल आई। उसे बेटी का चेहरा देखकर ख़ुशी हुई। सपना के चेहरे पर यात्रा की थकान नहीं थी। उसका चेहरा चमक रहा था। वह तीन माह बाद आगरा से आई थी। अलबत्ता हर माह दो-तीन पत्र वह माँ को लिखती थी। उसने एक पत्र में माँ को बता दिया था कि उसके स्कूल में एक सहयोगी है जो उससे विवाह करना चाहता है। उसका नाम

इरफ़ान ख़ान था। नाम सुनकर चन्द्रा अचकचाए। फिर उन्होंने कहा कि जब सपना ने एफ.आई.आर. दर्ज कराने से पहले माँ-बाप से नहीं पूछा तो विवाह करने से पहले उसका हमें बताना ही बड़ी बात है। इरफ़ान की तस्वीर से कुछ पता नहीं चलता था। जब तस्वीर आई तो सपना की माँ उसे देखती ही रह गई : एक सुन्दर युवक लगातार मुस्करा रहा था ! उसका नाम सुन्दर लाल भी हो सकता था। आँसू आहिस्ता-आहिस्ता भीतर की सीढ़ियाँ चढ़ते हुए आँखों में आ गए। अगले दिन मुकदमे की तारीख़ थी।

'क्या इरफ़ान को इस मुकदमे के बारे में पता है ?' चन्द्रा ने पूछा।

'हाँ', सपना ने कहा, 'उसे सब मालूम है।'

उसने कुछ छिपाया नहीं था। जब उसने अपने शहर से कुछ नहीं छिपाया था, तो इरफ़ान से क्या छिपाती ? यह फ़र्क ज़रूर था कि शहर को बताकर वह अपने शहर से दूर हो गई थी और इरफ़ान को बताकर वह इरफ़ान के और नज़दीक पहुँच गई थी। दोनों के बीच कोई अदृश्य सेतु बन गया था, जिसका दोनों को पता नहीं था। ऐसा ही कोई सेतु था जिस पर चढ़कर होली की दोपहर सपना रतन की अटारी में गई थी। रतन खाट पर लेटा था। वह उठकर बैठ गया और मुस्कराने लगा। सपना हँसी।

'बहुत सुन्दर लग रही हो', कहते हुए वह उठा।

वे दोनों आमने-सामने खड़े थे। सपना हँस रही थी। उसके चेहरे पर गुलाल का रंग खिल रहा था ! रतन की आँखें झपकना भूल गईं।

उसने पीछे मुड़कर मेज़ पर रखी थाली से गुलाल उठाया और दोनों हाथों से सपना के गालों पर मल दिया। सपना खिलखिलाते हुए गुलाल की थाली की ओर गई और हाथों में गुलाल लिए खिलखिलाते हुए लौटी। उसने रतन के नज़दीक जाकर आँखें ऊपर उठाईं और दोनों हथेलियाँ उसके गालों पर रगड़ दीं। रतन ने इस बीच अपना चेहरा नीचे झुकाया और झुकाता रहा। वह हँस रही थी। सहसा उसकी हँसी रुक गई जैसे कोई झरना ठहर गया हो। फिर उसके हाथ उठे और रतन के गले में लटक गए। सपना की हथेलियों ने उठकर रतन के सिर को पीछे से थाम लिया।

जब वे अलग हुए तो सपना ज़ोर-ज़ोर से साँस ले रही थी और हँस रही थी। रतन उसके सामने चुपचाप खड़ा था।

फिर रतन खाट पर बैठ गया। सपना उसकी बग़ल में बैठ गई।

'कोई नौकरी मिली ?' सपना ने पूछा।

'नहीं।'

रतन ने सपना की ओर देखा। सपना ने उसकी आँखों का ख़ालीपन देखा। वह सिहर गई। उसने गुरु को पिछले दस वर्षों में आहिस्ता-आहिस्ता छीजते देखा था। वह—गुरु की चेली—दस बरसों में चेली से गुरु हो गई थी। एक चक्र दो दिशाओं में उल्टा घूमा था। जब पहली बार गुरु ने उसे चूमकर शादी के लिए पूछा था, तो उसे लगा था कि वह गुरु के सामने बच्ची है। अब रतन ख़ुद एक हारा हुआ बच्चा लग रहा था। सपना के मन में रतन के लिए एक लहर उठी जैसे कड़ी धूप में माँ बच्चे को अपना आँचल उढ़ा देती है। वह रतन के कुछ और पास सरक गई। ठंडी हवा का कोई झोंका छत से आया। रतन ने उठकर किवाड़ बन्द कर दिए। वह खाट पर वापस आकर बैठा नहीं, लेट गया जैसे बहुत थक गया हो। सपना उसके बालों में उँगलियाँ फिराने लगी। रतन ने आँखें मूँद लीं। वह भी लेट गई। उसकी उँगलियाँ रतन के बालों में फँसी थीं और उसका चेहरा रतन की ओर था। रतन आँखें बन्द किए लेटा था। सपना के जिस्म के कुछ कोने और सीमाएँ उसे छू रही थीं।

तभी रतन ने सहसा आँखें खोलीं और सपना की ओर देखा। कुछ देर वह उसे देखता रहा। वह मुस्करा रही थी।

'ऐसे देख रहे हो जैसे कभी देखा नहीं !'

'नहीं !' आवाज़ तीखी थी।

वह एकटक देख रहा था। फिर जैसे बगुला अचानक मछली पर झपटता है, वह सपना पर टूट पड़ा। सपना की आँखें हैरान हिरनी की आँखें हो गईं। उसने कुछ कहने के लिए होंठ खोले। रतन को लगा, वह चीख़ेगी। उसने अपना रूमाल उसके मुँह में ठूँस दिया।

उसने बार-बार सोचा है कि यदि रतन उसके मुँह में रूमाल न ठूँसता, तो शायद रेप न होता।

क़ानून की नज़र में रूमाल कोई सबूत नहीं था, चाहे वह रतन का ही रूमाल क्यों न हो। क्योंकि रतन और सपना का पन्द्रह साल का सम्बन्ध था जिसमें एक का रूमाल दूसरे के पास होना कोई ख़ास बात नहीं थी। रूमाल में सपना का थूक भी बेमानी था। असली बात रूमाल का मुँह में ठूँसा जाना था, जिसका कोई गवाह नहीं हो सकता था। जब सपना को यह बताया गया, तो वह क़ानून की दुनिया की निरीहता पर सन्न रह गई। जो रूमाल बलात्कार का मूल कारक था, उस रूमाल का क़ानून की नज़र में कोई मूल्य नहीं था। सपना सायबान में खड़ी सोच रही थी कि कल अदालत में वह अपने बयान में जज से यह ज़रूर कहेगी। धूप चली गई थी। सड़क पर साए नहीं थे। सड़क मोहल्ले में दूर जाती हुई ख़ुद एक

साया लगती थी। उसी साए से एक सफ़ेद मारुति निकली और इसी ओर धीरे-धीरे बढ़ी। वह सायबान के नीचे से निकलकर आगे बढ़ी और रतन के घर के सामने रुक गई। उसमें से कोई काली दाढ़ी वाला आदमी बाहर निकला और घर में घुस गया। घर में घुसने से पहले उसने एक बार सपना के घर की ओर देखा था। शायद उसने छज्जे में खड़ी सपना को देखा।

बड़े ने अन्दर घुसकर अम्माँ और पापा के पैर छुए। वे दालान में बैठे थे। चाय पी रहे थे। बड़े भी तख़्त पर बैठ गए। गायत्री ने चाय का एक कप बड़े के सामने रखा। बड़े ने चाय का घूँट लेकर पूछा, 'छोटे कहाँ हैं ?'

'ऊपर।'

'ठीक है ?'

'हाँ', अम्माँ ने कहा, 'क्यों ?'

'थोड़ी देर में उसे लेकर वकील के घर जाऊँगा।'

गायत्री नूर और मुन्ना के बारे में पूछती रही। चाय ख़त्म हो जाने पर बड़े ने बाँके बिहारी की ओर देखते हुए कहा :

'सपना आ गई है।'

'सुबह आई थी', बाँके बिहारी बोले। उन्होंने अपने घर में घुसते हुए उसका ऊपर उठा हाथ देखा था।

बड़े ख़ाली आँगन में देख रहे थे। वहीं देखते हुए उसने पूछा—

'क्या आपने सपना से बात की ?'

'क्या बात ?' बाँके बिहारी ने हैरानी से ख़ाली आँगन की ओर देखा।

'अम्माँ पहले उसे एफ़.आई.आर. वापस लेने को कह चुकी हैं। वह नहीं मानी। अगर अभी वह आगरा लौट जाए, तो रतन बच सकता है।'

वे कुछ देर ख़ाली आँगन में देखते रहे। फिर जैसे अपने-आप ये शब्द उनके मुँह से निकले, 'मैं सपना से कुछ नहीं कह सकता।'

बड़े की निगाहें पिता के चेहरे पर ठहर गईं। पिता पुत्र की ओर देख रहे थे। बड़े ने आहिस्ता-आहिस्ता अपनी निगाहें नीची कर लीं। दालान में अँधेरा घिरने लगा था।

'सुना है', गायत्री ने कहा, 'वह शादी कर रही है।'

'अच्छा है', बाँके बिहारी ऐसे खुश हुए जैसे अपनी बेटी के ब्याह की ख़बर सुनी हो। फिर एकदम सहम गए।

'उसकी ज़िन्दगी बन गई', गायत्री ने पति की ओर देखते हुए कहा, 'तो क्या वह छोटे को नहीं बचा सकती ?'

'मैं उससे कुछ नहीं कह सकता !' वे चीख़े।

चीख़ की कोई ख़ास तुक नहीं थी। गायत्री की आँखें भीग गईं। अगली सुबह जब बड़े की मारुति अदालत की ओर चली तो उसमें आगे बड़े के साथ छोटे बैठे थे और पीछे गायत्री और बाँके बिहारी थे। छोटे अपने शहर में मारुति की अगली सीट पर विजेता की मुद्रा में बैठे थे और आहिस्ता-आहिस्ता मुस्करा रहे थे। वे राजनेता की तरह कभी सामने देखते, कभी बाएँ देखते। दो-तीन बार उन्होंने दोनों हाथ जोड़कर काँच के पार किसी को नमस्कार भी किया। मारुति हार्डी गंज की भीड़ को चीरती हुई दाएँ मुड़ी और फिर बाएँ मुड़ गई। दाईं ओर रानीमहल का अजायबघर था, जो अंग्रेजों के ज़माने में कोतवाली हो गया था और जिस पर बाँके बिहारी ने सन् '42 में तिरंगा फहराया था। पीछे बैठे हुए बाँके बिहारी अभी कोतवाली और अजायबघर के बारे में नहीं सोच रहे थे। उन्हें पता भी नहीं चला कब गाड़ी फिर आगे मुड़कर मिनर्वा टाकीज़ के सामने पहुँच गई, जिसके सामने सड़क के परे पहाड़ी पर क़िला खड़ा था। मिनर्वा में 'दिल चाहता है' के पोस्टर लगे थे, जिसमें आमिर ख़ान और प्रीति ज़िंटा क़िले की ओर देखते हुए हँसते लगते थे। क़िले के काई लगे पत्थर जाड़ों की गुलाबी धूप में चमक रहे थे जैसे उन्हें किसी से कोई मतलब न हो।

मारुति दोनों ओर दुकानों के बीच सड़क की चढ़ाई पर आगे बढ़ी। चढ़ाई के बाद सड़क के दाईं ओर रेत और पत्थर की पहाड़ियों की शृंखला थी, जिसके दूसरी ओर तालाब था, जहाँ एक रात रतन ने लखनऊ और मुम्बई के सपने देखे थे। रतन इस वक़्त सीधा शान से मारुति में बैठा था और सामने धूप में चमकती ऊबड़-खाबड़ सड़क को देख रहा था। दस मिनट बाद झोकन बाग़ और ईसाई अस्पताल पार करके गाड़ी अदालत के परिसर में घुसी। जब एक पीपल के पेड़ के नीचे मारुति रुकी और खादी का झक्क पाजामा-कुर्ता पहने रतन गाड़ी से उतरा तो ऐसा लगा जैसे कोई युवा राजनेता अदालत में आया हो। जब घर पर रतन ऊपर से तैयार होकर आया तो बाँके बिहारी को उसका लिबास देखकर कुछ विचित्र-सा अहसास हुआ था। उन्होंने कहा कुछ नहीं। वह बच्चा नहीं था कि उसे कपड़े बदल आने को कहते। असल में इधर कुछ दिनों से अपने चारों ओर और भीतर उन्हें इतना कुछ विचित्र लगता रहा था कि कभी-कभी उन्हें अपने पर ही शक होने लगता। जब रतन अदालत के प्रांगण में एक विहंगम दृष्टि डाल रहा था, तो बाँके बिहारी ने उसका चेहरा देखा : वह एक पर्यटक का चेहरा था, जिस पर धूप का काला चश्मा चढ़ा था !

धूप का चश्मा बड़े ने उससे लेकर अपनी जेब में रख लिया।

जब अदालत में सुनवाई शुरू हुई तो अभियोजन पक्ष को यह साबित करने में दिक़्क़त नहीं हुई कि रतन ने सपना के साथ सम्भोग किया। रतन और सपना की चिकित्सकीय जाँच के सबूत साफ़ थे। मुश्किल यह थी कि किसी चोट या नोच-खरोंच के निशान न रतन के बदन पर मिले थे, न सपना के बदन पर। इसका कोई सबूत नहीं था कि सपना ने प्रतिरोध किया था। अभियोजन की यह दलील वाजिब थी कि सपना जैसी सम्मानित महिला जब थाने में बलात्कार की प्राथमिकी लिखाने गई, तो वह अपना सम्मान दाँव पर लगा रही थी। कोई स्वयं अपने आत्मसम्मान से नहीं खेलता। यह पश्चिमी समाज नहीं था, जहाँ स्त्रियाँ बलात्कार को भी पुरुष के विरुद्ध एक अस्त्र के रूप में इस्तेमाल कर लेती थीं। यह भारतीय समाज था—वह भी झाँसी जैसा क़स्बा जिसमें सब एक-दूसरे को जानते थे। यही कारण था कि सपना ने एफ़.आई.आर. लिखाकर झाँसी छोड़ दी थी।

जब आरोपी के वकील निगम ने सपना से पूछा कि क्या यह सच है कि वह आगरा में एक मुस्लिम युवक से विवाह करने वाली है, तो सपना ने स्वीकार में सिर हिला दिया।

'आप उसे कितने दिनों से जानती हैं ?' वकील ने पूछा।

'तीन महीने से।'

'आप रतन को कब से जानती हैं ?'

'पन्द्रह साल से।'

'क्या रतन ने कभी आपसे शादी की बात की थी ?'

'हाँ।'

'कब ?'

'छह-सात साल पहले।'

'क्या इसीलिए आप उससे रिश्ता बनाए रहीं ?'

'नहीं।'

'फिर सोचिए', वकील ने कहा, 'होली के दिन सम्भोग के बाद कहीं उसने शादी के लिए मना तो नहीं कर दिया था ? तब अगले दिन आपने एफ़.आई.आर. लिखाई।'

'नहींऽऽ', वह चीखी़।

'मी लॉर्ड', वकील ने जज की ओर मुख़ातिब होकर कहा, 'ज़रा देखें, एक स्वस्थ, सुन्दर लड़की अपने लिए वर की तलाश में थी—जो अन्ततः उसे जल्दी ही आगरा में मिल गया, चाहे वह किसी भी धर्म का हो। यह हमारे समाज की विडम्बना है। लड़की यहाँ प्रेम शादी करने के लिए ही करती है। प्रेम में वह कुछ

भी करेगी। सम्भोग भी। सपना ने कोई प्रतिरोध नहीं किया था। वह राज़ी थी।'

सपना का चेहरा सफ़ेद हो गया।

अदालत में सन्नाटा था।

आरोपी के वकील ने यह भी कहा कि रतन को पिछले दस बरस से शिज़ोफ़्रेनिया है। उसका इलाज होता रहा है, जो अभी भी जारी है। उसे कभी-कभी दौरे आते हैं। जब उसने होली की दोपहर अपने घर की अटारी में होली खेलने आई सपना से सम्भोग किया तो वह दौरे की गिरफ़्त में था और सपना ने उसे रोका नहीं। जब रतन से पूछा गया कि बताओ, तुम्हें क्या बीमारी है, तो उसने मुस्कराते हुए कहा :

'बेकारी।'

उसके वकील ने अदालत के सामने उसके इलाज के पर्चे रख दिए थे।

'क्या तुमने सपना का बलात्कार किया ?'

'मैं उसे प्यार करता हूँ।'

मेडिकल कॉलेज के मनोचिकित्सा विशेषज्ञ डॉ. गुप्ता ने कहा कि हम लक्षणों के आधार पर इलाज करते हैं। 'क्या कोई अन्तिम निश्चित जाँच है ?' अदालत ने पूछा। 'नहीं,' विशेषज्ञ ने कहा।

'क्या रतन सचमुच बीमार है ?'

'हाँ।'

'क्या इतना बीमार कि उसे हिंसक दौरा आ जाए ?'

'यह कहना मुश्किल है !'

जब सपना का बयान शुरू हुआ तो दर्शक-दीर्घा में केवल उसके माँ-बाप और रतन के माँ-बाप और बड़े थे। उसने कहा कि वह रतन को पिछले पन्द्रह बरस से जानती है। वह बीमार है या नहीं, वह कभी समझ नहीं सकी। उसने कहा कि रतन उसे शुरू में गणित पढ़ाया करते थे, इसलिए उसके मन में उनके लिए सम्मान भी रहा है। वह पहले रतन के घर पढ़ने जाती थी। फिर पढ़ाई ख़त्म हो गई, मगर वह रतन से उसके घर में और बाहर कभी-कभी मिलती रहती थी। होली के दिन भी वह इसी तरह चली गई थी जैसे कोई अपने पुराने दोस्त से मिलने जाता है। उनके सम्बन्ध सहज थे—इतने सहज कि उसे रतन की खाट पर उसकी बग़ल में लेट जाने में कोई दुविधा नहीं थी। उसने अचानक उछलकर सपना के मुँह में रूमाल ठूँस दिया। यह हमला इतना अप्रत्याशित था कि वह सन्न रह गई। उसने यह बिलकुल नहीं सोचा था कि रतन कभी एकाएक ख़ूँख़्वार जानवर भी हो सकता है ! एक लम्हे को उसकी संज्ञा गुम हो गई। उसी लमहे में रतन ने उसके शरीर में प्रवेश

किया। जब वह होश में आई तो उसने उसे दोनों हाथों से परे धकेल दिया।

'सच पूछिए जज साहब', सपना ने कहा, 'तो मेरा सबसे बड़ा गवाह रतन का यह रूमाल है जिसमें मेरा थूक है और जिसकी आपके सामने कोई क़ीमत नहीं है।'

उसके हाथ में रूमाल था।

'क्या कोई इस कहानी की गवाही दे सकता है ?' आरोपी के वकील ने अपना काला गाउन झुलाकर मुस्कराते हुए पूछा।

'मैं दे सकता हूँ', बाँके बिहारी अचानक खड़े हो गए।

सब हतप्रभ थे।

बाँके बिहारी ने अपने बयान में कहा कि उस दोपहर सूने घर में वे छत पर एक बार गए थे। चूँकि अटारी अन्दर से बन्द थी, इसलिए उन्होंने खिड़की के छेद से अन्दर झाँककर देखा : सलमा ने राम कुमार को धक्का दिया और अपने मुँह में ठुँसा रूमाल निकाला !

दोनों वकील और जज मुस्कराने लगे।

निगम वकील ने फ़ौरन जज की ओर देखते हुए कहा—'मी लॉर्ड, रतन के पिता बेटे के ग़म में सनक गए हैं। वे नाम भी भूल गए। उन्हें रतन-सपना राम कुमार और सलमा लग रहे हैं !'

'मैं कुछ नहीं भूला', बाँके बिहारी चीख़े, 'मेरे घर में मेरे बेटे ने मेरी आँखों के सामने बलात्कार किया।'

उनकी सफ़ेद दाढ़ी लगातार हिल रही थी जैसे वे रो रहे हों।

कटघरे से वे घर नहीं लौट सकते थे।

वे दर्शक-दीर्घा की बेंच की ओर नहीं जा सकते थे, जहाँ गायत्री और बड़े बैठे थे। वे सीधे बाहर चले गए जहाँ खुली धूप थी। अदालत में मुकदमा चल रहा था। वे अदालत से बाहर आ गए थे। एक क्षण धूप में वे किंकर्तव्यविमूढ़ खड़े रहे। फिर इससे पहले कि कोई भीतर से आकर उन्हें छेड़े, वे आगे बढ़े और अदालत के परिसर से बाहर आ गए। वे घर की ओर नहीं मुड़ सकते थे। इसलिए दाईं ओर सड़क पर मुड़ गए। वे सीधे मुँह उठाए चल रहे थे। धूप में सफ़ेद दाढ़ी चमक रही थी। केश भी। चेहरा सफ़ेद बालों से घिरा था। वे चलते रहे। कुछ देर बाद दाईं ओर कैमासन की टौरिया नज़र आई। एक मन हुआ कि वे दाएँ मुड़ जाएँ और दूर पहाड़ी की चोटी पर चढ़ जाएँ। पहाड़ी पर थोड़ी हरियाली थी। चोटी

ख़ाली थी। चोटी उन्हें फ़िजूल लगी। वे सड़क पर आगे बढ़ते रहे। चोटी की तरह उनका मन ख़ाली था। सड़क भरी थी। लोग और वाहन आ-जा रहे थे। वे लोगों और वाहनों को देखते रहे, जिन्हें कहीं-न-कहीं पहुँचना था।

'कहाँ जाना है ?' टिकट-खिड़की के अन्दर से आवाज़ आई।

'कहीं नहीं', बाँके बिहारी के मुँह से अचानक निकला।

टिकट-खिड़की हँसी।

'अमरा...अमरा का दिकट दीजिए', बाँके बिहारी हड़बड़ाए।

टिकट लेकर वे बस की ओर बढ़े। वे सड़क पर अचानक बाईं ओर बस-स्टैंड देखकर उसी ओर मुड़ गए थे और क्यू में खड़े हो गए थे। जैसे कोई काम मिल गया हो, वे बस में आकर बैठ गए। बस भरी थी। एक सीट पर एक ही जगह ख़ाली थी। बाँके बिहारी उसी ख़ाली जगह पर बैठ गए थे। बस में मूँगफली, चने और पत्रिकाएँ बेचनेवाले लड़कों का शोर था। उस शोर के ऊपर अचानक एक मर्दानी आवाज़ गूँजी। मर्दानी आवाज़ ने बताया कि जाड़े सिर पर हैं, बुज़ुर्गों को जोड़ों का दर्द सताएगा। उसने अपनी हथेली पर शीशियाँ फैलाए हुए कहा कि यह उस दर्द की अक्सीर दवा है। दर्द ठीक न हो, तो दाम वापस। दाम प्रति शीशी दस रुपए। जब किसी ने पूछा कि दाम कब वापस होंगे तो जवाब आया, 'अगले जाड़ों में।' लोग हँसे। कुछ ने दवा ख़रीदी। बाँके बिहारी को याद आया कि जाड़े जब बढ़ते हैं तो उन्हें भी दर्द होता है। मगर उन्होंने दवा की ओर देखा भी नहीं जैसे किसी और का दर्द याद आया हो।

जब बस चली तो उनके पास बैठे अधेड़ व्यक्ति ने खिड़की से अपना चेहरा अन्दर घुमाकर पूछा, 'दद्दा, कहाँ जा रहे हैं ?'

बाँके बिहारी चौंके। फिर उन्होंने कहा, 'अमरा।'

'आपका गाँव है ?'

'हाँ।'

'बाल-बच्चे वहीं हैं ?'

'नहीं।'

'फिर', अधेड़ ने उनके चेहरे को घेरे झक्क सफ़ेद बाल देखते हुए कहा, 'फिर कौन है ?'

'अपना गाँव', वे हँसे।

'रिश्तेदार होंगे ?'

'हाँ', वे फिर हँसे।

वे झूठ बोले थे। गाँव में कोई रिश्तेदार नहीं था। बचपन के दोनों दोस्त—

सीताराम और बलराम—मर चुके थे। एकाएक उन्हें अपनी उम्र का अहसास हुआ। बहुत तेज़, चाकू की तरह। उन्होंने अपनी दाढ़ी पर हाथ फेरा। वे अचानक अस्सी बरस के हो गए। उन्होंने चेहरा घुमाकर अधेड़ की ओर देखा, जो बस की खिड़की से बाहर देख रहा था—जहाँ सड़क के किनारे पेड़ों की क़तार थी और क़तार के पार खेत थे, जो ख़ाली पड़े थे। ख़ाली खेतों में सूखी मिट्टी और मिट्टी के ढूह दूर-दूर तक नज़र आते थे।

गेहूँ बोने का वक़्त आ रहा था।

अस्सी बरस के बाँके बिहारी ने आँखें बन्द कर लीं। भीतर कोई उम्मीद नहीं थी। उम्मीद की ज़रूरत भी नहीं थी। कानों में बस की भर्र-भर्र गूँज रही थी। उसी पालने में वे झूलने लगे और सो गए। वे बैठे हुए सो रहे थे। अधेड़ उनकी ओर देखता और मुस्कराने लगता। उसे ताज्जुब इस बात का था कि बस में इतना शोर और हिचकोले थे और बुज़ुर्ग सो रहे थे। शायद बहुत थके होंगे, अधेड़ ने सोचा।

ऐसा न जाने कितने दिनों बाद हुआ कि बाँके बिहारी सोए और उन्होंने कोई सपना नहीं देखा। जब उनकी आँख खुली तो उन्हें हैरत हुई। चिरगाँव पर बस रुकी थी। काफ़ी चहल-पहल थी। वे नीचे उतरे। सामने ढाबे पर जाकर उन्होंने चाय पी। फिर वे वापस आकर अपनी सीट पर बैठ गए। बस चल दी। फिर पेड़ों और ख़ाली खेतों में पड़ी सूखी मिट्टी का सिलसिला शुरू हो गया। ख़ाली धूप में फैली सूखी मिट्टी देखते हुए उन्हें फिर नींद आने लगी। एक बार अधेड़ ने उनका सिर अपने कन्धे से हटाते हुए पूछा :

'दद्दा, लगता है आप महीनों से नहीं सोए !'

'ऐं', बाँके बिहारी ने आँखें खोलीं, 'हाँ हाँ...नहीं, नहीं।'

वे कुछ झेंप गए। उनकी आँखें आहिस्ता-आहिस्ता फिर बन्द होने लगीं। हिचकोले खाती हवा ठंडी थी। बस की सीट न नीचे गड़ रही थी न पीठ में। गर्दन उसी से टिकी थी। उन्हें लगा जैसे कोई उन्हें थपकियाँ दे रहा हो। साँवला समय घुलने लगा।

'अमरा आ गया', सहसा अधेड़ ने उनका कन्धा हिलाकर कहा।

बस रुक गई। वे हड़बड़ाकर उतरे। पेड़ों की क़तार लाँघकर वे खेतों के बीच पगडंडी पर उतर गए। वे पगडंडी पर तेज़ चल रहे थे जैसे उन्हें अपने रिश्तेदार के घर पहुँचने की जल्दी हो। अधेड़ ने दूर तक उनकी श्वेत केशराशि को देखा जैसे कोई ऋषि जा रहा हो।

बाँके बिहारी गाँव में नहीं घुसे। वे सीधे पीछे की ओर चले गए जहाँ लम्बी

घास का मैदान था, जिसमें वे पहली बार बचपन में घुसकर खो गए थे। वे चकित थे। लम्बी घास मैदान में उसी तरह खड़ी थी गोया कुछ भी न बदला हो। समय हाशिए पर चला गया था। घास पर धूप उसी तरह चमक रही थी। लम्बी घास हवा में आहिस्ता-आहिस्ता हिल रही थी। उन्होंने एक-एक क़दम बढ़ाते हुए घास में प्रवेश किया जैसे वे स्वयं घास की पत्ती हों।

●●●